ADVANCE PRAISE FOR *PACKAGING BOYHOOD*

"I love *Packaging Boyhood* for professional and personal reasons. As an educator, I am impressed by the depth of its social critique, which is fortified with numerous examples of how the consumer industries provide boys with emotionally stunted and cartoonish ideas about manhood in order to sell products. As the father of a young son, I learned practical tips about how to talk to and with him about these narrow definitions. And as a grown man who carries deep scars along with fond memories of my own boyhood, I am grateful for the empathy the authors show in these pages for all the boys and men who struggle daily in this culture to be happy, healthy, and socially responsible human beings, despite all the pressures to the contrary."

—Jackson Katz, Ph.D., creator of the award-winning video *Tough Guise* and cofounder of Mentors in Violence Prevention (MVP)

"*Packaging Boyhood* is one of the most important books ever written about the inner world of boys. Lyn Mikel Brown, Sharon Lamb, and Mark Tappan challenge all caring adults to educate our sons about the pervasive power of the media and to give our boys strategies for countering the harmful images of boyhood and masculinity that they receive on a daily basis."

—Mark S. Kiselica, Ph.D., H.S.P.P., N.C.C., L.P.C., professor of counselor education, the College of New Jersey, former president of the Society for the Psychological Study of Men and Masculinity, and coauthor of *Counseling Troubled Boys*

"If you read one book this year about how to be a better parent to your son, then it must be *Packaging Boyhood*. Unlike other parenting or 'boys books,' it reveals that boys do not naturally or biologically like violent images and don't have to do poorly at school. Rather, a bath of hurtful media images is overtaking them— and you can help save them, teaching them methods for resisting this gender mediocrity so they can grow into the unique, successful young men they truly wish to become!"

—William S. Pollack, Ph.D., Harvard Medical School, bestselling author of *Real Boys: Rescuing Our Sons from the Myths of Boyhood*

"The authors of *Packaging Boyhood* make a strong case that the media are selling our sons a steady diet of distorted dreams: power, domination, misogyny, pornography, and self-mutilation. I found *Packaging Boyhood* to be a well researched, thought-provoking study of the media's attempts to stereotype boys. As someone who worries about the academic underachievement of boys, I was particular interested in the marketing of the 'slacker' image to a generation of our sons."

—Michael Thompson, Ph.D., author of *It's a Boy! Your Son's Development from Birth to Eighteen*

"An eagerly welcomed sibling to *Packaging Girlhood*, *Packaging Boyhood* is informative, accessible, and above all a must-read for any parent, educator, and caring adult concerned with our boys' well-being."

—Dafna Lemish, Ph.D., editor of *Journal of Children and Media*

"Every parent of a son needs to know about the world of boys in twenty-first century America. It is a world in which boys are bombarded with harmful, damaging messages that come to them via movies, advertisements, music, fashion, and a host of other pop-culture sources. The desire of every parent is to help our children enjoy childhood and grow into responsible, balanced adults. But to do so today we need to help boys deal with the stereotypes of the superhero, the playa, the slacker, and other roles that can harm our sons. In *Packaging Boyhood*, Lyn Mikel Brown, Sharon Lamb, and Mark Tappan give parents—and grandparents—exactly the information and guidance we need in order to help our boys make their way safely through the pop culture minefields."

—Carmine Sarracino, author of *The Porning of America: The Rise of Porn Culture, What It Means, and Where We Go from Here*

"A thoughtful and provocative look at just how ruthlessly the media and marketing industries target boys, the negative consequences of that targeting, and what we can do about it. Essential reading for parents and anyone who cares about how childhood shapes the adults our children become."

—Susan Linn, Ed.D., author of *The Case for Make Believe: Saving Play in a Commercialized World*

Packaging Boyhood

Also by Lyn Mikel Brown, Ed.D.,
and Sharon Lamb, Ed.D.

Packaging Girlhood

Packaging Boyhood

**SAVING OUR SONS
FROM SUPERHEROES, SLACKERS,
AND OTHER MEDIA STEREOTYPES**

Lyn Mikel Brown, Ed.D.,
Sharon Lamb, Ed.D.,
and Mark Tappan, Ed.D.

ST. MARTIN'S PRESS ☙ NEW YORK

To other people's children and to our own,
Maya, Willy, and Julian

PACKAGING BOYHOOD. Copyright © 2009 by Lyn Mikel Brown, Ed.D., Sharon Lamb, Ed.D., and Mark Tappan, Ed.D. All rights reserved. Printed in the United States of America. For information, address St. Martin's Press, 175 Fifth Avenue, New York, N.Y. 10010.

www.stmartins.com

Library of Congress Cataloging-in-Publication Data

Lamb, Sharon.
  Packaging boyhood : saving our sons from superheroes, slackers, and other media stereotypes / Sharon Lamb, Lyn Mikel Brown, and Mark Tappan. — 1st ed.
     p. cm.
  Includes bibliographical references and index.
  ISBN 978-0-312-37939-1
  1. Children's paraphernalia—Marketing—Social aspects—United States.   2. Boys—United States—Social conditions—21st century.   3. Boys—United States—Psychology.   4. Child consumers—United States.   5. Mass media and youth—United States.   I. Brown, Lyn Mikel, 1956–   II. Tappan, Mark B.   III. Title.
  HD9970.5.C483U654 2009
  339.4'7083410973—dc22

                                                        2009016923

FIRST EDITION: October 2009

10   9   8   7   6   5   4   3   2   1

Contents

Preface

As soon as *Packaging Girlhood* was published, our book on how marketers and media sell girls a commercial version of girlhood, and we began talking with school and community groups about our findings, parents asked us, "What about the boys?" It was a good question but not one that we were fully prepared to answer at that time. Still, we couldn't explore how the media packages a narrow form of girlhood to girls without noticing how boys are sold a different but equally damaging version of boyhood. Marketers and media have invested billions in the crass commercialization of gender, using the most basic gender stereotypes to convince a generation that girls should be hot shopping divas and boys should be violence-loving "players," jocks, and slackers. Parents are told that their sons and daughters have nothing in common, and so they need separate games, toys, books, music, movies, technology, and even TV channels.

So we decided to go back to the malls, hit the movie theaters, and enter cyberspace to answer the question posed to us in 2006: what about the boys? We listened to popular music, watched horror movies, looked over the shoulders of boys playing video games, and tuned in to reality shows and sitcoms. As we did while writing *Packaging Girlhood*, we conducted an online survey—to which over six hundred boys responded. Through it all we couldn't miss the version of boyhood up for sale. It was louder, rougher, more arrogant, crass, and sophomoric than anything marketed to girls.

We asked Mark Tappan to join us as our investigation began. A father, teacher, and Harvard-trained developmental psychologist and educator, Mark brings a wealth of knowledge and experience to this project. His ongoing work with the Maine Boys Network, a statewide coalition focused on promoting boys' academic achievement, has given him the opportunity to conduct discussion groups with parents and teachers about the boys in their lives. Teaching courses at Colby College on boys' development and education, as well as facilitating focus groups and media literacy trainings with middle-school boys, Mark has heard firsthand how boys make sense of media and understand what it means to grow up male.

There is unprecedented concern right now about boys—particularly about their education and their development into healthy, productive, and fulfilled men. Popular books have generated a steady stream of magazine and newspaper articles commiserating about a national "boy crisis." Nearly every state's Department of Education has taken on the issue of boys' flagging achievement levels; nonprofits and boys' advocacy organizations are popping up across the country; documentaries and TV specials are addressing boy issues and parental concerns; and funders are creating a range of new opportunities for boys' programming and research. Not surprisingly, there are sharp disagreements about just what the problem with boys is all about. Is it low academic achievement, disengagement from school, and decreasing numbers of boys going on to higher education? Is it increased bullying and violence among boys and toward girls? Is it a struggle over identity, direction, and focus in a brave new world shared with competent and academically driven girls? All of the above?

Depending on how the problem is framed, some blame schools and teachers for not addressing boys' learning styles or needs, others blame parents for not taking boys' academic or emotional lives seriously enough, still others blame the women's movement for eroding gender boundaries or even girls for moving in on territories once monopolized by boys. Nearly everyone gives lip service to the role of media and its impact on what it means to be a man in this culture, but few do more than point to the most egregious examples, such as violent video games or sexually degrading rap lyrics. However, we saw all too well when researching *Packaging Girlhood* that media and marketing are far more insidious and pervasive. The impact has as much or more to do with the subtle repetition of images and messages that cross all forms of media and become a part of public knowledge than it has to do with any one or two obvious or sensationalized products or celebrities that kids are enamored of. Sure, media and marketers listen to what boys and their parents want, but the goal is not healthy development; it's to sell something. And because of that, the stories they tell and the images they serve up will reflect only a few aspects of "what boys want" and even more rarely what parents want for their sons.

Together we did research to find out what boys are listening to, reading, watching, and doing so that we could make sense of boy culture and think about what it means to our sons, students, and to us as parents and mentors for the next generation of boys. In addition, we drew from the insights of experts on boys, popular culture, and the influence of media and marketing on children. Mark's understanding of boys and experience with boys' groups was an invaluable addition to our own parallel understanding of girls. Sharon's two sons provided ample opportunities to try out the conversations we suggest to parents. Lyn's nonprofit regularly teams with Portland-based Boys to Men on education and advocacy projects. And for their insights and observations we certainly thank the boys who took our survey. In the end, as with *Packaging Girlhood*, our goal is not so much to convey the specifics of our investigations—although we analyze and report a lot of what we found—but to present the version of boyhood the media packages and sells, make transparent marketers' ploys, and teach parents how to read this world for the ways it channels their sons' interests, frames their options, and defines their relationships with one another and with girls. As a result, we offer something more systematic: a way of looking at the world that is both simple and revolutionary, a habit of seeing, understanding, and questioning the world around us.

We believe that parents and caregivers can do what we've done in this book without any particular training: they can observe and analyze what their son sees, hears, wears, reads, and does in terms of how boyhood is packaged and sold to him. *Packaging Boyhood* explores how media and marketing targets boys and affects them as they grow up. Most important, this is a book designed to help mothers and fathers engage with and *talk* with their sons in developmentally appropriate ways about the over five thousand media images and messages that confront boys daily.

Boys are major consumers of certain kinds of media, such as sports, video games, and music, proud of their facility with technology, and invested in believing they're immune to or above being affected by any of it in any deep way. For example, when we've talked in middle and high schools about *Packaging Girlhood*, boys as well as girls argue that media has little or no impact on their choices and behaviors. What they don't realize is that marketers wouldn't spend so much money if they didn't know how effective a good ad campaign is. They are skilled at taking a subtle gender difference and making it an absolute, detecting an interest and turning it into a craving, sensing wariness or uncertainty and transforming it into full-blown anxiety—just to turn around and sell the antidote for a nice profit. They are deliberate in their efforts to make boys feel as if parents want to take away their freedom and marketers want to enhance it. They use what we as psychologists and parents know and admire about boys—their sense of fun, adventure, and camaraderie—to sell a parody of manhood, steeped in anxiety about being big enough, strong enough, crazy and wild enough. Risk taking shows up in the form of MTV's *Viva La Bam*, a love of sport and action becomes World Wrestling Entertainment or Spike TV's *Ultimate Fighter*, fascination with technology is channeled into *Grand Theft Auto*, *World of Warcraft*, or *Halo 3*.

For these reasons, writing about boys and media is different than writing about girls and media, and we've had to address the difference head-on. While writing *Packaging Girlhood* we were confronted over and over again by the marginality or near absence of girls in images or stories of power, from G-rated movies to TV sports programs, from video games to the fist-pumping winners on board game covers, from cartoon superheroes to toy store action figures. If you don't count the action girls get as sexy-shopping-bootie-shaking-diva-mean-girlfriend types, girls live a relatively marginal media existence. Boys, on the other hand, are virtually everywhere and almost always the center of attention.

As a result the messages about power that boys and girls get from media and marketers are very different. We found in *Packaging Girlhood* that marketers had co-opted girl power and sold it to girls as the power to shop, make themselves over, and look sexy for boys, rarely offering girls pathways to real and lasting power in the world. Boys, on the other hand, are given more avenues to power than just sexuality and appearance. So what's the problem? you ask. The problem is that it's a version of power that entices boys into a world of absolute control, dominance over others, and stunted emotional development. Boys who can approximate this version of manhood might have more power in the world, but it's not a world that serves twenty-first-century reality very well.

Packaging Boyhood explores the images of power offered to boys through various forms of media and marketing and examines how these images entice boys with offers of big money, hot girls, and complete control, or give them a way out by assuming a cool, slacker dude mentality. We haven't covered every last bit of media that boys encounter, by any means, and we have probably left out one or more of your son's favorites. But we've done a good deal of homework, and we're eager to share what we've found. In the end we offer a bit of at-home media literacy training that encourages honest conversations between you and your son. It's not high tech, not over-the-top in terms of excitement, and it won't give your son a sense of "ultimate" power. But it will help to empower him in this marketing- and media-dominated world.

Introduction

Does your little boy want to grow up to be a superhero because they're strong and they fight bad guys? Does your teen son slip and sometimes call you "dude"? Is he a slacker? A player? A geek? A jock?

It's likely that your son is not any one of these things. Boys are complex, interesting, and hard to pin down. But the way popular culture defines what it means to be a boy has become narrower and narrower. That's because media and marketers spend billions of dollars every year promoting a version of "cool" that requires the latest fashions, technology, and lots of money and then takes advantage of his fear of not matching up or being called a wuss or a "faggot." In effect, they promote stereotypes. And stereotyping works for them because the bigger the net they can throw, the more boys they can capture with a certain image. The more boys they can capture, the more money they can get boys and parents to dish out. *Deadliest Catch* isn't just a reality show, it could be you or your son!

Don't get us wrong. The billions of dollars spent to entertain and market to boys doesn't produce only trash. There's plenty in boy culture to like—wonderful lyrics and music, artistic designs on sneakers and T-shirts, great messages in superhero films, challenging video games, and diverse role models on TV. But many of these wonderful images are packaged with an identity story that involves values and behaviors that are not so great—partying, pimping, playing people, and slacking. It's a story in which those with the most power too often have the wrong kind of power—they are the bullies, narcissistic athletes, "dogs," or "players"—the ones who call the shots and get the scantily clad, booty-jiggling, music video girls. It's a story that teaches boys that they need to avoid humiliation at all costs, seek revenge if wronged, dress to impress and intimidate, be tech savvy, show wealth, and take risks, all the while pretending they don't care about any of it. This is the media's version of boy power, a phrase you're unlikely to hear unless it means out of control and "over the top" or the power to do and buy whatever they want.

Parents want to raise boys who know themselves and feel powerful, but in the current testosterone-saturated media climate they wonder how to do this without encouraging that tough-guy aggression, top-dog persona, or cool-guy indifference about academics and school success. Increasingly, this notion of manhood reaches down to boys as young as preschool age, defining power as control, and too often control over girls and women. These images saturate boys' media from kids' cartoons to World Wrestling Entertainment (WWE), from MySpace to violent video games. So how *do* parents empower their boys when the media relentlessly sells their sons authority in the form of fighting, pimping (girls or rides), drinking, taking drugs, or looking "the big man on campus" with six-pack abs and cut biceps?

In the following chapters we scrutinize the media and marketers' version of boy power. On the surface, many of these things seem innocuous and even fun, but our argument is that being bombarded by these messages has a harmful effect on our sons. It's not the individual TV show that you hate for your son to watch or the most awful rap lyrics that you can't stand to hear. Journalists will grab on to these horrifying, sensationalized examples of media or marketing to boys (who hasn't heard about the *Grand Theft Auto* prostitutes?). Awful, yes, but these stories give us a false notion that we can clearly identify and avoid the bad stuff. It deflects attention away from a steady stream of more subtle messages that are never challenged because they don't reach the level of shock and awe that lands them on talk shows and the news. We are talking about the everyday messages. The ones they see and hear over and over in all forms of media—the bumbling fathers that frequent TV shows, the sports stars talking trash, the dark and angry action figures lining toy store aisles.

We think that the devil is in the details. We celebrate the positive song lyrics about struggles in men's lives to make a mother proud, the cartoons that encourage him to be himself instead of following the crowd, and the movies that tell him not to give up on his boyhood dreams or those that tell him to do the right thing. But we're also concerned about how, in the same song lyrics, TV shows, and movies, a boy will hear statements and see images that undercut these positive messages. Our survey and analysis of boys' media have led us to explore themes that, even as they tell boys, in Spider-Man's terms, that "with great power comes great responsibility," undermine boys and detract from their real power. This is the power to live life fully, to treat others well, to be in relationships that are good for them, and to be a positive force in the culture.

The Good and Bad of Media Boy Power

Consider the following media messages. They sound good or appear positive but also come with a set of competing messages that can make boys feel trapped and anxious, encourage them to ignore their feelings and needs, close down on the range of options available to them, or offer them a dangerously false sense of power.

BOYS ARE SUPERHEROES

Many of the stories presented to boys in comic books, cartoons, and movies show a boy or man as a "chosen one"—chosen to rescue, battle, or seek justice. Often this chosen one is misunderstood in some way, or wrongly accused, and outcast. But he is almost always on the side of good. And his battle will lead to glory. Good, right?

Sort of. Such stories typically turn into narratives of battle and revenge, so boys also get the message that being on the side of justice is an excuse for aggression, for harming or even killing others. Boys are taught a lesson early that when they feel wronged or when they or someone they know has been treated unjustly, it's all right for them to seek revenge. Often, it is incumbent upon them to seek revenge, especially if that wrongdoing involved some sort of harm to a person the hero loves. Whether it's revenge after being shamed or posing as invulnerable, one of the most important motivators in such stories is to avoid humiliation.

BOYS ARE BRAVE

Boys see a range of male heroes on TV, in movies, and in books who are brave and protective. They jump into battle, risk their lives, and sacrifice for others. Loyalty tests are everywhere in boys' media, and the hero always passes them, willing to put himself in harm's way to stand with a friend in need or to save the world.

Loyalty is good. Excitement and danger can be fun—think roller-coaster rides and rock climbing—and it's good to encourage boys to be brave and take risks. But right along with these messages is the assumption that boys should take it to the limit and not be afraid, or at least they shouldn't express fear. Fear, of course, is a natural and protective response, and while it may be funny to watch someone take crazy risks in reality shows like *Wildboyz*, imitating the over-the-top stunts that call for shutting down fear is dangerous for boys in real life.

BOYS ARE EXPECTED TO BE THE BEST

Competition is a good thing. It's part of the American spirit. So it's no surprise that competing and winning are a huge part of boys' media. Whether it's rapper Lil Wayne, Olympic swimmer Michael Phelps, or the Master Chief in *Halo*, boys are invited into the glory of being the best. Like so many popular rappers, winners can rise up from the school of hard knocks, or they can struggle, as Phelps did, with attention deficit disorder, or like *Halo's* Master Chief, they can simply be lucky. What's wrong with celebrating that effort or that luck, cheering the competition between those who worked hard enough to be there in the final contest?

Nothing, actually. The problem isn't the competition. The problem is that the media doesn't celebrate the hard work and effort it takes to get there. There may be a back-story mention, but all is forgotten when the winner wins—the cheerleaders come out, the flags wave, and the fans go wild. As they say so often on the sports shows that boys watch, no one remembers second place.

As a result, the other message boys get from these stories is that if they're not on top, they're on the bottom, or they might as well be. The media is full of top dogs, but in actuality, the world of the best is a rarefied one. A Tiger Woods comes along maybe once in a generation, so it's a problem for boys when the media world of winners is filled with disparagement for those who don't quite make it. Forget the long hours alone in the pool, the struggles in school, the bullying he experienced growing up; the Olympic Games announcer tells us that Michael Phelps is a winner who not only beats his opponents, he "demolishes them." Winners in the media don't tell us what it's like to get up at 6 A.M. to train every day (and who drove you there), to put your heart and soul into every competition, to never make the final heat. But the reality is that losing is a much more common experience than winning. While parents try to inspire their son to play fair and do his best, knowing in most cases he's not going to be the one on top, the media hits him daily with the glory of winning and the anonymity of losing. The shame of not being the absolute best is so great that even if they're not on top boys are sold an image that tells them they better arrogantly announce it anyway, as we saw reflected on a T-shirt slogan: GO HOME AND PRACTICE. COME BACK WHEN YOU'RE MORE OF A CHALLENGE.

With all this pressure to be on top or to at least pretend to be, it's no surprise that an alternative to the hero or the winner is a defensive position: the slacker. Its attraction in media comes from a desire to create a saving-face alternative to the humiliated position that a boy might occupy if he can't compete or is afraid to compete to be the best. It's a cultivated "I don't care" position, and it's a space that we let boys live in through messages that glorify slacking off, sometimes called "typical boy" behavior. The dilemma for boys is that they are told they need to be at the top—but in real life it requires hard work to get there. Plus, hard work in school is not only hard but also, as boys see everywhere in their media, entails behaviors that are considered "girly," such as studying, being in study groups, and taking notes. We pay special attention to messages about being a slacker throughout this book because we are convinced it's an image that contributes to boys' underachievement in schools. Rather than blaming girls for stealing away the attention that boys sorely need, or pointing at the fragile biology that makes reading harder for boys, we look to the media and marketers who teach them reading isn't cool and that trying isn't what boys do.

BOYS LOVE ACTION AND ADVENTURE

Any parent of a boy knows why media pitches them loads of action and adventure. From his rough-and-tumble toddlerhood on, he's running, jumping, and raring to go. Once you clear out the breakables, what's the problem?

Again, the problem is not the action and adventure, it's how far the media takes it and how much of it they dish out. Almost everything boys read, watch, wear, or listen to has to be not just action filled and awesome but also superextraordinarily awesome. One car crash isn't enough, but twenty crashes involving buses, trucks, exploding oil trucks, multiple police cars and a helicopter should do it. By the same token, something just a little embarrassing won't do when a boy can watch someone being totally humiliated. Gross is simply not gross enough when boys are offered material that's totally crude, crass, and disgusting. The message that boys want and need action that's over-the-top is repeated in all forms of media, from the little Valentines five- and six-year-old boys pass out to their classmates to the crass YouTube videos teenage boys forward to their friends. It's not just that violence in their video games and movies has to be way over-the-top, but even their personal adventures and the risks they're encouraged to take have to be extraordinary or not worth watching or doing. Risk taking is just another way for boys to be over-the-top and show that they're not afraid of anything or anyone.

We are particularly tuned in to media and marketing messages that encourage forms of self-harm. Risk taking, drinking, drugs, punching walls when you're angry, and doing crazy things are often driven by an interest in being over-the-top, beyond parental control, and impressing others. They're also about harming oneself. Media targeting boys are filled with what boy theorist R. W. Connell calls "iron men" who need to convince themselves that their bodies aren't hurting as much as they are.

We look at both sides of the self-harm dilemma. Boys are encouraged to hurt themselves to prove they're invulnerable and that their bodies can take it, but they also are shown a view of self-harm that legitimizes being vulnerable. For instance, they see grown men getting drunk and telling pals while in a total stupor that they love them. They're shown teenagers who can't find the words to express themselves so they punch a wall or a car until their fists bleed to show that they're hurting on the inside. The way to feel real, the way to feel *something*, they're told, is to bleed, to hurt oneself or someone else.

BOYS LOVE TO LAUGH

Whether it's the pratfalls popular on cartoons and Teen Nick, the slackers in movies like, well, *Slackers*, or the political humor of Jon Stewart and Stephen Colbert, if it's popular with boys and men it has heavy doses of comedy. Boys we see in the media are silly, funny, irreverent, and into practical jokes. Generally that's a good thing. We need humor in this life. Some of the best social commentary comes in the form of satire and spoofs.

Boys, especially, need humor to reduce the intensity of all those unrealistic expectations. The slacker image has an important function for boys as a comedic escape. Being a slacker takes the pressure off a boy who sees he must be a "heroic" jock or player to feel important. It also allows a boy to poke fun at the pumped-up hypermasculine dudes—the ones who think they're so hot but aren't. Slackers, like Jack Black in *School of Rock*, Seth Rogen in *Knocked Up*, and Steve Carell in *The Office* are supposed to be funny and endearing; everyone laughs at them or with them. Of course they don't study, read, or have ambitions (except perhaps to be a rock star), but they also offer boys a way to talk back to authority figures who demand way more than a boy can give.

While it serves an important purpose, comedy in boy-targeted media also acts as a conduit and justification for cruelty and unfairness. Animated films are filled with bullying and teasing between male characters designed to get a laugh, often at the expense of a character who doesn't act masculine enough. As boys turn from cartoons to the preteen and teen shows, they're invited to laugh at jokes with an increasingly sexy edge, like the girl on an episode of Nick's *The Suite Life of Zach & Cody*, who comes on to Cody because she's "drunk" on too much sugary soda. Online, boys can access the Axe Video Vixen Web site where they can choose a vixen to sniff his body. Or they can watch a steady stream of Will Ferrell movies where men act like horny, impulsive stereotypes of adolescent boys.

Boy humor is also a part of that over-the-top message sometimes called "inappropriate" by the adults around them. It's an "extreme sport" of sorts. From the fart and poop jokes encouraged in the youngest of boys, to the crass humor of adolescent boys, in all sorts of media boys are invited to join with other boys in laughing about some of the most profane or debasing things. Debasing humor is often focused on weaker boys or girls, and while this brand of humor may cause boys to be titillated, disgusted, grossed out, or freaked out, maybe even uncomfortable, feeling morally outraged or refusing to watch isn't an option, for risk of being the wet blanket at the party. In the name of "fun" it seems as if anything goes, and boys are asked to turn off their sense of fairness, justice, and compassion.

IT'S A MAN'S WORLD OUT THERE

On both the production and the consumption side of media and marketing, boys and men dominate. Boys get the message that they live in a world that wants them and needs them. It gives boys permission to desire and to dream big. It's an invitation to participate, to be involved, to be important, which are all positive. We don't want to stop boys from desiring or feeling these things, but we do want to temper these messages with an awareness and knowledge of those not given the same space and opportunity in the world.

We want boys to notice that all too often the media conveys a world that wants a certain kind of boy—the one who is stronger, braver, cooler, the winner, the hero. We want them to be aware of the not-so-subtle messages that they need to change to match up to a ridiculous expectation of what a boy should be. Even when the story is about turning masculine hype on its ear (as in many a Will Ferrell movie), boys get the message that the hype dominates their world and resistance to it is the exception.

We want boys to notice that they're being invited into a world where best friends for boys are often sidekicks, not equals, the clown to complete them if they're serious, or the straight man to set them right if they're the clown. After the cartoons and PBS shows boys watch when they're little, friendship is distorted to mean "I've got your back," "let's party," "that dude is crazy and that's why I love to hang out with him," and, in the case of groups of boys, a sense of belonging, "we cool." In the sections ahead we pay close attention to how the connection between boys is portrayed in the media, through the parallel play of video game play on the couch, to the daring stunts of adolescence.

We also want boys to notice the way girls are treated and how rare it is to see a boy among a group of girls in boys' shows and movies. In real life, many boys have strong friendships with girls, but in the media, girls are treated as annoyances in the lives of little boys, and rarely as friends. When girls are friendly with boys, they often stereotypically remind their male friends to be good and honorable, nag them to do their homework, try to prevent them from fighting (annoying detractors when "a man has to do what a man has to do"), or, later on, they become hot babes to be lusted after or good girls to bring home to Mom. These limited roles that girls are allowed to play in boys' media discourages boys from real relationships that can be a source of fun and connection.

BOYS ARE INDEPENDENT

In media, boys see and hear lots of messages about the importance of being independent, trusting and relying on no one but themselves. Nearly every superhero story reminds boys of the danger of being too close to someone or relying too much on relationships. A superhero who loves and needs is vulnerable. If the bad guy can get to a girlfriend or family member, the story goes, he has power over the superhero. But there's a clear problem in this message: while there are times in life when all kids have to stand on their own and make choices apart from the crowd, no one can survive without relationships.

In all the battles to prove their strength, competitions to be the best, and tests to prove they need no one, boys are rarely shown seeking out a friend or having a heart-to-heart. They're told that they must handle problems on their own. Just as "cutting" is seen as a form of self-soothing with girls who can't or won't reach out to others, hurting themselves through extreme risk taking can be seen as soothing and/or numbing the emotional pain that boys feel. Our friend and colleague Bill Pollack talks about the toughening up of little boys and the emotional harm this does. In their world, it's rare to hear messages that boys need people to help them sort through their problems.

In media for younger boys, we've noticed a real absence of relational play materials. Sure the earbuds and iPods of older kids suggest they're living in "their own private Idaho," as the 1970s song suggested, but the lack of connection and relationships suggested in toys for little boys is alarming too. Trucks, cars, and buses are a staple of boy play and marketers make sure boys see the fun of speed and danger. But if a boy wants to imagine that there are drivers with feelings, pedestrians with fears, and passengers with places to go, he has to invent these himself. Sharon once asked her older son, who loved to play the computer game *Flight Simulator*, what he imagined as he was flying, taking off, and landing. He talked about the weather conditions, the way the city looked below, the general handling of the plane, but most important, he added, "I imagine I'm a father flying my family on a vacation with two kids in the backseat." How heartening. But why couldn't *Flight Simulator* have introduced the opportunity in the game to be that relational pilot. Why did he have to invent it?

And for years dolls have been off-limits to boys. Why should we protest, given that the most popular dolls today come dressed in outfits fit for a prostitute on a street corner? Because dolls and dollhouses just like the kitchen and dress-up corner in the nursery school are the best places for kids to work on their feelings about what's most important to them—their families, their home, and their identities. Sadly, when boys in therapy are encouraged to play with the dollhouses, they often reenact the scenes from TV and movies that have invaded their lives, and therapists get stories of murder, mayhem, and robberies. Sure, wrestling and action figures are kinds of dolls, but what kinds of stories do they generally evoke?

BOYS EXPECT TO SUCCEED (EXCEPT IN SCHOOL)

It would seem that next to athletes and rappers, Bill Gates is a guy boys want to grow up to be. It's not his charity work—the Bill and Melinda Gates Foundation has supported HIV/AIDs prevention, college scholarships for minorities, and a range of projects around the world designed to lift people out of poverty. It's his billions. A constant message in much of boys' media is the importance of having wealth, getting stuff, and knowing how to work the system. As sociologist and masculinity theorist Michael Kimmel tells us, the biggest media message boys get these days "is that the world is absolutely overflowing with cool stuff. Material abundance seems to come without consequences." Whether wealth is accumulated through drug deals or ingenuity, the important message is that wealth gives a person power.

Boys are promised a fantasy world, pressed to imagine that someday they will be Donald Trump, Bill Gates, if not 50 Cent, a rapper with his own clothing line, million-dollar ad campaigns, and bevy of hot girls. It's promised to them not through hard work and sacrifice, not through a love of knowledge or the desire for a better world, but by knowing how to be tough, how to "play" people, play the game and win. In real life there's only one winner, one number one, one top dog. In real life the odds are against them. The promotion of wealth in boys' worlds almost tops the promotion of action—in fact, these days the two are closely entwined. But in media it's not the kind of action he must take toward his goal of acquiring wealth, it's the action he gets once he's there.

BOYS LOVE TECHNOLOGY

Think of the ingenuity and creativity of today's technology and it's hard not to think about all of the male inventors, scientists, and engineers who have made these advancements possible. We want boys to continue on this path, but we don't want them to be limited in thinking that they need to love technology or that it's a "boy thing" to love gadgets.

We found in our work for *Packaging Girlhood* that the message that "girls love to shop" was ubiquitous. But there's a parallel message for boys. They may not love shopping, but they're definitely spending—and spending a lot on technology. The guy with power is the one with money to burn, or as the T-shirt says, HE WHO DIES WITH THE MOST TOYS WINS. The way that many boys show their spending power is by purchasing the coolest new technology. Like bling hanging from the neck of the richest rap stars, most boys represented in the media accessorize themselves with technology like cell phones, iPods, and laptops. A recent *New York Times* article points to marketers targeting tweens with these items: "Tween boys want products that have an electronic, Internet, video or sports component; and there's a premium for portable toys and electronics because most tweens spend time traveling to after-school activities." You'll never hear a marketer advocating for more playtime, talk time, or admitting that drawing boys away from these pastimes might be harmful to them.

BOYS ALWAYS WANT SEX

Helping your son develop a healthy sexual identity is a critically important part of his adolescence. In fact, being able to laugh about sex and not feel ashamed about desire is a good thing. When it comes to boys' media, however, there's pressure not only to want sex all the time, but also to feel shamed or wrong if you don't.

Marketers and media producers like to portray boys as ready for sexual action, with cartoon little boys ogling (usually older and taller) girls and boys in preteen shows openly pursuing "hot" girls. Marketers have remade pink for little girls into a come-hither hot-pink and black, and they've also ensured young boys will notice. Because of girls' sexualized media image, and because of a concomitant focus on girls' vulnerability, parents may have been all too willing to focus on girls and buy into a stereotype the media encourages, which is that boys are invulnerable when it comes to sex. They're animals, or they're machines. They always want it and are always ready to go. They'll have sex anywhere with anyone.

Authors Dan Kindlon and Michael Thompson write about how sex is a vulnerable issue for boys. While music lyrics invoke players that can keep a girl satisfied "all night long," slacker movies tell boys that they're dirty and smelly. So what does that mean when they start to think of themselves as sexual partners? How do marketers get them to "clean up" for a girl? In our exploration of boys' media we pay close attention to the increased pornification of the media and, with this, the messages boys get about how to be a sexual male. All the themes we discussed already (the need to be over-the-top, take risks, be invulnerable, wealthy, and seek revenge when humiliated) spill over into the world of sex and relationships as depicted by the media.

MORE THAN ANYONE ELSE, A BOY NEEDS HIS DAD

Media and marketers promote the relationship between a boy and his father as the most important of all. We're told over and over again that father approval (also in the form of coaches, mentors, teachers, neighborhood drug dealers, whoever is an adult male) is central to a boy's well-being. We don't question the importance of fathers, but we do question the ways fathers are represented in media, and we're not the only ones.

Fathers have told us how resentful they are that they are constantly represented in media as bumbling idiots, absent, too busy, aggressive, and scary, or if they are to be perfect, the kind of dad who "never missed one of my games." Never? That's a tall order. That quintessential American phrase—"My dad never missed a single ball game"—captures the shallow and empty core of what the media promotes as a good father-son relationship—one in which a boy makes his father proud, and one in which the father lives through his son or supports the boy in a typically male activity.

A particular problem in media presentations of boyhood is the absence of fathers as positive, *realistic* models of authority. Stereotypically, boys forgive fathers their anger and their absences. In real life, as psychologist Carol Gilligan explains, fathers struggle with their own authority, wanting their sons to achieve and do well and participate in the world, but they are embarrassed and hesitant sometimes to offer themselves as real people with their own losses and vulnerabilities. Media images encourage them to hide behind a veneer of unquestionable authority or superstar status, and encourage their sons to package themselves as men according to the fantasy he-men, players, and winners they see on TV.

Fathers are hungry for ways to be present for their sons. They want their sons to know and develop the complexity of their feelings, their friendships, the qualities that make them whole. Yet because they live in this world, fathers also know the risks—the teasing, hurt, and shame boys can experience if they're not the right kind of boy.

But let's not forget mothers. We've watched and listened to moms in movies and TV who are fairly absent except as people who provide snacks to roving bands of boys. Female teachers are the bad cops. Grandmas and aunties, forget about it. They're nowhere to be found. We're not saying that fathers aren't important—boys without strong fathers miss them and want them. But this "father hunger" gets milked to death in the media, setting up unrealistic expectations for the real dads who are available and downplaying the role of women in boys' lives.

The Influence of Media and Marketers

Media and consumer psychologists evaluate how marketers get their messages across and how media affects kids or adults in general. One of the primary ways in which marketers grab kids' attention is by selling freedom. Psychological research on "reactance theory" has taught us that telling kids that someone doesn't want them to have something makes them want that item more. Marketers set up parents as the ones taking away freedom of choice, when in reality the choices marketers offer are not in the service of freedom at all, but in the service of selling stereotypes for their own profit.

One stereotype they bank on is "the Mook." Mook is a "term introduced by Douglas Rushkoff in an episode of PBS's *Frontline* entitled 'The Merchants of Cool.' Mooks are archetypal young males (teens–early twenties) who act like moronic boneheads." If marketers can provide slacker, disgusting, moronic humor and reckless behavior, they can make a buck off a "mook." We refer to this as slacker humor, and it gets under our skin as much as the over-the-top action and violence sold to younger boys.

As developmental psychologists we've examined child development research to try to understand how these messages influence boys at different ages and the impact they have. It's important to consider that the vulnerability of younger boys may make viewing traumatic and overstimulating material difficult for them. It's important to know that adolescents are particularly vulnerable to freedom, choice, and identity messages as well as messages indicating that they are inadequate if they don't buy such and such or act in a certain way. It's also important to be aware that feeling intellectually inferior is one of the best predictors of injuring a female partner. These vulnerabilities explain the need for narratives of boyhood that calm the overstimulation, explain the violence, undermine the emphasis on stupidity and slackitude, and offer pathways for boys that challenge old stereotypical scripts.

Our bottom line about the harmfulness of these messages is not that media or marketers are solely responsible for all that's problematic in boyhood today, but that they're a significant factor. These repeated messages limit boys' potential for developing a variety of human emotions, skills, and responses, and these depictions of boyhood and masculinity desensitize boys, celebrate problem qualities, and reinforce behaviors that are damaging to them and others: dominance, exploitation, violence, and slacking.

In This Book

The chapters that follow develop these contradictory themes by pointing out details and messages in a variety of media and marketing bids for attention. The media is filled with representations of boys as players, who talk about "hot" girls, joke about their drinking problems, flex their muscles, and go partying. Funny beer ads that pepper sports programs reinforce the same messages and images and show the youngest of boys, watching on their dads' knees, what they can look forward to and even expect: a grown-up life full of sexy girls, fast rides, and drinking buddies mixed in with promises of power and control. All of this is offered to boys who are too young to understand the implications, too young to use their power well, too young to know what it means to judge a girl hot or not, too young to know that shutting off a way of relating isn't good for them. It's not good for their developing brains, their social relationships, or their psychological health to be exposed to these messages so relentlessly.

In our section on movies we discuss how boys are taken to movies and exposed to violent material when they are too young to have the capacity to deal with it. As developmental psychologists, we maintain that because they're exposed too early, they develop psychological defenses toward these experiences—some grow to love this over-the-top excitement and some of them develop traumalike reactions to it. It may sound ridiculous to compare their reactions to movies as trauma reactions, but the two have a lot in common. One kind of trauma symptom is a reversal of fear, an exaggerated "I'm not scared" response that's often accompanied by a preoccupation with violent images. Some say that watching violence helps kids to vent aggression vicariously. But most of the research says that it's not venting that's going on but priming. Priming means that watching violence or listening to violent lyrics primes a boy to be more violent and to express more violent feelings. In our sections on violence in cartoons, movies, and lyrics we explore just what kind of violence they are primed to commit.

The pressure to pose as tough, nonchalant, or crude, and take on a superficial stance of power and control, leaves little room in media for the very real uncertainties, questions, and anxieties boys feel. Parents who see and value the complex, vulnerable boy underneath don't want to be the ones who shoot him down by saying no to that power; they want him to feel big and important and good about himself. What can we do to support our sons without reinforcing these media stereotypes?

We separate this book into five main chapters: What they wear; What they watch; What they read; What they hear; and What they do. In each of these chapters we look at the "stuff" in boys' worlds, the messages this stuff sends, and what it means for boys. We may write about products, artists, sports stars, or trends that are outdated by the time you read this book, but unfortunately we're convinced that many of these same messages will continue to be sent in new packaging for years to come.

A caution. This isn't just another book about the "boy box" or "boy code," the "gender straitjacket," the "tough guise" or "Guyland"—that is, the ways boy theorists describe how boys are socially and emotionally restricted by pressures and expectations regarding what it means to be a "real man" and feel "boxed in" by conventional masculine stereotypes and ideals. These concepts and ideas represent some of the most powerful and important contemporary work on boys' development; they appear in books like William Pollack's *Real Boys*, Daniel Kindlon and Michael Thompson's *Raising Cain*, Michael Kimmel's *Guyland*, and documentary films by Byron Hurt, Jackson Katz, and Sut Jhally. When these descriptions of masculinity reach the light of popular media, however, they portray boys only as victims. That doesn't sit well with us. We are worried, incredibly worried about boys, not only because they are being "victimized" by these messages but also because they are being enticed to develop their power and privilege in ways that are harmful to others, to society, and sometimes to themselves. In the conclusion, we address the importance of talking with our sons about a version of masculinity that promises control, dominance, and limitless opportunities and other narrow stereotypes that hurt boys and limit their emotional and social lives.

In the end, our argument is not the simple one of seeing your son as a victim of violent video games and a male culture that can turn him into an emotional cripple or turn him away from school success. We want parents to help their sons critique these images in the media and by doing so develop a number of alternative paths to empowerment—alternatives that may not only help him but will also help others and the world around him.

CHAPTER 1

Big, Bold, and Branded: What Boys Wear

When most of us think about boys and clothing, we conjure up images of grass-stained pants and shirts torn from climbing trees. Maybe it's all those laundry detergent ads reminding us that boys are especially active and get dirty. The stereotype is that boys don't care what they look like; they throw on jeans and a tee, grab a doughnut, and run for the bus. Only girls shop and stress over appearance.

In real life boys care very much about how they look and what image they project. Little boys long for T-shirts with images of their favorite cartoon characters and ballplayers. Older boys check themselves out in the mirror before their first dance to ensure their jeans fall just the right distance below their waist; many work hard to create an image that says they could care less about their image. The MasterCard ad of a young guy heading out to a club nails it: "Haircut, vintage tee shirt, and designer jeans: $238.00. Looking like you just rolled out of bed: priceless." Because boys don't want to look like they're trying too hard, marketers have to be careful not to blow their cover.

Anyone who thinks fashion isn't important to boys hasn't checked out the latest in tees, hats, hoodies, and sneakers or noticed the range of pant styles, hair lengths, piercings, and tattoos that boys are sporting. They've missed the significance of brands and the importance of logos. In fact, when we asked boys to list their favorite clothing brands, they named as many, if not more, than the girls we surveyed for *Packaging Girlhood*. Their tastes cover a wide range, and they most readily admit to buying stuff wherever they see something they like—from big department store chains like Wal-Mart, JCPenney, or Kohl's, to popular teen clothing stores like Abercrombie & Fitch and Hollister, to Southpole or indie clothing lines like Mighty Healthy that sell a more edgy, urban look.

The clothing marketed to boys says something more than "I just rolled out of bed." For the youngest boys, their Bob the Builder– and Thomas the

Tank Engine–themed slippers, tees, and coats say more than that these are their favorite TV shows. After all, little boys love Dora, but you won't see her on their pj's. That's because these themes say something about a boyhood that marketers think is important to three-year-olds. Boys like construction and transportation? Maybe. More like, boys will be boys. And that's innocent enough. As they get older there are the fast and furious themes—race cars—and the big and scary themes—dinosaurs, sharks, air commandos. And, as always, there are the superhero themes, clothing that advertises PG-13 movies little boys beg to see and sports-themed attire that tells them it's not enough to be a team player; he also has to be "Team Captain." These all fulfill some fantasy of what it means to be a boy and what it means to be powerful. As boys enter the preteen years, they're given a choice of colognes and deodorants to wear that tell them they're powerful in other ways, promising them that hot girls will go crazy for them. And finally, as teens, the flair and style of hip-hop fashion and the sneaks to go with it scream "bigger, better, best" with bling and designer labels.

Are clothing stereotypes harmful to boys? It would be hard to make that case, especially in comparison to the overtly sexualized clothing marketed to girls. But there's more than meets the eye here. Clothing is a form of communication, and he knows his clothing speaks volumes about the kind of person he is and the groups and interests he identifies with. Parents ought to notice that he's also expressing who he feels he can't be and what he feels he can't communicate as a boy. From an early age marketers capitalize on these boundaries and the anxieties that keep them in place.

Clothes Make the (Little) Man

Why is it so hard to treasure the sweetness and vulnerability of little boys? Ask clothing manufacturers who insist on assuring us from infancy that boys are tough, rough, and ready. We visited the infant, toddler, and 4–7 boys' clothing sections of large department stores, like Kohl's and JCPenney, as well as specialty children's clothing stores, like Gymboree and Children's Place, to examine the themes. And here they are, as if a parent of a boy couldn't have guessed: transportation; sports; funny, scary, or gross animals; superheroes; and competition. All-boy, all the time.

From day one, cars and all forms of transportation cover little boys' stuff, and especially their clothes. Vehicles are virtually absent from girls' clothing, but on boys' clothes it's a dizzying display of planes, trains, automobiles, and more. Cars need to be racers. Trucks need to be big and scary (no smiling ice cream trucks). Except for friendly Thomas the Tank Engine, vehicles mean speed and danger. Could they have made the Disney movie *Cars* without speedy racing car Lightning "I eat losers for breakfast" McQueen? We don't think so.

What kinds of animals symbolize boyhood? Dinosaurs, lions, frogs, lizards, bugs, dogs, giraffes, and sharks. No kittens. Not even a cat, which presumably is too girly. From early on boys know that cats are girls and dogs are boys. Why? Because the distinction is made for them from infancy on. As we all know, cats and dogs come in both genders. But this is part of a gender split that sets up a girl-boy boundary that gets increasingly harder to cross and that can only be defended by referring to the brain or the planet Mars. There's nothing in boys' brain chemistry, or dogs' either for that matter, that says dogs are male, but big, goofy, loyal, and high energy suggests male. It's also easy to see why frogs, lizards, and bugs are all-boy. Marketers assume that boys like yucky, slimy things—they're not afraid of them, like girls are supposed to be. Dinosaurs, lions, and sharks? They're big and scary, but a boy can handle them! Thus starts the pressure to be big, bigger, biggest.

In our exploration of young boys' clothing, it was surprising to see how many tiny T-shirts boasted winning some competition, being the best, the most successful. The tiniest of tikes will wear clothes that announce boys should be, wanna be, *will* be in "First Place"; they'll be "Champions," "All-Stars," "All Pro," "World Champs," and "Team Captain." No team players— only team captains. They're taken up into an all-American culture that brags about being number one, that needs to be number one instead of one among many.

If they're not winning, they're proving themselves through adventure. Marketers assume boys will drive their cars at "full throttle" with "Maximum Speed 250" before their parents even let them pedal a tricycle. These shirts tell boys to go "off road" in jeeps, go on "Safari Adventures" (a summer theme in all the stores we visited); they can be little versions of surfer dudes "Catching" a "Big Wave" or a "Wild Animal Explorer" in the jungle. Of course they can always find that adventure in the military, as many an advertisement for the National Guard points out, and as their small camo-patterned pj's, T-shirts, pants, hats, fleeces, coats, and sneakers reinforce. They too can aspire to be on a special military team—"Air Commanders."

Whereas little girls learn that to be noticed or important in this world they don't need to act but simply to look pretty as "special" princesses, action is a priority for boys. Sports themes abound as the quintessential action for boys, so at The Children's Place the parent of a 0–3 month old can choose between "Fourth Quarter," "Nine Innings," and "Second Half" onesies. But soon, as they get a little bit older, they'll find that just any action isn't good enough. It has to be wild and crazy action, and in the end boys have to rule, to win, to be the champion. There's never a suggestion that he might not be into speed, that he might like art or music, or, God forbid, reading. Just wild, fast, action-packed everything.

Superheroes have always been a popular theme in boys' clothing, all the way down to their first Spider-Man pull-ups. No wonder. Superheroes are champions. They're the best at something. They seek out danger. And they are called to adventures. They rescue others, but they stand alone. At the age of three, little boys look to identify with fantasy figures that are big and dangerous and powerful—the Hulk, a Teenage Mutant Ninja Turtle, a Power Ranger. Developmental psychologist Erik Erikson wrote about this phase in boys' development, of identification with powerful fantasy figures as they work hard at feeling competent in the world. Sigmund Freud wrote about it too, as the bulking up of the little ego in competition with the Oedipal father before joining the father in civilized pursuits. It's telling that this is the time of nightmares and night terrors, psychoanalytically understood to be the boy's own aggression projected outward onto some terrifying monster. But let's understand this in a different way, as a response to their early notions of what it means to be a boy. They are told they must rule, seek danger and be dangerous, identify with fighters and winners and terrifying beasts, sharks and T-rexes. It's all they see; it's what's expected of them. How can such a little being contain that much aggressive energy or become that aggressive? And how does he contain the shame if he can't or doesn't want these things?

As little boys respond to the world around them, propping themselves up to be big and unafraid, parents and adults respond to them by propping them up too. It may seem like self-esteem building—"brave little man" and "you can do it!" Yet there's little in our responses that confirms to them that they are vulnerable and have a right to be afraid of a T-rex or a car going 250 miles per hour, that it might even be okay to feel as little as the kitten on their sister's tee shirt.

Boys are not only victims of the pressure to rule but are encouraged to believe in their worthiness to rule. It may not seem obvious at this point in their lives, but they are consistently fed messages that they are born to take the lead, to have authority, and always to be in control. For some, this translates into entitlement. They may feel the need to grab the authority they're told they're entitled to, to take power rather than share it or yield to someone else. Others might use authority to take risks, compete, and do well. Still others may see themselves as failures or "less than" a real man if they don't fit the stereotype of those who are invited to take power and rule.

We wonder if anxiety about their sons' masculinity or parents' need to prop them up is behind the latest trend—clothing for little boys that reflects the humor and attitudes of very big boys. Through their clothing, little boys are encouraged to be the ultimate players. "Chicks Dig Me" says a onesie for a three to six month old. "Playground Pimp" says another—*pimp* spelled out in cartoon alphabet blocks. Similar to the increase in the "little hottie" version of clothing for girls, these messages on boys' clothing say something about the erosion of the boundary between childhood and adolescence, and also about what some are calling the general "pornification" of the culture. One has to wonder about companies that promote onesies and tees that say things like "My Mom Is a MILF" (definition: Mother I'd Like to Fuck), "All Daddy Wanted Was a Blow Job," or "Hung Like a Five-Year Old," but they're easy to find online, and of course someone's buying them. These kinds of tees account for 20 percent of T-Shirt Hell's sales. Gary Cohen, T-Shirt Hell's director of operations, justifies them by saying, "Younger, hipper parents are looking for something that's not the same, that has a little more attitude." Why is this particular attitude the definition of hip?

Of course, these tees say more about the parents than the child, but given that little boys aren't interested in shopping, that's generally true of most any article of clothing a boy younger than, say, six or seven wears. In that sense, T-shirt Hell isn't any different from the companies selling high-priced couture infant and toddler tees. Marketing to parents' interests and nostalgia, Crib Rock sells colorful versions of baa baa black sheep and three blind mice in styles "reminiscent of your favorite souvenir concert tee from those head-banger days. Hard rocking never felt so soft."

Whether they base their purchases on their own loves or whatever stereotypes designers and marketers dream up, if they think about their little tike as a whole person, smart parents will begin to notice what's missing, what part of their son's imagination and interests isn't represented in his clothing. Imagine tiny tees for boys that say "Best Friends" and show two boys with their arms around each other's shoulders, or a boy and girl throwing a Frisbee. Imagine a "jump into a book" toddler tee, an "I'm smarter than a fifth grader" slogan on an infant onesie—imagine anything that says he's clever, thoughtful, intellectual, kind, or loving. Also imagine the little face of a three-or four-year-old boy as he ponders a T-rex or a backhoe. Clothing for baby boys needn't only portray fierceness, but could also show awe and wonder, vulnerability and sweetness too.

Special Forces Jungle Fighter Child

Surf the Web, flip through the many catalogs, or walk through department stores beginning in early September to look for a Halloween costume and Boyhood (that's with a capital B) will assault you at every turn. Take him to any big box store like Wal-Mart or Target and your little boy can choose among a dizzying array of costumes. When boiled down, his choices include scary characters, fighters, and heroes—either in superform, like Spider-Man or Batman, or the real-life version, like police officers, military personnel, or sports stars. For the youngest boys there's the occasional Pooh Bear or SpongeBob, even a cute puppy or lion, but they are buried in an avalanche of ninjas, special Delta Force soldiers, and Transformers.

Thanks to marketers, Halloween for boys is about embodying a sense of power and full-throttle action. Boys dress up as men, and the version of manhood presented to them is one in which superheroes and warriors are ready to save the world. Their costumes come with every weapon they need to control, dominate, and save, and just to prove they're physically up for the challenge, costumes come complete with fake muscles. "Bulging padded 'muscles' are stitched into torso, arms and legs," announces a catalog description. "Transform your little hulk into the most powerful human-like creature."

Most powerful. Every costume says extreme action! Being a soldier is tame, almost boring, compared to being a Special Force Fighter Child, complete with ragged, ripped camo pants and "3-D foamed muscle top jumpsuit" that fakes six-pack abs—"A great costume if you want to be Rambo." Of course few boys today know who Rambo is, aside from those who have seen Stallone's recent R-rated sequel with the tagline: "Heroes never die; they just reload." Even if he's not allowed to see the movie, the little boy posing in the costume—his camo headband off-kilter, his hands on his hips, his best five-year-old "don't mess with me" expression—conveys the idea pretty well.

It's no surprise that Halloween invites boys to dress up as the superheroes they watch in movies or sports stars they admire on TV, but it's striking how many costumes are just variations of tough guys carrying all manner of weapons. Fighting crime like Superman and imagining you can dunk a basketball like Lebron James or win the Daytona 500 like NASCAR's Jimmie Johnson is great fantasy, but just as pink and princess have overrun all manner of girls' costumes, boys' costumes have to come with some kind of ninja attitude and fighter paraphernalia.

And more is always, always better. More stuff, bigger muscles, tougher-sounding descriptions. Who wants to be just any ninja when you can be Shadow Ninja Bounty Hunter? This extra-tough guy costume includes a jumpsuit with muscle torso, attached belt, sword, shin guards, apron, hood, and badge. The red and black mask covers all but his eyes: "You'd better hope this ninja isn't on your trail if you're a fugitive on the run because he always gets his man."

Perusing the Halloween costume catalogs sent to homes across the country, we're also struck by the images of little boys posing for these costumes. They must be told by the photographer to give him or her their hardest, scariest, meanest looks, to show the world how big and strong and frightening they can be, how fearless and intimidating. Like WWE stars, they model threatening poses, some showcasing their fake muscles, others in aggressive battle stance, their guns, swords, knives, light sabers, and blasters at the ready or their fake boxing gloves raised, as if to strike the next blow. Many are made up to look like they've just been in a fight, but they're still standing, hair messy, an eye blackened with makeup to show toughness, torn shirts and fake muscles pumped and ready for more.

Looking closer, however, we can see a hint of a smile play around the lips, even a smirk on some. The littlest boys can't help themselves. Many smile openly at the camera, loving the fun of this playful moment when someone takes their picture and tells them how cool and tough they look. The older boys are better at the menacing looks, more practiced and polished at faking invulnerability for the camera, but even then it's clear that this is a performance, an opportunity to imagine the glory and satisfaction of knowing all who come their way will quake in fear or run for their lives. Who wouldn't let their son enjoy a bit of this kind of fantasy?

Halloween is about the stark commercialization of gender. *All* boys go through this door; *all* girls go through that one. It's something we thought we'd left behind years ago. There is no neutral space, no crossing gender lines. Just look straight ahead and march, people! Even animals and insects are coded tough guy and pretty-sexy girl. No colorful butterflies and gossamer wings of dragonflies for boys. No black spiders and bats for girls. Dinosaurs and dogs are for boys. Cats, sexed up in black fishnets and full makeup, are for girls. Everything and everyone is elaborately and distinctly gendered.

Crossing over to the other side, as some do, is possible—boys *can* be dragon-flies, girls *can* be ninjas—but the distinctly male and female poses, the carefully worded descriptions in the catalogs and on Web sites, the clearly labeled "boy" and "girl" categories, alert us to the consequences of not dressing in a gender-appropriate way—they'll be out of synch with their friends and set up for teasing and rejection.

Of course there's something especially pernicious about paying good money to box in our children's worlds and limit their choices at such an early age. Fantasy for children is about trying on new roles or imagining the unusual or impossible, and Halloween is a chance to be whatever wild and crazy identity captivates him in the moment. After seeing costume after costume, he may desperately want to be Super Scary Special Forces Ninja Bounty Hunter Fighter World-Saving Man. Marketers know the promise of all that action and power can be irresistible, especially to boys who don't get the chance to feel that way very often (which is to say, most boys). But, given a real choice—a choice that builds action, fun, and adventure around other options—he may not. If we don't offer the alternative, how will we know?

Since these costumes will be part of his play long after Halloween is over, help him invent stories that include those parts of him you want to nurture, stories that include a range of feelings, his own and others'. Power can be about physical strength and dominance, but it can also be the power to change someone's point of view, persuade evil to be good, to challenge others to do good things. Remind him that every superman has his Kryp-tonite, and it's okay to feel afraid. A superhero needs to listen, pay attention, and show compassion. These skills distinguish a true leader from a despot, and it's never too early to help him know the difference.

Fashion with Attitude

As boys get older, their clothing choices point to a sense of independence and authority, as if they're saying "no one, especially my un-hip parents, has a hold on me." Yet they know a lot about fashion and what it can mean to their image or social standing. They know when they buy American Eagle's distressed jeans and baseball caps they project a casual, preppy, "whatever" attitude; they know when they go for Southpole's hoodies, they're giving off a more urban image, and that Hollister or Pacific Sunwear says "surfer dude."

In our survey, boys told us what they think is cool, sometimes in general terms, like "baggy jeans and baseball caps," "punk stuff," and "band T-shirts"; sometimes in specific terms, like "Bathing Ape hoodies," "Timberland boots," and "DC sneakers." They also told us that "the only cool thing is wearing what you want," "I have my own style," and "I don't know and I don't care." Marketers are well aware that cultivating an image a little too carefully or obviously could suggest that a boy is feminine or gay, so they've carefully waded into these waters by promoting "lifestyle" or a way of living rather than just "style" or "fashion." Selling a lifestyle draws attention away from "feminine" concerns about appearance and refocuses the gaze on more traditionally masculine activities, like risk taking, sports, hip-hop, and girls, girls, girls—because, of course, nothing says you're a real boy more than a lifestyle that includes lots of "real hot" girls. The message conveyed? It's not what you look like that matters; it's what you have, what you do, and who you're doing it with. This is a message that marketers of fashion and image hope boys can get behind.

This attention to "lifestyle" is brilliant because it connects clothing to all kinds of other products and activities, which means big money for those doing the selling. Music, technology, bling, and sports equipment all work together with fashion to create an overall image for boys. Just like those full-page spreads in girls' teen magazines that show a halter top with the right jeans, shoes, accessories, and makeup to create a "type" of girl, boys' fashion online or in magazine ads is displayed with all the right stuff—the cool watch, belt buckle, the expensive sunglasses. The difference is in the overall presentation. Whereas girls pose in passive, sexually provocative ways, boys are shown in action or power poses, showing off, displaying their "lifestyle"— throwing a football, skateboarding, texting friends, holding spray cans in each hand, posing with sexy girls leaning on his sports car. In this way, fashion for boys is more complex and expensive than it might at first appear. The calculated message and well-crafted surface says, "whatever," "I don't care," "it's cool"; but scratch that surface just a little, and parents can catch a glimpse of the desire and the anxiety he feels and the sea of products designed to create and reduce both.

All-Boy, All the Time: Graphic Tees and Jerseys

For most boys graphic tees are about attitude. Their tees announce who they want others to believe they are or aspire to be, or what they find funny, cool, or hip. When T-shirts originated in the 1950s as casual wear, they were strictly a guy thing, and in certain ways they still are. After a brief period of unisex tie-dye in the 1960s, manufacturers of girls' clothing have taken tees in a different direction altogether—tighter fitting, lower necklines, stretchy fabric, lots of glitter and glam. But marketers know very well what the boys in our survey told us en masse—that they'd never wear anything remotely girly, nothing that says, as they put it, "I'm a pussy" or "I'm gay." Even in stores that sell sports tees or Life is Good wear, there's a clear, stereotypical gender divide in color, style, and message. Girls' tees sport pink daisies and that smiley Life is Good stick figure in various forms of stillness or relaxation, like taking bubble baths or practicing yoga poses. By contrast, the boys' tees display funny slogans and lots of action. For example, one tee sports a skater grabbing his board in midair and says: "board silly"—the perfect combination of goofy humor, action, and that "I don't care" image found in so much of boys' media. On another there's a football player in midthrow; on another a hockey player in midfall. Life is Good projects the boy who loves adventure and sports, who's part of a team but working on his individual skills.

But is this the image that boys themselves like to present to the world? None of the boys in our survey chose sporty versions of Life is Good as a favorite tee, although many, especially middle schoolers, chose professional sports teams or favorite sports figures like the NBA's Shaquille O'Neal, the NFL's Brian Urlacher, and, WWE's self-proclaimed "Doctor of Thuganomics," John Cena. Maybe the generic message in a Life is Good tee doesn't say enough about who a boy is or who he wants to be. So let's take a closer look. If we read tees as a store window into marketers' views of how little boys can become big guys, they tell us a number of things:

Being a guy means being better and tougher than the next guy.

This "top dog" message crosses a lot of tee styles and brands. It can be said in a funny, straightforward way, when tees say things like "Go home and practice. Come back when you're more of a challenge," "This is what awesome looks like," and even "Humble, but still the Best." "Being the best" is a loaded term, and it can be performed or implied as well as said directly. It can mean being the best at a sport, being the most sexually desired, being edgy and in the know, getting a subtle satiric message, or staying ahead of the (music, skater, hip-hop) curve. Whether it's about performance or knowledge, cocky or humble, it's all about throwing down the gauntlet or, rather, announcing you've already won the competition.

Being a guy means being into sports.

Sports tees and jerseys are some of the most popular for boys in our survey: favorite players, favorite school, college, or professional teams, or just favorite sports brands like Nike and Adidas. In some ways they're a version of the "I'm the best" message, especially when the players (or numbers) boys choose to wear are the best in their sport. But these tees can give off a range of meanings not obvious to the uninformed. Wearing John Cena on a tee can mean more than that a boy's into wrestling, or even that he identifies with Cena's public persona as a hardworking good guy (in the good-bad column WWE promotes) and winner of Wrestlemania's XXV World Heavyweight Championship. It might also mean he's announcing his interest in hip-hop, because Cena's known for challenging rappers to compete with him onstage and has ventured into the recording studio. Similarly, a boy wearing the Nike swoosh might identify with their "Legend" ads because they highlight the success of athletes such as Michael Jordan and Tiger Woods and he too wants to become legendary someday, or he may simply like the no excuses, "just do it" philosophy Nike projects.

Wearing Nike, Patriots, Peyton Manning, LeBron James, or John Cena tees, boys announce their desire to be serious competitors and winners. Choosing these tees also shows that they identify with a position, an attitude, or a philosophy of the NFL, NBA, or WWE athletes they admire (as offered through marketers, of course). Wearing tees that say things like "I support 2 teams: The Red Sox and whoever beats the Yankees," they claim a place in a wider community of men, while displaying their knowledge of the game with the players and teams they choose.

Being a guy means being confident, cool, and cocky.

Some boys announce their comfort with themselves in funny, sweet ways through their tees. "It's just the way I am" says one boy's favorite. Others announce their difference from the norm with the slogans that reject or deflect others' judgments or criticism. Guys who lean toward goth can find tees that say "Ignoring you" and other similar messages designed to project a kind of aloofness, even if they might not be feeling so sure of themselves. These tees tell us that being a guy means not showing uncertainty, doubt, or fear.

Abercrombie & Fitch (A&F) tees display team jersey–style numbers and project an image of the big man on campus defined as a player. Their tees have slogans like "Save a Cherry, Pop a Collar" (popping a cherry is code for breaking a girl's hymen), and "One Man's Junk Is Another Woman's

Treasure" ("junk" here is reference to a boys' private parts), which are designed to be clever and edgy at the same time. The Hollister look is that of a laid-back surfer dude in tee, jeans, and flip-flops with images of surfboards, girls in bikinis, and a few suggestive sayings, like one we saw that had "Calif" down the side intersecting like a crossword puzzle with "Fornia" along the bottom (suggesting fornication) and the slogan "if it swells, ride it." This tee suggests that one of the best ways a guy can look cool is to be funny in an irreverent kind of way by announcing his interest in girls and sex.

Some of the most popular tees associate an urban feel with a distinctly masculine hip-hop image, and while younger boys might not be reading magazines that promote them, they are looking to older boys for their style, and those guys can find these brands marketed in *Vibe*, *XXL*, and *Skateboard*. In fact, the coolest tees these days, like lots of boys' media, pretty much require *Urban Dictionary*, an online searchable archive of the latest slang, to interpret. Parents might want to bookmark this Web site or sign up for their "word of the day." Boys wearing hip-hop–inspired clothing say all kinds of things about their image, and that's because hip-hop isn't a monolithic style but one that's blended and crossed with different kinds of styles. Mighty Healthy, an increasingly popular clothing brand, is a Brooklyn-based company founded on the integration of hip-hop and skater wear. Boys wearing Southpole, Mighty Healthy, and other urban brands can have a clean, cool, sporty image, even when the graphics suggest a darker, tougher street gang/graffiti–inspired look, such as an image of an apple split down the middle with a knife, revealing a rotten core, or a decaled photo of a blinged-up Tupac.

Being a guy means being into girls.

Lots of guys wear tees that give the impression that they're players: "Here I am. Now what were your other wishes?" says one boy's favorite tee. A pink Kohl's Urban Pipeline tee popular with a few of the guys in our survey announces "Chicks Dig Pink," making fun of the obvious and hoping to cash in on the sea of pink products marketed to girls. Other popular tees playfully invite girls to "talk nerdy to me" or announce, "Every 3 seconds a girl thinks about me." These messages are a little cheesy—and not unlike the bad pickup lines one might hear in a bar—but they make a boy feel funny, cute, and clever, especially in contrast to the more provocative girl-focused tees out there.

Other tees objectify women as sex objects or are demeaning in some way. They say things like "You can have my sister" or "Let's flip a coin. Heads I get tail. Tails I get head," and "Let's play Army. We get bombed, then you blow the crap out of me." Why is it funny for guys to imagine actually saying something so crude? Not because they can imagine actually saying this to a girl, but because they can imagine a bunch of other guys laughing at it. A lot of guys in our survey told us they won't wear these kinds of tees or their parents won't let them. Still, a good many list them as favorites.

Being a guy means having a sense of humor.

Humor is a big part of boys' media, and tees are a popular place for boys to announce what and whom they find funny. Psychologists who study humor cite its many and varied uses: it can be used to reduce tension, connect people with others, and contribute to social acceptance, attract attention, and help one survive in stressful circumstances. It also can be used to make a point, support an argument, or reveal what kind of person you are. Marketers targeting boys use all of these tactics. A boy teased at school for being into emo or goth can diffuse the pain or express his alienation with a shirt that says "I hear voices and they don't like you" or can make a statement about violence and aggression they might experience or see with a tee that says "weapon of choice" accompanied by an image of a guitar.

As we've written earlier about the slacker dude, it's all right to humorously loathe oneself, because it's an alternative to the "cool popular player" persona. In fact, even the cool popular players love the slacker dudes who might wear self-deprecating tees like "I bring nothing to the table" or "I'd do your homework, but I don't even do mine" as a way to reduce the anxiety boys may feel when expectations are too low or they're struggling academically. This way a boy can announce slacking or embrace checking out as a choice and not the result of a struggle to learn or a teacher's assumption that he can't or won't learn. Marketers also know boys desire desperately to be funny, because to be serious, especially in school, is to be "girl-like" and responsible, studious, or boring.

Like sports tees, funny images and slogans imply more than the message. "I know hippies, I've hated them all my life," for example, tells other people that a boy likes the parodied, raunch humor of *South Park* and knows the episode "Die Hippie Die" where Cartman utters the phrase.

Of course humor can also be abusive or used as a way of expressing rage or inciting aggression toward a group of people, as with some racist slogans or images. Only a few boys mentioned such tees (and more chose sexist ones than any other off-color slogans), so we were glad to hear that most drew a line somewhere. When we asked boys what T-shirts they wouldn't wear, a number said they avoid slogans altogether, a few said they avoided anything racist or sexist, and some avoided drug or alcohol references (although there were a few favorites in this category, like the McDonald's sign parody, "Marijuana, over 1 billion stoned"). But there was one message most boys agreed they wouldn't or couldn't joke about. The clear majority said directly and forcefully that they wouldn't wear anything that says "I'm gay."

And lest we forget, being a guy means being straight.

With humor boys can say almost anything they want in a way that diffuses pressures they may feel to be a certain kind of guy. But they know that no manner of humor can protect them against the threat of being THAT kind of guy. How a boy announces he's not gay isn't always clear—the code differs for boys in certain cultural groups and across race lines. For some boys pink polos are in; for others wearing pink is okay if the tee announces "Chicks Dig Pink" but not okay without this clear intention to attract girls or to fit in with a certain group of straight guys. Neat shirts with collars in bright-colored stripes are okay for an urban look, but only if they're oversize and the wearer is sporting other signs of a hip-hop image, like low-riding baggy pants, a baseball cap to the side, and untied sneakers. However it's defined and agreed upon within a particular group of boys, humor is often used to ensure they're "read" as straight. In this way, humor can be a way to reinforce an accepted image that not only excludes gay boys, but can also justify verbal and physical harassment toward this group. Of course this image also justifies all those sexist images and phrases so often used by boys to assure the rest of the world they aren't gay.

Tees are a great place to begin a conversation with your son about the kind of boy he is or wants to become and whether he wants to announce this to other people. Humor is fine, and sports can inspire some of his best qualities, but there are funny, sporty, and other messages that reduce him to something not so inspiring and contribute to a climate that makes others feel unsafe, demeaned, or anxious. You might want to tell him about David Shepherd and Travis Price, two high school seniors from Cambridge, Nova Scotia, who rallied their classmates to support a ninth grade boy who was called homophobic slurs and threatened with violence for wearing a pink polo shirt to school. The "sea of pink" campaign started when the two boys learned of the incident. They e-mailed their classmates and used various social networking Web sites to ask students to take a stand against such behavior by wearing pink to school. More than half of the school's 830 students wore pink polos, tees, and other paraphernalia the following day.

Since then, the "sea of pink" campaign has taken on a life of its own, and schools across North America are implementing "wear pink days" to show their solidarity. Now that's a statement.

Smells Like Teen Spirit?

It used to be that boys smelled like boys—all dirt and sweat. But these days fragrances for boys are gaining momentum, and at younger ages. Hoping to capitalize on their popularity in Latin America, Disney has a line of cologne and body spray for four- to eleven-year olds, primarily marketed to U.S. Latino boys. It's hard to make cologne attractive to any six-year-old boy, but they give it their best shot: "Fun and great for kids! Your child will love to spray and play!" Fun? Great for them? We think that's probably a big stretch. With all the youth marketing experts over at Disney, certainly they know that little boys have better things to do than shop for new ways to smell good. Disney is really targeting moms and grandmothers, who hold the purse strings, and who most likely have to endure the pungent smell of a boy after a day of playing outside. And who knows? Maybe little Jorge or Billy really would go for a splash of Donald Duck over a bath? But it's hard to imagine what the *Cars*, Buzz Lightyear, or *Pirates of the Caribbean* cologne Disney is selling would actually smell like. (Aren't pirates supposed to stink?)

To be fair, Disney's not the only one in the boy's cologne market. Marvel Superheroes cologne has been around for a few years—ah, get a whiff of their "Hulk Eau De Toilette Spray" in the cool green bottle. But what do these companies mean when they tell us that the age of male customers for cologne and eau de toilette is getting younger? They're saying more than just "boys get dirty" or "little boys want to be like their dads." They're suggesting there's a certain kind of image making it's way down to younger ages. A spokesperson for Disney's cologne distributor makes the link explicit for us in *Brandweek*, a marketing publication: "Look at the success of Axe [body spray]. It targets [males] 18–24 years, but ages 12-and-up are buying it like it's going out of style. The age of [male] fragrance wearers is moving down."

Remember the Aqua Velva TV commercial from the late 1970s featuring "babe magnet" Pete Rose seductively telling a cute female sportscaster that "a man wants to smell like a man"? We don't see a lot that's different in more recent cologne advertisements. David Beckham's Intense Instinct and Antonio Banderas's Diavolo use smoldering good looks and physical sex appeal in magazines like *Marie Claire* to entice women to buy the scent of masculinity for their men. Unforgiveable by Sean John targets men and is more sexually explicit, showing P. Diddy slipping between the sheets in a menage à trois with a white woman and an Asian woman (an ad that prompted protest from his own community). This ad can only be seen online because it was deemed "too hot for TV."

While teens may see ads for adult male fragrances on TV or in magazines, they are actually the target consumer for those that accompany popular teen clothing lines like A&F and Gap. Not surprising, given its history of employing very young models in very sexy ads, A&F markets their Fierce fragrance as an "attention getter" (the bottle sports a black-and-white image of perfectly cut abs), Proof as "packed full of dominant masculine attitude. . . . The Proof is in the man," and 41 as "a rich masculine scent" for that "rush of energy that pulls through and wins the game every time." While these may sound more like energy drink slogans, the marketers have been able to combine three attitudes at once—"don't fuck with me," "I'm a winner," and "don't I smell nice?"

Smelling good makes boys feel good because boys do get smelly and because they've been told "boys are gross; boys are smelly" since they were little kids. Of course they would be insecure about the way they smell, so cologne addresses that insecurity. Cologne ads for young and old are about attracting women, being sexy and sought after, even winning; they're also about proving dominance or expressing instinctual desires and uncontrollable urges.

So how do marketers sell their product to the younger set, to boys not yet sure how to get a girl's attention or what to do with those newly felt urges? These brands are the ones with the sophomoric PG-13 themes, full of base humor and raunch sexuality. They're the ones that do away with the anxiety of being "cut" enough or masculine enough. You can be just an average guy, riding your bike, getting on the bus, hanging out—spray a little product, and the hottest, sexiest girls *will come to you.* They won't of course, and that's the funny part (and probably a relief to most middle school boys!). But this is male fantasy in the making.

The makers of Axe, the fragrance and body spray that twelve-year-old boys buy in droves, know this. While parents might approve of Dove's Campaign for Real Beauty for the "love your body" messages it sends to girls and women, they may have missed the fact that Unilever, Dove's parent organization, doesn't give such a healthy message to boys about themselves, or about girls. While Axe insists their target audience is college guys and they aren't looking to market to the younger set, it's hard to take them seriously. Moms tells us their twelve-year-olds have Axe bottles lined along their bureaus. The college-aged young men we teach chuckle at the ads, but generally they don't play the simple Web site games (Naughty to Nice Program), read the *Axe Wearer's Handbook* ("Handling Multiples: How to tell triplets apart in bed? Write their names on the bottom of their feet—use permanent ink if you're planning to go in a hot tub"). Most say they don't use the stuff. Middle school boys, however, love their funny ads about packs of girls sniffing out and hunting down guys. Check out Axe on YouTube and you'll see the full collection, with porn-inspired names like Girl Fight and Hot School Girls.

The earlier Axe ads—the most famous, at least until recently, about a guy marooned on a beach who sprays on Axe and hordes of half-dressed women, like animals, stampede through the jungle to get to him—were unusual and visually clever. But the newer campaign aimed at making nice girls naughty is crass, funny, and absurdly sexist. The Bom Chicka Wa Wa campaign is designed around a scantily clad girls group, à la the Pussycat Dolls, who sing (undress, pole dance, fondle guys) about the effects of Axe on nice girls. *BusinessWeek* called it "edgy humor" (why does "edgy" equal "sexy" in boys' media?) and praised the company for "coming to grips with doing business in this complexly wired world." And on a purely marketing level, that's true. The Bom Chicka Wa Wa girls commercials were designed to be watched on YouTube, featured on Axe's Web site, shared among friends— that is, to be everywhere a teen boy is these days, and everywhere most parents are not.

Other brands have followed suit, like Gillette's TAG Body Spray and deodorant. In one ad a woman in a sexy white lab smock and spike heels feeds hot red peppers to an unsuspecting guy with electrodes attached to his armpits. A red triangle warning sign (a girl with her head on fire and the logo "consider yourself warned") accompanies the copy: "Tested under the hottest conditions. WARNING: Product's scent may turn already hot hotties hotter than a habanero." A boy who sends a friend the link to TAG's Web site does so to share the games at the "TAG testing facility." Here he enters the Body Spray Field Testing site, invited in by a buxom blonde scientist in a tight white vinyl jumpsuit with a gas mask. He can click on one of the many products and spray an average-looking guy's various body parts to watch a bevy of sexy cheerleaders, or lingerie-clad girls, or sexy Catholic school girls run onto the scene, jump on him, knock him over, fondle him, and fight over him. After watching some good romps, he can move on to Show & Tell and choose a product, each represented by a different pornlike silhouette of a dancing woman in a bikini. He might click on a product called Body Shots ("It's locked. It's loaded. It's in your pocket. Think of the possibilities.") Then there's the "anti-perspirant surveillance video," where three unsuspecting TAG-wearing guys on mountain bikes are sent into what looks like a desert nuclear-testing facility. They find hot women jumping on trampolines who pick up their scent, sniffing the air like dogs. Instinctually the women squirt their mouths with whipped cream and chocolate, do limber yoga stretches, and rub them down.

Parents need to talk with their sons about the appeal and the demeaning nature of these ads. In the world of middle school, lots of girls (like the Axe and TAG women in their scientist outfits doing experiments on guys) may seem, and in some cases may really be, more in control, more put together, more aggressive, even smarter. Girls develop earlier than boys, and at this age they're likely to be more into dating. They are sometimes more likely to be the one calling, flirting, or initiating talk about romance, even sex. These ads play on this part of middle school life in the cleverest kind of way. Beyond the hot girls and the lowest-common-denominator sexism, the shock on the faces of guys being attacked and tackled by girls may seem kind of familiar. But the girl in the Axe video shaking her bootie and humping household appliances is not the girl in your son's classroom and never will be. How he treats her and nurtures their friendship or their budding romance—even how he chooses to handle her aggressive advances—is something you'll want to help him think through.

These ads offer something else to middle school boys—a sense of being welcomed into a club at a time when fitting in and being a regular guy is pretty important. They say, "Hey, we're guys, this is what guys want; I watch these videos, I pass them around, I get the joke. We're in the guy club where hot girls are used to show us just how cool we are." Even the "nerdiest" guy who doesn't really think about hot girls can be part of the club by just knowing, sending, and receiving that "edgy" humor. But you can appeal to your son's sense of decency by pointing out how unfair it is, even just joking around, to use girls as props to make boys feel cool or a part of a special club. In the end, of course, it's fine to talk about smells and "smells"—his more funky growing-up smells—and that it's okay to want to smell better. It's just important to bring it all back to earth—you can smell nice so people don't get up and move to a different row of the movie theater, but it's probably not going to get the girls in the back row to fight to sit on your lap.

Keepin' It Real: Hip-Hop Fashion

> Money, hoes, and clothes all a nigga knows
> —NOTORIOUS B.I.G

P. Diddy has Sean Jean, 50 Cent has G-Unit, Eminem has Shady, Jay-Z has Rocawear. As Notorious B.I.G. tells us in his rap "Big Poppa," hip-hop is as much about fashion as it is about music. In fact, hip-hop as a lifestyle could take up a big section of every chapter in this book—it's what a lot of boys wear and listen to, but it's also what they watch and what they do. A parent may love it, hate it, fear it, or just want to avoid it, but hip-hop is a big part of your son's world, and so it's very important to understand it.

Rap music's beginnings in the 1970s drew from African rhythms and culture, and whether it was the green, yellow, and red colors of the African flag worn by early political rappers Public Enemy, the balloon pants worn by MC Hammer, or the gang colors of Tupac and Biggie Smalls, fashion has always been at the heart of hip-hop culture.

Hip-hop as a commercial fashion style began in the 1980s when certain brands, like Nike and Adidas, attached themselves to popular rappers. Since then it's been all about expanding and conquering. The genre moved in the mid-1990s from an important political commentary and socially dangerous response to racism and poverty to become a very big business for white-owned companies and fashion designers. Tommy Hilfiger was the first major designer to actively court rappers to promote a line of street wear—he's known for being the first to sell mass-market baggy jeans—and Biggie Smalls (or Notorious B.I.G.), part of the East Coast gangsta rap scene, became a part of Hilfiger's attempt to tap urban youth. Hilfiger gave free wardrobes to rappers, and his name was mentioned in rhyming verses and "shout-out" lyrics (shout-outs are where rap artists chant out thanks to friends and sponsors in performances). And the rappers were indeed influential—in 1994 New York City stores sold out of a Hilfiger sweatshirt the day after Snoop Dogg wore it on *Saturday Night Live*.

Black designers benefited as well. Karl Kani was the first black designer to receive national attention, and his 1990s baggy jeans and casual oversize knits found an unexpected white suburban audience. FUBU (for us by us—four young black male designers) made 350 million in 1998.

But it was inevitable that "mixing"—the musical technique of sampling and combining others' music at the root of the movement—would impact hip-hop fashion. The colors of the African flag gave way to American red, white, and blue (significantly, the Hilfiger colors), and hip-hop style became absorbed into the white youth culture. As hip-hop musicians and producers themselves became fashion designers, art, commodification, and materialism became further mixed. Phat Farm, created in 1992 by Russell Simmons, Def Jam Records cofounder and producer, for example, sells a version of black authenticity that pictures black men as a public threat, but does so by using the red, white, and blue of Hilfiger and Ralph Lauren. P. Diddy's clothing line, Sean John, is one of the most successful companies, initially branding and marketing the hip-hop lifestyle, but now transcending the look to compete successfully with the top American designers.

But Simmons, P. Diddy, and the like have to deal with white producers selling authentic blackness in a way that suppresses the reality and diversity of black culture, spitting out a popular version of hip-hop that appeals to white boys. The gangsta/pimp image defined by bling, drugs, and crime has an appeal to white male listeners, in part because it fits the stereotypes of black masculinity and because this stereotyped life is romanticized. But the clothes have moved beyond these stereotypes to influence more mainstream fashion like polo shirts. Whenever any subversive style becomes popular it's redone in ways that meld with a variety of other styles to be more acceptable to the mainstream. Some call that co-opting what was rebellious about it in the first place, thus undermining any hint of rebellion.

Today, hip-hop fashion reads like this description of a T-shirt brand: "In this hypebeast kind of world the Mighty Healthy can stay ahead of the curve with spot-on parodies of skate designs and thought provoking hip hop referenced mottos. Inspired by the sounds of the so-called golden age of hip hop, Mighty Healthy also embraces traditional brands from the era, such as Polo, Timberland and Hilfiger." Hip-hop is increasingly about the latest fashion. Those wearing the clothing it inspires announce their awareness of this fact with sneakers and the all-important goal to be "fresh" while showing a certain steez (style with ease). Ironically, to pull off that ease and "keepin' it real" look takes a bundle of money and a lot of conspicuous consumption. In fact, a hypebeast (according to *Urban Dictionary*) is "a kid that collects clothing, shoes, and accessories for the sole purpose of impressing others," and more than anything else, this is the image that a boy who is into urban style projects to the world.

The staples of hip-hop fashion have been fat-laced or no-laced shoes, platinum and white gold bling, baggy jeans, and oversize hoodies, even though recently, rappers like Common, will.i.am, and Kanye West are wearing suit jackets, tighter jeans, and fitted tees. There are some pretty clear and consistent messages this style sends to boys—about fashion and its relationship to money and lifestyle, about history and belonging, about masculinity and its relationship to violence and relationships with girls.

One of the best messages is that boys can have style, that their clothes can be imaginative, that they can mix it up, create an image, even be ironic and political in subtle, clever ways. If they look at their fathers in work uniforms, suits, and the button-down attire that most men are required to wear, they're likely to think growing up is about becoming boring, practical, and having no flair. All the restrictions a boy sees about what kind of flair he can have, such as avoiding any pink or frills, turns into a major restriction to look (and act) like everyone else. So when ads for clothing by companies like LRG (Lifted Research Group) come along with cool hip-hop styles and copy that reads "a company designed to overthrow the masses with our influence" and "a support group for the independent and underground culture," it's a pretty attractive message.

Flair, style, and originality don't *have* to mean conspicuous consumption. But the stylish clothing advertised to boys today is awfully expensive (LRG says they "focus on the ones that are trying to pay their rent with their passions" but sells lots of clothes that those struggling guys couldn't afford, like $100 hoodies) and suggests an unreachably extravagant lifestyle complete with girls, sports cars, expensive sunglasses, watches, jewelry, and clothes.

Such conspicuous consumption is most clearly seen in the bling that hip-hop artists wear in their magazine spreads and ads for their clothing lines and is reinforced in their lyrics and videos. As Lil Wayne raps in "Got Money," "Take it out your pocket and show it, then throw it . . ."

Boys themselves are less likely to have money to throw around or own that amount of bling—usually big ropes and medallions made of platinum, jeweled rings, earrings, piercings, and sometimes "grills" (removable metal covers molded to fit over teeth). More likely their bling will show up emblazoned in rhinestones on their T-shirts. But the constant display of wealth, connected to a certain kind of tough masculinity and power, is incredibly enticing, creating desire that's impossible for the average boy to fulfill.

But whose desire? Who are these clothing ads aiming for, and what impact do they have when they hit their target audience? We know from economists' research that blacks and Hispanics will spend more than whites of the same income level on luxury items like clothing, cars, and jewelry. Originally, urban boys bought high-priced sneakers, clothing, or jewelry to signal status and wealth. When white middle-class boys buy hip-hop fashion they like to show they have money too, but they also want to signal an image of an "authentic," edgy, tough urban guy.

There are some rappers who are openly critical of the commercialization of hip-hop. In his 2006 "Hip Hop Is Dead," Nas raps:

> *Everybody sound the same, commercialize the game*
> *Reminiscin' when it wasn't all business*

But in hip-hop, wearing certain fashion, either to follow the crowd or to identify with a certain artist, can mean demonstrating support of someone's line; thus loyalty can cost boys a lot.

Loyalty can mean something more positive than belonging to a gang. When a boy is loyal to a brand like Jay-Z's Rocawear, he could be conforming—simply buying rather than really living their "Be heard" and "I will not lose" messages—or he could have investigated the entire line on the Internet, learned about the designers, and even the lifestyles of the designers. Take an expensive West Coast brand of original hoodies and T-shirts sold in specialty stores called Upper Playground. As in an art show catalog, the Web site talks about the designs and the designers in ways that connect that sense of belonging to a sense of artistic appreciation. Look across different sites and the graphics tell stories, allude to significant historical moments, people, and places, and play with symbols that hold meaning to the initiated. This kind of belonging is about history and a sense of place and purpose.

Baseball hats, sneakers, and jerseys are also part of announcing with whom a boy belongs. There's nothing wrong with a boy announcing his team (or geographic) loyalty through his clothing or the name on the back of his T-shirt. Going to school and walking the streets can produce a car honk, a thumbs-up sign, or a serious conversation about statistics. But keeping tags and authentication stickers on this merchandise while wearing it means something else. It is intended to show that your gear is real rather than a knockoff, and that it's "fresh" or new, and, perhaps more importantly, that you're not just posing as cool.

Hip-hop fashion is all about having what's hot, and tags, authentication, and real vs. fake bling show this. It's also about "keepin' it real," as in staying true to yourself and your roots, even if your roots aren't in poor urban America. In fact, many middle-class black boys try to pass as "real," like hip-hop artists before them, by hiding their middle-class status. Marketers know the authenticity message sells hip-hop, especially when they can connect realness with edgy, original, and *exclusive*. Atlanta rapper Young Jeezy's frowning snowman promotional tee, banned for its alleged cocaine references, was one of the most bootlegged T-shirts of 2005–2006. Exclusivity sells, which is why hip-hop clothing marketers announce specific locations to increase the hype and consumer value of certain brands and products.

"Real" has its roots in hip-hop and has come to mean an almost mythic sense of virility, danger, and physicality. Clothing ads almost always feature black rappers and black models in tough poses, promising this "authenticity" in the form of gambling (a Lot29 ad features playing cards), graffiti (an Ecko model with spray cans in each hand), roots (Akademiks Native Warriors clothing), black power (P. Diddy modeling his clothing line, Sean John, in the now famous Tommy Smith pose, one fist in the air), and dance moves (Rocawear's B-boy poses). These cool, tough images clearly attract young white men to the clothing, but they also drive home stereotypes of young black men and fear and dread of violent black culture by white consumers. Jeffrey Ogbar argues in *Hip-Hop Revolution* that fashion spreads in *Vibe* and other popular magazines place the hip-hop body in "a state of constant leisure and play," and he connects this image to old stereotypes of shiftless, lazy blacks. But it appeals to boys because they aren't ready for the world of work, and indeed, they are in a state of constant leisure (save for school). Moreover, many feel oppressed by their parents, worry about the police (whether on the streets or with their new licenses), and are frustrated with their limited finances.

Hip-hop fashion opens up a space for boys to care about their appearance without seeming "gay," because it does so by announcing a hyperheterosexual masculinity. The prevailing theme in this genre, pimp wear (e.g., Phat Pimp Clothing Company's tees that say things like "I got it 4 cheap" and "go down south") underscores or perpetuates this image in boys' clothing too.

For parents, sorting out the good from the bad is nearly impossible. So much of hip-hop fashion seems to honor a history of oppression for black people in our country; so much seems to exploit that history and stick black boys permanently in it. For this reason, hip-hop fashion offers a smorgasbord of possible conversations to have with your son, from the wonderful creativity of clothing styles and the use of fashion to craft an identity, to the rags-to-riches trajectory of rappers with their own innovative clothing lines, to the origin of baggy beltless pants, to the sexualization of women, to conspicuous consumption in the midst of poverty and need. Not one of these alone defines hip-hop fashion, and it's unlikely that just one of these defines his interest in or love of this kind of clothing. So if you can find a way to both enjoy his interests and help him question some of the questionable stuff, perhaps you can redefine "keepin' it real."

Sneaker Lifestyle

From young to old, sneakers are almost exclusively what boys wear on their feet. Why is that? Because they're practical? Sure. But wearing only sneakers also shows a certain narrowness of being that pervades boys' worlds, which can be easily captured and exploited by marketers. That's unfortunate, because diversity is not only the spice of life and freedom of expression a right, but wearing something unique also makes boys vulnerable to the humiliation of being different, or worse, being "girly."

While we challenge the "Law of Sneakers," we also have to admit that there's a ton of creativity within the market. Perhaps this expresses a tension: boys have to conform, and yet they yearn too, like girls, to express themselves with a little flair, color, and personality. So to keep it "fresh," boys are sold amazing new designs and colors, sneakers that integrate graffiti artists' work. They are offered sneakers promoted by sports stars or hip-hop artists or "vintage" and rare sneakers from the 1980s and 1990s. There's some variety, but that comes at a cost—literally. Many sneaks cost $100 and upward, and when your son *has* to have a new pair every three months or less, when the sneaks he buys make him feel like a pimp rather than a star or a B-boy or a DJ, then a parent starts to worry.

It may seem like a good thing when marketers play up the uniqueness and originality of sneakers, but this also means that they are justified in setting up limited releases so that only a few kids can get them and show them off. Controlled roll-offs and hyping are done by releasing, say, 25,000 shoes in a "pop-up store" before releasing 250,000 of the same shoes later on. Moreover, companies can then keep coming up with new and original variations on the same theme, because new and original becomes old and clichéd very quickly. Marketers support the idea of new and original by creating ads around insider information, so that small differences in style or technology become big differences for the subculture. (And since hip-hop itself is about a new mix, they hardly have to say anything to sell the product—as long as it's part of a hip-hop line, or their favorite "boys" are wearing them, they'll want them.) They also hardly need to pay for advertising if they can create street buzz about a certain design or series, as was true for Air Force Ones. Fifteen million shoes were sold before Nike spent a single dollar on advertising. Planned obsolescence will result in collectors' glorification of a shoe and the need for newer, cooler shoes for each season.

Sneaker hunters, collectors, and many a teen boy seek out cool sneakers by going to specialty stores. With new money to spend, and multiple sneakers to sport, teenage boys hang out and admire stores like Harputs in the Fillmore district of San Francisco for their collection of original sneakers and the stories about who wore what when. The idea that white boys can belong to a subculture, even if the sneaker fad has become totally mainstreamed, is played up by some of these smaller places. In Boston there's a specialty store that sells street wear, and it looks like a tiny grocery store, a Bodega, which is the store's name. But as you stand around, confused by the stacks of laundry detergent, cereal, and Moxie bottles, looking shiftily at the thuglike character behind the counter, a secret passageway opens through which you pass to the well-lit wooden-shelved store in the back. Everyone gets in, but it sure gives a kid the illusion of being a part of an exclusive subculture.

Far be it from us to criticize boys for wanting to look fashionable or fresh; in fact, we kind of like the trend. But where did these fashion ideas come from, and what's the message in the advertising to boys? How do their kicks make them feel?

It used to be that sneakers were all about performance, jumping higher and running faster; higher and faster, by the way, are relative terms, and that's a good thing. In the past there were very few promises made that a boy would be the best, a champion. Sneakers were rugged footwear for boyish activities. But in today's hyped-up world of extraordinary promises of prestige and entitlement, sneakers make the boy. Even sneakers have to be over-the-top.

While the marketers sell the idea that sneakers give a boy both ankle and arch support for the sports that he plays, only 20 percent of sneakers sold today are actually sold for athletics. Instead, they are the most sought after fashion accessory, says Bobbito Garcia, editor of *Bounce*.

The sneaker industry grew out of basketball, break dancing, and hip-hop, but really, out of the urban African American community. As hip-hop scholar Koe Rodriguez puts it in the movie *Just for Kicks*, "brothers like to coordinate." And Scoop Jackson, the author of *Sole Provider*, claims that this has been true of "brothers" even as far back as the 1920s, when black men would step out for a night on the town in Harlem. It fits into a capitalist belief that people can create who they are, and they can do that through buying and wearing the right clothes. As a member of the break-dance group Rock Steady Crew more kindly claims in *Just for Kicks*, in a society that puts you down, when you step out, you want to be visible, to be "larger than life." Sneakers were a way to be just that.

How did this interest in a fashion accessory become mainstream? That has to do both with basketball and the mainstreaming of hip-hop music rather than the break dancers who first showed them off. But it's a good story to tell your son, if he doesn't already know it, a story that will help him separate the hype vs. the "hip" around a shoe.

The rap group Run-D.M.C. were the first to dress on stage as if they were from the streets, looking like what was then called a "stick-up kid." They wore Adidas. Many others were wearing their sneakers without laces at that time, imitating guys just released from prison (because shoelaces weren't issued in jail). In 1983, the rappers' fans began to notice their shoes, and audiences of thousands of kids would wear Adidas to their concerts. An upper-middle-class African American doctor named Dr. Deas also noticed. He was an amateur musician who thought this sneaker craze was detrimental to the community because black boys were dressing like ex-cons rather than like the lawyers and doctors they should be aspiring to become. As a result, he wrote, performed, and distributed a rap song called "felon sneakers" to which the famous Run-D.M.C. "My Adidas" song became a reply. The legend goes that Russell Simmons, manager of Run-D.M.C. at the time, was high on angel dust (he's clean today) when he called the band to him on the street and told them they had to write the song "My Adidas." They knew he was high and were confused about why they were getting this command, but they said that they would write it if they could put out a positive message and "flip the stereotype" of kids wearing Adidas. Simmons told them, "whatever," as long as they mention "my Adidas." They wrote it, they performed it, and a marketer from Adidas attended one concert where about 20,000 kids waved their Adidas in the air in response to a cry of, "All y'all wearin Adidas, let me see them." This marketer went straight back to the conservative German company to convince them to make a deal with the rap group, which they did, and in 1986, $1.5 million later, Adidas started the Run-D.M.C. collection, which also included apparel. Other groups and businesses followed suit, including Fresh Gordon with Filas and LL Cool J with Troops.

In 1987 Nike, way behind in the game given their association with white runners, signed on with Michael Jordan *before* his first NBA game. Smart move. Air Jordans became the most popular series; number 23, Jordan's own jersey number, was released to great fanfare. At one point one out of twelve Americans owned at least one pair of Air Jordans.

Following these events came media stories of guys stealing other guys' sneakers. Today this is lore. How frequently were people knifed, gunned down, or killed for sneakers? We don't know specifics, but we do know it was perceived as a problem and journalists pounced on it. It could just as well have been a marketing strategy to let mainstream America know that expensive sneakers were hot while at the same time selling the "authenticity" stereotype of the violent black man.

New, fresh sneakers represented a flamboyant lifestyle that only rap stars or drug dealers could approach. Today Damon Dash, cofounder with Jay-Z of Rocawear, states he doesn't like to wear the same pair twice. In the film Just for Kicks, he explains his confusion in the morning when he stares into his roomful of shoes. Rent this film if you can. Watching him stare at hundreds, probably thousands, of shoes will make you hope for a moment that his confusion is about how absurd it was to spend so much money on shoes. The truth is, he's just confused about which pair to wear that day. Too many choices; over-the-top.

These backstories form the basis of marketing to your sons regarding the sneakers they wear. Marketers use sports stars in their campaigns, but only the very best. Michael Jordan was considered the best and could do things nobody else could do in basketball at the time, so he was the perfect representative for a sneaker boys would love—he was a legend. Marketing indicated that it was less the idea that boys who wore those shoes could make those amazing flying dunks, run faster, and jump higher, and more that those who wore them had a touch of the athlete's greatness. In fact, a commercial with both Spike Lee and Michael Jordan specifically indicated it was not the shoes that contributed to Jordan's greatness. Spike's character from She's Gotta Have It, Mars Blackmon, keeps insisting "it's got to be the shoes" while Michael retorts, "No, Mars."

These backstories also create a gangsta feel that help marketers sell a street kid urban lifestyle through sneakers. The tension between the positive vs. negative messages of this lifestyle are ever present, from the creative riffs that are a part of black culture in language, art, and music to the thug, gangsta references in a Reebok ad we'll describe in a moment. Then it gets confusing when so-called gangsta rappers become entrepreneurial role models.

What our sons probably think when they see rap stars like Jay-Z walking away with millions from a shoe deal is that he is cool; he lends his name and celebrity status, and after that, money starts pouring in. But you can explain to them that Jay-Z cut a smart deal. He didn't want to be used by a major company and as a black man was keenly aware of the possibility of being exploited. Because of this, Reebok gave him his own division. It's the story of a deal made by a guy who became "the man" rather than being bought by the man. But it's also a story of segregation. RbK is a division of Reebok that is more independent and can make all sorts of ads and products, because it doesn't always have to answer to the more conservative parent company. It's not seen by the public as representing what Reebok stands for, but as the "black sheep" of the family, supported and enabled. In *Soul Provider*, Scoop Jackson argues that companies see athletics as a universal part of life, whereas hip-hop is a trend. As such, athletic shoes are a part of the major company, and smaller divisions take care of the hip-hop style.

One very troublesome recent sneaker endorsement is the deal Reebok made with 50 Cent. We guess that it's not just 50 Cent's popularity but also his "authenticity" factor that made him appealing to RbK. He's known to have been a street hustler and gang member who was shot nine times. He feels "real" to boys. But there's a fine line between our sons admiring a guy for what he's been through and the history of suffering he represents, and admiring a spokesperson who continues to glorify violence through his rap lyrics like "I'll still kill" to reassure his fans he hasn't changed with commercial success. And we suspect he reassures them because his street hustler persona is a brand, worth plenty of money to him.

50 Cent's Reebok ads show him scowling and give a close-up of his fingerprints. (Perhaps that's why Jordan's fingerprint is on his new shoe too. After all, fingerprinting is, of course, what is done when a person is arrested.) The ad reads: "Where I am from, there is no plan B. So take advantage of today because tomorrow is not promised." Take advantage of today, and buy some sneaks? This commercial tells kids from hard environments that buying sneakers is a source of control and power. It suggests to white suburban kids that Reeboks are "for real," authentically black. Selling 50 Cent's gangsta image as the face of this authenticity also suggests a relationship between powerful black men and criminality. Sociologist Gail Dines and others are right when they argue that black men are the faces of the new masculinity, because they are connected for white people with things like danger, hyperheterosexuality, physical dominance, and power—now both physical and commercial.

You won't see a big cut-out cardboard figure of 50 Cent at Finish Line in a Vermont or Maine mall, however; nor one of Nelly, whose song "Air Force Ones" helped to sell fifteen million pairs of the namesake shoe. The mall stores keep up the appearance that these are stores for athletic shoes not a place for marketers to decide for kids which sneakers are cool. The stores are divided by sport in order to keep up the illusion for parents that these expensive shoes will add needed support for their sons in P.E. class. Salesclerks seem to be trained in the backstory of each shoe, emphasizing info like "these are LeBron's tribute to his favorite team, the Yankees." But they probably won't say, "Did you know that LeBron James got ninety million dollars for his deal with Nike? And maybe that's why he's wearing these shoes at every game?"

That there is a certain shoe for each sport is a marketing ploy to diversify the brand. In actuality, in terms of performance, designers can do only two things: give a shoe more or less structure and more or less cushion. It comes down to personal preference, like mattress firmness, and some people like more or less of each. Nevertheless, there are fourteen categories of sport with multiple types of shoes for each sport, even though 80 percent of these shoes are not even used for sports. At Finish Line, for example, the Air Jordan Men's XX2 PE Basketball Shoe is "on sale" for $119.98 and promises superior performance with "unsurpassed grip." It has "I.P.S.," which is interpodular suspension technology, we're guessing in case someone's taking their shoes into space and battling the pod people. Or it may otherwise be that some marketer thought that since boys like technology they should put some techno-astronaut term in the description.

Most sneaker aficionados know that an engineer was responsible for the design of many of the earlier Jordan series and that engineering and technology play a huge role in the imagery evoked in sneaker descriptions. So does war. The 12.5 is the "ultimate basketball shoe for the ultimate basketball warrior." Converse has its "Weapons" line. There are also abundant over-the-top messages as we noted earlier. A "Kid's" version of the Air Jordan's XX3 is inspired by Michael Jordan's thumbprint and hyped as "The ultimate basketball shoe for the greatest player." Nike Air Flair Flightposite is billed as the "most innovative basketball shoe on the planet. Just in time for the basketball revolution." Old Skool shoes made by Vans play on a kid's desire to be part of a heritage, a subculture, so a white boy in the mall can feel a part of black history or borrow a bit of the glory and honor of truly super players.

Plenty of other sports stars now have their own shoe collections.

Converse boasts a Dwyane Wade series. There's the Nike Air Jordan Melo (Carmelo Anthony) collection, one variety with a gold blinglike rim. Le-Bron James has a Nike collection, and Nike's Kobe Bryant collection is supposedly "hot" this year.

It takes a hell of a lot more than hard work and practice to get to the NBA, so it would be really wrong to insinuate to kids that as long as they work hard, they too could reach these heights. However, that's not why marketers choose not to emphasize practice and hard work. As Robert Thompson, founding director of the Center for the Study of Popular Television at Syracuse University, reminds us regarding Nike's strategy, the hard work message doesn't sell style: "The idea that people don't get good at something because of practice and the right genes, but rather with the right attitude and the right shoes—it was brilliant."

There are also sneaker lines for alternative, artistic, rebel, punk rocker goth types. Converse led the way, made famous by Kurt Cobain and groups like the Ramones who wore sneakers called "one stars" or "chucks" for Chuck Taylor, the basketball player who designed them in the 1920s. Called a "niche" market, these shoes are made with designs for boys who want an alternative look. It's the rock star "role model" that sells these shoes. One unisex pair of Converse has a red tongue, and 10 percent of profits goes to a global fund to fight AIDS. Others have little red riding hood, plaid, abstract art. But it's alternative gone mainstream if it's sold at Finish Line. And why aren't the sports legends supporting AIDS prevention? What would be wrong with creating an Air Jordan shoe that supports HIV-AIDS research on behalf of his former competitor Magic Johnson? Why isn't there a Magic Johnson "Support HIV Research" shoe? Perhaps because it would not suggest "champion" but rather a vulnerability that marketers just don't want to touch.

We'd love to celebrate the freedom and artistic expression of the sneaker, pointing our boys away from the kind of sneaker that promises them legendary entitlement and esteem, and pointing them toward a fun, colorful pair of Pumas, high-top Converse, or Greedy Genius sneaks. Then again we'd also love our sons to understand the value of a dollar and realize they don't need ten pairs of brand-new sneakers at all times. We should also help them to think about the wages of factory workers who put these shoes together, the forced overtime, verbal abuse, working conditions, and the harassment they endure. Sneakers are so much a part of a boy's daily wear, you should talk about them with your son. Knowing the history, the backstories about race and oppression out of which the love of style and freshness came, as well as the hyping of sports legends as invulnerable machines, can help this conversation get a running start.

Image and Self

There's much for parents to love about boys' fashion, and also much to question and talk about. Sure there are messages about authenticity, action, and fun, the camaraderie and invitation to be part of something big. And with hip-hop and sneaker fashion, boys are invited into history as well as a world of art, design, and vibrant and bold color. As boys get older, messages about keepin' it real and making it against all odds are combined with messages about having and showing off bigger, better, and more expensive items, and about playing and dominating others, especially girls.

Parents need to appreciate this complexity and understand the attraction of certain clothing lifestyles for their sons—the desire they may have to project and protect a certain image and their fear of what might happen if they don't. Before marketers and media co-opt the meaning of important ideas like "keeping it real," and before they use their versions of "loyalty" and "freedom" to grab his attention, parents can help their sons define what these concepts really mean to him and his family. They can help him understand that keepin' it real isn't a commodity to be bought and sold, that being authentic says something about who he is on the inside, and that loyalty is something someone has to earn and is probably best applied to friendship rather than fashion designers. Such conversations can help him be more discriminating and, when the time comes, give him the support to cultivate an identity less about image and more about who he really wants to be.

CHAPTER 2

Super Size Me: What Boys Watch

TV. Movies. Ads. Video games. Computer screens. Comics. Like no generation before, kids today are fed a constant diet of visual stimulation. When Bruce Springsteen sang "Fifty-seven channels and nothing on" years ago, he wasn't counting on digital TV and other new technologies to come along. Even with the explosion of reality shows, we might still think there's nothing on, but with kids watching three to four hours of TV per day and forty thousand commercials each year, we have to take the visual impact of media in the lives of our children seriously. In this chapter we explore the shows and movies the boys in our survey tell us they like to watch, and how marketers target boys as viewers. Then we offer parents a way to navigate this brave new visual world.

The familiar adage that girls will watch shows about boys but boys will not watch shows about girls continues to prevail, even though there is evidence to suggest it's not entirely true. Boys loved *Dora the Explorer*, for example, at least before she became a sidekick to Diego, started babysitting her younger siblings, and selling princess stuff, makeup, and talking kitchen sets. They got the message that if they *really* want to explore, it's all *Go Diego Go!* Still, a study of young children's favorite television programs found that boys liked and remembered adventurous girl characters like Eliza Thornberry in *The Wild Thornberrys*, and that it only takes a few such characters to alter gender stereotypes. It seems that what a character does is more important to boys than the character's gender. Of course, with an onslaught of princesses on TV, it may be hard for them to find those less stereotypical girl characters on Saturday morning. The assumption thus lives on, and it's the reason why boys see themselves (or boys who they think they should be like) in media far more often than girls see themselves.

The advantages to this privileged place in the culture are of course obvious. Both boys and girls come to see boys as central players in the world. When asked to write about their favorite TV shows, both boys and girls refer more to male characters, use more male than female pronouns, and recall more masculine than feminine behaviors. In TV and movies boys and men engage in more action and adventure, instill more confidence and project more authority; boys come in every shape and size, master every gadget, and play every role, from hero to brainiac, to villain, to funny sidekick.

But just as with the super-size-me world of junk food, more isn't always better or healthier. Exploring TV, movies, and ads targeting boys, we find a number of themes that should concern parents, some assumptions they'll want to question early, and some disturbing messages they'll want to talk about with their sons. TV shows and films beloved by even the youngest boys offer up messages about dominance and control, acting tough, partying hard, and being distant and cool. These are all played out in ways that set the groundwork for the same behaviors (with more mature themes) they'll eventually see in shows like *Family Guy* and *Two and a Half Men,* in PG-13 and R-rated films, on MTV and BET (Black Entertainment Television) videos, and on World Wrestling Entertainment, NASCAR, and Monday Night Football, as well as in the ads between them.

So Hyper So Soon: Boys and TV

Pediatricians don't recommend screen time of any sort for children under two years old, but we know that lots of parents of young children take advantage of the time and space a little television can offer—even if it's just the time to take a shower or get dinner ready. The reality, according to a Kaiser Family Foundation national survey, is that 43 percent of children under age two watch TV every day, and 83 percent of kids under age six average about two hours of screen media per day.

Psychological studies tell us that children who watch a lot of TV hold more stereotypical views of gender roles. So what are little boys watching and learning? Let's start with educational TV, which is, all things considered, an okay place to hang out. Boys see boys twice as often as they see girls in the shows they watch, which is actually an improvement from over ten years ago, when it was closer to a 3:1 ratio of boys to girls. Shows with central characters like Big Bird and Elmo, Caillou, Clifford, and Arthur prevail, but educational TV is also one of the few places little boys can engage with male caregivers, if only virtually. Mr. Rogers still gently guides the neighborhood, Joe on *Blue's Clues* helps solve mysteries, Johnny hangs out with the woodland Sprites, and Barney and The Wiggles sing and dance with abandon. In fact, most educational shows targeting toddlers and young children, like *Wonder*

Pets, The Backyardigans, Little Bill, and *Little Einsteins,* offer up some nice messages to boys about compassion, friendships with boys and girls, sharing, helping, and close relationships with siblings, parents, and caregivers.

The sensitivity and relational acuity of little boys, acknowledged in psychological studies, find support, even room to grow, in educational TV, perhaps because developmental psychologists and educators often help to create the shows. Little boys can learn that heroes don't have to be "super" and that they come in both genders and all shapes and sizes on *Higglytown Heroes,* and that little boys can be well liked, into music, and smart in *Little Einsteins* (a combination they'll rarely see again). They can learn about initiative and team work with *Bob the Builder* and friendship and community with *Thomas the Tank Engine.* They can enjoy art, learn about gravity, sing, appreciate differences, try a new game or sport, cook, solve conflicts peacefully, become environmentally aware, sometimes all in one episode of *Sesame Street* or *Bear in the Big Blue House.* Life is rich with possibilities and nobody is saying "don't do this because it's a girl thing" or "other boys will laugh at you if you do that." There may be quite a few more dad figures than mom figures, but we're guessing the producers think that kids get enough of mom at home!

But in what feels like the blink of an eye, *Bob the Builder* gives way to *Ben 10, Dragon Tales* to *Dragon Ball Z,* and *Mr. Rogers* to *Rugrats: All Grown Up.* These TV shows are no longer about scaffolding the emotional and social life of your little boy—no "I love you, you love me, we're a happy family" as Barney still sings—but are all about promoting a commercial version of boyness in which such "sissy" sentiments are embarrassing and pushed aside, along with the girls who now are likely to embody them. *He* hasn't changed that much, but the shows targeting him are altogether different.

We suspect kids of all ages won't register the messages about diversity in these shows. Unlike educational shows like *Sesame Street,* these cartoons have little or no race or social class diversity. When there *is* a character of color, he's usually subordinate to a white lead character—the sidekick effect we see a lot in grown-up movies. For example, Arnold's friend in *Hey Arnold!,* Gerald, is African American, *Back at the Barnyard's* sidekick mouse, Pip, is Latino (why do Latino characters tend to be small and annoying like mice and Chihuahuas?); *Fairly OddParents's* Timmy Turner's friends are African American AJ and white Chester, who lives in a trailer park; *Chalk Zone's* Rudy Tabootie's best friend is Latina Penny Sanchez; Jimmy Neutron's best friend is Latino Sheen Estevez.

The message to boys is that girls can't even be sidekicks. If they appear in by cartoons they're likely to be mean and nasty, like Cindy Vortex in *Jimmy Neutron* (the second smartest kid in Retroville), Icky Vicky, the cruel babysitter in *The Fairly OddParents*, vacuous girly sisters like Dee Dee in *Dexter's Laboratory*, meanies like the Kanker Sisters in *Ed, Edd, n Eddy*, or just marginal, like cousin Gwen, the only female character in *Ben 10*.

In this new world, comedy is rich in satire, slapstick, and slacking, and the noise and excitement level is ratcheted up to make action/adventure about winning every battle with more dazzling power or a more spectacular weapon. Poor Pooh Bear never had a chance against all those bullies and pumped-up ninjas. If he even dared or cared to fight back, they'd just reproduce and gang up on him. Because really, what's better than one superhero? Four superheroes! *Fantastic Four! X-Men! Teenage Mutant Ninja Turtles!* What's better than four superheroes? TEN superheroes! *Ben 10!* And if *Ben 10* brings in the big bucks, what will *Ben 10 Alien Force* bring in? And so it goes.

It's not to say these cartoons aren't fun or don't speak to the humor, energy, and imagination that boys bring to them. They do. But as with so much of what's marketed to boys, a parent has to ask what all that satire, speed, action, adventure, and danger is suggesting to their son about growing up male, and whether a steady diet of such programs might have something to do with the decreased interest in school, the increased aggression teachers are reporting, and psychological studies that tell us that by early elementary school boys begin to hide what are perceived to be "weak" human emotions, like sadness.

Boys are more likely than girls to watch cartoons, especially "action" or "adventure"-driven cartoons and comedies. The boys in our survey indicated that they watch a lot of Nickelodeon, the most popular children's cable network, and its main rivals, Fox 4Kids TV (also now on the WB), Disney (also now on Disney-owned ABC), and Cartoon Network. It's not all bad. There are some really inventive shows where boy characters are complex and interesting, show their loyalty to friends and family, and solve problems creatively in ways that avoid unnecessary violence. In *Hey Arnold!* (alas, only in reruns) for example, fourth grader Arnold, who lives in the city with his motley crew of friends, his quirky grandparents and neighbors, is a dreamer, a peacemaker, and a jazz lover. Twelve-year-old Aang in *Avatar: The Last Airbender* is a sensitive, curious, and fun-loving boy who befriends a girl and her brother in a quest to save the world from the cruel Fire

Nation. Even the Nintendo-owned anime series *Pokémon*, originally designed as a role-playing video game, underscores the central character Ash Ketchum's closeness to his friends and his love of his little yellow Pokémon, Pikachu. The Pokémon fight, yes, but only until they faint from exhaustion, and then they recuperate, Ash at their side, in a Pokémon hospital. But all too many action and comedy-based cartoons (or a combination of the two) on the traditional Saturday morning lineup support what the research tells us—that cartoons are the most violent of all kids' TV.

You might ask, what's the big deal? It's just a cartoon for heaven's sake, the stuff of fantasy. Kids need fantasy, and this is as good a way as any to work out those aggressive impulses. After all, most of us grew up with cartoon violence—anvils dropping on Wile E. Coyote's head, Elmer Fudd blasting his rifle at Bugs Bunny, Tom stuffing Jerry into his mouth.

Back then, our parents didn't really like the violence, and now that we're parents, we don't like that the new violence has become darker and the animation more realistic. We don't like the crossing of boundaries in children's media where what's thrilling for a twelve-year-old is assumed to be appropriate for an eight-year-old or even a four-year-old. We're not talking Tweetie Bird outwitting Sylvester, but cartoons showing kids resolving adult problems by fighting Terminator-inspired cyborgs, extraterrestrial autobots, and otherworldly warriors capable of the worst kinds of cruelty. We also know more now than we knew then about the impact of violence, even cartoon violence. For example, we know that age matters when it comes to fantasy, especially fantasy that gets its energy from violence and aggression. Preschoolers are attracted to fast movement, vivid colors, and sound—which are all present in violent cartoons—but they can't really appreciate social context or understand a character's intentions. Perhaps it's no surprise then that preschoolers play more aggressively after watching violent TV. We also know that children over eight years old are better able to appreciate subtle motivations and they're less likely to imitate violence that is portrayed as evil, causes human suffering, or results in disapproval. Still, if the action reflects real life, if he identifies with a violent hero—and there are many, from Teenage Mutant Ninja Turtles to Transformers—or if he comes to the screen with a headful of aggressive fantasies he's more likely to act aggressively. Parents can't let marketers and producers define what's "kid TV" for them simply by putting it on a certain channel during a certain time slot. And because it's so hard to discuss satire, stereotypes, and stupidity with a four-year-old, it might be best not to watch along with your son but rather to channel surf until a big purple dinosaur or a bunch of colorful wiggly guys sing about friendship, love, and rainbows!

Saturday Morning Mayhem

It used to be that kids looked forward to Saturday morning cartoons—the one time in the week when TV programs were devoted just to them. But things have never been quite the same since the advent of the twenty-four-hour Cartoon Network. Competition for viewers is high, and channels like Disney and Nick have cleverly targeted little kids, tweens, and teens with special afternoon and evening programming. Not that these time slots really matter. Once summer kicks in, age is out the window, and what Disney calls their "totally rockin'" programming brings precocious preteen shows like *The Suite Life of Zach & Cody* and *Hannah Montana* into living rooms and bedrooms every morning. And because kids are watching in their bedrooms, away from adult supervision, parents might not be around to comment.

Beyond the superheroes fighting evil, we looked at the "regular kid" cartoons. Whether it's Ben in *Ben 10: Alien Force*, Danny in *Danny Phantom*, Timmy Turner in the *Fairly OddParents*, Dexter in *Dexter's Laboratory*, or Chris in *Sonic X*, boys who aren't special in any obvious way suddenly find themselves with, in superhero lingo, awesome power and responsibility. It's a familiar story, and a successful one. As comic book writer and best-selling author Brad Meltzer explains in an article for *USA Weekend*, the best part of Superman for him as a kid wasn't the man of steel as much as it was "the Clark Kent part: the idea that all of us are so plain, so ordinary, but we know what it's like to want to rip open our shirts and do something to better the world." This is obviously true for a kid connected to the problems of the world and not only the problems of *his* world.

While the desire for justice is commendable in superhero wannabes, the desire to transform oneself from someone unremarkable, maybe small, maybe even bullied at school, into someone powerful and not to be messed with is probably a stronger motivator. These cartoon regular boys become invulnerable, fearless, muscular, aggressive, and tough and use these qualities to fight for justice. Caring about injustice doesn't translate into going to court or mediation or even talking things out. In these cartoons, most problems will be resolved by physical violence. The qualities parents want their own boy to have—the ability to think through his problems and come up with creative nonviolent solutions, or simply to consider violence as a last resort—are pretty much absent, because these solutions aren't exciting enough.

Action cartoons targeting boys can have a cocky, sarcastic tone, where the characters sound a lot like younger versions of the characters in *Rambo* or *Die Hard*, offering up funny, glib comments when the characters are in the most danger. Remember, the writers of these cartoons aren't hanging out in school yards; they're watching their own media. In fact, excluding the steady stream of vile language in the R-rated versions, someone reading the scripts would have a hard time telling the difference:

See if you can match up the dialogue with the correct speaker.

"Any of you boys plan on shooting, now would be a good time."	Mike Lowrey, *Bad Boys*
"We got all afternoon to duke it out, buddy boy."	Rambo
[after shooting someone] "Any one else want to negotiate?"	Raphael, *TMNT*
"Don't like green, huh? How about black and blue?"	John McClane, *Die Hard*
"Now back up, put the gun down, and get me a pack of Tropical Fruit Bubblicious."	Sonic the Hedgehog, *Sonic X*
"There're three things I refuse to tolerate: cowardice, bad haircuts, and military insurrection."	Frieza, *Dragon Ball*

"Don't like green, huh?" is a Teenage Mutant Ninja Turtle giveaway, but you get the idea. Long gone are the days when Kermit the frog sang "It's not easy being green" to teach about racism. Someone's a racist now? Clobber 'em!

The wise-guy banter covers the fear these characters would naturally feel in these moments, and adds levity to pretty intense situations. But there's a thin line between cool and callous. While it doesn't matter so much if that line gets fuzzy in R-rated films—in fact, that's what gives them a lot of their appeal—it matters a lot that little boys see a steady stream of characters who define cool as invulnerable, unafraid, and unconcerned about the hurt they inflict on others, evil or not.

Cartoon comedies have always worked on both the adult and child level, from Daffy Duck's Errol Flynn–inspired Masked Avenger to Shark Tale's spoof of the *Godfather* movies, but the ones popular with boys these days take their pop culture references not from adults but more from action films and the stereotypical slacking and partying world of teen boys. This means they look and sound a lot like the young men who Michael Kimmel writes about in *Guyland*—that *Entourage* culture of slackers, where boys are goof-offs and want to spend their time chilling, checking out hot girls, and hanging with their bros. Little boys are invited into a teen world where Timmy Turner uses his fairy godparents to get cool stuff and popular friends, where Jimmy Neutron uses his super brain to impress the girls, where Edd and Eddy teach Ed how to be a "swingin' dude," and where Otis affirms his "party cow" status in *Back at the Barnyard*. So many boy characters get their laughs from the way they try to be cool in a teen-boy way (the kid version of *Knocked Up* or *Superbad*). They bumble their way through a slacker world and somehow come out on top, farting and burping as they go—just to ensure they bring the younger boys along. And we're talking *lots* of farts, burps, and bad breath. This is the trope of boys' TV, the leitmotif of marketing boyhood. Entire shows are based on bodily smells, like when SpongeBob and best friend Patrick scare everyone away with their onion breath, only to discover "we're not ugly. We just stink!" and when Pig in *Back in the Barnyard* has a chance to become royalty but would rather fart and burp on the farm with his friends.

We can laugh with the best of them, and we admit we do LOL at some of these cartoons. SpongeBob's innocent cluelessness, *Fairly OddParents*'s Cosmo's ditsy antics, or not so smart Sheen Estevez's obsession with his Ultra Lord action figure ("He's not a doll! Get it?!!) can be funny, but it strikes us that we're laughing a lot at the stupidity and anti-intellectualism of boys. "Brilliant" boys may be the heroes of a few stories, but they're also the unpopular nerds, and their "genius" takes them far, far out of the ordinary realm of boyhood. This makes all the rest (the slackers) normal by comparison.

Parents play an important role in the lives of children and preteens, but the cartoons kids watch promote a stereotypical version of teenage independence and sarcasm. Parents are represented from the point of view of a mortified teenager—as clueless, annoying, and intrusive—as when *Fairly*

OddParents's Timmy Turner's dad says, "Timmy, I'm respecting your privacy by knocking, but asserting my authority as your father by coming in anyway." If the boys are modern teens, the parents are, by contrast, relics of the past. In one cartoon after another, boys dismiss overly attentive 1950s-style moms (complete with pearls and aprons) and argue with vacuous newspaper-reading dads.

Fathers come off especially bad in these shows. Jimmy Neutron's idiotic dad loves pie and ducks and says inane things after he burps like "Well, at least it's coming out of the attic and not the basement." Timmy Turner's dad says things like "neat" and "I'm hip." It's hard to know who's insulted more, girls or dads, when Mrs. Turner says: "Timmy, you know you're not supposed to make your father scream like a girl three times in one day."

Because most of the main characters in these cartoons are little boys (Timmy still needs a babysitter) and not teens, they come off as sassy and rude smart alecks. And because they still have little boy bodies their obsession with the hottest, most popular girls (who are always taller and more mature than they are) and their desire for a buff body are especially weird. Clearly these cartoon comedies are designed to be spoofs and even social commentary, often about masculinity, as when SpongeBob buys oversize blow-up muscles to fit in with the macho guys at the beach. But by repeating the same themes—the desire for hot girls, the wish to be super strong and super cool, the laughter at nerdy characters—they have the odd effect of supporting the very image of boy and manhood they spoof.

We suspect kids of all ages, and probably lots of the adults who tune in now and again with their children, won't register all of these messages, just as most watchers rarely think about how boys and girls of color are marginalized in these shows. But once you see them, you can't not see them anymore, and once you share your observations of them with your preteen son, he won't be able not to see the same old messages too. It's akin to reading the labels on the side of cereal boxes. Once you start examining sodium or sugar content disguised in all their various forms, you start limiting the junk, and you start explaining to your son why too much of it might not be good for him. The point is not to take away all the fun, "grown-up"–seeming media from kids, but to put it in its place. Call it what it is. Show them the problems, and let the superhero lessons lead you into higher-level discussions about what to do when forty gazillion aliens want to fight him. No, don't invite them to dinner. Use your own super parent fantasy life to read their minds and understand that they love anything green, and turn them into a super gardening coalition at the house. Well, that might be a super parent's fantasy, but you get the picture!

No Girls Allowed! Saturday Morning Commercials

It's not unusual for cartoons to be half-hour adver-shows for dozens of products, but these days entire channels are commercials unto themselves. Disney shows are punctuated by ads for Disney movies; ads for movies are also ads for Disney toys; shows and ads together serve to promote Disney pop stars like the *High School Musical* crowd or bands like Jonas Brothers. It's enough to make your head spin.

But beyond *TV* commercials, competitors also invent newer and cooler portals to an online universe. In 2007, for example, Fox's 4Kids Entertainment introduced themselves as "The Game Station" because, as Alfred R. Kahn, chairman and CEO explained, "Kids don't just watch TV anymore—they want to get involved, interact—experience the characters, the stories and the action for themselves . . . either on-air, online, or in a multitude of ways." Kids are asked to go online to solve mysteries ("Who is this mysterious [black ninja] Pop-Tart? You can unmask him on poptart.com!"), to spread funny videos of products like the *Gummi Bear* song, or to create their own commercials, putting online their reactions to shows, or taping themselves singing a pop star's song. The companies will put "YOU" online! And all they ask in return is for kids to do their marketing for them, invest lots of time thinking about their products, take their marketing surveys, and send their links to their friends.

Saturday morning commercials make no distinction between three- and thirteen-year-olds—they go after them all with a wide sweep. That means lots of older teen messages are offered up to the youngest children along with those little boy products. Take a look at the *Gummi Bear* ad that kids pass to each other online, the one where the bear grabs his crotch and booty shakes like the rappers and dancers in MTV videos; even the youngest kids are brought up-to-date on what's "hot." PG-13 film fodder leads the way into tweendom. At the time of writing, *The Hulk* (PG-13), *Iron Man* (PG-13), and *The Dark Knight* (PG-13) were just out, and so nearly every commercial break on Saturday morning Nicktoons had at least one related ad, underscoring one of the most common complaints we've heard from parents: the youngest boys are sold on the action and excitement of films way too mature for them to see. Indeed, little boys who have yet to see Indiana Jones fight the Nazis will see ads of other little boys playing with the toys hawked at Burger King, eating from the color-changing spoons planted in their Frosted Flakes, listening to the movie theme song while chasing little brothers and sisters in the backyard and cracking the Indiana Jones Electronic Sound FX Whip ("You can make every day an adventure!").

It's that "pester power" advertisers are counting on: "Can we see it? Can we? Can we?" Some parents tell us they were convinced by all the fun superhero film product ads punctuating their son's favorite cartoons, so they gave in to the begging, figuring their brave little boy could handle the action, only to walk out with a crying son after the first twenty-minute onslaught of intense sound and aggressive action. Who cares? Not the advertisers. Even if a father holds out and doesn't take five-year-old Johnny to the film, he can appease his son by buying him Incredible Hulk and Dark Knight action figures. The ads have already showed him what to do with these figures—fight, fight, fight!

However, PG-rated movies like *Kung Fu Panda* are the kinds of movies the littlest boys *do* see. *Kung Fu Panda* features the voice of wild and crazy Jack Black as Po the Panda, famous to little kids less for his roles in movies like *School of Rock* and *Nacho Libre* than for his TV antics as MC for 2007's Nickelodeon's *Kids Choice Awards*. *Kung Fu Panda* ads are filled with the fart and burp jokes designed to pull in little boys. One commerical for the movie shows the scene where Po adds funny martial arts moves to the old "pull my finger" joke by shouting: "The belly! The butt—get ready to feel the thunder! The wuzi finger hold?" With a combination of kung fu, silly slapstick, and goofy jokes, this movie could sell boys anything, and it did, from Intel computers and wireless T-Mobile to role-playing toys, including Po's Power Paws (a set of sparring mitts), the Sword of Heroes, and the Commander Crossbow.

FAST-FORWARD ADVERTISING

Most parents complain about this unconscionable ploy of marketing PG-13 movies' "violence, sex, and coarse language" through toys to little boys during their cartoons, but other less obvious messages are marketed as well. Almost every product targeting boys gives them the message that a world of "turbo speed," "mayhem," and "awesome excitement" is theirs to control and that winning is everything.

Speed Racer, a rare movie appropriately targeted to the ten-year-old set, reportedly had over $80 million in marketing support from the likes of General Mills, McDonald's, Target, Mattel, and LEGO. Lined up on TV at al-most every break were commercials for the movie-related toys like Hot Wheels Casa Cristo 5000 Maltese Ice Caves Track ("with dangerous frozen curves"), *Speed Racer* turbo cars as prizes in GM cereals like Lucky Charms and Apple Jacks (like the boys in this commercial, he can position his cars on the track to just miss each other in an exciting "criss-cross!"), and a *Speed Racer* video game, where he can take the seat of his favorite driver and "per-form wild tricks and pull off insane stunts."

These and all toy vehicle ads give a constant message about risk taking, mayhem, control, and winning. "Race ahead and leave the competition in the cold," Hot Wheels tells him, along with, "*You* choose the car. *You* race the world." LEGO asserts, "*You* control the adventure . . . It's in *your* hands . . . It's up to *you*." And Nintendo Wii exclaims, "In an unstable world, action explodes! Starring the biggest hero of them all! *You!* Grow, grab, blast your way to over 300 levels!" Maybe little boys do feel they're in an unstable world; if so, one would think, experiencing a sense of power and control would offer security. But so can good relationships, connections to family, a teddy bear to hug, and time to play without the pressure of having to win.

SATURDAY MORNING REAL

While some commercial messages about being a boy seem to stay the same year after year, others evolve. We were taken by the increase in images of boys of color and the urban edge given to lots of products in the past few years, sometimes in a positive fun way but sometimes in a stereotypical way. For example, the life-size glass pitcher with a face and feet that's been selling Kool-Aid for decades is now a basketball player in baggy shorts and fresh sneakers playing in a pickup game under the city lights. A largely African American team and audience cheer wildly when he tosses the ball high so a fellow player can dunk it: "Nobody shakes it like Kool-Aid. Oh yeah!"

It's good to see the neighborhood scene, the fun and the action, but observant parents will notice the same old roles for boys of color in Saturday morning ads. They're almost always shown to be into sports—or toting guns. The Banzai's Color Stream Blaster Water Gun commercial (complete with "color fusion technology" and "rock load activator") is also set on the urban streets. Here boys of color way too old to be into squirt guns shoot at one another from behind buildings and from stairwells. Martial arts flips, tricks, and kicks punctuate the action. All in good fun, right? Water guns aren't REAL! But wait—a boy is hit in the chest and grimaces in pain, an expression designed to tell the young boys watching that this is a serious blaster. "Bring color to battle!" the male announcer shouts, oblivious to the double meaning. And, it seems, bring pain!

Whether the product sells itself or the message sells the product, toys for boys are increasingly about an imagined urban life that includes guns, fast cars, technology, and sometimes comedy. Boys, like girls, are attracted to products that say teen or mature, and marketers capitalize on this whenever they can. Anything active is made over-the-top exciting and, like the blaster, features boys older and tougher than any boy who would actually play with the toy. This lends an air of authenticity to "just toys," teaching little boys that this is what the big kids are doing.

Part of this urbanization of messages to boys derives directly from music video culture. This may explain why even the youngest boys who have no romantic or sexual interest in girls are urged to begin thinking of them as accessories or objects that enhance their esteem. If girls are present in ads targeting boys, they're likely to be dressed in pink or in cheerleading attire, fawning over a boy who's the center of the action. So how do you market ring pops (a hard candy on a plastic ring) to preteen boys? It's surprisingly easy in the present world of hip-hop bling, sexy girls, and sports stars, where championship rings signify consumption and status. Start with a hot twenty-something announcer, pink clad and blonde, interviewing a preteen boy dressed as a professional baseball player. As he strikes manly poses in his uniform and flashes his "ring," she hangs on his every word. Do we imagine that this is the dream of most ten-year-old boys? We understand the desire to achieve sports star status, with the ring to signify it, but what purpose does the hot girl serve?

BUY ME SOMETHING BOY

In the girls-are-anathema commercial world of boys' media, it's no wonder that one of the most common ways to get a laugh is for something to happen that transforms a guy into a pink princess or makes him look feminine or girly. Occasionally media girls can cross over to boy territory and be into the stuff marketed to boys, like sports, cool technology, and even fast cars, but boys don't have the same option in the media. There are *no* boys, *ever*, in ads targeting girls—the ones where girls sit in a circle and laugh, where they hug a stuffed animal, or play online games like Carrie the Caregiver, who looks out for all those campers at Camp Funshine.

It seems unfair that after hours of being told they have to win, control, and compete, there's no possibility that boys might enjoy a little mutual friendship and noncompetitive play with girls. Real boys do, of course. Our grown-up students and some of the boys we spoke to tell us that they remember fondly the games they played with their sisters and the girls in the neighborhood, the dolls, the playing house, the board games, and the jump rope, even if sometimes they worried that other boys might find out. Why wouldn't they love these games? Boys have imagination. They like other people. They even think babies and kittens are cute. The only difference is that they need a safe space to express it, where they won't be mocked or bullied.

After watching hours of gender-specific commericals, we may have to give props to two sugary cereals—Lucky Charms and Trix. Even if the product they market is nutritionally questionable, in this strictly boy-or-girl world, they at least feature cartoon girls and boys, white and of color, running, laughing, and playing together. They've figured out that they might be able to make a wider sweep if they include everyone.

Here's an exercise to do with your son when watching a morning of cartoons. Teach him that commercials want to sell him things that might not be so good for him by making that stuff seem fun and wild and full of excitement. While you watch commercials together, ask him to identify what is actually being sold. Then teach him the genre of jokes that go like this: you state what the kid does, and then say, in a phony narrator's voice:

> (after kids joyfully drink Gatorade) One hour later: "Mom, my stomach hurts . . ."
> (after kids chow down their Trix) One hour later: "Mom, can I have breakfast? Again?"
> (after fun with a water blaster) One hour later: "Dad, my arm has a bruise on it."
> (after boy zooms a small car across a Hot Wheels track) One hour later: "Dad, *now* what can I do with this?"

And maybe even suggest that "one hour later," after "fight fight fight" between Spider-Man, Hulk, Batman, and Superman, he might want to give them a rest in a doll cradle and play a board game with his sister.

Me TV

Tween is not a real developmental stage, it's a marketing concept designed to encourage little kids to make the leap to all things teen. And nothing says "teenager" better than tween TV. It's funny, totally entertaining, and after the onset of cable and digital TV diversified viewing, it's one of the last places on TV where a huge percentage of the targeted audience return week after week to watch the same shows. Nickelodeon and Disney have almost the entire market share, and their competition for your kids' attention is fierce. (Nick is the highest-rated network on all of cable, although when it comes to tweens, Disney has them beat.)

Tween TV taps into that teenage "it's all about me" psyche—hence Nick's moniker ME:TV. Even though most preteens aren't *really* feeling it— to them, "me" is still very much defined by closeness to family, friends, and school—TV shows targeting this age group are about how well you can *imagine* being a teenager. Imagine what it's going to be like when the hot babes want you. Imagine the fun, the parties, the clubs, the dorms, all without those pesky, dopey, intrusive, nagging parents, all without homework or after-school jobs or actually working hard at anything. Cool! That's what's different about these shows and shows of yesteryear, for example *The Partridge Family* or *The Brady Bunch*. Parents and the value of school are pretty much ignored in today's shows. Even when the show is based in school, like *Ned's Declassified School Survival Guide*, it's the version of school one might see on a T-shirt marketed to middle school girls: "My favorite subject is Social Studies."

The tween moniker stands for "wannabe teenager." Just ask forty-something Dan Schneider, producer of Nick's *Drake & Josh* and *Zoey 101*. You may remember him as the guy who played a smart high school kid in the 1980s sitcom *Saved by the Bell*. But what does his version of teenager on these tween shows really look, feel, taste, and sound like? It's pop culture, man. It's partying, dude. It's coffee addictions and drowning your woes in soda binges. It's really just a twelve-year-old version of the hedonistic womanizer Charlie Harper, the Charlie Sheen character in *Two and a Half Men*. Adolescence, these shows suggest, isn't a developmental period, it's a lifestyle.

In 2006, The Kaiser Family Foundation found that two-thirds of all eight- to eighteen-year-olds had TVs in their rooms; Nick reports 77 percent of tweens do. Add to that the fact that prime time for these shows is just before or after dinner, and we suspect the makers of these shows like their odds that most parents aren't watching. So maybe that's why we see *The Naked Brothers Band*, a Nick show about a group of precocious mostly preteens living the rock star dream, imitating the kind of problems colleges are doing their best to control. In their first movie, a mockumentary of their rock star rise to fame, then six-year-old bad boy drummer Alex develops a lemon-lime soda addiction. When their original band breaks up, he binges in a bar scene, chugging like a frat boy, and ends up in a luxury rehabilitation Soda-holics at Sea program. Then there's bad boy Zack on *The Suite Life of Zack & Cody*, a show about twin tweens living it up in a luxury hotel, who sets up his own underage dance club in the hotel lounge. The boy "bartender" pushes sugary soda on shy, nice girl Barbara, and after chugging root beer—"Hit me again!"—she takes her hair down, whips off her glasses, and starts dancing suggestively while the crowd shouts, "Go Barbara! Go Barbara!" It's a nerdy boy's dream when she staggers to Cody and kisses him hard on the mouth. Does it matter at all that the guy who wrote this episode, "Club Twin," got his own start in the raunchy 1983 film *Screwballs* and the TV takeoff of the movie, *Police Academy*? Does it matter that study after study connect alcohol consumption and sexual violence? Of course not. How dare we imply something so crass—this is just harmless entertainment for tweens, right?

Most of these preteen shows feature eight- to 12-year-olds running their own lives in a world created for them by adult guys (the writers) who know how to create a pseudosanitized version of a twenty-something's fantasy. All the themes, expectations, and desires are there—but it's okay because the drinks they're chugging aren't *really* alcoholic and the come-ons and references to hot girls don't *really* lead to the party-house bedroom. But there's no missing the staggering around and slurred speech or the wild, loose behavior as anything but an imitation of the real thing.

The real problem here isn't the humor—this is what boys love about these shows; the not-quite-able-to-pull-it-off hilarity, the slapstick, the over-the-top silliness—it's the stereotypical version of teen boy they're imitating, the Tom Cruise in *Risky Business* fantasy. Indeed, many of these shows revolve around pop culture references and stereotypes of mature teen life taken from movies you'd never let your preteen see. Take Alex's binge drinking in *The Naked Brothers Band: The Movie*. Losing your band of brothers (okay, there's a token girl in the band) is cause for sadness, even acting out, but to throw the whole scene into a bar and set up what looks like a preteen version of *Entourage* is just bizarre. Sure, it's funny, but also a little perverse, and it models a coping mechanism that won't be helpful to him in the future. Same goes for the reality show *Kid Nation*, a one-season wonder that was quite popular among kids we spoke to. In this show, in which kids were set up virtually alone in what appeared to be a wild west ghost town, some brainiac thought it would be a good idea to give eight- to fifteen-year-olds a saloon, so they could drown their sorrows in root beer. How did the kids on the show know to fill shot glasses and float them in the "beer"? Having a preteen gathering place makes perfect sense, but suggesting they use drinking *anything* as a crutch when they're down and depressed has to be some childless adult producer's idea of funny.

Lots of tween shows are set in teen fantasy worlds of luxury, even when the kids themselves aren't wealthy. In *The Suite Life*, Zack and Cody live at the Tipton Hotel because their mom sings in the lounge. The TV sequel, *The Suite Life on Deck*, is set on a luxury cruise liner, perfect because now babes in bikinis and hot tubs can give the show a more grown-up feel. The kids on *Zoey 101* and *Hannah Montana*, shows that boys in our survey tell us they watch too, hit the dorm rooms, beaches, and juice bars, and even, in the case of *Hannah Montana*, "after parties."

But not everyone plays to the party scene. Parents love Disney's group Jonas Brothers as much as their daughters because the brothers are squeaky clean in an openly Christian way. On most of the other shows, however, bad boys rule. The other side of *The Suite Life*'s good boy Cody is bad boy Zack; the other side of *Drake & Josh*'s good boy Josh is bad boy Drake, the other side of *The Naked Brother's Band*'s good boy Nat is bad boy Alec. The good boy is the moral compass of the shows. Good boys are responsible and smart, and they date smart girls. But we know also that they are weak, a little nerdy, and corruptible. Their girlfriends are mean or controlling or both. Their bad boy counterparts shame them into doing things they would never do on their own. In the "Club Twin" episode with the soda-chugging scene, Cody says to Zack: "This is great! The salty snacks are making everyone drink more and the sugary drinks are fueling their energy. It goes against everything I believe in, and I couldn't be happier!" That's the fun of it. How unnerved can the good boys get? How far will the bad boys go? With no parents around, with new hot girls for the bad boys in every episode, with endless dumb messes for bad boys to create, they go pretty far, get pretty unnerved, and pretty stoked too.

Preteen TV has given us a steady stream of good girls gone bad, ever since (and probably before) the *Micky Mouse Club* spawned Britney Spears. Since then we've watched girl after girl make the transition from innocent to sexy diva or teen momma, and as a culture we worry about the messages these "role models" send our daughters. Not so for boy stars, and it's not because their forays into teen life haven't been provocative or questionable. Zac Efron of *High School Musical* fame showed a lot of skin and "hotness" on the cover of *Rolling Stone*. Drake Bell of *Drake & Josh* went over the top in the raunchy R-rated movie *College*. These choices may garner some attention, but we don't really worry about them. Why not? Why don't we worry about boys' behavior in these shows and what it suggests to our sons about drinking, drugs, and sexuality? Why don't we make the connection between these preteen antics and more serious misbehavior that could get them kicked out of clubs or colleges, or worse, when they're older?

There are positive aspects of these shows too. Boys can be best friends with girls, like Mosely and Ned in *Ned's Declassified School Survival Guide* and Meena and Cory in *Cory in the House* (although there's typically a tinge of romantic interest), and boys tell us they like to watch shows with girl leads like *Hannah Montana* and *iCarly*, upending the deeply ingrained assumption that boys won't watch shows that feature girls. Even though there are a lot of boys who are smart alecks and smooth operators, not into responsibility or school, there are also boys who at times show their honest, sweet, smart sides. There is diversity in some shows too, where a boy of color can carry his own show, like *Cory in the House*, about the son of the African American White House chef (and the president is Latino). It's important to remember that most of the episodes in these tween shows don't focus on hot girls and drinking; that would never fly with the parents who are also watching. Regardless, this is a tween consumers' paradise, oddly punctuated by commercials for everything from little boy Power Rangers Jungle Fury Helmets to very grown-up teen stars singing the latest Disney-promoted CD. As novelist and *New York Times* contributor Jonathan Dee writes in his article "Tween on the Screen," "Children go from being a kind of cultural protectorate to the Junior Auxiliary of the tube-watching nation at large, and programs are designed for them on the same principle as they're designed for grown-ups: as a way to sell eyeballs to advertisers." The message to advertisers seems to be, come on, anything goes, we've got 'em ALL.

WWE TV

There are some shows, however, that make it very clear they don't want 'em all. They not only don't want the girls, they don't want boys who aren't the right type of boy. If there's any doubt about what that type of boy is, consider the following scene.

Vince McMahon, CEO of World Wrestling Entertainment (WWE), stares into the camera, microphone in one hand, his other hand on his grown son Shane's shoulder. They stand in the middle of the wrestling ring, in front of a cheering crowd of thousands in the arena, and millions watching on cable TV. Shane and his father insult "Stone Cold" Steve Austin, one of the most popular professional wrestlers of all time, calling him a bastard and a jackass. As the father-son duo continues for several more minutes, the crowd grows restless and starts chanting their own insults, directed not at Austin, but at the McMahons: "Asshole! Asshole!" Men, women, and children are shown scattered throughout the crowd, taking part in the taunting. Onstage, Vince, who plays the character of Mr. McMahon, evil owner of the wrestlers, then does the unthinkable: he takes away Austin's chance at winning the World Heavyweight Title at the upcoming Wrestlemania Pay-Per-View event. The enraged crowd showers the stage with boos.

Suddenly, the fans hear the sound of glass shattering over the loudspeakers. It's Steve Austin's theme music. The self-proclaimed "Texas Rattlesnake" makes his way down the ramp to the ring, an enraged look on his face. Austin wastes no time—he confronts Shane and delivers his signature move, the "Stone Cold Stunner" (in which he reaches over his shoulder to grab his opponent's head, pulls his opponent's jaw above his own shoulder, falls to a seated position and forces his opponent's jaw and neck to slam onto his shoulder). Austin then does the same to Vince. Both McMahons now lie unconscious on the ring mat. A beer is tossed to Austin. He cracks it open, pours some over Vince, and then chugs the rest himself. The crowd responds with a near-deafening roar of approval. The Texas Rattlesnake sticks his middle finger up at both McMahons one last time and leaves the ring.

Ladies and gentlemen, girls and boys, welcome to WWE.

This scene, and countless others like it, define the world of WWE. Several times a week, thousands of fans in major arenas around the country join millions of viewers at home to witness what Vince McMahon calls "sports entertainment." Bulked, buffed, and scantily clad "professional wrestlers" (both men and women) engage in a series of elaborately staged and choreographed matches that are made to appear realistic, and sometimes spontaneous. During a typical show, one can expect to see a wrestler's head smashed with a metal chair, beer chugging, women wrestlers (called Divas) getting their clothes ripped off, demoralizing taunting and name-calling, countless orchestrated betrayals, and loads of profanity. Professional wrestling bears virtually no resemblance to amateur, interscholastic, intercollegiate, or Olympic wrestling. It is not a sport, but, as author of *The Macho Paradox* and antisexist male activist Jackson Katz explains, "a powerful story, about how 'real men' prevail—through intimidation, humiliation, and control, all accomplished by verbal, physical and sexual aggression. Manhood is equated explicitly with the ability to settle scores, defend one's honor, and win respect and compliance through physical force."

WWE is very popular, especially among boys between the ages of twelve and seventeen, who make up nearly 40 percent of all viewers. The three "branded" shows produced by WWE, *Raw* (Mondays on USA), *Smackdown* (Fridays on the CW), and ECW, *Extreme Championship Wrestling* (Thursdays on the SciFi channel), are some of the most popular regularly scheduled shows on cable. On a typical week, for example, more than four million viewers tune in to an episode of *Raw*.

How can we understand and explain the phenomenal popularity of WWE? Everyone knows that the matches are fake, that the good guys (what WWE terms "faces" or "babyfaces") always triumph over the bad guys (the "heels"). In his documentary *Wrestling with Manhood*, Sut Jhally offers at least one plausible answer: the WWE is popular because it offers a "soap opera for guys." Each season is scripted, with specific characters playing specific roles, in the context of specific plotlines and action sequences; there are bones to pick, revenge to seek, demands to make, and enemies to humiliate. The big title matches occur at the monthly Pay-Per-Views, after weekly shows build up the tension between the two opposing sides through backstabbing, verbal confrontation, and physical fights. In the end, there are clear winners and clear losers, and all conflicts are resolved by physical confrontation, aggression, and violence.

For most, it's hard to take WWE seriously. But, as Jhally argues, we have to, not only because of its popularity, and its ability to draw and engage a largely male audience (nearly 90 percent), but also, and most importantly, because of the messages it sends to boys about what it means to be a man in today's world. In his article "Masculinity as Homophobia," Michael Kimmel argues that "masculinity must be proved, and no sooner is it proved than it's again questioned and must be proved again." This is the essence of WWE. Wrestlers are constantly calling one another out to the ring so they can talk face-to-face. These face-to-face encounters are filled with intimidating comments, each man trying to come off as the toughest, biggest, and scariest. In one such encounter, Edge, the self-proclaimed "Rated-R Superstar," calls out to Triple H (aka, King of Kings, The Cerebral Assassin), "I will fight him if he has the guts to accept the challenge!" Of course, no wrestler can ever back down from a challenge; he'd be called a wimp and the crowd would happily greet the decision with boos and chants of "Pussy! Pussy!" Triple H does in fact meet Edge's challenge: "You came out here to talk, I came out here to fight." Real men don't talk; conversation is for wimps. They take action. As

Jhally points out, because WWE's version of masculinity must be proven again and again, no one is ever safe. The soap opera drama demands it. Those who show fear or fail the test are teased mercilessly by other wrestlers and by fans.

Boys watching WWE learn that, whether good or bad, you have to use mental and physical humiliation to scare, intimidate, and defeat your opponent. "Stone Cold" Steve Austin is one of the most powerful bullies in WWE. He routinely taunts and humiliates his opponents, and the crowd loves it. To earn respect, a guy needs to look tough, be larger than life, more muscular, taller, and more intimidating than the next guy. This is a fantasy world in which giants rule over men and men can turn themselves into giants. When the wrestler, The Big Show comes out, for example, the announcers are heard saying, "Weighing at nearly five hundred pounds, with hands large enough to crush a skull. . . ."

Muscles make the man. When men verbally confront one another and situations heat up, one common response is for a man to rip off his shirt to show off his muscles, as if to say "you do not want to mess with this." "This," of course, is what all those fake muscles sown into boys' Halloween costumes are designed to imitate. To underscore the point, WWE shows are inundated with commercials for exercise machines and high-performance supplements that suggest to boys that they too can get an intimidating physique. The exercise machines are never ones that improve cardiovascular fitness but instead stress the increased size of one's muscles. Intimidating spokesmen shout at the viewer, telling them what they need to do to look the part, capitalizing on the anxiety of boys and men watching, who fear that they are not big or tough enough.

By contrast, wrestlers who are not big, muscular, and intimidating are viewed as jokes, like the all-male cheerleading team, the "Spirit Squad." Smaller than the other male wrestlers, wearing (male) cheerleading-style outfits and entering to cheesy music as opposed to the hard rock and rap music of other wrestlers, the five-member Spirit Squad endures the jokes, homosexual taunts, and boos of the announcers, wrestlers, and fans. Similarly, Chuck and Larry, two explicitly gay wrestlers, are taunted and ridiculed. Jhally argues that wrestlers like Chuck and Larry serve a very real purpose in WWE, namely, to counteract the homoeroticism that runs just beneath the surface of professional wrestling: buff men wearing skimpy trunks, locked in close physical contact. When Chuck and Larry are taunted and teased by the other "straight" wrestlers, the message is: "That's what gay looks and acts like, and that's not me."

The messages about women are just as clear. While men resolve their conflicts by physically assaulting one another, the "Divas," as they're called, accompany men to the ring and evoke jealous competition between the men. Once an episode or so, women wrestlers will fight (there is, in fact, a Women's Championship Title), but the matches usually result in ripping one another's clothes off while the crowd yelps with excitement and the announcers make sexual comments. While there's a section on the WWE Web site for the "Divas," they're all posed as sex objects and toys, or, as Ivory likes to refer to herself, "Athletic Barbies."

Boys love WWE for the excitement, the power, the fearlessness, and the clear message about what it takes to win or lose, all within high drama and identity stories of trauma, destruction, and revenge. Boys can go online to read lengthy bios of their favorite wrestlers, which include made-up biographies, stories of wives taken against their will, unborn babies lost, hatred simmering, disappearances, and transformations. Like soap operas, each episode promises something more to come—ongoing feuds, interconnected lives, and cliffhangers. WWE is as much about these identities and the questions swirling around them as it is about the actual fights. Will John Cena make it as a rap artist? Will the Undertaker really die or will he reappear? And boys can buy the lifestyle products that encourage identification with these guys—Triple H's ring tone, and T-shirts, action figures, and DVDs of other favorite wrestlers.

Does everyone love a good fight? Godzilla vs. King Kong? Alien vs. Predator? The Red Sox vs. the Yankees? Even the kids on the playground who circle around the two kids fighting after school, choosing sides instantly? Just go to YouTube and type in "backyard wrestling" and watch kids banging stop signs on one another's heads and jumping, flipping, and careening off one another.

How is WWE different from Godzilla vs. King Kong, or Olympic boxing for that matter?

Of course, in boxing both competitors are skilled, trained, disciplined, and fair. WWE ultimately is not at all about who wins, or who's strongest, or a fair fight. It's about humiliating an opponent and earning respect. Participants remake their bodies into invulnerable machines and prove their superiority through tricking, cheating, raging, demeaning, and utterly destroying one another. The boys at home most likely aren't re-creating the story lines, but they're attempting to show themselves and one another that they can feel no pain.

In WWE, boys are identifying with the worst qualities in men. They are enamored of acts that would land any real person in jail. Since when did we ask boys to root for the bad guys?

Boy vs. Discovery Channel

We weren't planning to turn on the Discovery Channel to do research for this book, but the boys we met and surveyed told us how much they enjoyed the shows there—*Man vs. Wild, Dirty Jobs, Deadliest Catch*—so we had to check it out. Once we watched some episodes, we got a glimpse of what the producers are aiming for, and it isn't pretty.

But it *is* action packed! Well, kind of, or so much so that there's a warning before *Man vs. Wild* airs saying that Bear Grylls and crew receive support when they are in potentially dangerous situations, as required by health and safety regulations. Oops, there goes that "one man alone against the hostile environment" premise. The warning also indicates that some of the dangerous situations he finds himself in are setups so that he can demonstrate survival skills. Why doesn't wrestling have these preshow caveats? For example: Warning—Most of the wrestlers are on steroids. Seemingly dangerous moves are practiced setups. No one actually gets hurt. Winners are decided beforehand. After all, it's far more likely that a boy is going to try to put his friend in a headlock and flip him than he is going to attempt to jump over an eight-and-a-half-foot gully in Copper Canyon or eat a scorpion.

Bear Grylls is one man alone against the environment (one man alone that a crew ironically seems to capture from every angle, in every river, and on every mountaintop). He has served in the British Special Forces and climbed Mount Everest, which gives him status in spite of his wiry, almost nerdy look and purple backpack. In *Man vs. Wild*, he shows us that the wild is full of dangerous animals, gross things to eat, treacherous climbs and falls, and mind-dazzling statistics. Statistics? Take Zambia for example. The Zambisi River is the fourth longest river in Africa; "beneath (him) 85,000 feet of cubic water is pouring over the falls every second"; there are more than 75,000 crocodiles there; ten people a year are trampled or gored by elephants; elephants can be as tall as thirty feet and weigh as much as eight tons; they also can run at nearly twenty miles per hour. In this all-male, all-danger adventure, size matters; everything gets measured, and the viewer will know how close each thing is to being the biggest, longest, worst, highest, or most dangerous. The appeal to all those *Ripley's Believe It or Not* fans and preteen collectors of stats and cool stuff is obvious.

And that's part of the hype of this educational show. Along with the ingenuity of the adventurer Grylls, we get a running commentary that uses superlatives faster than a running elephant.

- "Black ants. These aren't just ordinary ants. They're vicious!"

- ". . . home of the biggest and most dangerous animals in the world"

- "[this river] snakes its way through some of the meanest terrain in the world"

- "face-to-face with the largest killer in Zambia"

- "They're one of our planet's most ruthless and efficient killers."

- Wilderness is "unforgiving" and

- In the outback, "if [something] happened here, no one would hear you scream."

To highlight how extreme these environments are, we're reminded at every turn how many people have died or how the viewer or even the all-knowing Grylls might die if he were to do the wrong thing.

But there's also the all-important comic relief that we see in almost all boys' programming. Bear Grylls survivalist refuses to eat the gorp (or more likely turkey club sandwiches) that his camera crew carries with them. He chooses to eat from the land and then describes to boys watching exactly how what he's eating tastes, doing so while the green pus of whatever bug he chews runs down his chin. Of the rhino beetle larva, a delicacy when fried, he says to the viewer after taking a bite, "No wonder they fry them." It's the "worst" thing he's "ever, ever" eaten: "It's as if all your friends got all their bogies [boogers in Brit speak] together, squeezed them inside a sausage, and then you put it inside your mouth." Now tell us that this show was written for adults after THAT line!

The show is filled with exciting predicaments, lots of ingenious uses for the natural world, creativity in the face of imminent disaster, and moments of awe. In fact, if we had our druthers and HAD to give our sons he-men adventurers to look up to, Bear Grylls ranks a lot higher than Batman or Hulk Hogan. That's because he laughs at himself, like when he slips in the mud, or when he poops off of a cliff while dealing with a bout of diarrhea. And sometimes he even says he feels vulnerable—"If only they [the herd of elephants] could know how completely defenseless I am"—and reflective—"What a privilege to see them!" A mountaintop "makes [him] feel pretty small here." Lovely, we think, for a moment. And then, as if to underscore the unmanliness of such admissions, "Suddenly, I'm up to my neck in fetid water."

Speaking of which, *Deadliest Catch* is all water, all the time, and it's got a huge, mostly male viewership of over three million. As we write, season four is coming to a close; we're taken onboard fishing boats called *Wizard*, *Northwestern*, the *Cornelia Marie*, *Early Dawn*, *Time Bandit*, and the *North American*. It's king crab season, and this quasi-documentary follows the guys (the show is predominantly composed of men) on their trips on the Bering Sea. Unlike reality TV, which invents survivor competitions, *Deadliest Catch* camera crews simply tag along and narration is added later. The narration and clever editing make the most of dangerous runs, stormy weather, fifty-foot waves, counting the catch, the rivalry among the boats as well as among crew members, the cussing and fussing when the guys are exhausted, a few fistfights, and the ka-ching of a full pot: "that's 156,000 bucks of crabs." A sign on one boat says: CHECK YOUR FEELINGS AT THE DOOR, giving any boy watching a message about what it means to do "men's work."

But if a boy stops and analyzes what feelings are "checked," he'll note that they're the softer ones. Some feelings are allowed and are expressed in problem behaviors. It's par for a sailor to punch a fish with frustration, insult his brother, haze a greenhorn (new guy) for laughs, and explode with anger when tired or scared. But the truth of this series is that the guys seem real, it gets scary out there, and fishing does seem to be an adventure (albeit a tiring, sometimes boring, sometimes very disappointing adventure). Crew members are not made out to be superheroes or even heroes, although they have plenty of viewing fans. They're just guys doing what truly looks like a difficult job.

But because the docu-story focuses almost exclusively on adventure and danger, a certain version of male work washes over the deck of every episode. It goes something like this: The work is over-the-top (work twenty hours and sleep four), dangerous (e.g., when the block breaks and a cable falls, we're shown through a cartoon how, if the block had broken five minutes earlier, it would have snapped off the head of the greenhorn working there), and hierarchical (to pump up the drama, the show emphasizes who's the captain, who's the greenhorn, and who's working harder than who much more frequently than it shows the teamwork). And there's the opportunity for the "little guy" to make it rich! Or so it may seem. "It's all about the working-class guy," says Beers, executive producer. "What they're doing is modern-day prospecting, and nature, in all its violence, is the great leveler. It's about how a working-class guy makes it rich."

If *Man vs. Wild* does docu-adventure and *Deadliest Catch* does docu-danger, then *Dirty Jobs* does docu-gross! Mike Rowe, the host, is a different kind of man on the edge than Bear Grylls or any of the guys on the crab boating crew. While Grylls aims to always look smart and daring as he battles nature, and the boating crew really does appear to be in harm's way, Mike Rowe of *Dirty Jobs* is an upper-middle-class, somewhat intellectual guy who roughs it up a little to bring his audience some really gross footage.

Rowe doesn't pretend to be someone he's not. He introduces one show by quoting Chekov and alliterates constantly, "murkiest, muddiest, most miserable," "damp and disgusting," and "nefarious nautical nightmares," much akin to Alton Brown of the Food Network. But he makes fun of himself while he spends serious time trying to do the dirty jobs of honest working men and women. As he works he lets viewers in on what's particularly disgusting. Grinding mackerel into a mush of blood, bones, guts, and scales makes him throw up. A shark flopping on the deck "scares the hell out of [him]." A dead catfish he's skinning feels like a "giant hunk of snot." And when Ed Palmer, an oysterman, teaches him how to walk in mud he ends up falling over and getting stuck in it. During a catfish noodling episode (*noodling* means to catch catfish by wading in snake-infested waters and getting them to bite onto your hand, essentially catching you!), he asks, "Am I just being a big baby about it?" Afterward he directs a self-deprecating warning to the kids watching: "Kids . . . if you're thinking about noodling, don't. Don't go running off in some swamp and stick your arm in a muddy hole just because you saw me do it on the TV. Remember, I'm an idiot. I'm a moron."

Like a lot of boy TV, *Dirty Jobs* is over-the-top. The septic tank technician takes him to the "most disgusting thing" he's ever seen: a basement three feet deep in human excrement. Another hardworking guy brings him to a woman's basement where all of the neighborhood sewage exploded and covered the entire room. Amid the hype and hoopla over how disgusting everything is, Rowe introduces viewers to people who seem worthy of admiration even though—maybe especially because—they do the dirtiest jobs in the world. And in a shocking turn that one rarely sees in reality TV, he even introduces us to his cameraman who, he admits, does everything he does in order to film him in the trenches! Most boys need to see more behind-the-scenes, "behind the man" (fear, vomit, disgust, awe, and respect) footage like this, even if it's in over-the-top, crazy places.

Slacker Satire and Offensive TV

When *The Simpsons* debuted in 1989, some parents were up in arms about smart-alecky ten-year-old Bart. Others praised the character's originality and humor. Today Bart is the poster child for wisecracking, ironic, mouthy kids everywhere, and this clever satire is now into its twentieth year. Compared to Stewie, the trash-talking baby in *Family Guy*, and Cartman and his band of bleeping friends on *South Park*, Bart looks downright angelic. Cowabunga, dude.

In our clinical and educational work with kids we're struck by how many preteen boys are watching "R-rated" animated comedies. *Family Guy* and *South Park* are especially popular with middle school boys. Don't get us wrong. We love satire and spoofs, and so-called wholesome middle America provides some of the best material. The fictional towns of Springfield, USA (*The Simpsons*), Quahog, Rhode Island (*Family Guy*), and South Park, Colorado (*South Park*), seem like good places to start.

Animation has a way of tripping up even the best parents. It seems so child-friendly at first! Check in on him to be sure his homework is done, get a "yes, Mom" or "yes, Dad," glance at what he's watching and see a cartoon baby and his dog on the TV, and it all seems cool. How adult can a cartoon be? Very. *Family Guy*'s opening song says it all. Parents Lois and Peter invoke Archie and Edith Bunker of the great satire *All in the Family*:

> LOIS: It seems today, that all you see, is violence in movies and sex on TV
>
> PETER: But where are all those good ol' fashioned values
>
> ALL: On which we used to rely?

The answer, of course, is "not here." That's probably the best bit of satire in the show, because unlike *All in the Family*'s 1970s challenge to war and bigotry, or even *The Simpsons*' clever spoof on the all-American family, *Family Guy* just doesn't seem to have an agenda—unless, of course, the agenda is nonstop poop, sex, and barf jokes, with a few ironic twists and a bit of violence thrown in for good measure. Our college students say that's why they love it—"it's so random." Because there are plenty of references to pop culture and a steady stream of offensive jokes, a middle schooler doesn't have to be an intellectual to get it. He can just laugh at the stinkers and shockers. A high schooler will understand the subtle references to TV, movies, and pop culture, but since everything is so crudely displayed, whether or not a kid gets most of these, he too can feel clever and ironic without having to think too much.

The real problem with this show is that, in spite of the funny bodily noises and crass antics that invite boys in, the viewer never knows how he's supposed to feel about any given activity except from the perspective of whether or not it's funny. Every offensive statement or act encourages the audience to laugh at the person doing it rather than support or question it. Every character is laughable. Does this offer a kind of anything-goes nihilism to those watching, or does it just normalize some really horrific statements? So many times you can imagine a boy saying, "That's so not funny that it's funny." There's even a Web site for the most offensive statements that each character has made, because the show is all about being over-the-top offensive. And because so much of boys' media supports an over-the-top message, lots of boys are watching.

Take for example a single 2006 episode called "Brian Sings and Swings" in which Brian, the dog, and often the only "normal" character in the family, begins singing in a nightclub with Frank Sinatra and drinking too much. First, as always, there are the poop jokes: Stewie, the diabolical baby, to Brian, as he dons a tux in which his tail sticks out between the tux's tails: "When you wear that suit it looks like you're making a white poop—but it's stuck." Then there's homophobia, racism, or anti-Semitism, which are all meant to be acceptable if put in the mouths of people we're supposed to think are stupid. For example, Peter, the father of the family, pretends to be Jewish and remarks to a rabbi, "How about all those coupons?" and— referring to the anti-Semitic phrase "I jewed them down"—he says, "I 'us'-ed them down [since he's now a Jew] to five hundred dollars." Then there's the funny violence: a Care Bear splattered in the street has an ear gnawed off by a deer. When he won't share electricity, Thomas Edison's neighbor threatens, "How about if I come over here and kick your ass?" Of course, there's lots of offensive sex and sexism: A song about Allen Funt alludes to the "C-word"; regarding Jessica Alba, a narrator says, "If I were forty years younger I would plow that till next July"; a teacher accidentally shows a sex tape of himself and his wife to the kids, in which he's wearing stockings and a garter belt; Brian the dog says to the woman next to him at a bar, "Those are huge—those are huge boobs." Meg the daughter, trying to be a lesbian to be accepted in the Lesbian Alliance Club at school, looks at *Penthouse* with a girlfriend in her room. Her mother, trying to convince her she's not a lesbian, shows her how she would be kissing her girlfriend if she were a real lesbian, and then begins to make out with the girl visitor, at which point her son pops out of a closet and runs off to masturbate. (The idea is that whenever a girl kisses a girl, even if it's your mom, that's "hot.")

In another episode, a gay gynecologist looks at a woman's vagina and says, "Eeeewww, it looks like a sad old man"; in another Peter does a musical revue number with his barbershop quartet around the bed of a man dying of AIDS.

It's slacker humor—humor that's not especially witty or satiric but merely has to be offensive, absurd, or outrageous to get a laugh. We mean, who would run over a Care Bear? (Okay, that's kind of funny; who doesn't remember reaching a certain age and seeing those bears as a little insipid.) But who would almost say the word c_ _t on prime-time TV? Who would deliver a diagnosis of AIDS in song to a dying man? It's funny because they're selling rebellion. If do-gooders think they can have a hold or contain teen boys in a web of political correctness, think again. No one "owns" them, they might think. They're freethinkers and don't need to live by any rules of civility, not exactly the definition of freedom the founding fathers had in mind.

South Park is over-the-top too, but sometimes it's story lines become clever satire with a moral message. Its Comedy Central, 11 P.M. time slot (at least until it was syndicated and some greedy exec decided 7 P.M. was now an appropriate time for adult fare) suggested pretty clearly that it was aimed at the college crowd and older. We can vouch for the fact that college students of color found the token black character Chef (voiced by the late Isaac Hayes) hilarious rather than insulting, especially when he reluctantly dished out advice to the town's white children.

South Park aims for social commentary, and although gross, it manages to achieve that goal. For example, when Obama won the 2008 election, an episode featured all the old 1960s grown-ups so happy about the win that they took to the streets to celebrate, leaving the kids at home to wonder what came over them; in another episode "Sexual Harassment Panda" gave a very lame talk to the young boys at school. The joke works because the children struggle to make sense of some of the stupid, crazy, and terrible things the adults do. In one of their most controversial episodes, "Red Hot Catholic Love," a bumbling counselor asks the boys if a priest ever put anything in their butt. The boys can't figure out what the heck she's talking about (which is a commentary on the idiocy of some forms of sexual abuse interviewing), and they somehow come up with a theory that there's a way to eat through your butt and poop through your mouth. By the end of the episode, all the adults in town have taken up the habit of pooping out of their mouths as a metaphor for what adults say to you. It's disgusting and gross, yes, but it's a satire about the horrors of child molestation in the Catholic Church, where people in authority haven't owned up to their misdeeds and are not speaking straightforwardly about it. In the end a good priest says, "When they have no mythology to live their lives by, they just start spewing a bunch of crap out of their mouths." The parents listen, regain their faith, stop pooping from their mouths, and go to church again.

There are other offensive plots with good messages. For example, *South Park*'s Bebe has the first signs of breasts, and all the boys think she's cool, but the catch is that none of them realize why. Here the writers poke fun at boys' obsession with breasts and later, when other girls want the same attention that Bebe is getting, the insanity of plastic surgery. When *High School 3* mania takes over *South Park*, the perfect Zac Efron–like star, Brydon, who'd rather be playing basketball, is forced to act in the school musical by an abusive theater-crazed father. In these and other episodes, there's a small morsel of a moral somewhere at the end of all the offensive nonsense. While we would be morally outraged at some of these characters and events in real life, for now we're laughing.

It's important for parents to appreciate the connection between all those early poop and fart jokes on their son's TV, the irreverent remarks between characters about the way they look and who they like, the pseudo-drinking and risk taking, the assumptions that boys and men will be stupid, take dares, and will laugh at anything over-the-top or gross, and the reasons why these more adult shows appeal to boys. It's all the same really, just more or less extreme, and boys are invited onto this pathway through all forms of media. The problem, of course, is that it takes more (grosser, stranger, more offensive) to be over-the-top with each show, with each season, and it's easy to forget that, as many a parent has said, "It's all fun and games, until some-one gets hurt."

Humor is at the heart of most marketing to boys, and at its best it's very effective. So talking with your son about humor and, when he's old enough, satire and spoofs, is important. Having cheap laughs at another's expense is never a good idea. Good satire has a goal, a social or political point to make; it's not just a string of pop culture references or humor for humor's sake. So do we still stand by our claim that you should watch along with your son? Sit through the poop jokes, the boob gags, the offensive insults to people of all races, sexual orientations, ethnicities? Of course. How else can you discuss them with him? It's a good exercise for a teenage boy to explain why he likes something that he can tell is cruel or insulting. And in a way, perhaps it's better to view these things bluntly in a cartoon, than more subtly in TV shows that either have no awareness or don't care that they may be support-ing sexism, anti-Semitism, racism, and more.

Not the Sharpest Tool in the Shed

Tune into VH1's *Tool Academy* or MTV's *From G's to Gents* and you'll get a heavy dose of one of the most popular themes in reality TV these days: re-making a jerk, a gangsta, a geek, or a slacker into a different kind of man. What kind of man that is depends on the premise of the show, but it usually involves a transformation into some stereotype of "cool": a guy who looks the part, acts aloof, doesn't bend under pressure, and impresses or seduces the ladies. In MTV's *Made*, for example, you'll see plenty of computer nerds transformed into cool rappers, ladies' men, and prom kings, but never the other way around. Once a guy is "made," so to speak, by becoming the best boyfriend, the most sophisticated gentleman, or the master pickup artist, he can head on over to male reality shows on the Discovery Channel or His-tory Channel like *The Contender, Ax Men, Ice Road,* and *Deadliest Catch* to compete with even more manly men to see who's the toughest. Or maybe if he's more hot than brave, more player than tough guy, he'll forgo the punch in the solar plexus, the smelly fish, and the dangerous roads to vie for the attention of sex kitten Tila Tequila on her MTV show *Shot at Love.* Or why not compete to be the new best friend of former *The Hills* star Brody Jenner on *Bromance*? If he has any musical talent, he can parlay his new-found manhood into a regular gig, then cash in and show off his cool stuff on *Cribs.* Better yet, maybe he'll become the next Bret Michaels or Ray J, host his own version of VH1's *Rock of Love* or *For the Love of Ray J,* and get to choose from a bevy of big-breasted girls so dazzled by him they'll grovel, cry, fight, and do virtually anything he wants.

Seems like a lot of choices, doesn't it? Gent, player, rock star, tough guy, bro, or slacker? The more stereotypes producers can play across genres, the more they can keep them going. These reality shows have an incestuous streak, where the most outlandish contestants from past shows like *Flavor of Love* and *I Love New York* appear on new shows like *I Love Money.* They be-come celebrities of a sort, making their way into the tabloids. And why not? It's just entertainment, right? We all know there's very little reality in reality TV shows. We know that producers choose competitors and edit situations carefully to pump up the drama and that they even prevent contestants from sleeping enough so they can ensure plenty of blowups. As NPR *Morn-*

ing Edition reported on May 14, 2008, reality show producers are well aware of the research showing that people deprived of sleep are likely to be emotionally volatile. Sleep deprivation is just another tool to incite drama, like putting a control freak in the same room with a slob; it is, as Lincoln Hiatt, executive producer of the Fox reality show *Solitary*, said in the NPR story, "a producer's ally on almost any show."

Reality shows work so well because they take that small piece of reality behind every stereotype and run with it. In the 2009 season of *Tool Academy*, which is a show about remaking "tools" into husband material, the competitors have names like "Loudmouth Tool," "Slacker Tool," and "Power Tool." One of the two black guys on the show stands in for the stereotype of all black guys as "Playa Pimpin' Tool." Funny thing is, he's a nice guy—even tempered and respectful, and he even wants to marry his girlfriend—that is, he's not convincingly in need of retooling. But the show needs a playa/pimp so it seems as though any black guy will do. As the show progresses it actually becomes a problem. He's not like the other guys who diss their girlfriends, fart, get drunk, yell, and start fights, and because he does so well in the "maturity challenges," he doesn't make for good reality TV, so off the show he goes.

Whether it's geeks in need of makeovers, players looking for the hot girl, or demonstrations of cool toughness, reality shows offer boys some of the worst messages about what it means to be a man. In show after show, boys get the message that women are there to please, serve, or sex men up. In *For the Love of Ray J*, girls with nicknames like Cocktail, Chardonnay, and Danger will do anything to be chosen by this younger brother of R&B singer Brandy. In what sounds like a middle school dating game, Ray J asks each girl "to pretend I'm out of town and you have to keep me interested" via computer Web cam, while the other girls watch and make catty comments. Of course the girls do everything from a striptease to sexy raps to making a "human banana split"—even Ray J is so shocked by that one that he can't stay in his seat to watch. (A voice-over invites the viewer to go to the show's Web site to watch the stuff too racy for TV.) There are a few girls who keep it clean—one paints a portrait of Ray J, another does a ballet— but of course it's banana split girl who wins the day. Shocking, yes, but even more shocking is the implication that boys should be attracted primarily to girls who act like porn stars.

The same naughty fantasies drive *Rock of Love Bus* with forty-five-year-old Bret Michaels, the front man for former glam metal band Poison. Sexy twenty-something-year-old women follow him on tour in their own pink and blue buses loaded up with cameras, and so we're privy to a steady stream of "ugly ass" and "stupid bitch" commentary behind the scenes to compare to the sweet sexy posturing the girls show on the individual and group dates they win with Michaels. In one episode, Michaels takes the "little hotnesses," as he likes to call them, to Larry Flint's Hustler Club, divides them into three groups, and gives each group a dowdy girl to transform into a "megahot goddess." The team leader of the group that best turns nice into naughty will win a date with him. Each group does such a fine job that not only do all three group leaders get to go on the date with Michaels, but much to the disappointment of the competitors, those once dowdy girls are so hot that Michaels invites them to join the tour too.

This fantasy is as much about having control over the situation as it is about being surrounded by hot girls. Speaking directly to the camera, Bret Michaels and Ray J pass judgment on the girls who try too hard or not hard enough, who they dislike for being catty or overly dramatic, or who are skanky or not giving enough "love." In the end, the girls line up and wait for the verdict: "Are you here for the love of Ray J?" Ray J asks each before handing her a glass of champagne, and the girls respond with wide-eyed sincerity, "Oh yes, Ray J, I am." "Would you continue to rock my world?" asks Bret with the coveted press pass in hand, and each girl assures him, "Oh yes, Bret, yes." To the loser? "The tour ends here."

Of all the reality shows we watched, a few stood out, offering a twist on the same old themes and something a little more complex. In *Bromance* (with a heart in place of the *o*) guys compete to become Brody Jenner's new BFF. The winner will be included in Jenner's entourage and will be gifted with a "sick-ass apartment and a life he can only dream of." That life is right out of the HBO series *Entourage*—a fast-paced LA lifestyle of hot girls, cool stuff, and paparazzi. The guys are put to the test. Can they handle a conversation with *Playboy*'s Playmate of the Year or talk up chicks in a bar? Are they committed enough to wear Brody's fake jean line in front of the paparazzi, even though the jeans are tight and "girly" and the T-shirt is pink, and are they loyal enough to tell him that the jeans are terrible? Can they go on a camping trip, fish, and act like outdoorsmen? Can they do crazy fun stuff like ride a rolling chair down a hill? Most of all, can they be real with their potential new bro? Will they choose him above all others, especially that pesky girlfriend back home? Brody is looking for true friendship, and he'll do whatever it takes to get it, including meeting the finalists' families, submitting the guys to a lie detector test, and making sure they pass muster with his own mom.

The whole concept of a reality show star (Brody was on *The Hills*) picking a best friend on another reality show is a bit absurd. The new best friend doesn't need skills of any sort. There's no talk of education or a work life or what he offers Brody in return for the surprise new ride and the new life. At least Vincent Chase in *Entourage* is a talented A-list actor and his best friend, Eric, has the skills to act as his manager. What does *Bromance* winner Luke Verge, self-proclaimed "party animal," bring to Brody Jenner's life? He can slack with the best of the bros? He can play sidekick to a star? The real answer is what makes this show so interestingly different. Luke really likes this guy, and Brody likes him back. The guys on this show hug, they struggle, they even cry. They are in real relationships, sorta. Sure, there are lots of hot girls around so that we are constantly reminded which team these guys play for, and the same old stereotypes about what boys are into are prominent on the show. Still, a show that in the end suggests that male bonding and friendship is simply about really getting to know and liking another guy does break some kind of new ground.

So does *From G's to Gents*, created by actor/singer Jamie Foxx. Like all reality shows, this one is over-the-top. Bring twelve gangsters (hence the G) to a mansion to meet suited-up and sophisticated Mr. Fonsworth Bentley (P. Diddy's personal assistant), who will introduce them to the finer things in life, put them through etiquette, diction, fashion challenges, and whip them into gentlemen. The difference between the gangsters—covered in tattoos, wearing grills and bling, barely decipherable between the cusses and slang—and Mr. Bentley, whose version of proper is more Thurston Howell III of *Gilligan's Island* than smart, irreverent Benson of the 1970s soap opera parody *Soap*, is magnified for effect, but there's still something real about this show. The guys chosen are from the street, and they are both tough and vulnerable at the same time. There are no "types" among them—they all want out of bad neighborhoods and hard lives and think this is their one chance. They have young children to support, fathers or mothers who abandoned them, grandmothers and girlfriends rooting for them. They recall painful memories, telling stories of prison and drugs, of people who gave up on them, and mistakes they want to put behind them. Sure, the guys are often out of control—no thanks to all the liquor lying around the mansion—but Mr. Bentley constantly invokes the hard work that stands between them and admission to "The Gentleman's Club." He's also perceptive and compassionate in a way the other reality show hosts aren't, and guys watching—whether G's or Gents—can learn not only a little about how to dress, behave, and speak if they want to pass as members of conventional society, but also a little about second chances.

Reality shows, like all media, have some of the good, the bad, and the ugly (okay, more of the bad and the ugly). They're best turned off unless you're prepared to watch with your son to discuss the content. If you watch these shows together, let your son know how reality shows work, how clever editing can create almost any reality, and how smart decisions on the part of a producer can suggest volatile moments or even a sense of intimacy. Do we know if the romance or bromance is real; if a fight was justified? No. But you can talk with him about what seems real to you—an emotional reaction, a behavior that interrupts the usual goings-on, a refusal to play or be played— and highlight what you value about these things. It seems like a weird way to initiate a conversation, but the only way reality shows can work for you is if you make the effort to insert a little of your own reality when watching.

From Superman to Superbad: Boys and Movies

Google "movies for boys" and it's not too surprising what comes up— everything from *Rocky* to *Star Wars* to *James Bond* to *Spider-Man*. Indeed, "boy movie" means almost anything except *Sisterhood of the Traveling Pants*– type "chick flicks." However, there are genres marketed especially to boys, and our survey tells us these are the ones boys say they love to watch. While parents might wish their sons would choose inspiring movies with great messages, like *Holes*, *Hoot*, and *October Sky*, or discuss interesting characters like Napoleon Dynamite or Donnie Darko, left to their own devices their sons are more likely to go for comedies punctuated with lots of loud bodily noises, action-filled superhero adventures, blood and gore horror flicks, real-life sports stories, and funny slacker films. We can't review all the movies boys watch, so we examine movies in these genres, paying close attention to the messages about boyhood and manhood they deliver.

Films are, for the most part, a man's world translated for boys. Men comprise 83 percent of all directors, producers, writers, cinematographers, and editors of the top 250 domestic grossing films; the writers and story crews of animated films are overwhelmingly (or completely) male; 90 percent of animators are men, and 75 percent of characters in G-rated animated movies are male. You'd think these men would pass down messages to boys they've learned in their lives about the things that really matter. Sometimes they do, but it seems as if they all, from directors to marketers, buy into the notion that male stereotypes sell tickets.

Consider, for example, the G-rated movie *Cars*, one of the highest grossing animated films to date. The DVD release includes a bonus features section titled "Inspiration for *Cars*" in which creator and director John Lasseter describes how his summer road trip with his two sons inspired the "get off the fast track and appreciate the journey" message of the movie. But since life's racetrack is exactly what boys are encouraged to jump on in every form of media that targets them, this sentimental midlife message wouldn't fly unless it came to boys as an over-the-top action adventure. Sure enough, Disney/Pixar pitched the movie as a "high octane adventure-comedy that shows life is about the journey, not the finish line," and it was promoted as the movie to corner the boy market in a way that Disney's princess-focused empire had been unable to do. In the largest promotional program ever created for a Disney/Pixar film, *Cars* was responsible for sales of one billion dollars worldwide, most of it on products emphasizing a pedal-to-the-metal image (e.g., PlayStation, Xbox, and Game Boy race car games, street racer sets, even car-shaped ice cream bars called Burn Outs) that directly countered Lasseter's inspirational moral.

Cars has a message about the importance of friendship as well, and as we reviewed animated movies boys said they loved we discovered that this theme was both plentiful and powerful. Perhaps male filmmakers are remembering the importance of their male friendships; maybe they're longing for the days when these relationships marked an all-male world full of adventure and fun. Whatever the reason, buddy films have a lot to say to boys watching about what a friendship should be like.

BROS BEFORE DOES

Buddy stories traditionally involve two male characters with different backgrounds and personalities forced to live or work together. Classic examples are of course the Bing Crosby, Bob Hope *On the Road* films, *Butch Cassidy and the Sundance Kid* and *Lethal Weapon*, but in recent years the genre has given comic energy to a steady stream of PG-13 and R-rated films like *Wedding Crashers*, *Superbad*, and *Step Brothers*. Buddy stories have also made their way down the ratings ladder to PG and G-rated animated films. Of course we want our sons to have buddies when they're little tikes and especially as they grow up. Buddies offer comfort in new situations and protect them from teasing in middle school and the awful loneliness of adolescence. But the films popular with little boys offer such a narrow depiction of what buddies are for real boys. They might have an overarching theme that a boy needs another boy, or a man, another man, which is all good, but when we take a look at the details, some of the messages are not so friendly.

Nearly every popular animated buddy film can be classified as a search for some version of that different kind of journey Lasseter longed for—to be a better, braver, more genuine and trustworthy person, to learn how to love well, to see that life's about more than being a winner. They're also journeys into the unfamiliar, the wild, the untamed, the new and scary—that is, stories about growing up and leaving home. A friend is essential to the journey and the underlying message of all the films is that making it, being the best, winning all alone, is not only impossible, it's no fun. These are messages that appeal to parents, and for good reason. Boys need friends, support, and love.

But the buddy relationships in these films are less about mutual friendship than an opportunity for a dominant male character to work out his issues. Like the quarterback on the high school football team, the star of these movies can afford to learn an inner lesson or two because he's already proven his masculinity in a whole variety of important ways—he's the scariest ogre (*Shrek*), the best child scarer (*Monster's, Inc.*), the biggest and strongest mammoth (*Ice Age*), the fastest race car (*Cars*). Not surprisingly, the buddy is typically what the main character isn't: smaller, weaker, needier, more emotional, not as smart. He's a sidekick, Tonto to the Lone Ranger.

We are tuned into race and class difference in these movies, when they exist, by who voices the characters, their mannerisms and slang, and the humor that arises from the clash of cultures. In all but two of the movies that showcase these differences, the sidekick is African American or from a lower social class, a pattern we also saw in TV shows and nonanimated movies. For example, Shrek the Ogre's sidekick Donkey, an easily frightened, needy, fast-talking operator, is voiced by Eddie Murphy (*Shrek*); Lightning McQueen's sidekick tow truck, Mater, is the self-named redneck comic Larry the Cable Guy (*Cars*); Alex the lion's sidekick, Marty, a bored and dissatisfied zebra, is Chris Rock (*Madagascar*).

Only two movies we watched reverse this trend: Martin Lawrence plays the "mighty grizzly" Boog in *Open Season* (to Ashton Kutcher's Elliot the deer), and Will Smith plays the lead fish Oscar in *Shark's Tale* (to Jack Black's Lenny the shark). In both movies African American culture is marked by hip-hop expressions and lifestyle. In *Open Season*, Boog talks about his crib to Elliot, and in the end affirms the ultimate buddy message: "Bros before does" (a parody of "bros before hoes," an urban phrase that suggests that there's something wrong with putting your girlfriend or any girl ahead of a brother). Everything about Will Smith's Oscar in *Shark's Tale* is hip-hop—his slang, his clothing and backward baseball cap, the bling and parties he covets, his put-down references to anything "old school."

Interestingly, the buddy relationships in these two movies are more mutual. Oscar the fish needs Lenny to fake his own death and create the illusion that he is a "shark slayer" so he can leave the car wash and "move on up" to a life of girls and parties; Lenny, who hates to kill, needs Oscar to escape the burdens of his Mafia family. *Open Season*'s Boog, the performing grizzly, is afraid to be on his own in the wild; his buddy, Elliot, is a wilderness survivor but he's small, effeminate, and needs protection from hunters. They bond in the woods one night when they confess their vulnerabilities and debate who's the biggest loser. In spite of the hip-hop bravado, the African American leads in these movies share more vulnerability and a richer expression of emotion than the white male leads. Unfortunately, they're also, as we'll see, more likely to invoke a "bros before does" story line, make reference to partying, and draw on stereotypes of girls.

In spite of these differences, the buddy relationships in all of these films provide the opportunity for characters both to prove and worry about masculinity. Friendship is tested via wild and crazy troublemaking that gets passed off as fun and games but which can encourage young boys to invest in problem behaviors. When Elliot dares Boog to leave home, they trash a country store and get "drunk" on candy bars. As in tween TV, drinking is a repeated theme: Woody in *Toy Story* tries to sober up Buzz Lightyear when he drinks too much "tea"; SpongeBob in *The SpongeBob Square Pants Movie* has a hangover from an ice cream bender. The friends in *Madagascar* set up a cool bar on the beach.

In addition to troublemaking, bullying and shaming are used to create tension between the buddies, and also to mark their emerging closeness. In *Cars*, Mater dares McQueen to go tractor tipping, squawking like a chicken and calling McQueen a baby when he hesitates. Buddies, especially the more emotional and uncertain sidekicks, are called names like losers, girls, divas, goldilocks, and versions of "mama's boy." Others who aren't cool enough, in control, or fearless are the butt of jokes and taunting as well. Bad guys—almost always hypermean, hypermasculine, hyperarrogant, hypersexist characters—get their comeuppance, but not before those watching have been exposed to an hour's worth of messages about how not to behave unless you want to be made fun of, shamed, or hurt. No matter how the story ends, the journey is fraught for any character who isn't man enough.

The message that violence is justified is common in these movies. Buddies fight out their differences but over time bond against a common foe.

Hypermasculine guys end up looking like dopes and getting their due, but the final showdown is less a challenge to their macho image than a comment on good or bad use of power. Evil guys abuse power, are bullies, and use brute force to get what they want and enjoy the consequences. They must be challenged by someone with the heart and courage to fight back, a man of the people who is loyalty tested (hence the buddy; before the end of every film there will be a test of loyalty) and who will replace the tyrant with a new and just world order.

"I LOVE YOU, MAN"

For her book, *Dude, You're a Fag,* sociologist J. C. Pascoe listened to high school–aged boys say that "'fag' was the worst epithet one guy could direct at another" and "since you were little boys you've been told, "Hey, don't be a little faggot." Characters in these G- and PG-rated movies don't call one another fag or gay, as characters do in R-rated movies, but they contribute to the everyday warnings little boys get about how to behave if they want to avoid "being a little faggot." In the vernacular of everyday life in schools across the country, "that's so gay" means lots of things—stupid, incompetent, too emotional, feminine, weak—in short, the characteristics given to most of the sidekicks in these movies. In the face of Sid the sloth's physical struggles in *Ice Age*, Manny the Mammoth says, "You're an embarrassment to nature, do you know that?" When Sid questions why he has to be the baby's diaper changer, Manny says, "You're small and insignificant—because I'll pummel you if you don't."

Buddy relationships in these movies provide a special opportunity to define what's okay to do and say between male friends and to show what "normal" friendship between guys looks and sounds like. Alas, what boys see is that shaming and teasing are okay. Physical closeness isn't. When one night by the fire Sid says, "How 'bout a good night kiss?" Manny is speechless and uncomfortable, which maybe we can understand. But the reason Sid asks is to underscore a neediness he'll be shamed for throughout the film. In *Surf's Up*, when mentor Z saves surfer Cody's life and Cody tries to hug him, Z says, "Hey, hey, man, none of that" and calls him a loser. It's a joke, it's always a joke, but we get the picture. In *Open Season* a pair of macho beavers (manly laborers that they are) call Boog a diva and tease the buddies about their closeness: "Keep on prancing you panty-waistin' cow." Maybe adults can distinguish the kind of cruel bullying the beavers deliver from the buddy to buddy warnings, but to little boys they all say loud and clear that physical closeness between boys is a no-no.

There is some variation when it comes to what's considered normal male behavior, but there are always boundaries to understand. In *Madagascar*, Alex the lion and best pal Marty the zebra embrace, skip, wrestle with each other, even run together on the beach to the soundtrack of *Chariots of Fire* without any indication that this is anything but affectionate fun. But against the playful and energetic "boys," the giraffe, Melman, is positioned as one of the girls, whining and complaining about his various illnesses and lounging in a waterfall with Gloria the hippo. In *Cars*, masculinity is represented by dark colors, aerodynamic edges, and lots of "flash"—flames, lightning bolts, and thunderclouds. In contrast, Luigi and Guido, two male cars with European accents and lots of style, have curved bodies in pale colors, like the female cars. The message is clear: "real boys" should be active, cool, edgy, and tough (and American).

Gender bending of any sort invites teasing and laughter, and cross-dressing (almost always a tough guy in frilly girl's clothing) is comic relief in movie after movie. So we were surprised when hip-hop–inspired *Shark's Tale* avoided the stereotypes and offered the closest thing to a genuine "coming out" story. Sensitive shark Lenny, the son of a mobster and next in line to inherit the family business, tells Oscar he's a vegetarian: "In case you haven't noticed, I'm different from other sharks. You're the first fish I've ever told. I'm sick and tired of keeping it to myself." Lenny hides by dressing as a dolphin, and it's Oscar who confronts Lenny's father: "So your son likes kelp; so he has a fish as a best friend; so your son likes to dress like a dolphin. Everybody loves him the way he is. Why can't you?" To which the moved father replies, "I love you, son. No matter what you eat or how you dress."

Girls are an important part of buddy movies, primarily because they counter that fearful possibility of an "unnatural" relationship, especially for the weaker sidekicks. Girls show up as hot babes, love interests who need to be saved from mean guys or evil women, or comic relief. And female comic relief usually has a sexy edge. In *Cars*, twin superfans Mia and Tia giggle and hang on either side of Lightning McQueen. (Kids can even buy the threesome in a gold "bling" toy gift pack: "Mia, Tia and Lightning McQueen are all dressed up and ready to hit the town." Who cares that in the movie Lightning moved beyond a life where hot girls are status symbols?) In *Ice Age*, Sid sits in a hot tub with three "hot" female sloths and tries to impress them by bragging about caring for a human baby. *In Shark's Tale*, gold digger Lola, who calls herself "superficial," is pitted against genuine, practical Angie, who loves Oscar for who he is. In the end Angie gets Oscar of course, but not before we've been introduced to an age-old stereotype of good vs. bad girls.

Overall, the prevailing theme for boys—because girls in these movies are either absent or marginal—is, in fact, "bros before does." When in *Monsters, Inc.* Mike becomes jealous of buddy Sully's attachment to Boo, the little girl he's protecting, Sully reassures him: "I'm your pal, your best friend, doesn't that matter?" In the end, it does. They team up to save Boo because, as Mike says, "You and I are a team, nothing is more important."

NOW THAT WE'RE MEN

The *SpongeBob SquarePants Movie* is perhaps the most obvious boy-to-man journey movie of all. The TV show characterizes SpongeBob as an innocent, gullible type, and his friendship with dopey Patrick is openly, sweetly affectionate—so much so that it's raised the ire of social conservatives who call the pair gay and critique the show for promoting a homosexual agenda, as if there is such a thing. This made the movie all the more interesting. Will the friendship be changed to appease the show's critics? Will the characters be tougher and less affectionate?

True to form, the movie is a very funny satire about manhood. To prove his manliness (to become the MANager of the Crusty Crab), SpongeBob and buddy Patrick risk a journey to Shell City—a dry land souvenir shop. Fearing failure because they're only kids, seaweed mustaches convince them they are now men and "are invincible." They sing:

> *Now that we're men, we have facial hair*
> *Now that we're men, I change my underwear*
> *Now that we're men, we've got a manly flair*
> *We got the stuff, we're tough enough to save the day*

But in this movie, as with many others, there's a difference between the creator's intent and what children see and hear. It's important as parents to be ever mindful of the gap between the stories told and retold through media and marketing and the complexities of our sons' lived experience, and how certain story lines, repeated over and over, invite children to see certain relationships and ways of behaving as normal and good, and others as unnatural and bad. Do they understand satire? Or do they relish in the "now that we're men we're invincible" theme as it's played? They can get it, but a parent has to be right there by their side, laughing at how funny it is when boys think that being a man means shaving, wearing clean underwear, and acting tough. Alas, when they view the Burger King commercial, a sad partnering of SpongeBob and BK, "I like Square butts and I cannot lie," the joke falls flat.

We suspect that the men who create these movies have a lot of things in mind—their own interests, relationships, and boyhood memories; a desire to make movies children will love but that are also entertaining to adults; pressure to make a big profit; the creative interplay among well-established genres and themes; a wish to promote lofty messages. But regardless of their intent, for children, as we've seen before, the devil is in the details. The messages repeated over and over—the ones about troublemaking, risk taking, bullying, drinking, checking out hot babes—are the ones most likely to impact boys.

Little boys' friendships are filled with possibilities. Sure, there will be competition and struggles over power, as well as teasing and risk taking. But boys will also show affection, share fears and vulnerabilities, and build genuine bonds. Given the messages in the movies they watch, it's important to be reminded that if we want them to experience real friendships, we'll have to intentionally create the space for them.

With Great Power Comes Great Responsibility

Superman, Batman, Spider-Man, Fantastic Four, X-Men! What's not to like about superheroes? They fight evil, they stand for justice, they show compassion, they use aggression wisely or at least only defensively, and at heart, they're all vulnerable beings. Perhaps this explains why moms and dads are so willing to allow their four-, five-, and six-year-old boys to watch these movies, even though most of them are rated PG-13. Sure, watching the car chases, crashes, and explosions with their dad or big brothers lets young boys know that this is what boys with a capital B love and ought to love, but witnessing the uncertainty and even angst behind all that action and violence may actually teach them a good lesson about what it means to be a man.

Superheroes come with ready-made vulnerabilities. Created in comic book form, superheroes are for any boy who's ever felt like an underdog, an outsider, a loser, but knew that deep inside he had talent, capability, and intelligence. With the ability to stretch and twist, Reed Richards of the Fantastic Four is brilliant but very timid and passive, and his friend Ben, The Thing, has real issues about how unattractive he looks in rock formation.

Bespectacled Clark Kent is bumbling and laughable, but even as the Man of Steel, Superman, he has an innate vulnerability to Kryptonite. The X-Men are an oppressed minority. Batman was traumatized as a child when he fell into a well and was attacked by thousands of bats. He has to overcome PTSD (post-traumatic stress disorder) symptoms, such as flashbacks. Spider-Man was bullied as a kid, and Peter Parker is a nerdy science genius. Most have problems with their fathers.

These vulnerabilities lend a special sense of what it means to struggle in real life for each superhero, just as their superpowers give them a special gift. But parents need to look closely at the messages to boys about how to live with and respond to one's own vulnerability. In these movies vulnerability hides behind superpower, guarded and secret because it's a superhero's greatest weakness, the key to his downfall. The overriding message to boys is that one has to hide or turn vulnerability around because it is, in the end, humiliating. The answer to vulnerability is to find some way to pretend it doesn't exist or to prove that really, in actuality, one is stronger, better, abler than others in spite of it.

While it's important for all children to know what it means to persist in spite of hardships, it's the "I'll show them!" mentality that bothers us most about these movies. This revenge theme is not as present in the comic books, and we wonder if by form-fitting superhero movies to action movies, some of the good work that these comics did for boys gets lost.

This revenge mentality is dangerous for two reasons. First, it reflects a pattern we see in real life. An inner need to deny their vulnerability through power is the way some men come to violence. Second, this way of dealing with trauma—coping by turning it into its opposite; what some psychologists refer to as "reversal"—doesn't really address the frightening feelings of vulnerability that all of us need to learn to master as we grow and develop. Batman turns his PTSD around by becoming the very thing he is most afraid of, a bat. Quite a few superheroes fight against traumatic fears through reversal. They avert plane crashes, global warming, car accidents, and in *Superman Returns*, stop and reverse a 9/11-type disaster and wreckage to a city, Metropolis, much like New York. They teach that the way to undo vulnerability is through proving their superiority and their power, and aggressive power at that.

But there are discussions and limits to the use of power, and superheroes are always struggling with using power wisely. We see this in the use of moral language in these films. Spider-Man's theme, "with great power comes great responsibility," reminiscent of the biblical "to whom much is given, much is required"—is indeed a moral message. Mr. Fantastic, Reed Richards, and the Invisible Woman, Susan Storm, chide her brother, Johnny Storm, constantly for wanting to seek the limelight, warning him not to show off his powers or use them for personal gain. Hulk goes into hiding for specialized training to control his anger. In *The Dark Knight*, the theme "you either die a hero, or you live long enough to become a villain" speaks to how difficult it is to remain good. Batman sees "what he has to become" to stop men like the Joker. As far as we can deduce, superheroes only kill in self-defense (or accidentally). When fighting mano a mano with a villain, they almost always show compassion or a limit to what they will do aggressively in order to demonstrate the line between good and evil. The Joker says, "I want you to do it. Come on. Hit me." And of course Batman won't. When Batman's childhood friend Rachel Dawes tells him that if he seeks revenge instead of justice he's just a coward with a gun, we might approve. Villains kill willy-nilly, but superheroes use violence in the service of justice. Will Smith as Hancock in *Hancock* is hilarious as a down-and-out superhero because his behavior is so unsuperhero-like. He's not very careful with his power. He picks up a car and hurls it, and calls little old ladies the *b*-word.

Speaking of women, along with the little old ladies that most superheroes help, there are two types of women for superheroes: good girls and bad girls. The wrong kind of girl to love is featured clearly in all of these movies, and boys learn that while these girls might look hot and can be used as status symbols, the girl one really wants is moral and sweet and good. Sometimes these good girls are independent women, such as Lois Lane, the reporter who never takes direction from chief editor Perry White, or Rachel Dawes, who grew up with Batman and is now an assistant D.A. who believes in the rule of law. These women do these kinds of jobs because they too are fighting injustice, only on their own, less heroic terms. The good woman is also someone with the emotional power to soothe the beast within the superhero. But there's a not-so-subtle message about those other girls, such as Lex Luthor's Kitty, who's sexy, superficial, and stupid, or the bimbos that Johnny Storm, the Human Torch and playboy of the Fantastic Four, likes to have around him. The message is that power is *enhanced* by trophy broads fawning over you. This is true not only for the jokester characters, like Johnny Storm, but also for those who are evil. When evildoers are presented as cool with awesome equipment, as they so often are, one piece of that "awesome equipment" is the sexy trophy girl. Does this teach little boys that only bad guys use women? No. Good guys use 'em too. Bruce Wayne, in *The Dark Knight*, arrives at a fund-raiser with three gorgeous models in tow. Iron Man sleeps with and discards a woman at the beginning of his movie. He has a stripper pole on his private jet for the hot flight attendants to use for his entertainment. Sure, he loves Pepper Pots, but we learn that he also needs his playmates when he's asked, "Is it true you went twelve for twelve with playmates last year?"

Parents in these films also play stereotypical roles. Over and over we hear the message that fathers are terribly important figures in boys' lives. "He is his father's son," someone says of the Incredible Hulk, "every last damn molecule." Fathers, however, are mostly absent in their superhero sons' lives, even though their sons are constantly criticized for not living up to their fathers' expectations of them ("Your father would be ashamed of you," Rachel Dawes says to Batman, or "The apple's fallen far from the tree"). When fathers or father figures are murdered, sons feel guilty for whatever part they feel they may have played in their fathers' deaths, and guilt turns quickly to anger and thoughts of revenge.

"Son" imagery is also important—that is, religious imagery about Jesus as the son of God. Superman is called his father's "only son" sent to Earth, both a man and yet not a man. The supersilvery guy of *Fantastic 4: Rise of the Silver Surfer* martyrs himself for humanity. In so doing, Jesus gets reinvented not as the loving prophet who urged forgiveness, but as a guy who took one for his buddies, threw himself in front of the bullet, brave as any soldier. This, of course, is a theme in many an action hero movie. Just as the movie *Dogma* had Buddy Christ, here we have Superhero Christ.

But religion plays a small part compared to the almighty dollar. Bruce Wayne has no special powers, but the playboy millionaire has enough money to buy and pay someone to invent for him the coolest car, tools, suit, and devices to fight evil. Villains have the "biggest" computer or the "fastest" car. Every time the audience is asked to hate the evil person for his greed, whether it is Victor von Doom in *Fantastic Four* or Lex Luthor of *Superman*, they are simultaneously asked to admire all the cool stuff he has.

Every one of these blockbusters has car crashes and multiple explosions with lots of fire. Missiles explode, guns explode, cars and buildings explode, rockets explode, oil trucks and sometimes even people explode. (This sets them apart from their comic book counterparts, where explosions happen in a panel or two before moving on to plot.) There is cool equipment galore and often a semiautomatic gun that's larger than life. There are spectacular visuals of screens within screens that evoke the computer and video games viewers will be encouraged to buy. Then there are remarkable fight scenes where the superhero can take on hundreds of men at once all in self-defense until that inevitable point in the movie when he and the evil villain will be face-to-face, going at each other with only their hands or their superpowers. Reaching out to fans of wrestling, drag racing, martial arts, and fireworks, these movies have it all. They are designed to be over-the-top, all-male for the boy who is all-boy, and they are a far cry from the comic books from which they came.

That's because comic books are for a niche market, and superhero flicks aspire to be blockbusters, and therefore need to appeal to everyone. So we get romance scenes next to car crashes. These movies need to *almost* receive an R rating to be successful (to appeal to grown-ups and to create a controversy over the rating as part of the movie's hype). Thus, the youngest of boys who see these movies at home or even in the theater are inundated for 120+ minutes with scenes of sexy seduction, mature language, terror, irrational anger, villain tantrums, car crashes, and explosions, and are encouraged to develop an attitude of excitement toward them. These scenes introduce something into the lives of young boys that mimics playground threats. Can you take this? Or are you a wuss? The boy who turns his head away from a worm being squished or who won't challenge himself in risky ways, the one who doesn't thrill to noise, violence, and explosions, is weak, a "puny human" as Hulk calls himself when he sees Bruce Banner in the mirror.

Even though these events are presented in a stylized way, in make-believe cities or outer space, they evoke real-life traumas, such as when, in *Superman 3*, a tall building trembles, windows shatter, and a man jumps out of the building, his arms flailing. How many of us will remember the 9/11 video footage of those who had no choice but to jump from the Twin Towers? Superman saves the man before he reaches the sidewalk, but does that undo the reference? Each multiple car crash or explosion teaches kids to invest in the fun of destruction. One can almost hear a voice urging, "Isn't that cool?" In *Fantastic Four*, that voice is Johnny, who says "cool" and "awesome" at every explosion. Of course this stuff is not generally terrifying to older kids, and it may even serve as a release from the stresses of school or the pressures of home to some. But for younger children who don't yet distinguish fantasy from reality, it is terrifying, not only because in reality it's scary stuff, but also because of the expectation of what it means and what it takes to be a boy and become immune to the loud, the scary, the gigantic, the fearful, so that later movies will need to up the ante.

Film companies most likely would say that the PG-13 ratings are a warning to parents not to let their young children see these films. But this is hardly a convincing argument when these same companies advertise incessantly to young children during their TV shows, in their fast-food restaurant kids' meals, via E-rated video games, and in aisle upon aisle of movie-driven action figures in toy stores. With all the advertising directed at children, how could they not beg to see these films?

It's interesting to note one exception to this genre, at least with respect to some of the most prevailing themes. *Hulk*, the first Incredible Hulk film, was directed by Ang Lee, and it is qualitatively different from other super-hero films. In the hands of a more thoughtful director, gone are the bimbo trophy broads and joking sex references. Scientists look a little more like scientists, not the sexed-up or nerdy stereotypes. Unlike other films where the power awarded the superhero goes unquestioned, Hulk expresses feel-ings of "why me?" and desires to rid himself of the responsibility and anguish of his terrible strength. Unlike other superhero films, where absent fathers are idolized and loved, in *Hulk*, father and son have a tortured relationship, the father envying the son's power, and the son untrusting of his father's motives. When angered, Hulk turns furious, violent, and destructive, with no control over the expression of his anger, harming most things in his path (as if in a super toddler tantrum). But rather than treat this as a superpower, Ang Lee treats this as a problem of manhood, one that makes Bruce Ban-ner, the vulnerable man beneath the hulk, ashamed and confused. Strug-gling with a poor role model of a father, the film ends with his memory of his father kissing him and saying "Let's play trains." We think this may be a more realistic view of the difficulty for boys of wanting and exercising power, their desire to be invulnerable, and fear and shame of their own aggression and greed. Unfortunately, this more realistic view of aggression is discarded in the sequel that stars Edward Norton. Fights. Explosions. Constant ma-chine gun fire. Bullets bouncing off green skin. A car torn in two. More fighting. Hulk roaring. We hear: "As far as I'm concerned, that man's whole body is property of the U.S. Army." We know that Hulk has not been suc-cessful in reining in his "temper," and as viewers, we're meant to be pleased.

These films are exciting, and their defenders may point out that at least on the surface, the moral messages are good. But the moral nuances of these films are most likely lost on the younger set. When we asked one six-year-old why he liked Spider-Man he said, "He fights good." And, perhaps even more importantly, he wins.

Men Will Be Boys

What is more telling that we are at a crucial stage in America when it comes to our feelings about masculinity than the number of movies and TV shows that spoof manhood. As we've seen, TV cartoons like *South Park*, *Family Guy*, and *The Simpsons* make it their business to set up bumbling dads, macho guys, and narcissistic loser playboys. In the movies, stars like Jack Black and Will Ferrell often play lovable losers who aren't really men but adolescent boys. It's not as if being a "real man" is at all celebrated though; these and movies with adolescent boys, like *Superbad*, show that attempts to become "real men" are simply ridiculous.

Will Ferrell movies are quintessential masculinity spoofs and satirized statements about what "real men" do and don't do. In *Step Brothers* for example, John C. Reilly's character Dale complains to his recently engaged father that getting married will put an end to all their father-son fun, like fishing and "talking about pussy." His father looks at him quizzically and replies, "But we've never done any of that." Later in the film, *adult* masculinity is imagined thus: "I want to make bank, get ass, and drive a Range Rover." The guys who talk about what it means to be a man are particularly pathetic, and the guy who has all these things is the biggest loser of all. That's because the characters in these movies who represent "real men" are almost always real jerks—mostly jocks and he-men who have no sense of humor and who bully little guys. They're brawny and brainless players or arrogant businessmen who eventually get their comeuppance when we see that they didn't get where they are because they worked hard or deserved it, but through Daddy's favor or money. When hypermasculinity is revealed as a pose and those "real men" are exposed, it reassures every boy who feels he doesn't and could never measure up to that ideal.

The arrogance and stupidity of "real men" are especially mocked. Take Ben Stiller's White Goodman in *Dodgeball*, who says dumb things like, "You can't be my boss. Nobody's my boss. I'm my own boss. I created myself!" and "Nobody makes me bleed my own blood, nobody!" In *Anchorman*, Ron Burgundy says, "I'm very important. I have many leather-bound books and my apartment smells of rich mahogany." And later, when Veronica, the feminist anchorwoman calls him a baby, he asserts: "I'm not a baby, I'm a MAN, I am an ANCHORMAN!" Later, in reference to women, he proclaims, "The only way to bag a classy lady is to give her two tickets to the gun show *[kisses his biceps]* and see if she likes the goods." Like Ron Burgundy, Ricky Bobby of *Talladega Nights* is a buffoonish narcissist, raising his sons to be just like him. His son Walker Bobby tells his dad, after he says grace before a meal, "Daddy, you made that grace your bitch."

Everyone's immature in Will Ferrell movies, though, not just the narcissistic he-men. Ordinary guys who are stuck in adolescence are also satirized and stereotyped. In *Step Brothers*, bonding between males is satirized as peeing into the same toilet, measuring their penises, drooling over cool technology and hot chicks, and watching gruesome movie violence together. After lying around the house for twenty years post high school, their plan for success is starting a multimillion-dollar international corporation and making a rap video. The writers got it right. This is the masculinity to satirize: the choice of either being a player or being a slacker, which comes with the firm belief that success is deciding to and then instantly making millions or becoming a rap star, preferably both.

Authoritative masculinity is also spoofed. Again, in *Step Brothers*, the father of one stepbrother gave up his boyhood dream to become an internationally renowned doctor, who now can't wait to retire and sail around the world. When the stepbrothers get "real" jobs, they become soulless and talk about boring things like their cholesterol levels.

In the end, the message for boys is not to give up their dreams—that being an oddball is better than being an arrogant fake. The dream for Ferrell's Brennan?—singing without fear of being teased for not being masculine. For his stepbrother it's drumming in a rock band. Fine enough, even gratifying to see—but they achieve these dreams not by standing up to gendered injustice or even by practicing the drums. They just magically are given that one opportunity to shine, and their natural talent always somehow prevails. Boys watching this movie and others like it learn that even though these guys are some of the most ridiculous, foulmouthed, unmotivated, lazy, socially inappropriate, and immature slackers on the screen, they have hearts of gold and never give up their dreams. So while the movie tries to give boys permission to be who they are, "who they are" is usually defined as wild, immature, farting, burping dreamers. You can see the problem—it's a celebration of slackerdom even while we laugh at how over-the-top their multislacking gets. Consider this line from *Anchorman*: "What? You pooped in the refrigerator? And you ate the whole wheel of cheese? How'd you do that? Heck, I'm not even mad; that's amazing."

If anxious, authoritative, and narcissistic masculinity are all spoofed, what about gay masculinity? In *Talladega Nights*, gay jokes are directed at French racing car driver Jean Girard, played by Sasha Baron Cohen. On men holding hands with each other: "It is a sign of friendship in many cultures, it is not sexual at all. Do not be bothered by the fact I have an erection right now. It has nothing to do with you." But in many other movies, gay masculinity is something that causes anxiety, anguish, and trouble. In *Step Brothers*, Brennan is crushed for life when in high school, while singing a pirate song onstage, the entire audience, prompted by the football team (paragons of masculinity), start chanting "Man-gina" at him. The message is that you risk being taunted when you say or do anything out of the normal.

If guys are anxious about how masculine they are and can be, how do the women hurt or help? In superhero movies, girlfriends are submissive and prop up the good guy. In slacker movies, girls are the sensible ones who point out the stupidity and immaturity of guys. Sometimes, in slacker movies they outdo the men at being masculine by jumping on guys, riding them like a bucking bronco, and then lifting up their skirts to pee in the urinal. They put these posers in their place by showing them what "real men" are like!

We suspect most high school boys watching these movies get the spoofs and the satire. But, as David St. Hubbins says in *This Is Spinal Tap*, "it's such a fine line between stupid and clever," and these movies make a ton of money blurring that line. Even as adults, it's hard sometimes to know the difference between laughing with the characters or laughing at them as nerds, geeks, and losers. And when a kid calls a grown man a "fagstick," do our kids understand the joke? Do they use the word themselves later on, or do they simply acknowledge that they'd better watch their step around jerky guys? Even though the jerks are spoofed, we all know that in the real world, jerks get away with a lot. In the face of their arrogance and strutting, a slacker lifestyle can look like the best defense.

Last *Girl* Standing? Horror Flicks

Is watching horror films, like watching slacker comedies, a guy thing? So we hear. Although horror films are made for all audiences today, boys from middle school through high school tell us these films are some of their favorites. So we watched the gore, the bio-disasters, the slashings, and the ghosts to figure out what kinds of messages these films might be giving to boys about what it means to be a boy. Who gets killed? Who survives? And what are boys learning in between?

But first, consider that while parents get up in arms about the prostitute killings in *Grand Theft Auto*, we hear nary a peep about the killings that go on in horror films. Is that because in *Grand Theft Auto*, it's our sons who are invited to do the killing as part of the game, while in most horror films, it's a bad guy or creature that does the killing and such killings are purposefully horrific? In horror films our sons aren't meant to identify with the killers but rather to fear them. The killers are, after all, "pure evil."

So exactly who are boys supposed to identify with? Unlike so much of boys' media, in this genre (and we recognize that it's a wide-ranging genre), girls or young women are often the lead characters. Boys are meant to identify with *them*. How unusual that they're smart and they now fight well too! Long gone is the cliché of teen girls running through the woods and tripping. In fact, the first ten minutes of *Scream* satirizes the old-fashioned horror movie by mocking the stereotypical dumb white girl. Beautiful, blonde, and helpless, Drew Barrymore does every dumb thing stupid white girls used to do in horror movies when confronted with a killer in the house. After this beginning vignette, the lead character, brunette Sidney, played by Shannen Doherty, is shown to be much smarter than that. While the movie script outsmarts her at times, she triumphs in the end with wit, power, and ingenuity.

Film scholars have discussed the "final girl" phenomenon, a term coined by Carol Clover, describing horror films that leave a seemingly empowered girl standing at the end. However, critics disagree about who she is and what she means to boys. By identifying with her at the end of the movie, are boys let off the hook for enjoying the slashing, torture, and sexual violence against the other women in the film? That explanation certainly fits with the murders in *Final Destination 3* or the remake of *Halloween* in which the "bad girls" are killed in very pornographic ways. The sole survivor (final girl) is often a virgin—she doesn't have sex, do drugs, or talk trash like the girls who are killed off and tortured. Are filmmakers affirming the old good girl/bad girl distinction and suggesting only good girls are worthy? Or is the final girl supposed to be more like the boys who watch? Clover points out that many of these girls have boys' names, more androgynous bodies, and by the end of the movie, pick up something akin to a penis (sword, machine gun, chain saw) and use it well. In *Hostel: Part II*, it's an actual penis that the final girl hacks off a very bad guy. Some have argued that she has to be a girl because her earlier terror (which gets transformed into power by the end) is too "unmanly" to be realistic. Others say that she's androgynous because adolescent boys are vulnerable and still fragile, and this way they can relate to these "feminine" emotions. So maybe with this confusion about the last girl standing, we should look at what boys are learning about *all* the girls and boys in these films, as well as about who deserves to be killed and who doesn't.

Horror films abound with assholes, jerks, and mindless jocks who boys as well as girls don't like because they're so obnoxious and arrogant. Whether these jerks evoke the bully types that populate most every school or just bring to the surface pent-up anger, the audience is waiting to see them eviscerated for what they say and do. We're meant to dislike them, but we do watch them, and these guys get a chance to say and do some of the most macho and offensive stuff that ever hit the big screen. They are sexist, racist, and homophobic, and are allowed to say whatever they want because they're going to get killed for it. For example, there's a scummy guy in *Final Destination 3* who sees women as "nothing but funbags," and so he gets killed. In *Scream*, an obnoxious boy says, "There's always some standard bullshit reason to kill your girlfriend. . . . Maybe Sidney wouldn't have sex with him." (By the way, this theme of men going mad because women won't have sex with them recurs. In *Hostel: Part II*, one of the killers is angry at his wife because she hasn't had sex with him for a year.) There are also a few jabs at "yo mama," with guys calling people's mothers' sluts; for example, "How's your mom doing? My old man said for a buck she'd rub her tits on his face." The killer in *Scream* tells final girl Sidney that her mother "was a slut-bag whore who flashed her stuff all over town like she was Sharon Stone." So is the message to guys "watch what you say about girls and mothers" or "this is what a jerk sounds like"? In the end, does the excitement of the message get separated from the moral?

The jerks in these films are always challenging other boys' masculinity. Whether it's just a guy or the killer himself, boys and men, left and right, are being told that they're not man enough. In *Scream*, a boy is called "a lapdog" by an obnoxious boy in school. In *Halloween*, a bully calls a young Michael Myers, a "fucking pussy." Challenging a man's masculinity is the worst possible insult and can, in these films, drive the victim crazy mad. We know the power this kind of humiliation holds because triumphant final girls also get a poke at the evil guy's masculinity. In *Scream*, when one of the killers says he's going to rip Sidney up, calling her "you bitch," she counters by calling him a "pansy-ass mama's boy." After all, a killer who thinks he is really something big needs to be cut down to size.

Cockiness most definitely is punished in these films. The boys who are assholes, jerks, and mindless jocks get it and get it early. That they are jerks can be portrayed in subtle ways, for example, like when Darry runs a stop sign at the beginning of *Jeepers Creepers*. Girls are also punished for being too cocky, too sexy, for being a tease, or for even talking about sex. For example, the two "popular girls" in *Final Destination 3* get burned alive in tanning booths after admiring their bodies in pornlike fashion. But if girls who are too conceited about their bodies get killed, so do the he-men who work out and strut around, like the buff guy in *Final Destination 3* who is killed when two weights crash down and crush his head.

There may be a double standard in horror films for boys and girls when it comes to who gets it, how, and when. Boys tend to get it much worse. Because our society is so sexually violent, and so many victims in real life are women and girls (one in five by some reports), film directors may be more cautious about portraying such violence in film. Although they would probably argue us down with regard to whether or not horror films inform or influence serial murderers and rapists, we're betting that it's a bit of a worry. Or maybe they're just going against type and figure it's too predictable to victimize only the girls. After all, there's a rape a week in *Law & Order*–type TV shows. Whatever the reason, the worst violence is saved for teenage boys.

Why? Because they can take it? Because we already know girls are vulnerable so it's scarier to show vulnerability in boys? Or sadly, perhaps it doesn't matter as much nowadays if *a boy* is ripped in two when tied between two trucks that then move apart, as in *The Hitcher*. Better maybe to see the terror and upset reflected on his girlfriend's face. That gruesome scene is probably meant to evoke some mixture of "yikes," "gross," and "awesome" from kids who are interested in gory special effects.

These horror films are for the "little guy." Filmmakers bank on the audience identifying with Average Joe, the guy who is not the macho, hot, big man on campus. But there's no celebration of the little guy; the films keep boys in line by telling them that they better not be strutting their muscles out there like some kind of superhero or thinking they're better than anyone else, because there's always someone willing to cut them down to size or point out that they're just another asshole. Even worse, there's a feisty girl waiting around the corner ready and able to point out that they're a pansy-ass mama's boy.

But are horror films also for the other "little guy," that elementary school or preadolescent kid who sees his big brother enjoying these films? With the availability of these films on cable TV, how many of the youngest kids watch them? And how traumatic are they? One survey of third through eighth graders found that as the amount of TV viewing per day increased, so did trauma symptoms related to post-traumatic stress. In studies of college students looking back on their lives, 90 percent reported an intense fear reaction to something in the media, and a third of these fears were long-lasting. In her article "I'll Never Have a Clown in My House: Frightening Movies and Enduring Emotional Memory," Joanne Cantor reports that the majority of college students' longest-lasting fears come from entertainment rather than news! The movies cited by students most frequently as causing long-lasting fear are *Poltergeist*, *Jaws*, *The Blair Witch Project*, and *Scream*, even though *Scream* is somewhat satirical. Why do these college students still experience fear of clowns ten years after they saw *Poltergeist?* Why do some of them worry about stalking maniacs even if *Scream* is highly unrealistic? Because these movies about attacks on helpless victims invade their memories, especially if and when they feel vulnerable. Those who study the brain now speak of emotional memory and say that kids can have a conditioned fear response that is "indelible" and highly resistant to change.

We're not saying do away with horror movies. But as pornography invades the lives of younger and younger children, let's also be careful about the horrific images they're exposed to, and especially those horrific images that are intermingled with porn, as in the remake of *Halloween,* a movie that a middle schooler in our survey calls his favorite. It's different if a *teenager* wants to scare himself, although he should be warned that sometimes his fright will last longer than the ninety-minute film. But when children's vulnerability is messed with, and little boys are asked to master seeing unthinkably scary and gory things, it's time for parents to step in.

We don't recommend that little boys watch horror films. If your middle schoolers are watching, watch with them. Discuss with your son what kind of goo they use to make brains and answer his questions about how the special effects people animate the evil characters or the prop people make fake blood spurt. Don't forget to talk about the sexist stuff and the insults to mothers and manhood. These are some of the real horrors your son will face growing up.

Heroes and Antiheroes in Action Flicks

ONE MAN ALONE: QUOTES FROM ACTION MOVIE TRAILERS

How far would you go to protect your family?

Live for nothing or die for something.

He's a hero. He's a menace. He's what the world needs.

Nobody owns me.

Disobey and you die.

Don't think of it as just another job; think of it as a mission.

God be with you, Frank./Sometimes I'd like to get my hands on God.

My boss said you're the man for the job.

They tried to kill my wife.

It's not vengeance; it's punishment.

Win and get your freedom, or die trying.

Do you feel as if you were meant for something better? Something special?

Greatness comes to those who take it.

In a world where machines control man's destiny, imagine you were the only one who could stop it.

There is only one, who punishes them all.

"There is only one, who punishes them all." Only one? From the sound of it there are plenty of guys out there ready to blow things up, exact a little vengeance, and crash a few cars to save the world! When we wrote about superhero movies, we entertained the notion of justice. What action movie lovers tend to see as a "complex moral message" is just a sham. Don't buy it. There's nothing really complex about the movie version of justice in action films; there's a mixed message, perhaps, but it's not complex. It's mixed because heroes do some horrible things in the name of justice, and antiheroes occasionally do some nice things in the name of their gangster code even as they break the law. When it comes right down to it, whether good guy or bad, justice is just an excuse for aggression; and as violence in the movies gets worse, the justification for violence has to match it.

Let's take a closer look. When we last left James Bond in *Casino Royale*, Bond's girlfriend, Vesper, had been blackmailed, which led to her suicide. In the latest film, *Quantum of Solace*, M, the spymaster now almost motherlike toward Bond, is nearly killed. Of course the hero Bond will want vengeance. The comic book vigilante who is turned into the star of the film *The Punisher* is also obsessed with revenge. His family was killed. Who wouldn't want to punish the culprit? In *Transporter 2*, a child is kidnapped and infected with a deadly virus. Now that's going too far! Time for sweet justice. Sadly for Will Smith in *I Am Legend*, everyone's dead, including his lovely family, and zombies want to eat him. Go get 'em Will. And for video game–inspired, former cop Max Payne? "When the people a man needs get taken away from him, you can't ever go back to who you were before." Who wouldn't get violent? This is injustice, and it's very personal. While these personal vendettas fuel the motivation of most movie heroes, large-scale injustice is ultimately at the heart of each film.

The largest-scale injustice reaps the largest-scale violence. In the 2008

Rambo IV, the stage for violence is set by using what appears to be real footage of the atrocities that were part of the genocide in Burma. This background is designed to justify what critics have called a "gorefest" and a movie "sickening, almost degenerate in its savagery." While coproducer Sylvester Stallone said he wanted the world to see the horrors taking place in this "hellhole" against peaceful citizens at the hands of the military, the antimilitary message gets lost, both because Rambo's reputation and training came in Vietnam and because the film glorifies the use of military weapons and grenades. In this film, Rambo agrees to bring Christian missionary medics into Burma after warning them that nothing they do will bring change. The missionaries' moral message of nonviolence is proven so naïve and ineffective by the end of the movie, that a missionary is seen uncontrollably bashing the head of an attacker.

What's the message here? That when given a righteous cause, anyone will resort to violence? It's okay to put forth violent scenes in movies, as long as it's justified violence? While many a teen boy might benefit from an understanding of violence in Burma today and the horrors of such a military dictatorship, how can he understand it when it's put in the form of entertainment and escapism? When it comes from a gun-toting guy who says, "When you're pushed, killing's as easy as breathing"? What provides the escape? Endless, horrific, realistic violence showing heads severed and limbs blown off, a man strung up so that a wild pig will chew off his legs and he'll die slowly, a child shot in the head, a village burned, prisoners asked to run and then machine-gunned down. By one critic's count, over 250 people are killed. Cool? Neat? Awesome? What will teen boys who rent this R-rated movie think when and if they hear of the peaceful protests of the monks there? Most likely they'll think of the idiotic, helpless missionaries in the film who learn that violence is the only way to stop this genocide.

There are other solutions to this violence that he'll never hear from the likes of Rambo. One blogger recommends that anyone interested in the plight of these Burmese groups check out the Web site of the FBR (Free Burma Rangers)—a multiethnic humanitarian service movement that brings hope and help to people in Burma. They are trained themselves (no need for John Rambo) to go into areas under attack to provide emergency assistance and human rights documentation. Great minds have made serious arguments for peace and human rights assistance, which is quite different from sending in the tough guys.

It's hard to have conversations with your teens about the big issues raised in the most violent of these films—the murder of loved ones, drug cartels, genocide—and the feelings of loss, rage, and helplessness one feels in the aftermath. It's incredibly frustrating when, as parents, we're put in the position of having to explain or counter the messages in R-rated movies they shouldn't be watching anyway. How can our information and explanations compete with the graphic mayhem and grisly violence they see on the big screen? Though we encourage you to talk with your son about these films, it's even more important to prepare him for the messages they convey before he sees them. If you begin discussions with him from an early age about fantasy and realism in films and filmmakers' motives, and if you model an attitude of critique and disbelief when watching with him, you won't have to worry quite so much when he watches them at some other kid's house.

REVENGE IS SWEET?

Talking with your son about violence in PG-13 movies means first thinking about the messages these movies offer and, since you may not see them all, knowing which themes come up over and over again. Longing for justice is a wonderful quality to nurture in our children, but as we've noted already, the kind of justice that we find represented in most PG-13 movies is often about revenge. A lot of the violence is done in self-defense, and unlike R-rated movies, there are warnings about impulsive and over-the-top behavior, but these come as sidebars to the bigger issue of vengeance. In *Quantum of Solace*, for example, M has to warn Bond that his violent overreactions in self-defense mean that he's killing off all their leads. Some of the violence in Bond movies may not look like self-defense; it's done to fight the "bad" guys who usually want to take away our freedoms. But that's a form of self-defense and if you watch carefully, a lot of it looks vengeful and feels personal. This is acknowledged in the script, through lines about what revenge does to a man or about how vengeance seekers get out of control and lose sight of themselves. For example, M asks Bond if he can still work, given that his girlfriend was killed by the people he's after. Will his need for revenge lead to bad decisions? Will he be reckless? Not to act in the heat of anger and not to act out of vengeance are probably good lessons to teach teen boys—but that doesn't stop Bond.

In many of these films, the women, girlfriends, back-talking sassy pickups, moms, and kidnapped daughters all provide reason for revenge. *How far would you go to protect your family? Your girlfriend? That pretty blonde you met this morning?* It would be too selfish only to seek revenge for oneself. As one hit man in *Hitman* says to another hit man's corpse, "I told you to leave her alone." Men are protectors of women and children, so they seek revenge on behalf of them, and even, as in *Quantum of Solace*, alongside them, helping them seek their own vengeance. Women also provide moments in these films to show the hero's humanity. We were struck with how the two latest Bond movies had him posed identically, seated next to a woman after some mayhem, with his gentle hand around her head, protecting her, and how others, like the Transporter, throw their bodies over those they are meant to protect.

For all that longing for justice, what happens to longing for order? Order, in action movies, is untrustworthy. In movie after movie, our hero has to go rogue! The government that supported him may be corrupt as in *The Bourne Ultimatum*, or the agency he works for is trying to hold him back from doing what a man has to do, as in *Quantum of Solace*. In the end, the hero either goes completely rogue or just doesn't listen to the authority figures with good judgment. "Are you a cop or something?" a bad guy asks Max Payne. "Not tonight," he replies. He doesn't have to pay attention to those giving orders, because, after all, he's the chosen one, the one assigned to the onerous task of saving everyone and everything.

"Chosen one" imagery abounds in these movies, much as in the fantasy and superhero movies. In *Wanted*, guys reach "heights reserved only for the gods of men." In other movies, religious music and images, almost campy at times, are subtly and not so subtly present. For example, the main character in *The Punisher* twirls around with arms outstretched in Christ-like fashion, a gun in each hand shooting bullets, thousands of bullets. This imagery helps boys to see these guys as both good and as wronged. The words to Jason Bourne, spoken at the end of *The Bourne Ultimatum*, when he discovers he's been a part of a secret program to train expert killers, are "We didn't pick you. You picked us." This twist on "the chosen one" becomes a worthy metaphor for boys buying into a form of masculinity that leaves them less than human and very alone.

Whatever the torture that heroes have endured that has made them who they are, heroes are not quite human. Sometimes they are simply "chosen" to be stoic killing machines. Some are part of elite groups of children who've been numbered and transformed at birth, of agents who have been behaviorally managed to be superkillers. And they often lack almost all emotions. "You can't kill me; I'm already dead," says The Punisher. Bourne has no memory of his love affair with Nicky Parsons. Rambo is dead inside; you can see it in his eyes. This is achieved through minimal words and an impassive face. Watch their faces during car chase scenes—these men are focused beyond belief.

Then count how many words are spoken by the hero. In *Quantum of Solace* even the witty repartees are reduced to two- or three-word comebacks. "You killed a man" Bond is told. "I tried not to" he replies. Or, "You were supposed to kill her" a bad guy demands. Bond: "I missed." "What the hell do you think you're doing?" asks M. "You're welcome," says Bond. As he picks up the unconscious heroine like a piece of meat and drops her into the arms of a passerby on the dock, he simply says, "She's seasick."

These characters are bizarrely stoic, which underscores their macho image, but what's most striking to us is how alone these heroes are. The imagery in the films supports this—Rambo on a hill looking down at the woman he helped, hugging her husband, knowing he can never have that kind of love; David Rice as the Jumper who can teleport himself anywhere, sitting alone on top of the Sphinx as he narrates his story; James Bond has M and Q, but his words "I have no friends" tell us a different story. He has learned not to trust anyone. The Transporter seems to have a friend, but he only occasionally touches base with him. Robert Neville in *I Am Legend* had a family once, but he's also alone. Bourne is alone, except for Nicky Parsons, the girl who will help him. When these guys are on top of the world they have "assistants," but most of them are utterly alone in their mission to save (or, in the case of antiheroes, to have) the world. Perhaps this is a requirement of the lead character in an action movie. But we think not. We think that these movies follow a narrative of old, the flawed hero who, because of his heroic nature and personal quest, must pursue his tasks as a loner. Talk about a mixed message to boys: the person who is most admired, most noble, and the coolest of all is the guy who's alone.

There are exceptions to these lonely killing machines, like the down-and-out *Live Free or Die Hard*'s John McClane, played by funny, fast-talking Bruce Willis. He's not a machine; he's actually suffering from his divorce and rejection by his daughter (she doesn't understand why he spies on all her dates to protect her). But although he's a detective, he needs to go rogue, and once the action starts, he's all-muscle and few words.

The minimizing of words is contrasted with the maximizing of action. Like every other action film, the chases and explosions are tremendous and over-the-top. Cars dangling and smashing. Cars flipping over not once or twice but five times before they land. Cars and people leaping across intersections, sometimes forty stories in the air. The travel is over-the-top too. Bourne travels around the world: London, Madrid, Washington. Bond is an "international man of mystery" in Austria, Italy, and Haiti. There's also over-the-top killing of women. For example, the totally sleek and black oil-covered agent, Strawberry Fields, laid out on a hotel bed like the horse's head in *The Godfather,* and all-black to remind us of the all-gold woman in *Goldfinger.* Then there's the Hindu woman in *Wanted,* who gets it right through the dot on her forehead from a sniper's bullet. See, it's fun to find creative ways to kill women!

FROM ROGUE TO GANGSTER

There's a fine line between the PG-13 and R-rated heroes of action films and the sympathetic characters in PG-13 and R-rated gangster films. In both cases, the clear message to boys watching is that sometimes you have to break the law, and that when it comes to justice, you need to take the law into your own hands. The moral message at the end of the gangster movies is that there are limits to what you can get away with. However, the ride before the downfall is awfully fun and includes lots of sexy girls and piles of money. Before taking on the three big gangster movies boys love, let's look at a couple of hybrids. These movies borrow imagery, dialogue, and explosions from more serious gangster films.

While *Wanted* and *Jumper* have a lot in common with superhero, action, and gangster movies, these 2007–2008 films appeal particularly to boys because the hero needs to overcome bullying. In *Wanted,* Wesley Allan Gibson is clumsy and called a pussy. In *Jumper,* David Rice is tortured by other boys in high school. All boys can identify with this. And wouldn't all boys want some special training or special powers to show those bullies who's really boss? Wouldn't all boys like to learn that their anxiety is actually a part of a secret power that has not yet been tapped? With the bullying at the start of these films, we hear once again that revenge is personal.

What makes these films closer to gangster films than their action-film counterparts is their obsession with money. In these films and the gangster films we will describe, having it all means not only killing whoever gets in your way, traveling around the world, and having every vehicle imaginable at your control, but also having lots of money. In *Jumper,* Rice lies down on a pile of cash on his bed. His bachelor pad has a huge TV screen, motorcycle, closet full of money, several computers and gadgets, a surfboard, a guitar, a bike (really, it's a souped-up boy's room, not unlike something we'd see on the MTV show *Teen Cribs*), and because he is in some sense modeled after the "international" man of mystery, postcards of all the places he's jumped to are taped to his fridge. He has a one-night stand with a "Polish chick in Rio" and another in London, "jumping" back to the States before the girl wakes up.

All that money is transformative. After Wesley in *Wanted* discovers three million dollars in his bank account, thanks to an elite fraternity of assassins, he says, "I guess I feel different." Only then does he have the nerve to confront his verbally abusive obese female boss and yell, "Shut the fuck up!" Once he has all this money and learns how to kill, he is told, "For the first time in your life, Wesley, you're in control." It's the message boys get everywhere from the media, even when they're little—"You take control"; "You have the power"; money gives you both power and control. Only here it's not control over his toy car; it's the power to blow people away.

Closer to gangster than rogue cop, these guys have the tricks and the money to laugh at law-abiding citizens: "I'm going to have to see a warrant" someone asks Rice, and he says "certainly" and punches him. This line in particular brought a huge laugh from the boys in the audience. You want a warrant? Here's your warrant—right in the kisser.

Gangster biopics, extremely popular with teen boys, follow themes that are similar to all gangster movies. The year we researched our book, boys said they were looking forward to watching the R-rated *American Gangster* with Denzel Washington and told us they also love gangster movies that predate them, such as *Scarface* and *Blow*. *Scarface* tells the fictional story of Tony Montana, a Cuban emigré. *Blow* is the story of the drug dealer George Jung. *American Gangster* tells the story of Manhattan drug kingpin Frank Lucas. All three of these films show the rise and fall of more or less lovable gangsters who are good at breaking the law. These guys are shown as super-talented businessmen (thus legitimizing their activities) who take risks (sort of like Donald Trump) that, until the end of their lives, pay off and pay off big. The money montages in all three films are excessive: money is counted by counting machines in piles and piles, briefcases overflow with money, big duffel bags of money are delivered to a crooked bank exec, houses are bursting to the seams with money, rooms in houses are devoted to money, closets have boxes and boxes of money, and money is thrown up in the air constantly—it's raining money! Money is also represented by a garage full of cars, more drugs than anyone would want, gifts of mansions and businesses for family members, and scores of beautiful women. Are the boys watching this movie supposed to shake their heads and think, That's disgusting? Heck no. They're supposed to imagine basking in it and wish it was theirs, forgetting about how the end of the movie is inevitably going to show there's a real serious problem with greed and excess.

Boys are meant to like these gangsters not only because they are self-made millionaires, but also because these gangsters represent "the little guy."

George Jung in *Blow* is getting back at society for how his dad, a hardworking small business owner who ended up bankrupt, was treated. We're reminded in *Scarface* that Tony's just an "immigrant spic" with a lot of moxie. For *American Gangster*'s Frank Lucas? Well, the detective who chases after him can't figure out for most of the movie that the kingpin of New York City is black because obviously no one thought a black man could be so successful. At the climax of the movie, some cop says "No fucking n_ _ _ _ _ has ever accomplished what the American Mafia hasn't, in a hundred years." George Jung stands in for working-class white guys; Tony Montana stands in for all immigrants called names like "monkey" and "spic"; and Frank Lucas stands in for all oppressed blacks whose talents have been underestimated and who have not been given access to mainstream moneymaking ventures.

If they aren't redeemed by their personal vendettas and self-made fortunes, like the Corleones in *The Godfather*, a love of family makes them more hero than gangster. They have loyalties and a code of honor. Frank Lucas loves his mother; he's shown at a Thanksgiving table at the house he bought her, surrounded by loving family. George loves his father. Tony Montana loves his sister. Against the power of all this love, the judicial system is cruel. George can't serve jail time because his wife is dying of cancer. The courts are cruel to him when they prevent a drug-dealing dad who hangs out with gangsters from obtaining custody of his daughter, whom he loves. So when these guys say things like "I never fucked anybody over in my life that didn't have it coming to him" or "All I have in this world is my balls and my word. I don't break 'em for no one," they come across as more honorable than crass or cruel.

What's the message when gangsters are lovable family men or have a code of honor? When there is a mixture of good and bad in them? We're supposed to believe their backgrounds and codes justify lawbreaking, living in excess, causing harm, and erupting in violent confrontations with gangs and police. Cops are corrupt, and other gangs don't follow codes. But *these* gangsters are "moral" (or so it seems). Are they getting revenge for the way people close to them have been treated, or is this really about playing the system to their own advantage? Does it matter that all the money Frank Lucas amasses comes at a cost to his community, to all the poor black drug addicts whose lives he is presumably ruining?

In the end, Tony Montana has a few defensive words for those who dare to ask, and his answer says a lot about the view of masculinity that pervades boys' media. Regardless of how they meet their demise, these gangsters don't back down. They stick with the code; they call it like it is; they remain at the top, if only in attitude.

You need people like me so you can point your fucking fingers and say that's the bad guy. . . . You're not good. You just know how to hide and lie. Me? I don't have that fucking problem. Me? I always tell the truth. Even when I lie. So say good night to the bad guy.

Yeah, okay. Good night Tony.

Now, ask your son, are we all just like him, only we know how to hide and lie? Sure cops, politicians, and the courts can be corrupt. But the guy who's saying this is the gangster who has lost everything in the end because of his drug habit, excess, and violence. The handsome black man, who shows you that you can be what you want to be, did this on the backs of his community. The cool, fun-loving, slackerlike George Jung looks awfully scary in the mug shot at the end of the movie, the one that shows how he really looks after years in prison.

There's No *I* in *Team*?

The Comebacks, the sports version of those teen parody films (like *Scary Movie, Epic Movie,* and *Date Movie*), spoofs the recurring themes in a genre boys love: the eccentric coach with the long-suffering wife, the ragtag team of losers, the quarterback with a heart of gold and the sweet girl he falls for, the disappointed father, the tragic injury, the over-the-hill jock who makes the team, the redeemed bully, the third-stringer who steps up to lead, the near loss, and the ultimate win.

Watching sports is something boys and men do together, and so we take up that activity in chapter 5. Sports *movies,* on the other hand, are part of the whole shebang of what boys watch, whether alone, on their computers, with their friends, families, or even teams on a bus ride to play an away game. And while a few of these movies pursue that "one man alone" theme, many of them deliver a buddy or team story. So what's not to like about team spirit, male mentors, and the company of other boys?

While sports announcers hype individual egos, rev up rivalries, tell and retell the worst kinds of stories—about steroid use, domestic violence, dog-fighting, and car wrecks—sports movies invite boys into the inner lives and relationships of players and coaches who anguish about life decisions, learn about loyalty and teamwork, break through personal or racial barriers, and consider messages about life played out on a field of dreams.

Additionally, sports are one of those rare public arenas where it's okay for boys and men to be emotional. Not surprisingly, there's a *lot* of emotion in these movies. Where else in boys' worlds would you hear a respected athlete (Timo Cruz in *Coach Carter*) sincerely invoke the famous Marianne Williamson quote, "Our deepest fear is not that we are inadequate. Our deepest fear is that we are powerful beyond measure. It is our light, not our darkness, that most frightens us."

Love amid pain, struggle, and injury is everywhere. In *Invincible*, thirty-year-old bartender Vince Papale goes to open tryouts for the Eagles and makes the team against all odds—he's too old, has never played beyond high school, has lots of self-doubt because his wife left him, and he has to borrow money from his friends and father. But his friends support and love him. He soon finds a new girl who loves him. More important, after harassing him, even the football guys start to love him. In *Remember the Titans*, jealousy and racism give way to genuine affection both between the black head coach and his white assistant coach, who thinks he should have had the top job, and between the two star players—one black, one white. In a hospital scene invoking 1971's *Brian's Song*, perhaps the most emotional sports movie ever, the black star player visits the white star player after an accident. When the nurse protests—"Sorry, only kin allowed in here"—the white player says, "Alice, are you blind? Can't you see the family resemblance, he's my brother."

Teammates overcome their arrogance, their fear, and their hatred, and come to love one another. They take falls for one another, give up coveted opportunities, and refuse to play when a teammate is treated badly. They are a team, and a team wins and loses as a team. Boys express love to girls in sports movies too, although it's a different story for older women. We wonder how all those wonderful, sweet young things turn into the beleaguered mothers powerless to help unhappy, judgmental dads or the nagging wives of overcommitted coaches.

The best of these movies are about facing our fears or working hard to be more or do more than anyone thought possible. The best parts of the best of these movies are when teammates and townspeople overcome differences and prejudice, or when players and teams confront and overcome difficult experiences and circumstances. These are the films where everyone watching knows winning isn't the point and that sports stands in for something bigger. In *Rudy*, the story of a too small guy with big dreams to play for Notre Dame, it's all about being a part of a legacy. All he hopes for is to suit up; his one moment in the sun is dazzling, sure, but it's all the little victories leading up to it that make it so. In *Coach Carter*, the team doesn't win the big game but ultimately learns that winning was never what it was all about. In *We Are Marshall*, a true story about the rookie team created in the wake of a plane crash that decimated the "Thundering Herd" football team, it's about honoring the past by giving your best in the present. They win their first home game, important as a dedication to their lost friends and teammates, then lose every other game that season, but it doesn't matter.

Boys learn a lot of good things from these movies. Putting history, relationships, power, vulnerability, and personal growth in the context of something they love, like sports, allows them to confront questions and reflect on issues that in any other context would be denigrated or called gay.

However, with all that love and loyalty comes a heaping helping of stereotypical boy fodder. For example, there's the anger and frustration at overbearing or disappointing fathers—fathers like Wilber Flatch in *Hoosiers*, who drinks away his failure to win the big game in high school, or like steelworker father Daniel Ruettiger, in *Rudy*, who dismisses his son's dreams, or Sam Moxon, the football-obsessed father of second-stringer "Mox" in *Varsity Blues*. Even the father/coach of team leader Troy Bolton in perky *High School Musical* is aggressive and insensitive, and that's not even a true sports movie.

Like every stereotype, there's some truth to these representations. There are fathers who pressure their sons to excel in sports and disparage and question their abilities. At least in the movies most fathers come around in the end. But there's so much more to any father-son relationship than this struggle over approval, and dads ought to sit up and take note of this misrepresentation. Where are the dads who are proud and amazed that their son has any athletic ability at all, given they were in the chess club when they were kids? Where are the dads who keep telling their sons not to take it all so seriously? They're not in these movies.

Given all these disapproving dads in sports movies, what's a boy to do? Every media source tells him that mom's not good enough; he needs a father figure. He gets something so much better: a coach. Sometimes the coach is a nightmare, like Bud Kilmer in *Varsity Blues*; sometimes he's goofy but passionate and smart, like Jack Lengyel in *We Are Marshall*; sometimes he's unorthodox and inspirational like Herb Brooks in *Miracle* and Norman Dale in *Hoosiers*; sometimes he's all tough love, like Ken Carter in *Coach Carter*, benching his players because they failed to meet his academic requirements, or Herman Boone in *Remember the Titans*, demanding precision, perfection, and respect.

Why are there so many *demanding*, *authoritative*, but *despised* dads in sports movies and so many *demanding, authoritative* but beloved coaches? Are they cooler than the fathers? Do they have a higher status? Lots of these coaches, played by some of the coolest actors, like Denzel Washington, Samuel L. Jackson, and Matthew McConaughey, come to towns that live for sports—the town's status and the people's self-esteem depend on the success of their teams—and so the coach's job depends on a winning streak. Coach promises a legacy. Coach is larger than life, better than a dad. Coach Boone in *Remember the Titans* reminds his players who's the boss: "If you want to play on this football team, you answer me when I ask you who's your daddy. Who's your daddy?" "You," the players reply. At first they may resist the demand for perfection, the total obedience to rules and the punishments for breaking them, but before you know it, sons can't wait to get away from their father's disapproving stares to take what's presented as "real critique and advice" about the game and about life from Coach.

Even when these movies present messages about teams and team spirit, they are still about individual heroes, and more often than not, that hero is the coach. Coaches, like superheroes and action heroes, have flaws and vulnerabilities and not-so-proud pasts, but they overcome these obstacles to do what no one else can. Whatever tragedy or challenge comes down the pike, Coach can deal. A country suffering from cynicism and fear? Coach Brooks can deliver a miracle Olympic hockey team gold medal. Self-doubt and lack of discipline keeping the team down? Coach Carter has the answers. Racism dividing a team, school, and town because of forced segregation? Coach Boone's team-building will overcome. A town and team underidentified with community and overidentified with winning? Coach Gaines can straighten out those priorities. An insecure, ineffective college president? Coach Lengyel can show him the way. How about that alcoholic loser dad? Coach Dale will give him an assistant coaching job. He'll even get himself kicked out of the game to give Dad a chance to prove his worth. If Coach can believe, demand respect, walk tall, and forgive, so can the son.

The coach determines how the players develop, both on the field and off, even when the coach is cruel, racist, and power hungry. Players too can rise to the level of hero. In *Varsity Blues*, the second-stringer, Mox, refuses to follow Coach Kilmer because he sacrifices his players for wins. "Never show weakness. The only pain that matters is the pain you inflict," Coach shouts at his team in the locker room. Mox, replacing the arrogant quarterback, who was himself injured, leads a mutiny that ousts the coach in the final game. His own locker room speech echoes the themes we heard in movie after movie:

We got the rest of our lives to be mediocre, but we got the opportunity to play like gods for the next half of football. . . . There's no room for fear in this game. If we go out there and we half-ass it because we're scared, all we have is an excuse. We're always gonna wonder. But we go out there and we give it absolutely everything, that's heroic. Let's be heroes.

Gods? Heroes? No fear. No excuses. These movies are great conversation starters. Does your son think that sports are about becoming a hero or god? Why are there so many bad fathers in these movies? What makes a coach good or bad when almost all of them demand perfection, call players wusses, and punish them for infractions? Is the difference one of degree only? Coach Dale, in *Hoosiers*, takes the injured player out of the game, potentially forfeiting the win, whereas Coach Kilmer patches him up and sends him back in. Is this the difference between good and bad? Dale thought about patching up his player too. Is it that second thought, that one last-minute choice, that redeems him? Can a "good" coach and a "bad" coach both shame their players, but only the good coach can shore him up after the game? We should ask boys to think about these relational and moral distinctions more carefully, to look beyond the emotional movie-ending wins and losses to consider the moral questions these films raise and also the ones they gloss over in the name of caricature and stereotype.

We wonder too after watching so many of these films—where is the emotional expression for the boy not into sports? Where are genuine boy friendships in films? On what other canvas, or rather, reel, might they confront individual differences and break down racial barriers? A few movies might speak to them, like the wonderful story of friendship and fate in *Holes*, but alas far too few. And even in *Holes* the boys find each other under the gaze of a ruthless prison warden. Later, boys will see that men band together through war if not sports, in films like *Band of Brothers* or *Saving Private Ryan*, and have officers now instead of coaches, and platoons instead of teams. Can we help our sons to imagine male friendship outside of competition? Outside of war? Outside of pain and peril? Sure. But maybe not at the movies.

What to Watch and How to Respond

It's impossible to capture the full world of boy-targeted TV and movies in one chapter of a book. We're all too aware of what we've left out, but also confident that the messages about boy and manhood aren't qualitatively different in *Rock of Love* than they are in Axe commercials or action movies. The patterns are easy to discern: the little players in *The Suite Life* are set up to become the big players in *Two and a Half Men*. The little thrill seekers sold on *Speed Racer* are primed for the fast cars in *Fast & Furious*. The farts and burps in Saturday morning cartoons pave the way for the farts, burps, and hurls in *Step Brothers*. When it comes to what boys watch, it's funny, it's fast, it's powerful, it's over-the-top, and it's virtually everywhere.

But it's not him. He laughs and begs to watch, but the desire has to do with the vast difference between who he is and what his media promises him. In the media world of superheroes, superpowers, superrich, and even super laid-back, it's not cool to be "just a boy." It's also not cool to dampen the over-the-top fun or to slow down the wild ride, and we don't think you always should. As we say over and over, it's more than okay to watch with him. You may not want to talk about the messages right at the moment, but we encourage you to find the right time, when you're driving him to a friend's house, playing ball, or even doing chores, to ask him about the shows he loves.

Just as important as a conversation about what's in these shows and movies, is a conversation about what's missing from them. Where are the girls who are leaders, friends, and not just concerned about being someone's supportive girlfriend? Where are the fathers who are more than newspaper-reading idiots or authoritarian jerks? Where are the moms who are everything to their sons? Where are the cool boys who play instruments or paint and who don't care about fast cars, risk taking, or sports? Where are the boys who like some of these things but who balance a lot of different interests, who do well in school, who volunteer? Where are the boys who both like to have fun and are respectful at the same time?

Often it seems that non-cookie-cutter boys aren't entertaining, unless they're geeky underdogs like Napoleon Dynamite. Writers don't like to put them in movies, unless they're the butt of practical jokes or they triumph in the end. Boys have been primed from day one to laugh at *those* kinds of boys. So how do you help him *be* uniquely himself? The more you affirm the complexity of his interests and personality, and notice the one-dimensional view of boys in media, the more room you'll make for his choices and for the things he loves and wants to do. Stay a step ahead. Talk with him about the stereotypes of boys, the over-the-top gross stuff, the fearlessness and posturing, and the risk taking before he sees a lot of it. That means talking to him when he's six and seven about the themes in Saturday morning comedy and action-based cartoons, and when he's nine and ten about the partying boys and hot girls in tween TV shows. Point out the nerdy good boy/partying bad boy setup and the slacker image in PG-13 movies. Watch with him and show him the patterns. Ask questions. And most of all use what you both see to affirm the many qualities you love in him and in his friends.

The bottom line is this: if you let your son watch TV and go to the movies, you're enrolling him in a course about how to be a player, slacker, wealth-adoring, over-the-top risk-taking tough guy. Is this the curriculum you want your son to be exposed to? Are these the right teachers for him? If you don't think so, then get in there and offer him a richer vocabulary; wider options; clear the way for his imagination through conversation, through careful selection of movies, and, whenever possible, by turning off the TV and getting outside.

MOVIES FOR BOYS THAT FEATURE COMPLEX CHARACTERS AND FEWER STEREOTYPES

FOR LITTLE BOYS

The Many Adventures of Winnie-the-Pooh

Finding Nemo

The Polar Express

WALL-E

Happy Feet

Wallace & Gromit: The Curse of the Were-Rabbit

FOR PRETEENS

The Water Horse

Sky High

Spy Kids

The Sandlot

Free Willy

Mad Hot Ballroom

The Lion, the Witch and the Wardrobe

Hoot

Holes

A Series of Unfortunate Events

A Bug's Life

Rudy

Bridge to Terabithia

The Incredibles

The Princess Bride

Spirited Away

FOR YOUNG TEENS

The Outsiders

August Rush

Elf

How to Eat Fried Worms

The Stone Boy

Remember the Titans

Harry Potter

Hoosiers

October Sky

Quiz Show

Love and Basketball

Girlfight

Billy Elliot

Field of Dreams

Stand by Me

FOR MIDDLE TEENS

Dead Poets Society

To Kill a Mockingbird

Napoleon Dynamite

This Is My Life

Crouching Tiger, Hidden Dragon

Step Up

Across the Universe

Big Fish

FOR OLDER TEENS

Dogfight

Boyz in the Hood

Ordinary People

Shawshank Redemption

Into the Wild

Good Will Hunting

Boys Don't Cry

FOR BOYS ALSO (ALTHOUGH INITIALLY RECOMMENDED FOR GIRLS)

The Wild Thornberrys Movie

Fly Away Home

Because of Winn-Dixie

A League of Their Own

Whale Rider

Miss Congeniality, 1 and 2

Erin Brockovich

DOCUMENTARIES

Game Over: Gender, Race & Violence in Video Games

Hip Hop: Beyond Beats and Rhymes

Mickey Mouse Monopoly: Disney, Childhood and Corporate Power

Tough Guise: Violence, Media & the Crisis in Masculinity

Wrestling with Manhood: Boys, Bullying & Battering

Consuming Kids: The Commercialization of Childhood

Kids + Money

Merchants of Cool (Frontline)

Raising Cain: Boys in Focus

CHAPTER 3

It's a Guy Thing: What Boys Read

"My name is AJ and I hate school."
—*My Weird School # 21*

We got a pretty clear picture of what authors (and marketers) are thinking when we looked at the books marketed to boys. They think boys prefer pictures and large print; they think boys want action adventures, gross or goofy characters, and fantasy. This may be in response to worries that boys aren't reading, but it also raises questions. Do boys really prefer books with action and aggression, explosions and farts, journeys and gadgets? Or do these things merely signal to boys that the book they're looking at is just for boys and they needn't be embarrassed choosing it?

We ask these questions because we've seen boys we know pick up those supposed "boy" books only to be bored to tears, while at the same time loving books with quirky, funny characters like *Junie B. Jones* or *Harriet the Spy*. We've read the arguments about smaller language centers in boys' brains, but we also know many boys who are avid readers, whose parents can't keep up with their demand for the next in the *Harry Potter*, *A Series of Unfortunate Events*, *Bunnicula*, or *Alex Rider* series. These boys talk about books, share books, spend their allowances on books. Do these boys share an altogether different brain chemistry from other boys? Do they somehow defy the biological odds? Or is something else at play?

If it's true that boys struggle with reading slightly more frequently than girls, it's also true that they struggle with the stereotype that reading is a girl thing. And who would be surprised, given the images boys see (or don't see) in their media? Research shows that boys who are exposed to men who read are more likely to read, hence the use of Shaquille O'Neal and others posing for the American Library Association's celebrity READ posters. But aside from these images, where do boys ever see guys reading? Does the Incredible Hulk or the Dark Knight ever pick up a book? When men do read, it's usually a sign of disconnection or work. Dads are often pictured ignoring their families, their noses buried in newspapers or doing some "serious" reading. How many cartoons feature fathers reading to their sons or simply reading a novel?

It's more than just an absence of images. Boys get the clear message that reading is for girls. Boys in books are described as hating reading, as in the *My Weird School* series. On a recent sitcom, *Yes, Dear*, one dad, Greg, says to the other dad, Jimmy, his brother-in-law, that while their wives and babies are out at "Mommy and Me," he's going to spend his time getting started on a book he's been wanting to read. Jimmy, flabbergasted, lays out the "male view" on this—"Reading's what you do when your kids are asleep and your wife wants to talk," and then he persuades Greg to go golfing with him. Upon their return he says, "Be honest, it was a little better than reading a book, wasn't it?" And Greg says "Yes." Says a lot, huh?

Beyond PBS cartoons, it's rare to see a boy or a man in visual media who openly loves to read. On TV the men golf or play poker; in the movies they drive fast cars and shoot; in fantasy games they may open a book to look up a magic spell right before they battle, and in *Grand Theft Auto*, we'd be shocked if the gangsters stopped at a local bookstore in between gunning down enemies and running over prostitutes. Back in the 1990s, literary education specialist Meredith Rogers Cherland examined images of reading that children are exposed to and found that almost all the images were of girls reading, either alone or with other girls.

Are parents immune to this media, or does it influence them to read less frequently to their sons or assume that their sons won't want to read? In one study of low-income urban boys and girls, Harvard researchers found that mothers of preschoolers engaged with and talked less to boys than to girls about the books they read together. Following these same boys into middle school, they found that boys' socialization "toward stereotypical masculine roles" had a significant impact on their literacy skills, in part because "being smart was more a cause for ridicule than for popularity." In the tightly scripted world of middle school, where boys are boys and girls are girls, this "demure activity" is difficult to integrate with the tough, competitive sport star. But more important was the fact that, when the research started, preschool boys and girls in the study were equally matched in terms of language and literacy ability, and these similarities held as the boys and girls progressed through school. The real differences were in the ways boys were socialized around literacy. The researchers conclude: "Parents and educators seriously committed to the preparation of children's success in school and beyond do students a disservice by attending to their needs without consideration of the greater social context in which learning takes place." Translation: it's not biology that makes boys not into reading; it's the stigma of being a boy reader.

We recently ran into two ninth-grade classes on a field trip to Barnes & Noble. B&N instead of the library? Maybe it's because libraries don't have toys and a coffee bar, while they do have that stereotyped image as BOR–ING! And in libraries there are librarians. (In media of all forms, librarians are usually represented as bespectacled, humorless, bun wearing, and constantly shushing.) Or maybe a bookstore simply has a greater variety of books labeled in ways that kids understand (better than the Dewey decimal system). Regardless, on this particular day, the students were all given coupons they could use to buy one book apiece.

Both ninth-grade classes started out in the young adult fiction section with their teachers, and we stood by, hoping to surreptitiously document their choices. But before we could make our way past the long aisle filled with *Gossip Girl*, *The Clique*, *It-Girl*, and *A-list* displays, the boys had disappeared. We found them finally in Sci-fi/Fantasy. One had a knee-deep pile of comic book *Star Wars* paperbacks and was sitting on a stool intently reading them, one after the other, utterly absorbed. Another longingly fingered the Tolkien books, as if a new one might appear from the grave. He obviously had read them all. His friend showed him a fantasy book that looked to be about eight hundred pages long (size matters!), to which the Tolkien aficionado bragged, "That would take me about two days." Perhaps good boy readers are cajoled into making reading a competitive sport!

Risking detection—it had to seem odd to be sharing this section with a gray-haired mom—we pretended to peruse the *Halos*, *Warcrafts*, and *Aliens* books where two boys lingered over the one in which Alien meets Predator. They discussed who killed whom. Based on video games and movies familiar to teen boys, the boys read off the titles to each other: *Resident Evil*, *Umbrella Corpse*, etc. "Look at this," one cried out, reading aloud, "In the world of hunters, who becomes the hunted?" The other replied, "Have you seen the mixed alien predator one? Does he kill them both?" Inquiring minds want to know.

The kind of books boys bought (in front of one another that is) was fascinating. Do boys feel pressure to look for a book they can be proud of or that says to their peers, they're boy enough? We overheard one boy asking another, "Do you think this one's aggressive enough?" (he really did use that word!) and the other confirmed that yes, this was a real boy book: "Look at him [referring to the picture of a fantasy evil figure on the cover], he's just about coming out of the cover to eat you!" Another boy unabashedly showed us that he was buying *Diary of a Wimpy Kid*, a book popular with much younger boys. Because it's popular and has a funny title and quirky stick figures, an older boy who has some trouble reading can read it in public and not feel ashamed. Another boy bought two *Hardy Boy* mysteries. We're guessing that newer titles like *Motocross Madness* and dark cover images of motorcycles and fast cars make this old mystery series more interesting and accessible to boys who are less advanced readers or more intimidated by longer books.

At Barnes & Noble that day there were a few serious readers who chose concentration camp survivor Elie Wiesel's autobiography *Night* and a biography of fourteenth-century Catholic martyr John Payne. There were the boys looking for action and excitement, horror or thrills, who chose *Dracula, Ghost Soldier, Streams of Babel* (enthusiastically telling us it was about terrorists poisoning the water in a city), *The Host, Alien, 30 Days of Night, Kujo, Dead of the Day* or *Day of the Dead, Criminal Minds*, and some Stephen King novels. And then there were the boys who chose the sports books *Legends of United*, "a book about the Red Sox," and *Facing Ali*.

So maybe authors and publishers are on to something. Most of the boys chose sports books and thriller/horror/fantasies—that is, when they were set in a situation with other boys. Finally there were those boys who chose books written for younger boys. We wonder about the lone boy who chose *Old Yeller*. We didn't have time to ask why before he got on the bus. Was it a brave choice in the face of all the others slathering over aliens and trolls? Was it his dad's favorite? Did his teacher place it in his hands? We don't know.

We do know that marketers and authors work hand in hand to get boys to buy books. In the books we review in this chapter, we've found the good, the bad, and the ugly in most all of them. There was a lot of good in "boy books" written by men and women who know what vulnerabilities boys might need to address through their reading. Some of the best moments appeared to us in books that did a bait and switch—a boy gets a "boy" book, and without even knowing it, he's in a world of real vulnerabilities, relationships, complicated conflicts, and problem solving with diverse characters and deep thinking. The bad? The same old stereotyping reappeared in many of these books: messages that *all boys must of course* like sports, hate school, want gadgets, see girls as sex objects, get revenge on bullies, have a special talent, be troubled by a missing or overly harsh father, have no relationship with their moms, and crave a male mentor that will teach them to be disciplined. And the ugly? The message to boys that when they're young they're all about farts, boogers, and burps, the juvenile humor version of explosions, crashes, and chases.

With both hopeful messages and unfortunate stereotypes in mind, we take you through some samples of boy books, young to old. We then move on to the magazines that boys page through and the comic books some adore.

Boys Who Dare . . . to Be Different: Little Boys and Reading

How can the popularity of the *Dangerous Book for Boys* be explained? Peggy Orenstein, an author and frequent *New York Times* contributor, has a reasonable answer to this question. The book is not so much for boys, she wrote, but to "induce nostalgia among fathers—who are typically the ones purchasing the book—for their own Huckleberry childhoods, those halcyon days before cable, Wii, Facebook, and cell phones." She goes on to point out that girls are allowed a little more latitude in their identities whereas boys "*must* be boys—unless no one is watching." She refers to a study by psychologists Isabelle Cherney and Kamala London that showed when boys were taken to a room alone, told they could play with anything at all there, and led to believe that nobody, especially their fathers, would find out what they played with, almost half chose "feminine" toys as often as "masculine" ones.

In a recent display at Barnes & Noble, some marketer jumped on the *Dangerous Book for Boys* bandwagon by featuring an "Activities with Dad" display on a stand-alone bookcase. In this bookcase were the following books:

For Boys Only: The Biggest Baddest Book Ever

The Curious Boy's Book of Exploration

Tinkertoy Building Manual

Lincoln Logs

The Encyclopedia of Immaturity

The Worst Case Scenario Survival Handbook, Junior Edition

The Kingfisher Book of Great Boy Stories

The Great Outdoors Games and Puzzles

Oh Yikes! History's Grossest, Wackiest Moments

Oh Yuck! The Encyclopedia of Everything Nasty

Jokelopedia: The Biggest, Best, Silliest, Dumbest Joke Book Ever

What do we learn about boys (and dads) from this list? Not only that they like things big, bad, gross, wacky, silly, and dumb, but that when things are big, bad, gross, wacky, silly, and dumb, they had better be the biggest, baddest, grossest, wackiest, silliest, and dumbest. That is, and here it is again, they had better be over-the-top! Moreover, if the worst, baddest, or grossest thing should happen to them, they'd better be prepared. As per stereotypes of old, boys are presumed to like the outdoors, exploring, and surviving. They build. They like humor, especially really immature, snotty, stinky, and gross humor. Except for the *The Kingfisher Book of Great Boys Stories* (in this media world of the best, most awesome, and amazing, "great" sounds almost humble), this display imposes on boys and their parents a vision of what boys are supposed to like and be like. Do these titles sum up what boys prefer? So say many, but how can we tell, when from left, right, and center these presumed desires are imposed and reimposed on them?

While in B&N, we watched a boy who looked to be about seven or eight perusing books with his mother. He picked up *Eragon* and said to her, "Have you ever seen a book like this?"—a curious question. He then walked directly past the big "BOY BOY BOY" display to a stand-alone bookcase right next door and said, "Mom, mom, do you see the stuffed animals of the characters from *Guess How Much I Love You?*" Why wasn't a sweet children's book about love and family included in the boys' books section? Most likely because seven- and eight-year-old boys who are readers are presumed not to like these sweet picture books anymore. They're ready for "real boy" stuff, like knock 'em, crash 'em car books, and speeding fire engines with loud sirens.

We took a look at the books for younger boys, the picture books and the books that are aimed at early readers. There is certainly a lot of sweetness there. Looking through the giant picture books, we saw little boys afraid to swim, hugging parents, loving their pets, fixing a bird's broken wing, hand in hand with their grandmas and grandpas. Boys sat on their daddys' laps and helped their moms. They played with girls as well as boys and showed all sorts of emotions.

Invading this peaceable kingdom were the books from movies that seemed to be poking their evil noses into the playground like a gang of bullies. There was a huge display of books from recent movies, some of them PG-13 rated, with the likes of *Incredible Hulk*, *Speed Racer*, *WALL-E's Rogue Robots*, and *Kung Fu Panda*. Battles, fighting, conquering, speeding, exploding. This display says, here is what *real* boys like—even three-year-old boys, given that one of the Incredible Hulk books came with thick crayons, the ones you stop using by first grade. Although there was a "Word Search for Justice" puzzle in the middle of the Hulk coloringbook, most of the thirty pages for little ones showed Hulk battling. He never even turns back into Bruce Banner at the end.

These movie books are problematic for a variety of reasons, most especially, as the Campaign for a Commercial Free Childhood points out, for the way they disingenuously acknowledge the PG-13 movie rating but then shamelessly market toys and books like these to the youngest children. In this way even the littlest boys get treated as teens. The marketers see no difference between a thirteen-year-old and a three-year-old except for the number of words on a page. Thus they have books with the same images and story lines for all levels of readers. Parents so eager to have their sons love reading might think they're helping him by buying him a "Level 2, Ready to Read" book on the Incredible Hulk, but there's some truth to "garbage in, garbage out." They're also teaching their little boys that it's okay to be aggressive (the youngest boys won't grasp the "aggression in the name of justice is okay" message) and that terrible, rageful anger is nothing to be ashamed of, as long as it's pointed in the right direction and at the right people (another distinction over the heads of younger boys). We say, get these "early readers" away from our young readers!

So many other early readers, like *Arthur*, *Little Critter*, and Dr. Seuss books stand in stark contrast. In fact, on the display right next to the Incredible Hulk were the *Henry and Mudge* books. A boy cuddles his dog. A boy cuddles his family. A boy hugs a bunch of grandpas. A boy has a sleepover. Not a hero, but a boy who dares to be, dare we say, gasp, a real little boy? Where's a father's nostalgia for that version of childhood?

We Know "Everyone Poops" but . . .

People complain that teens today are too cynical, that via *The Simpsons*, *Family Guy*, and *South Park* they appreciate little and mock all. Each one of these TV shows takes risks with inappropriate, gross, and crazily funny events that teens and, alas, even preteens love. Still, we're reminded of *Catcher in the Rye*'s Holden Caulfield's desire to protect the innocence of children from the corrupt world of adults. We feel the same way. Has the blurring of the lines between adulthood and childhood brought too much cynicism and too much inappropriate humor to our kids?

Many books today, especially ones marketed to young boys, celebrate the gross, the crass, the inappropriate, and the silly. Silly no longer is a Dr. Suess "seven hump wump" or a "moose kissing a goose down by the bay." It's bath-room humor, as in *Everyone Poops* and *The Gas We Pass*. Silly is *Walter The Farting Dog Book* and *Captain Underpants and the Big, Bad Battle of the Bionic Booger Boy*. These are books for the very young to the mid-elementary school kid that promise to make them giggle with the inappropriateness of it all. Step aside *Mrs. Piggle-Wiggle*, the babysitter who teaches children how not to beg, whine, talk with their mouths full, or leave their toys lying around. Move on *Berenstain Bears*, who teach kids not to pester their parents with the gimmes, and tell them what's wrong with lying, not doing your chores, and too much vacation, junk food, and TV. Get out of the way *Little Critter*, Mercer Mayer's animal/child with books like, *All by Myself*, *The Best Teacher Ever*, *Just Going to the Dentist*, *I Was So Mad*, *Just Grandma and Me*, and *Just My Friend and Me*. Say hello to a cadre of animals, kids, and objects that are vying for boys' attention with crass humor, body emissions, and supersize whining.

Sure kids of all ages get the giggles over farts and burps and underpants—that's not something marketers have to instill in them. But there's some-thing about the sheer volume of these books and the influx of this genre of children's book into the lives of very young children that we find somewhat suspicious. It's as if the sarcasm, sense of irony, celebration of mischief, de-struction, and disruption must all begin at once; that no matter your son's age, marketers are picturing him as a "cool," rebellious teenager. It's as if before a librarian can even say "shush" or a teacher can remind him to take turns, a boy has to be taught to express his right to be a troublemaker. This seems like a double bind for teachers too—they're encouraged to give boys books that equate boyness with disruptive and gross behavior, and then when they need to control the boys in their classrooms they're criticized for suppressing natural boyhood. Boys can't and mustn't be repressed. Politeness is for goody-goodies. Order is for wusses. And at the expense of teachers and boys, it has to be good for marketers if a boy learns early to shrug off a par-ent's choice or sees that pestering and a healthy case of the gimmes will net something fun.

We know that children's book author Jon Scieszka, who runs the Web site GuysRead.com, is doing all he can to help boys read more, and we appreciate the many good books he recommends, but we worry about the heavy dose of *Smash! Crash!* type of books for young boy readers, imposing on even the youngest boys the idea that they should, by nature, love noise and vehicle crashes and explosions. Says Amazon.com of Scieszka's *Trucktown* series: "It's a world where all the characters are trucks, all the stories are action driven, and boys and girls can imagine themselves in all their crazy, loud, funny, creative, excited, full-throttle glory! It's a world where . . . no one's afraid to get dirty or be LOUD! And it all kicks off with *Smash! Crash!* [and] best friends Jack and Dan."

Scieszka's argument is that we need to reach boys where they are, and if you listen to boys, they say they like car crashes, explosions, superheroes, information, and more. Of course this is the best kind of bait and switch possible, bait them with a car crash and, *voilà!*, they're readers for life. But perhaps he hasn't considered the reinstituting of the stereotypes that such pandering does for boys. Perhaps, like those boys in Cherney and London's experiment, what boys *say* they like is what they think they're *supposed* to say they like because it's all they see around them. If given a choice and permission, maybe they wouldn't only love these stereotypically "boy" things.

Consider Kate and Jim McMullan's *I Stink*, about a bigmouthed garbage truck. Like a rebellious teen gang member, he yaps at children in an aggressive, in-your-face manner: "Did I wake you? Too bad! Pistons? Bring on the crusher blade. Blade? Push back the bags! Squeeze them! Crush them! Mash them! Smash them!" Yup, he's one tough truck, and The Little Engine That Could probably couldn't (or wouldn't) hang around this dude. But just so a little boy doesn't get too frightened, turn the page to hear him go "BURRRP!" quite proudly.

I Stink's truck, like the annoying pigeon in *Don't Let the Pigeon Drive the Bus*, *Don't Let the Pigeon Stay Up Late*, and other pigeon books, is unapologetic. Pigeon spews a number of reasons, arguments, facts, whines, and tantrums that would torture any parent. But unlike the garbage truck, at least the parent reading this book is put in the position of the parent who stands firm. While we celebrate pigeon's persistence and ingenuity, we do not give in!

We can understand the appeal of these characters who disrupt the orderly, seemingly boring lives of children's books such as the old *Dick and Jane*. We love to watch children giggle over farts, burps, and poops. But let's look at this in the larger context as encouraging boys to be rude, loud, and over-the-top and depicting anything polite, thoughtful, or quiet as girly. These books are about self-expression and lack of restraint. They celebrate it. And adults, as children's book scholar Ellen Handler Spitz asserts, collude with it. She suggests this is an abdication on the part of the adults, a refusal to be the whistle-blower and adult role model. Adults find it easier to enjoy the messiness, "rather than undertake the more difficult challenge of curbing and channeling those feelings and impulses." Sure children love to get messy, but they also do this as a direct challenge to their parents and as a childlike request to parents to help them, teach them how to rein it in, and show them how to express themselves in socially acceptable ways.

Ultimately, marketers are marketing to the adults who hold the purse strings, not to their children. The parents must often enjoy the farting dogs and burping trucks as much as the kids, or else these books wouldn't continue to sell. When adults adore the immature along with the child, who is left to say no? Well, in picture books it's the mother or schoolteacher character, positioned not as the mature helper Mrs. Piggle-Wiggle used to be, but as the killjoy. As if to underscore what a bummer these stick-in-the-mud rule abiders are, we see an influx of teachers in books who are "cool," who don't really say no, and are even more immature, or at least eccentric, than the kids. If Miss Frizzle in the *Magic School Bus* series (described as a "likeable teacher") and Miss Daisy, Mr. Krups, Mr. Louie, and the rest in the *My Weird School* series are exceptionally cool in their eccentricity, then there really may be no adults at all.

It's difficult for parents who want to join in the laughter with their son so that he doesn't feel shame or humiliation and learns to love his body. But in a world where little boys will soon be marketed smash and crash nonstop, and given problematic types to identify with, like "the operator," "the slacker," and "the player," there need to be parents pictured in books who teach them to invest their giggles, intelligence, energy, and interest into worthwhile projects and endeavors. There need to be teachers who show them how to treat one another with respect and story lines that value compromise over manipulation and discussion over aggression; indeed, love over smash and crash, and as Ferdinand the Bull showed us, daisies over gore.

Real Boys in Fantasy

Boys love fantasy books too. In fact, to anyone who says boys don't read, the obvious retort is, "What about *Harry Potter*?" Boys not only read books, they read 800-page books, stand in line for them at midnight, and devour them, one after the other. And not just *Harry Potter*. The movie version of *The Lord of the Rings* trilogy reintroduced Frodo Baggins and friends to a new generation of young readers in much the same way film adaptations of *The Lion, the Witch and the Wardrobe* and *Prince Caspian* have put the *Narnia* series back on their shelves. The attraction is not only the high adventure, the battles, and the magical realms where humans are just one of many fantastic species; it's also the human drama, the friendships, challenges, journeys and quests, almost always led by brave boys and men.

We see in so many fantasy books a chosen one—the boy from humble beginnings, protected from evil by a wise mentor until he comes of age, his power invisible even to himself. The King Arthur legend is a prototype. Arthur grows up not knowing he is special, receives mentoring by Merlin, discovers he has a power—a legacy—that allows him to pull the sword from the stone and wield it in battle. Other fantasy series follow suit. *Pendragon* for example: "Bobby Pendragon is a seemingly normal fourteen-year-old boy. He has a family, a home, and even Marley, his beloved dog. But there's something very special about Bobby. He is going to save the world." (After reading chapter 2, "What They Watch," you can appreciate just how often boys get this message in media.) This unusual talent, ability, or possession is echoed over and over again in fantasy books, as with *Eragon's* special dragon, Charlie Bone's ability to hear conversations in photographs, Harry Potter's special status as the the boy who Voldemort could not kill. Perhaps that's what makes these books fantasies boys will read, and we don't fault them for that. All kids wish they were special or magical or more powerful than they really are. But we do think books like *Diary of a Wimpy Kid* get their popularity, in part, because boys get tired of fantasizing greatness and once in a while like to see their everydayness or mediocrity humorously reflected in literature.

Even the best fantasy books follow genre rules, so how do we differentiate between genre and stereotype? Given that no fantasy books we could find show boys or girls of color in leading roles (*Chasing Vermeer* falls under the mystery category), it's interesting to look at where these characters do exist. They tend to get bit parts. A dark-skinned golden-eyed giant, met in the second book of the Deltora Quest series *Lake of Tears*, gives Lief and Jasmine a puzzle. Dark-skinned beauties, like Loor, in *Pendragon*, exotic and sensual, are also spied, often bathing in a lake or needing to be rescued. Bobby Pendragon describes Loor as "totally cute like an Olympic sprinter. No fat, all muscle, totally awesome." (This evaluating of girls' bodies seems something new in boys' lit.) Those who are different from the typical white lead character are either dangerous or exotically attractive. Perhaps a white boy who identifies with the lead character doesn't even notice. But we think these messages, when seen over and over, make a difference in how white boys perceive kids who are different from them in their schools. And given that boys of color struggle most with reading, according to national surveys and tests, this lack of lead characters is just wrong.

Girls too get stereotyped as either the "girlfriend," as in the case of Courtney Chetwynde, "beautiful and smart" in *Pendragon*, or the exotic girl from another planet/tribe/world/galaxy, in the case of Loor. In *Pendragon* the lead character has just been kissed by Courtney but chapters later he is floating into some rapids with the dark-skinned, dark-haired Loor who is clinging to him because she can't swim. Girls can also be stereotypical caretakers, as in *Ranger's Apprentice*, where a girl is praised for her wonderful baked pies! Or they can be sex objects. For example, in comic book versions of the *Star Wars* series, girls are supersexy, busty fighters or bikini-clad captives, tied up waiting to be rescued—pumped-up versions of centerfolds. We wonder about that slightly pornographic image of the helpless girl, tied up, waiting for rescue. Even in the very popular *Eragon*, the story begins with a beautifully regal elf held captive, while her captor is "enjoying her helplessness."

In the best fantasy literature, girls can also be friends, and they're often good friends. In the *Harry Potter* series, Hermione "gets" Harry at a level his other good friend Ron doesn't, or maybe can't. In Angie Sage's *Magyk*, Jenna and "boy 412" work together to overcome dangers and fight evil, long before they discover that he is in fact Septimus Heap, a boy with with extraordinary powers. Girls who are real friends in books provide opportunities for boy characters to talk and explore their feelings without judgment or teasing, and book series with competent girls, often sisters like master fencer Malory in *The Spiderwick Chronicles* or inventor Violet in *A Series of Unfortunate Events*, offer one of the few places in boys' media where they can really connect with girls as friends or equals rather than as love interests they feel the need to impress.

While girls do appear in fantasy books that boys read, the main relationships for boys are with other boys and men. For example, in *Eragon*, after the regal, beautiful elf is freed at the beginning of the book, it's a world of boys, men, boys, men, and more boys. These male relationships are worth looking at more closely, because there are predictable patterns here as well. A bully or a boy who represents pure evil (think Draco Malfoy from

Harry Potter or Andy Mitchell in *Pendragon*) exists, in part to underscore the hero's goodness. A best friend (Ron and Mark, from *Potter* and *Pendragon*, respectively) exists to underscore the hero's loyalty. There's often a team of other boys to cheer one on if there's some schooling involved, as well as a male mentor to take the place of the father, which we discuss in our next section on battle schools. There's also some version of an absent father, either in a photograph or a memory. It might simply be the pledge made by a father before the lead character was even born, as in *Lake of Tears*, but he's there, looming over the lead character with either a sense of pride or unreasonable expectations and disappointment. There's no place for moms in the world of fantasy except when the boys return home from their adventures, as in *The Secrets of Droon*, or upon return from Hogwarts, when dinner is served.

Clearly some books defy all the stereotypes about boys as reluctant readers. What do these books have that others don't, and what does that say about boys and boyhood? Let's look more closely at one example: Harry Potter.

THE BOY WHO LIVED, AND STILL LIVES

Harry Potter is famous in the wizarding world as the boy who survived Voldemort's wrath, "the boy who lived," and he's famous in the Muggle world as the character in a book series that saved boys from the gross generalization that boys don't read. In a November 2008 article for *Publishers Weekly* aptly called "read this b-4 u publish :-)," thirteen-year-old Max Leone speaking for, as he says, "that population segment that is constantly derided as 'not reading anymore,'" mourns the "barren" terrain of teen boy books since the last Harry Potter was published. What J. K. Rowling's books had that so many others didn't, according to Leone, were "great characters, humor and action." In an attempt "to end this dark age of adolescent prose," Leone has decided to counsel would-be writers about what to avoid and what to embrace when writing for boys.

What to avoid? Leone says, please no "archaic language" like "Methinks" and "Doth," no story lines heavily laden with "fairness or honor or other cornball crap," and don't overdo the romance. Vampires are okay, he says. But not the *Twilight* series version or anything with, like, "100 pages of florid descriptions of romance and 100 pages of various people being emo." Leone likes his vampires to be "menacing badasses." What to embrace? Horror, action, and political humor, and "books with video game–style plots involving zombie attacks, alien attacks, robot attacks or any excuse to shoot something."

Hold on just a minute. In our perusal of books on the shelves for teen boys, there seems no end to those "excuse to shoot something" kinds of books, especially in the newer graphic novel series. But Harry Potter doesn't fit that genre and isn't what Leone says he's looking for. Lots of action and spells, but the violence is never gratuitous. There's emo (emotion) too, as Harry and his friends grapple with loss, sadness, and fear. There are no menacing vampires either, although Voldemort more than makes up for their absence. J. K. Rowling did a great job writing a contemporary story, although within a pretty "archaic" setting of castles, formal banquets, and ancient dusty libraries, but anyone reading these books would be hard-pressed to miss the morality throughout the series. To be sure, Rowling didn't "clumsily smash morals" into the stories—Leone tells us boys hate that, and we believe him—but moral questions and answers are the heart and soul of *Harry Potter*, and any really good fantasy novel. Harry confronts the struggle between good and evil in the magical world, but also within himself. He challenges the wizarding world's equivalent of fascism when he befriends and defends Hermione, a "mud blood" (half human, half wizard). He learns to embrace his power, but in his darkest moments he's reminded by his mentor, Dumbledore, to confide in and rely on his friends. He looks beyond the surface of things and people to love a clumsy half-giant gamekeeper, a werewolf teacher, and an ex-con godfather. Forgiveness, loyalty, and righteous indignation are everywhere. There's even more than a sprinkle of romance.

So what's the appeal to boys who, like Mr. Leone, seem to have taken on the marketers' view of their reading interests, who accept assumptions that they are only interested in shooting and menacing creatures? How about the intensity and complexity of the story line, the way Rowling taps into real adolescent angst, captures the uncertainty and urgency of a world threatened by evil, and gives Harry and friends, with the guidance of adults who trust and believe in them, the means to defeat it, while offering humor that deeply satisfies because it's not cheap or based on bodily functions? Leone reminds writers of "the cardinal rule of writing for young adults: Do Not Underestimate Your Audience." We like this rule a lot. That's why, when Max Leone says to his audience of potential teen boy book authors that if they follow his simple rules they'll be able "to cash in on the four or five minutes each day that teenagers aren't already spending on school, homework, video games, eating, band practice and sports," we don't believe him. Not just because those simple rules don't apply to the books he found "heart-poundingly intense," but also because any thirteen-year-old who writes about books with such clarity, maturity, and depth is reading a heck of a lot more than that.

Battle School

Although too many popular books try to get on boys' good sides by dissing school, there's one kind of school that pervades boy literature, no matter the genre, and that's battle school. It isn't called battle school outright. In fact, in some books there isn't even a recognition that boys are being prepared in a school for battle, but the culmination of the book in a battle permits us to reflect back on earlier lessons as lessons in war. And what's the message to boys? That it's a cruel world and you'd better be prepared? That to be a real man you need to know how to develop your fighting skills? That war is exciting and fun? All this and more.

You'll find this training for battle even in kitty lit. That's right, kitty lit, not kiddy lit. In *The Warriors*, a popular series that grade school and middle school boys read, cats are warriors that have become enslaved by the twolegs and turned into kittypets. Warrior cats must rescue them and bring them into clans to restore them to their natural wildness but also to live by "The Warrior Code." Eventually there is a battle in which a former kittypet will have to test his or her mettle. Be assured, most will leave the battle victorious.

There are countless competitions, wars, fights, and challenges, some hidden and some not so hidden, in the books written for boys. From fantasy literature with dragons or trolls or royalty, to sports books that lead to a final game, to funny books where there is a competition for class president, to science fiction books where the galaxy is at stake, boy literature includes battles. But before the battle there needs to be some training. Even *Harry Potter*, looked at one way, is a book about battle preparation, in this case leading to the battle of all battles. Of course, Dumbledore's Army prevails. Sure many subplots, including those in the *Harry Potter* series, contain other problems to be overcome; however, for boys' enjoyment, everything ultimately must converge in a battle of "epic proportions."

Sports books are popular with boys, so librarians and the boys in our survey tell us. When they're good, as in Mike Lupica's series, *The Comeback Kids*, they include all sorts of subplots that show boys struggling with the important relationships in their lives and with what it means to fight fair. But even these good books prepare boys for the battle. If the book is about basketball, the "battle" will be the final game of the series, against, for example, a team that doesn't play fair, and so the lead character is justified in wanting to obliterate them. There will always be a bully to overcome, and a lead character with a special talent.

In sports books, the mentor is usually the coach, though sometimes the mentor is the boy's own father. But typically in boys' literature, as on TV and in the movies, fathers and sons have very troubled relationships. In fantasy books, the teacher is never a father but a father figure, a wise teacher or warrior mentor who is typically strong and silent, giving the boy little and letting him fall on his face to teach him a lesson. (No overprotective mamas allowed!) In *Harry Potter*, Dumbledore gives Harry the space and opportunity to make mistakes and discoveries he'll need later on. In *The Ranger's Apprentice*, the Ranger allows a horse to throw young Will to teach him patience. This is "a lesson," as opposed to the humiliation meted out by bullies.

In battle school books (not just in *Harry Potter* or *The Ranger's Apprentice*), bullies also need to get back what they give to others. There must be revenge; retaliatory aggression is justified. We see this over and over, even though, as in superhero movies, there is often a moment when the hero has a chance to kill his bully and doesn't. Will has this chance in *The Ranger's Apprentice*, but he drops his sword and punches his aggressor instead. In these readable equivalents of action movies, the final fight is always mano a mano, one-on-one. Revenge is always sweet; after the punch Will says, "You have no idea how good that felt." A reader will know he's truly in fantasyland when the lead character doesn't look at his hand and say, "Ow, that hurt."

Battle school is generally a boy thing even though the plot usually allows the inclusion of a "pretty girl" who is noticed at the beginning of the book and who likes the lead character by the end. However, there are no real girls in the whole book unless she's a girl permitted into the world of boys as a true competitor, finally a girl a boy can relate to (of course, after she proves herself). An exception to this all-boy world is the *Harry Potter* series, which initially emphasized Ron and Harry's relationship, keeping Hermione as an annoying, know-it-all third party, but over time expanded not just to include Hermione, but also Ginny and Luna as real friends, all enrolled in a real school, all learning to use their magic wisely, and, alas, all needing to use their magic in battle.

Even in the series books for kids, there is often a battle that must be fought. When kids travel back in time in the *Time Warp Trio*, three boys need to do battle with an evil knight or a sabertooth tiger. In the *Magic Tree House* series, the kids do battle against three knights using a flashlight. In the *Secrets of Droon*, three kids do battle against the evil Lord Sparr using a soccer ball. In *Choose Your Own Adventure*, there will be choices that lead a reader into battle. In the Jack Sparrow series from *Pirates of the Caribbean*, Jack stands his ground "defiantly" against a murderous giant. In *Goosebumps* there are monsters that insist on a game of tag, and he who loses gets eaten. Even in Thomas the Tank Engine's *Diesel 10 Means Trouble*, a bully diesel with a "huge metal claw" says he'll have to "destroy all of them." Luckily, no battle ensues, but hey, this book is for three-year-olds! Let them wait until they're six or seven before they're required to fight back!

Boys are also reading battle school books based on action movies, like the *Star Wars* series, which come in comic book, graphic novel, and various other forms, and are marketed to all levels of readers. In these books the warriors are "the fiercest, fastest, and most fearless" and the boy characters are taught valuable lessons from both dangerous men as well as their mentors. As in *Boba Fett: The Fight to Survive*, a Scholastic Book, ten-year-old Boba's problematic warrior father has taught him that "life is hard for the small and the weak." Required to help his father in combat by shooting weapons from starships at Jedis, Boba would rather read books. (Ah, a boy who reads!) Still, when his father dies, he takes his dad's helmet and continues the battle. His father has left him a black book with a message: seek self-sufficiency, knowledge, and power. A final note informs him "money is power." The reader will soon find out Boba's father's code is all wrong and that books are good and money is bad. But is that the message a boy reader is going to take away from the book after reading about countless Jedi killed through several battles on various planets on cool starships? We guess a character can only be a reader if he's forced to put down his books and fight.

What's wrong with battles? With learning to fight fair? What's wrong with standing up to bullies and giving them a taste of their own medicine? After all, aren't most of the great works of Western literature about men going into battle, getting lost, and returning home the hero? Doesn't fantasy help children to cope with their fears? Yes, but reducing fantasy to battle scenes also narrowly defines those fears, leaving others, like the fear of abandonment or loneliness or loss, unexplored. Why does the battle have to invade every form of literature for boys? Aren't there other problems of childhood that need to be worked on? And what are we saying to boys when we teach them that every conflict ends in a battle that they must be ready for, that training to be a strong man will always involve bullying and humiliation, and that what boys need to learn is stoic discipline in the face of hard trials?

Sound like the military? Sure does. And although we may need men and women to fight in wars, we also need to appreciate what fighting does to human beings and how training to fight can affect a person. For a boy out of control, angry at his dad, and flunking out of school, the military can possibly be a source of self-esteem, a way to learn self-discipline and team spirit, and a place to find father figures (or at least that's what the advertising promises). But for those who actually go to battle, it can also be a source of trauma. Maybe when war doesn't look like such a grand adventure, and so necessary to forming one's adult male character, other forms of diplomacy will emerge and have a greater effect on the lives of boys and in our world.

We do, however, agree with author and comic book writer Gerard Jones, who wrote *Killing Monsters: Why Children Need Fantasy, Super-Heroes, and Make-Believe Violence*. Jones claims that we need to trust children to use these stories in a way that helps them to grow, and he adds that because children constantly wrestle with how small and powerless they are, fantasy lives of power are "thrilling antidotes to life's pain." He's right that even young children can desire power and need to fight, through fantasy and play, to understand their aggression. Even when the play becomes real, children learn through this experience the consequences of real fighting. But we object to the way this fantasy of violence becomes indistinguishable from a story we tell little boys about what it means to be a boy. Are these stories, as Jones suggests, really about "action, power, and mastering life," about "the joy of feeling big and strong"? Or are they about assuming a stereotypical masculine role that overemphasizes the need for power, control, and the joy of conquering? Perhaps both, but until authors disentangle the two, we're asking for a few less battles, and a few more conversations.

Fighting the Battle Within: Loneliness, Vulnerability, and Cruelty

Those who are quick to assume boys are being "boxed" into a bulked-up, silent, Schwarzenegger-type masculinity will find that in some YA (young adult) literature written for boys, this image is undermined rather than advocated. Perhaps this is one of those few media-safe havens where real boys are represented among the sea of superheroes, farting giants, battling robots, and predatory aliens. In these books, authors create lead male characters who are isolated, rejected, or vulnerable, who struggle internally as much as with the world around them; that is, they emphasize the inside battle as much as the one outside. Too bad, or so a *New York Times* article claims, it's mostly adults who are reading them.

Teachers and librarians, however, are still fighting the good fight to introduce boys to literature that speaks to the inner boy, in particular, to the boy who has a glimmer of self-awareness about his insecurities and vulnerabilities. In some of these books, the story lines never culminate in a real battle or fight. For example, in J. D. Salinger's *The Catcher in the Rye*, still required reading for many tenth-grade English classes, Holden Caulfield, struggles against the "phonies" out there in the world, against grief, the loneliness of male adolescence, and most importantly against growing up. The book actually ends before the inevitable confrontation, when his parents come home to discover he's been kicked out of yet another school. Similarly, in the more recent, 2007, *Some Day This Pain Will Be Useful to You* by Peter Cameron, a book that's been compared to *The Catcher in the Rye*, another isolated teen, James Sveck, struggles with understanding phoniness (his father's facelift, the "American Classroom" experience in which he has won a place, and his perceived difference from other kids—more subtly, his sexuality.)

Boys love *The Catcher in the Rye*, once forced to read it, but they can't always say why, just as when they watch a tearjerker movie and are embarrassed and surprised to find themselves crying. There's no battle. There's little suspense and little action. Instead, there's an inner monologue that's a mixture of self-hatred and superiority. Perhaps that's the clincher. What's recognizable to boys about boy books that require self-reflection during any journey is the form that self-reflection takes, the wiseass, I'm-above-it-all, who-are-these-jerks-anyway commentary these characters do so well. It's a kind of humor that allows the protagonist to maintain a level of superiority while at the same time, as the reader understands, he's going down fast. Through his witty judgment about everyone else, his sense of irony and ear for hypocrisy, a male lead character maintains his likability, but boy readers can see through to his vulnerability, uncertainty, and self-defeating self-deception. In real life, we might hate it when a boy becomes arrogant as a way to develop a form of armor, but these books can help boys understand this arrogance as a defense and as something that gets in the way of their relationships. To mock others, feel superior, and use satire and wit may win a boy a certain kind of respect, but it also leaves him lonely, unwittingly hurting the people he likes, and distancing himself from potential friends.

Vulnerability is a part of many fine books for boys, even books about superheroes and sports teams, but often the author seems to feel he or she must create some saving grace to hold the reader's interest. Sometimes, that saving grace is the clever wit and superiority of the lead character. Other times characters are lovable losers or slackers. More often the vulnerable boy is redeemed through a special talent. This can be magic, as in fantasy books, or athletic talent, which is often hidden until a make-or-break game. Unlike the wit that gets some guys through hard times, the special talent or power theme undermines the good work the book does for boys who need to accept their vulnerability. This theme says that even if everyone else thinks you're a loser, you're not because you have a secret weapon or power that makes you better than the rest. Unlike the sarcastic tone of superiority, which the reader can see through, these books that describe a secret talent reconfirm a form of masculinity that tells boys they must be the best to not be a loser.

Many times YA authors call attention to boys' vulnerability to cruelty at the hands of their peers. As the popularity of Greg Heffley's *Diary of a Wimpy Kid* affirms, every teen and preteen boy knows what it's like to walk into a place where there's a group of other boys, just hanging, looking you over. Will they be friendly? Will they make a wisecrack to impress the other boys? Will they try to provoke you? So many of the very best YA books for boys show how boys cope with this cruelty, but we cringe a bit when this very real problem for boys is solved by some superpower or special sword that incinerates the bully or proves the lead character the superior fighter.

In Robert Cormier's *The Chocolate War*, published in 1974, we see how youth cruelty is enabled by the adults around them, in this case a coach and teacher. A new boy, Jerry Renault, needs to prove himself through sports (a common beginning) and wins admiration for taking the most brutal of all hits on the football field. Throughout this book and others like it, there is always the feeling that "shit happens" while the adults aren't looking, so parents can't protect their kids. There's often a boy who represents every-thing evil about boy-to-boy cruelty, whose main goal in life is to humiliate others. In this case it is Archie, and even his own henchman is shown won-dering about his character: "Archie repelled him in many ways but most of all by the way he made everybody feel dirty, contaminated, polluted. As if there was no goodness in the world. And yet Carter had to admit that he was looking forward to the fight, that he himself had bought not one but two tickets. Did that make him like everybody else—greedy and cruel, as Archie said?" The book asks boys to think about their own attraction to greed, cruelty, and violence, and it culminates in a final "battle" between good and evil, a competition that's been rigged by the bully mastermind.

Similarly, in 2001's *Tangerine*, by Edward Bloor, the new boy, Paul Fisher, needs to prove himself in middle school. He is a talented soccer player. The cruelty of his older brother as well as other kids in the school looms over him, but it is invisible to his overzealous father. He struggles when his new school classifies him as disabled because of his very poor eyesight, thus preventing him from playing the sport he loves. He struggles with being different and fitting in. Even in this excellent novel, there's a final game as well as a fight at a school assembly where the bully brother begins to get his comeuppance.

In *Ender's Game*, the science fiction masterpiece about a boy (who's not actually adolescent but written to sound like he is because of his superior intelligence) chosen to save the world through *Star Wars*–like battles, vulnerability is ever present. In the beginning of his story, like Paul Fisher in *Tangerine*, Ender is cruelly abused by his older brother. He is "different" too, because he is a third child in a society where parents are not supposed to have more than two. When chosen to train at a kind of battle school, his wit proves him superior to the others, and he has a special talent that earns him respect. Even though, as in all these books that culminate in a competition, game, battle, or several battles, he is victorious, the book maintains its sad undertow of the loneliness of boyhood in the face of inevitable cruelty.

Leave it to fifteen-year-old author S. E. Hinton, however, to avoid pitting truly evil boys against the vulnerable ones. In 1967's *The Outsiders*, still required reading in middle schools across the country, the two gangs, Greasers and Socs, are more alike than different, and even the meanest of kids can be liked, or at least understood, in some way. On the fortieth anniversary of its publication, Dale Peck wrote in *The New York Times* that this book changed the way YA fiction was written, "empowering a generation to demand stories that reflected their realities."

Parents would do well to read or reread some of these books when their own sons reach adolescence, to remind themselves of the cruelty boys both face and mete out, as well as their bluffing arrogance, their love of wit, and their complex relationships. Such books help us keep in mind that behind those arrogant judgments of others is a desire to be close to others. And boys who have been encouraged to stick with reading through their teen years, who often profess to read only sci-fi or fantasy or graphic novels or adult novels, may also find themselves uniquely and deeply reflected in such fiction.

Read a Book, Read a Book Read a Mutha Bleepin' Book: Race and Reading

In July 2007, Black Entertainment Television (BET) aired a cartoon version of spoken word artist Bomani "D'Mite" Armah's satirical rap song "Read a Book" during its popular teen video show *106 & Park*. In what appears to be a public service announcement, a rapper performing at "Raphael De La Getto" high school ditches "hooks and concepts and shit" to "go blacker." He then raps "read a book, read a book read a mutha fuckin' book . . . not a sports page, not a magazine, but a book nigga, a fuckin' book nigga" amid all too familiar images of thong-wearing crumping women with BOOK written across their booties, gangsa-style rappers loading guns, and black kids hanging out in the 'hood. The images are shocking, the song catchy, the point made: this is what passes for a successful rap video these days—a simple repeated line, any line, a strong beat, graphic language and images—and this is how people sell anything and everything to black boys. Replacing a gangsta-type rap with "read a book" completed the parody. While lots of people, including parents and Jesse Jackson's Rainbow Coalition, didn't appreciate the social satire, pretty much everyone commenting on the video agreed that black children, especially black boys, are not encouraged to read enough.

It's clear from recent research on boys and reading that the literacy scores in urban schools with predominantly minority, poor, and immigrant populations are comparatively low. In fact, some researchers argue that the focus on boys' school achievement should be more on poverty and race than on gender. Blame the media. Blame the parents. Blame the schools and the teachers. Or blame years of "high stakes" testing. But what kind of books are we making available to these boys?

We asked a class of predominantly white sixth-grade girls and boys to think of all the books they've read in their lives and to name one African American character? Nothing. We reminded them that George, one of the two pranksters in the *Captain Underpants* series, is African American, and they said "oh yeah" but still couldn't think of any others. Maybe this isn't the right group for this question; maybe black characters weren't on their radar. But when we surveyed seventy-five African American middle school–aged boys on their favorite books, we heard essentially the same answer. Maybe this helps explain why nearly half said they didn't read at all. Either they left the section blank or they wrote "None," "No," "N/A." Yet the other half *were* reading, and a lot. They were reading wonderfully imaginative mysteries like *Chasing Vermeer*, hugely popular fantasies like *Harry Potter* and *Artemis Fowl*, classic fiction like *To Kill a Mockingbird*, as well as generic manga, horror, action, sports series, and the gross and funny stuff.

In boys' literature that includes African American characters, we found a striking bias: they all seem to be promoted for Black History Month. Where we work, our African American colleagues complain that February shouldn't be the only month in which black speakers are brought to campus to talk. Likewise, black history should not be the only genre in which one finds literature that presents interesting black characters. After Ezra Jack Keat's *The Snowy Day* and the lovely Faith Ringgold picture books like *Bonjour, Lonnie*, and *Tar Beach*, read to the littlest of children, there is *The Stories Julian Tells* for African American boys who might want to see themselves reflected in their reading. Otherwise, boys get history: *Henry's Freedom Box*, by Ellen Levine and Kadir Nelson, *Elijah Buxton* and *The Watsons Go to Birmingham*, both by Christopher Paul Curtis, and a number of books about Martin Luther King Jr., such as *Martin's Big Words* by Doreen Rappaport and Bryan Collier. Even in the fiction options, like *Bud Not Buddy*, a book has to incorporate a little history lesson. There's no doubt that these books are an important supplement to the history texts in school that do little to represent the rich and varied experiences of African Americans in this country, but can't a black character *just be* without carrying the burden of educating too?

Speaking of that rich and varied history, it's hard not to notice, in fact, that the contributions of African Americans to our country, aside from Dr. King, according to well-meaning biographies, typically come down to sports or music. One can choose from *We Are the Ship: The Story of the Negro Baseball League* by Kadir Nelson; *Jesse Owens: Fastest Man Alive* by Carole Boston Weatherford and Eric Velasquez; *Muhammad Ali: Champion of the World* by Jonah Winter and Francois Roca, or another on Ali, *Twelve Rounds to Glory* by Charles R. Smith Jr. and Bryan Collier; and *Satchel Paige: Striking Out Jim Crow* by James Sturm and Rich Tommaso. Or one can choose books like *This Jazz Man* by Karen Ehrhardt, *Dizzy* by Jonah Winter, and *Charlie Parker Played Be Bop* by C. Raschka.

Teachers tell us that boys love to see themselves in their books, and if the best education is an inclusive education, then the lack of boys of color as protagonists in their fiction is a huge problem. While we try to get kids away from TV and into a book, TV series, at least up to the preteen years, actually do a better job of representing boys of color! Maybe that's because advertisers see boys of color as possible consumers and book publishers see the writing on the wall. We fear that this absence of rich and varied characters for boys of color—and for all boys and girls—to consume in books reflects the low expectations of boys of color and the assumption that they aren't going to buy books when there's a new song to download or a cool new toy to purchase.

Action Books: A Contradiction in Terms?

It might seem that we're against action in boys' media, but we're not entirely. We're against action as the *only or primary* source of entertainment for boys. We also find troublesome the *way* this action is put forth. It seems just lazy, thoughtless, and suspect (is this purely about making money?) to repeat the same story line over and over when action can creatively defy stereotypes rather than reinforce them. Action and adventure stories don't have to contain rampant violence that's always justified in some revenge narrative. Action and adventure stories don't have to create all-male worlds where girls are pretty accessories and moms are clueless. And these stories can be written in gender-neutral ways that allow for both girls and boys to enjoy activities, books, and movies together. Some books succeed at defying stereotypes even when writing within a genre that is sold, stereotypically, "for boys only."

Take, for example, the best-selling children's novel *Artemis Fowl*, by Irishman Eoin Colfer. It's a crime caper fantasy novel modeled after a James Bond–type character, meant for the seven-to-twelve-year-old reader. It's one of the only children's books where the lead character is of questionable morality; his father, before he reformed, taught him that gold and power are everything but now wants him to use his intelligence for the good of the world rather than for selfish ends. Sure, the book is filled with gadgets and technology, and the lead character has a superpower—his intelligence. He's such a smart thirteen-year-old boy that he has invented his own language and a technology that the most brilliant minds of his time can't figure out. Still, he's underappreciated: "You're nothing but a thirteen-year-old kid. How did you do it?" one opponent asks. It's a male-focused fantasy, but female characters of interest abound. The commander of the fairy police force is a woman who Artemis must call on for help and rescue. (Yes, sometimes boys need rescuing too.) The eighteen-year-old sister of his bodyguard began training at the age of four to belong to an elite group of mixed-sex bodyguards and is there to rescue him from trouble. *She's* the one whose ADD diagnosis gets her into trouble. And the supreme mentor trainer of bodyguards is one Madam Ko.

This mixed-gendered and mixed-raced group of evildoers, authorities, helpers, and mentors stands in stark contrast to books in which authors seem to have felt that they must surround boys with other boys and men in order to interest boy readers. These other authors re-create the stereotype that boys will only read about boys and that boys think girls are either yucky or hot damsels in distress; they underestimate boys' interest in the social world around them, the girls that are interesting in their own rights, the women who mentor and teach them, and a host of characters of all walks of life, ages, experiences, and nationalities.

But sadly, as boys get older and look for more action, they're likely to be inundated by more stereotypes. Books based on video games or blockbuster movies promise violence on every page. Although some of these games are rated M (for Mature), and many of the movies are rated PG-13 and R, books get no rating; parents are likely to be happy that their sons are reading anything. But if they open the first page, their happiness might fade. For example, in a book based on the video game *Halo*, sold in a separate section on books based on video games, "Master Chief defends a besieged earth" while "myriad factions of the Covenant" want to "eliminate humanity." Of course the lead character belongs to a secret cell of Naval Intelligence and will fight off faction after faction. Why waste any time? In the first two pages, Tom remembers his trainer's advice: "Your training must become part of your instinct. Drill until it becomes part of your bones." Thus by paragraph six he has raised his assault rifle, by paragraph seven he has "automatically" reloaded his weapon, and by paragraph eight he has pulled out an additional sidearm. In paragraph nine we are reassured that he was wearing a full suit of "Semi-Powered Infiltration Armor." Are boy readers supposed to care? It doesn't really matter, because caring about the lead character in these novels, just as in the video games, is not an emotion that anyone's trying to evoke. Instead, boys are asked to identify with the fighting machine.

There are, of course, other books for boys that are action filled, mingling story with stereotype, and the real vulnerabilities of boyhood with special powers. These can be discussed with your sons for both the bad and the good in them. Consider Anthony Horowitz's *Alex Rider* books, a series in which a fourteen-year-old boy (with no parents) is recruited as a spy by Britain's MI6 and given all sorts of cool spy tools, as in *Point Blank*, in which he gets goggles, blasting cream, insulated and bulletproof clothing, and a DiskMan that converts to an electric saw.

First, "the bad": it seems as if the author feels the need to catch a boy's attention on page one by showing a "custom-made Mercedes" and a "Beretta sub-compact automatic pistol." This isn't the usual product placement; that is, these products are included in these books not because they're being marketed to boys per se—they're clearly out of reach. Boys are given the message that this is what they're supposed to like; boys should be interested in and know the names and brands of flashy objects and equipment like guns and cars, as well as detailed technological information about them. Later we'll hear about a Rolls-Royce Corniche and a "beautiful" "over and under shotgun" with "detachable trigger lock" handmade by Abbiatico & Salvinelli. There's also a Yamaha Mountain Max snowmobile equipped with 700 cc triple-cylinder engines and a Lockheed Martin C-130 Hercules aircraft. With equipment like that, how could there *not* be a chase scene? And how about an explosion after a crash? Gotta have it, if only so a new vehicle can be obtained in the next book in the series.

Other stereotyping occurs in the requisite bully scene in which a gang of rich boys tries to scare Alex and call him names. (We've seen these bullies ever since Thomas the Tank Engine had to deal with the diesels!) He, of course, gets the better of them. There's also the stereotypical beautiful older (fifteen year old!) girl who snubs him after she appears in a white bikini. (He gets to snub her back later, after she discovers how cool he is.) That's it for girls. The action takes place in a school for very, *very* rich boys, and the fights between Alex and the bad guys involve the same sorts of chases and getaways one would find in any Bond or superhero movie with the same old ultimate "mano a mano" scene near the end. The hand-to-hand fistfights are there so that the boy (or man) can prove his mettle without all the metal.

Now, for the good (of sorts): such books give boys what they promise: action, adventure, a wild ride in which a boy can imagine himself as a hero. Unlike the book versions of video games, boys in these books are asked to care and be aware—that the bullies get their due, that wealth can corrupt, that justice wins out. Granted, these valuable lessons are dressed up in old-fashioned stereotypes, and most of the creative energy is channeled into finding fresh twists on tired themes (not unlike the *Gossip Girl* genre of chick lit aimed at girls—there are only so many ways to imagine a shopping scene and a catfight), but there is a moral center to these books.

Finally, there are relationship messages specifically about boys and dads. In *Point Blank*, for example, boys are at a school because they can't get along with their powerful dads. They're rebels. And when the boys are made into Stepford sons, a few dads catch the change and don't like it. They want their old, rebellious sons back. The message that father-son conflict is inevitable and should be understood more deeply may be an important one, but it's rarely explored with any depth in an action novel. Instead, we get caricatures of dads, fathers who have gone bad, do bad, or are bad. When a novel like *Artemis Fowl* defies stereotype and presents a dad who encourages his son to settle down, do good, and value family, we appreciate the difference in quality and we might want to point this out to our sons and say, "No surprise really with that! Isn't this what most dads want for their boys?"

Boyhood for Sale at Your Local Newsstand

THE SHORT TRIP FROM EARTH TO MARS

Little boys and girls alike love to read about other children, imagine what it's like to explore the solar system, or learn about how a pair of colorful South American parrots raise a nest full of hungry chicks. For this reason, the most popular magazines for little ones aren't for boys *or* for girls but are designed to introduce all children to friendships, nature, and the wonders of the world. The National Wildlife Federation's magazine trio, *Animal Babies*, *Your Big Backyard*, and (in case you didn't know that boys could love animals and still be tough), *Ranger Rick*, are great examples. So is Cricket Magazine Group's literary series *BabyBug*, *Lady Bug*, *Spider*, and so on. Then there's *Highlights*, a magazine that today's grandparents may remember reading in the dentist's office waiting room when they were little kids. It's amazing that their cartoon feature Goofus and Gallant, about two boys who teach manners and "good conduct," has lasted all these years. (Perhaps there were slackers long ago under a different name!) Parents are looking for imagination, wonder, and yes, manners, in magazines for their little ones.

So what happens when children reach seven or eight? (1) Magazines with heavy pop culture advertising turn up, some of them endorsed by parent organizations that should know better; (2) Mars and Venus take over the solar system; that is, boys and girls become different "target populations"; and (3) the messages your son gets about the world, and himself, change. While boys at age seven may start looking for something a little different, something far more different than anything they've seen before is pushed on them.

Sports Illustrated for Kids is a perfect example. *Kids* is a misnomer—this is really a magazine targeting boys. In the sixty-page 2008 summer issue, there were one or two small photos of women athletes and just one story about women, an article about the Olympic basketball dream team. The first message boys get from this magazine, then, is sports are really a boys' thing. But what does that mean, "a boys' thing"? It means action and fun, of course, and competition. It also means looking and acting cool, like Florida Devil Ray's Hanley Ramirez, who graced the cover in sunglasses . . . "Made in the Shade." It means buying things, because looking cool and having fun requires lots of "stuff": "Fun in the sun . . . don't leave home without these cool summer items . . . sneaks, Boogie board, cool suit [just the boy style], cool glasses." Is this a boys' version of a shopping catalog? And it means looking tough, especially if you don't have the size (size matters, even at seven or eight) to really pull it off. Take the "faces in the crowd" story of an eight-year-old all-American wrestler, his freckled game-face on, his small body in bodybuilder pose to look tough, staring hard into the camera. It means "Living Large" and having "awesome power and speed." It's also means top-five lists and "power rankings," and hero worship of the biggest and best. What's Hanley's favorite food, movie, and music? An admiring boy wants to know. Whether it's in the stories or the ads, everything is "one of a kind," "full speed ahead," the "coolest," the "largest," the "ultimate," and "all-star."

Kids need to know what brands their heroes use, so they can pester their parents to buy the same. Advertisements are something *Sports Illustrated for Kids* has plenty of—ads for the kinds of movies, candy, toys, and video games a *Sports Illustrated* boy or his hero would like. In these ads, the boy and action hero merge into one. Ads for a bat and ball set say "mow 'em down" and "smack 'em deep." *The Dark Knight's* Got Milk ad—"others reload, Batman refuels. . . . body by milk"—sounds a lot like the R-rated Rambo tagline, "Heroes never die, they just reload". We're cajoled into momentarily thinking this hypermuscled plastic black bodysuit is his real body, which needs milk to keep it strong. Even ads for candy and junk food like Yogos sour bits are about the "super struggle" of sweet vs. sour. There's a battle in his mouth—which will win?

To be fair, there are a few "tips from the pros," healthy meal suggestions, and "hot reads of the summertime," including basketball player Lisa Leslie's autobiography, *Don't Let the Lipstick Fool You.* For an artistic kid there's even a "design an Olympic polo shirt" activity. But there's no doubt that the primary focus of the magazine is on winning, challenging, and being a sports superstar.

National Geographic Kids' tagline is "dare to explore." Well, maybe, if it's daring to explore these pages to find the product embedded in nearly everything. Over half the magazine is either full-page or sidebar ads for junk food, toys, and movies. You can't have a cover article about pandas without Jack Black and his character, Po, in *Kung Fu Panda* ("Panda-monium"), because really, aren't pandas more interesting when they're kicking butt? No article about the sea would be complete without Jack Sparrow of *Pirates of the Caribbean*—beats a deep-sea diver exploring those boring coral reefs. Even an article about happiness refers kids to the activities (and more ads) they'll find if they leave the magazine and go to the *National Geographic Kids* Web site. After all, nature isn't nature without space chimps and Ninja Pop-Tarts, and it's no fun if we're not grossing someone out or head-banging a few endangered species.

Unlike *Sports Illustrated* or *National Geographic*, *Nick Magazine* doesn't even pretend to be about anything "real." It's an entertainment magazine, which means it's primarily one big ad for Nickelodian shows and products. In fact, it's so *not* real that the publishers have to put a yellow and red REAL sign on sections that aren't ads. (We're wondering if they know about the research that shows kids eight and under can't distinguish ads from content or understand the persuasive intent of the images and messages they're seeing.) Even if they're taking responsibility for showing kids the difference between an ad and a story, there were only six REAL signs on forty-eight pages in the issue we previewed, and we think at least one of these doesn't count, since it's a story called "Inside Nick" about "what's upcoming on the network and show times." Come to think of it, is a story about a star real when it's a result of a recent movie or TV show on Nickelodeon that he starred in? If that's the case, maybe we should omit the *Nick Magazine* contest results (still kind of an ad for Nick). We're down to the "'Real' Stupid Things People Have Done"—okay, that's one we'll accept—but, of course, as in Nick's TV shows, it has to be of a bumbling dad who had to be rescued from his hide-and-seek spot in the family washing machine or the stupid cabdriver who followed his GPS into the river. Adult men (at least the ones who aren't superstars or super athletes) are almost always idiots in this magazine.

Nick Magazine reflects every stereotype of preteen boyhood available: they're gross, stinky, goofy, and if they're not wiseasses, like the adult men in feature stories, they're dumb and nerdy. Consider their "Hazy, Hot and

Stupid" summer issue. It's truly amazing how many ways *dumb* and *stupid* can be associated with boys and men. For example, celebrities are asked "What's something funny you can do that should become an Olympic sport?" Singer Nick Cannon chooses burping. Actor Seth Rogen likes spitting. How about a dumb frozen treats naming contest ("the burpee, the sludge bar"), or "Put to Duh test" brainteasers that show a cartoon of a smart and smartly dressed girl asking questions and a confused, sloppily dressed boy looking stumped. (Being smart is put down because it's associated with being girly or nerdy. Girls who are smart are annoying and controlling. Boys who are smart are sissies or nerds. Bad for girls. Bad for boys.) How about a *Fairly OddParents* quiz: "Who in the Fairy World do you think you are?" with choices like farts, boogers, and chimps in dresses, and scores like "you have the brain of Cosmo"—the dumb male fairy in the show. Then there's "The Village Idiot"—a fake newspaper—story in which Moronia's education chief, Ed E. Ott "Just Say(s) No to School." But unlike *Highlights* characters developed in the late 1940s there's no Gallant to this Goofus.

In forty-eight pages of this issue of *Nick*, thirteen contained references to being dumb or stupid or doing dumb or stupid things, and most of them referred to boys or men. Mind you, a full five pages were devoted to front matter, an invitation to become a member of the *Nick Magazine* club, and a *Nick* survey about the magazine; eight were full-page ads for candy and Nick-related shows and movies. Take away the eight pages contained in their "comic book section" and we're talking about half of the remaining pages. This magazine alone makes us wonder about how much of the current concern about boys' school achievement has to do with messages like these about how stupid boys are.

At first glance, the magazine *World Wrestling Entertainment Kids* is a bit of a surprise. Maybe because we were prepared for something way worse, with violence and mayhem. On the cover there's a cartoon wrestler in mask, bare chested with big muscles, in full midair wrestling mode, and the usual boy-targeted topics: "Sports! Pranks! Superstars!," "How to Win at Sports Every Time," and "25 Coolest Vids, DVDs, & Toys of Summer." But there are a few substantive stories too, maybe because the creators know that without them they'll have a harder job convincing parents that this is a magazine to get for their son. So he can read about eating well (fab vs. flab), about "history's mysteries," science ("know your muscles"), and how to "help like a champ." Just as *Nick* invites boys to design a polo shirt, *WWE Kids* readers can design a fighter's cape.

Even so, like the WWE itself, the volume is cranked up in the magazine.

Be "the first," "win every time," "be a champ," "a superstar," "you are in control," "gear up," "dominate" at sports, be "in the driver's seat." Even stories about being a friend or learning something new are sold WWE style, because it's not just new, it's awesome; not just gross, it's super gross: "we haven't figured out how to turn poop into video game store gift cards, but . . . we're working on it." Jokes are "wicked pranks" and designed to "make Mom freak!" Girls and women almost always serve as the goody-goodies or scaredy-cats that make boys' pranks even more fun. Give your teacher these "handy coupons to save your butt"—"This coupon is valid in place of (1) one homework assignment, which I did not complete because I was watching *SmackDown*." Imagine the woman teacher's pinched face of disapproval.

The only thing more hyped than the articles are the ads, and like *Nick*, there are lots of them. "Destroy dullness with the most eye gouging awesome games of the season," "meet the ultimate fun-slingers," "launch a foam-rubber offensive," ride those "power wheels," and these aren't even the ads for WWE stuff, the "Unmatched Fury of 8," "SmackDown," and "Adrenaline" action figures, the ultimate battle games, and all the ways boys can be ultimate slammin' WWE super fans! They can even "amp up those naked appendages" with the help of "The Planet's coolest new kicks and time-tellers"—sounds eerily like a Viagra ad.

But the most obvious problem with *WWE Kids* is the ripped, muscled wrestlers—both cartoons and photos of the real thing—on nearly every one of the magazine's forty-nine pages. We know they can't get that way by just "eating right," as the stories suggest, but do preteen boys? We know the scary stories about the increase in steroid use among athletes, but do they? A boy won't read about it here, or if he does in some silly form, it won't be in a way that would have boys questioning the adrenaline-rushed action of these Incredible Hulk–like figures. While there are no ads for all those high-caffeine energy drinks yet—candy will have to suffice—the language here is similar to those ads, and we can see the setup. *WWE Kids* gives lip service to the good stuff, but when it comes down to it, the message to "be a boy," or rather, "be a man" couldn't be any clearer than in the ad for its own magazine. If you want your parents to buy you the magazine: "(1) Hustle through all your chores; (2) Show loyalty by washing your dad's [not your mom's?] car; (3) Respect your parents all month; (4) Have your parents call . . . and skip all this nonsense." This is what passes as prankster fun for preteen boys: pretend to act in decent ways to earn a reward (the magazine) and then mock doing good. In case you need to reread that ad, it's the magazine writers saying "Skip all this nonsense," not us. For them, it's all about slackitude, man.

In the name of fun, entertainment, and literacy, these magazines appeal to the lowest common denominator. Why? Because after age seven or eight, boys are presumed to leave behind all that "sissy stuff" like, well, geography, nature, and friendship. These editors will argue that this is what boys love, as if eight-, nine-, and ten-year-old boys are paying for the subscriptions to these magazines; they'd rather use their money for candy. Of course they might love it to an extent. It may be amped, cranked, geared up, and funny, but it's also dumber than the magazine boys they stereotype. Parents can talk back to these editors and say, sure, every boy wants to dabble in what they're told is all-boy, about-boy, or every-boy, but listen, my boy loves our family cat, doesn't want to fight people, identifies with engineers, chefs, carpenters, and musicians too, likes his downtime, can curl up with a good book, and yes, while sometimes he's goofus . . . he sure can be gallant.

BIG, BIGGER, BIGGEST: TEEN BOY MAGAZINES

Most teen boys are not reading men's magazines like *Giant, King, Maxim*, and *XXL*, but they don't have to actually read them to get the message. Being a man is about being BIG, although it's hard not to wonder if the need to announce size in nearly every magazine title isn't compensating for something. *XXL* ("hip-hop on a higher level") seems to have street cred, at least judging by the letters sent in from prisoners that praise the naked and digitally enhanced apple-bottomed women in the "eye candy" section and the debates regarding the authenticity (and toughness) of the rappers. *Giant* ("the first entertainment magazine for guys") makes giants of players like clownish rapper Flavor Flav and touts every "object of desire" any urban guy could want, while *Maxim* goes right for the hundred hottest girls. They write in one article: "Show Time: This Valentine's Day, we wanted to give you a gift that keeps on giving—lingerie. Why? Because we love you, man!" The gift, of course, isn't lingerie per se, but nonstop photos of girls in lingerie. The message to readers is as clear as the Wild Turkey bourbon ads that grace their pages: "Gentleman, Check Your Skirts at the Door." No uncertainty, no nonsense, no sissy boys welcome.

Is this the message teen boys get in their magazines as well? What stands between the cranked-up, crazy, gross, and stupid stuff in boy-targeted preteen magazines like *Nick* and the highly sexualized babes and stories of wealth and status in men's magazines? Not much, actually. There are, of course, dozens of teen magazines for girls, and while parents of girls may not like the constant focus on unrealistic bodies and getting a guy, adolescent girls have magazines that speak to many of their other inner concerns. At least there's the assumption they actually *have* an inner life. There are no such general interest magazines for boys. Instead, teen boys buy magazines that speak to specific interests, like *Dirt Wheels, Skateboarder,* or *Game Informer.* What's missing in these magazines is any conversation about real boys and the real questions they have about the real issues in their lives. There's nothing about sexual decision making or what it means to be in a relationship, nothing that speaks to the uncertainty boys feel or the questions they have as they come of age. Asking those questions, these magazines assume, already makes him a guy who wouldn't read this magazine. Relationships? Once they're interested in girls, it's straight to *Maxim, FHM,* and *Giant,* where women are hard bodies and eye candy.

Most parents are happy to buy their sons special interest magazines, in part because they promote boys' budding interests and offer information and skills. Maybe they're hoping to distract them from the adult men's magazines a few steps down the aisle. But don't let the titles fool you into believing boys aren't getting an *XXL* eyeful of *Maxim* messages from these magazines as well. Yes, there's information, but the stories and the ads package their interests and skills in ways that speak volumes to boys about who they're supposed to be as men—in control, powerful, risk takers, and, of course, into hot girls.

Dirt Wheels, an all-terrain vehicle magazine, and *Outdoor Life,* for those into hunting and fishing, are especially popular with boys in rural settings, for obvious reasons. The articles cover equipment review and places to ride, fish, or hunt, while the ads show it all as the most exciting, action-packed, aggressive, and risky stuff a guy could do. In *Dirt Wheels'* many all-terrain vehicle (ATV) ads, for example, riders don't ride defensively, as parents hope and pray. They lean off the side of their ATV while skidding sideways and spraying dirt sans helmets and protective goggles. The copy announces that this little number "is ready to dominate." Buy these babies and you won't have to stay on those pesky marked trails. This is all about "performance" and "exhilaration." Boys in the photos ride over boulders, fallen trees, and into unmapped territory because, hey, screw the environment. These brute force ATVs have "the power to conquer practically any terrain. Game on."

Maybe a magazine called *Dirt Wheels* has to have some of this stuff. Yet one could imagine *Outdoor Life* would occasionally celebrate the quiet beauty of nature. Not a lot of contemplation here—all that Thoreau-like self-reflection is for wusses. Instead, speed around the lake in that "bad boy" fishing boat, then "put the hammer down," "kiss your hat good-bye and draw a bead on the next sweet spot. You're out of the hole before you can say, 'trophy catch.'" Once on land? Don't waste your time watching wildlife; scare the hell out of anything living by doing doughnuts in your desert racing truck with its "dominating," "toughest," off-road racing tires. Try not to hit a deer on your way out. Wait, points for you if you do!

Perhaps these kinds of magazines invite this Mach speed and power to counter the perceived boredom of nature. Maybe they pull boys and young men in who love nature but who worry that simply listening, watching, and well, just being, won't be cool or macho enough. Plenty of dads in our home states of Maine and Vermont tell us how much they enjoy sharing their love of nature with their sons, just being in the woods—the awe, the respect. But virtually every magazine targeting teen boys' and young men's interests, interests that might have been supported in wonderful ways by their families, finds a way to amp up the volume and transform respect into domination.

This is incredibly interesting when you think about the passive act of sitting in front of a screen and playing a game. How more quiet can an activity be? Yet the skill of video gaming is packaged as screaming, over-the-top action. *Tips & Tricks*, for example, the self-proclaimed "world's leading game strategy magazine," is filled with game and gaming system reviews that celebrate the fight and the hero who emerges. A fold-out ad for a fantasy fighting game, where the player challenges gods to save the world from destruction, claims, "Devastating combo attacks, powerful allies, and an arsenal of deadly weapons and magic are at your command, but will they be enough in a battle between gods?"

GamePro, described as offering the "most comprehensive gaming news," is filled with previews, reviews, and secret codes for games that will help him "blow out the competition," "destroy," and "burn baby burn." Articles highlight the latest hot game's fearsome creatures and awesome weapons, and show how to make the best use of them: "When backstabbing just isn't enough, the chain saw bayonet can now be surgically implanted into the spines of enemies. They'll never know what hit them!" Boys can check out *Gears of War 2*'s avatars with names like Butcher, Grinder, and Maulers and cool weapons like Gorgon burst pistols and scorcher flamethrowers. More into sports than fantasy? They can play *Shawn White Snowboarding*, and all those "beautiful, open world ski resorts" will be "yours to dominate." How about *UFC 2009 Undisputed*, a game that puts you in control of Ultimate

Fighting martial arts competitions, because "this game will punch you in the nuts."

The articles and ads for games speak to all boys as if they are made from one ultracool mold, obsessed with cranked-up action and confident they'll be the best at everything. Oh, and of course there are those sexy girls to be had and watched, represented by female avatars that look like Pamela Anderson. Girl gamers exist in these magazines, but like the avatars, they're showcased in ways that provide a kind of erotic entertainment for your son. In one issue of *GamePro* there's a sidebar interview with a busty gymnast who plays a "live Lara Croft model," a GameFly ad featuring the "5 Hottest Girls [avatars] Ever (#2 "Lara Croft, Tomb Raider Series—How many times have you switched camera view while she's running"), a sexy "catfight" between Sonya Blade and Catwoman (Mortal Combat vs. DC Universe), and an article called "Game Girls Gone Wild" featuring GameGirl.com's bloggers with sex-kitten Internet names like Raychul and Nikole. They pose porn-star seductively in black bustiers and hot pink micromini Catholic schoolgirl outfits, touching their *Rock Band 2* game guitars in a manner that suggests masturbation, and teasing their clearly excited male interviewer with answers like "my sexiest piece of video game clothing isn't actually clothing, more like panties." In a magazine that features lots of "E for Everybody" games that little boys love, what are they thinking? Even if occasionally a frustrated teen boy like Alex from Las Vegas writes in to complain that "nice guys never get the girl" in these games, he's drowned out by the scoffing testosterone-induced gun-toting avatars on the next page.

So what skills are boys getting from magazines like these? Are they buying them, as the old *Playboy* excuse goes, "just for the articles"? Well, sure. *Skateboarder* magazine will show him some "kick-ass" moves, teach him how and where to get his "shred on," will show him the coolest new decks (boards)—as well as help him develop an insider's vocabulary that you'd need a translator to understand. Parents are often just plain happy that their son is reading something. But what about the other messages about manhood being defined as a having cocky attitude, taking wild and crazy risks, dominating nature and people, and sexualizing girls? Learning actual skills and strategies of the sport are so important during these years that we hate to see it cluttered with the same ol' same ol'. Boys never see their love of the whole sport or activity in these magazines. The high-octane elements are all that get written about. Maybe the buzz gets kids interested, but once interested there are so many aspects of the sport to learn about than the magazines provide. Real learning includes yielding, waiting, and listening—things very hard to do when you've been told that the goal of everything you do, education included, is to physically dominate it.

The Amazing Captain-Super-Iron-Man-of-Steel

MARVEL-OUS MEN

"Depravity for Children—Ten Cents a Copy!" read one newspaper headline in the 1950s, back when comic books contained "lurid stories of crime, vice, lust, and horror, rather than noble tales of costumed heroes," David Hajdu tells us in his recent best seller, *The Ten-Cent Plague*. He writes that as one of the "first and hardest-fought" conflicts between kids and their parents, the fight over comic books was the harbinger for later conflicts over rock and roll, long hair, tattoos, and more recently, rap. Today parents can't get enough of comic book material for their kids, like Spider-Man bedsheets, *Captain Underpants* early readers, action figures, and movie after movie— from *Superman* to *Spider-Man* to *Batman* to *Iron Man* to *Hulk* to *X-Men* to the *X-Men* spinoff, *Wolverine*.

American comic books have always been associated with superheroes; in fact, the so called Golden Age of American comic books dates from the appearance of the first *Superman* comic in 1938, through the early 1950s. During this time comic books enjoyed considerable popularity. The archetype of the superhero was invented and defined, and many of the most popular superheroes were created (for example, Batman and Robin, Wonder Woman, The Flash, Green Lantern, the Atom, Hawkman, Aquaman, the Human Torch, the Sub-Mariner, and Captain America, among others).

Today, the two most popular comic book publishers in the United States are DC Comics and Marvel Comics. Each publisher has a stable of both classic and contemporary characters who function as the main heroes (and, to a lesser extent, heroines) and villains in their comics. The five most popular DC characters are: Superman (Clark Kent); Batman (Bruce Wayne); The Flash (Wally West); Green Lantern (Hal Jordan); and the Joker. The five most popular Marvel characters are: Spider-Man (Peter Parker); Captain America (Steve Rogers); Iron Man (Anthony Stark); Wolverine (James Howlett); and Silver Surfer (The Incredible Hulk is actually number ten). These characters represent a very small percentage of the total number of characters (both primary and supporting) in the Marvel and DC comic book "universes," but each is his own franchise. Since 2000 an extraordinary number of movies based on comic book superheroes have been released. The new *Batman* movie series, starting with *Batman Begins* (2005) and continuing with its sequel *The Dark Knight* (2008) has been so popular that the latter film is not only the highest grossing comic book film of all time, but also the highest grossing film domestically in the first decade of the twenty-first century.

Before jumping to the conclusion that a daily dose of supermanly superheroic figures is bound to make a boy feel a tad inadequate, consider that many of these superheroes were created by Jewish men at a time of pervasive anti-Semitism. Jewish comics creators and cocreators include Joe Shuster and Jerry Siegel (Superman), Bob Kane and Bill Finger (Batman), Will Eisner (The Spirit), Jack Kirby (Fantastic Four, Incredible Hulk, the X-Men), Jack Kirby and Joe Simon (Captain America), and Stan Lee (who helped create Spider-Man and other superheroes). In his book, *Disguised as Clark Kent: Jews, Comics and the Creation of the Superhero*, Danny Fingeroth says,

> You had a bunch of young men whose parents were immigrants, writing stories about a very idealized world, where force is wielded wisely and people are judged by their individual character, not by who they are or who their parents were. For the guys who made the comics, it was a way to transcend who you were and become locked into and involved with the American mainstream, to blend in.

So, comic book superheroes were originally a way for Jewish boys from the Bronx, deemed weak and inferior by the culture around them, to identify with a superior being and to fit in with American society, much like Comic Book Man on *The Simpsons*, and other stereotyped geeks who love to collect comic books and figurines. In *Disguised as Clark Kent*, Danny Fingeroth describes how, for Jewish boys, and presumably more contemporary geeks and freaks, the idea of a disguise, of having a double life, was essential to their attraction to comic books. While everyone in their world might see them as inferior, they knew that secretly they were strong, intelligent, masterly, and talented. And they knew that if they showed this side of themselves, they would be vulnerable to ridicule or would be shot down for aiming too high.

Thus what started as a way for Jewish boys and other outcasts to fit into American society has evolved into a way for *any* boy to fit into *male* society by identifying with a superior being—certainly the attraction of video games as well. All of the male superheroes now are drawn in ways that emphasize their hypermasculine physiques, including buffed bodies, broad shoulders, and bulging biceps. This includes Wolverine, who is about sixty years old but whose healing powers make him look younger, and buff, like an aging Rambo.

Heroes in literature have often been super, so comic book superheroes aren't so much new as they are technologically advanced. Take, for example, Hercules or Samson, or, as one of our teen boy informants reminds us, Gilgamesh, who was "crazy-ass strong," in this boy's words. He warned us, however, that Gilgamesh was "not anything like what you read today, because he was in the first book ever written." But Gilgamesh sounds *a lot* like something we'd read in comic books.

Even so, the stories of these crazy-ass strong guys have become more complex, and they last for years, actually decades. Boys grow up learning narrative life histories of a single character not only through their battles but also through their relationships and families. Unlike the quick exit and entrance of an auntie or the tragic relationship with a father that is only touched on in a movie, the comic book follows these relationships through their difficulties over a lifetime—well, longer than a lifetime, given that most of these superheroes never age.

The writing is also interesting. Although full of slick comebacks, boys who read comic books also will be exposed to metaphoric and sometimes quite evocative language: "the boundaries between what's real and what's illusion have come to seem as threadbare as a moldering shroud" and "But when I imagine how it must feel to him [the Joker], I think of a snake with a broken back, flipping and tracing intricate, agonized arabesques in the dust." (I SPY a couple of SAT words there!)

If it sounds as if we like these comic books, perhaps we do, compared to their movie counterparts. These comics are not nonstop aggression, crashes, and explosions. In fact, aggression is part of the narrative but not its raison d'être, which is more about justice and trying to do the right thing, and more often than not, coping with a lost, horrific, or absent father. If they're violent, the plot includes personal struggle with "berserk" rage, as with the Hulk or Wolverine. Besides, the real bullies are often the villains who are ready to shame or to put a superhero down for being a wuss: "I have to say I'm disappointed," says Atlas, Titan of Yore, "I expected more valor."

Fingeroth says, in an interview with "Mr. Media" on blogradio, that the violence we see in comic books is less about having a superpower and more about wielding power wisely. Not exactly upholders of the letter of the law, superheroes tend to be vigilantes who are struggling with what's just. In the latest *The Amazing Spider-Man*, for example (number 581, rated A, which means appropriate for age eight and up), of ninety-six panels there were only a handful of violent scenes. The police shoot at Spider-Man because they think he's gone bad. A molten man is strapped down because he's trying to control his aggression. Harry Osborne's son tries to cope with the death of his father and cuts off the heads of all his Spider-Man dolls. Then the molten man, brother-in-law of Harry's ex-wife, escapes to try to kill Harry Osborne because he believes Harry "hurt his family." Peter (Spider-Man) saves the boy as his molten uncle explodes. Violent, true, but full of the anguish of disappointing friendships and family relationships.

Aside from wives and aunties, in these A-is-for-all–rated comics, we continue to see slightly pornographic, stereotypical women drawn as hot babes, whether they're the shy, bespectacled "interesting" woman—Pepper Potts, for example, in *Iron Man*—or "a gaggle of Icelandic flight attendants [he] met snowboarding." Even Lois Lane, sharing coffee with Superman in the morning, jumps up to throw her legs around his waist and expose her thonged bottom to A-is-for-all readers. Similarly, the women who are superheroes are drawn in ways that emphasize their voluptuous bodies, including large breasts, long legs, tiny waists, and beautiful faces.

Do parents need to worry about the sex and aggression in these comics? There are barely clothed T & A shots galore, and some aggression, yes, but aggression and the "player" image are more ferociously represented in the advertisements in these comics than in the comics themselves. One ad boasts "Wrestling so real you feel the pain": *TNA Impact* (it's a video game). Another shows a sexy babe in an ad for the Fox show *Terminator: The Sarah Connor Chronicles*. Her tiny tee is ripped. Her back is full of wounds, and her metal body parts are showing through. And then there are ads for the "Mountain Dew Tour" featuring over-the-top motorbike feats. Finally, an ad for BVD thermal underwear features a test tube of something purple labeled "Machisium" with a square from the periodic table of elements giving the abbreviation "Ma." Like the potions that superheroes are exposed to that strengthen them, "trace amounts of Machisium can be found in every male; these can rise to dangerous levels when exposed to kung fu or hammers. Radioactive to women and unstable when mixed with caffeine, Machisium is famous for its comically low boiling point and its brute aromatic strength. It is typically found in rugby scrums, bikers, and BVD thermals." *Please.*

You won't see *nonstop* Machisium in most of these comic books. In fact, plenty of them poke fun at the concept. For example, the beginning of *The New Avengers* (Secret Invasion number 47) has a full-page drawing of muscular, black, and bald Luke Cage's angry and frightened face (he's PowerMan), with the tendons in his neck bulging out, swearing, "Sweet Christmas . . ."

Truly frightening. Turn the page and you find that he's been confronted with his baby's soiled diaper, his wife explaining to him that babies' poop is often green and yellow.

Turn to those comics rated T (for Teen), though, and you get guns, chases, crashes, and dark scenes with mercenaries, a veritable Rambo with shots of superfemales from the ass on up. Is this what "growing up" means in the T-rated comic world? In A (All, in comic book land) world, it means dealing with poop, protecting your family, and dealing with the shame of not always having done right. Not a bad message. But it's a message that comic book readers won't find when they move over to the dark side of T comics. "Mr. Media," a blogger, asked Danny Fingeroth, who worked for almost twenty years at Marvel about this recent "dark trend" in comic books (for example, *The Punisher*). Fingeroth recalled a quote on this topic: "What do you end up with when you take a child fantasy and incorporate adult sensibilities . . . what if Babar suddenly kicked butt and took names?" Good question. So what do you end up with? A good story ruined? A world stripped of humanity? Lost innocence? All of that and one man alone, dealing with yellow baby poop.

READING CLUBS, COMIC BOOKS, AND GRAPHIC NOVELS

A graphic novel is a type of comic book, usually with a lengthy, complex, and more "novelistic" story line, and often aimed at teen audiences. As such, the plot in a graphic novel typically has a beginning, middle, and an end, as opposed to a plot that continues through a series of comic books published periodically. Graphic novels resemble Japanese manga, which are comic books that typically have novelistic qualities. In terms of popularity, more boys in the United States read graphic novels than manga. Today, both DC and Marvel list a series of graphic novels on their Web sites, which include virtually all of their most popular superheroes.

Building on the popularity of these characters, and the comic books and graphic novels that chronicle their exploits, some concerned about boys' school achievement have been discussing whether comic books and graphic novels might be used to entice boys to read more. For example, Christine Welldon, author of "Addressing the Gender Gap in Boys' Reading," developed The Cool Guys Reading Club for older boys in her elementary school. She awarded symbolic colored belts, as in martial arts, to express levels of advancement, threw pizza parties, and handpicked popular kids to help recruit others. In advertising the club to the school, Welldon reports, "The message was that members could love or hate reading, it didn't matter, but they had to be a guy." Literally, no girls allowed. Her advice is to start boys out on *Captain Underpants*. Move them to graphic novels. Separate these books out from real books so a boy is tricked into thinking he's doing something other than reading. Allow him to see how he measures up to other boys. We get it—turn reading into a sport. Does she ask boys to form reading teams too? (For which they'll choose the poorer readers last?)

Sounding a similar note, Chris Brown, the author of *Boys into Books*, a reading report commissioned by the British government, has included many comic books and graphic novels in a list of the Top 200 new works he has drawn up for five- to eleven-year-old boys. In a London *Times* online story dated June 14, 2008, Brown's rationale for including comic books, graphic novels, and manga on the list of books for boys is that not only do such books appeal to many boys, but they also stimulate both visual responses to the pictures and intellectual responses to the words. Brown says that he regrets that schools and parents too often dismiss such books: "On the Continent, picture-strip books take up quite a high proportion of children's book sales and are very prominent in shop displays. But here [in the U.K.] we still tend to be a little nose-in-the-air about them."

There is, indeed, an entire series of manga Shakespeare, published by Self Made Hero (which lists, as its mission, "reinventing the classics as manga and graphic novels"). Here is the descriptive copy for manga *Hamlet*:

> In this manga, *Hamlet* is set in a dramatic futuristic world. The year is 2017. Global climate change has devastated the Earth. This is now a cyberworld in constant dread of war. The state of Denmark has grown prosperous and defended itself successfully against neighbouring states. But could it be that its greatest threat comes not from without, but from within the state itself? It is in this cyberworld that we find the young Hamlet. His grief over his father's recent death turns to something far darker when the ghost of his father appears to him. Hamlet is very soon to discover that something is rotten in the state of Denmark.

In manga *Macbeth*, the central warrior characters are represented as hypermasculine Samurai, replete with bulging biceps, headbands, swords, poles, and other martial arts weapons:

> "ALL HAIL, MACBETH, THAT SHALT BE KING HEREAFTER!" With that misleading prophecy, three witches plant the seed

of criminal ambition in the warlord Macbeth. Spurred on by Lady Macbeth, his wife, he embarks on a killing spree of former friends and rivals, until a final confrontation when he realizes too late that the witches have deceived him. In this version of Shakespeare's tale of murder and the supernatural, Samurai warriors have reclaimed a future postnuclear world of mutants.

So, in the end, we've gone from Superman to Samurai Macbeth. There is no doubt that comic books, graphic novels, and manga appeal to kids because of their eye-catching graphics and succinct dialogue. But reading a manga version of Macbeth is not the same as reading the real thing. They should coexist in a boy's world, but how can they when the manga version is the "real boy" version, and everything else is most likely characterized as being for nerds, geeks, and girls? There is no evidence we know of to suggest that boys who read the manga version will progress to Shakespeare's original. If we assume that these genres are all that boys will read, boys will be shortchanged by a culture that thinks they can't do any better. If we think that boys are slackers who will only read something that's short, "sexy," and filled with a lot of pictures, how will they ever learn to love reading anything else?

Reading Between the Lines: Why Boys Don't Read

It may sometimes seem as though we are picking on the best in boys' world, critiquing something they clearly need more of—books! And it may seem as if this is especially wrong of us at a time when teachers and parents are so worried about boys' reading habits and their low test scores. We are concerned about boys' reading too, but we're not convinced that gender is the key factor here or that just getting your son to read *anything* (like boy-stereotyped books and magazines) is the answer.

There's a lot of concern about boys' academic achievement these days, and much of it focuses on a gender gap in reading scores. But the gender gap favoring girls in reading is not new and it has not increased in recent years. In fact, according to the National Assessment of Educational Progress, fourth- and eighth-grade boys' scores have gone up, albeit not as much as girls'. Moreover, experts point out what research studies consistently tell us: the larger gap has more to do with race and poverty than gender. Age and racial differences lead some to argue that this is less about brain development than about the association between doing well in school and femininity.

It may be true that boys mature a little later than girls, but consider how difficult it is for children to defy expectations or learn something they think they're "bad at" or will be teased for. Think about how kids tend to cope with disappointment and shame when they can't do something they think they should be able to do. They either feel bad about themselves and get depressed, or they say something like, "I didn't like that or want that anyway." Boys can say things like "it doesn't matter if I read" or "I don't read because reading is a girl thing," suggests Jon Scieszka, children's book author, advocate for boy reading, and founder of the Guys Read project. Boys struggling to read before they're ready, living in a constant stream of video lures, being told in every media source that boys don't read, and trying to avoid being humiliated in front of other boys for choosing a "girl thing," certainly are going to shy away from reading early.

As we've seen, some advocates' solution to the problem is to give boys more of what they assume boys like. Yet we find that if teachers introduce boys to books they wouldn't normally choose on their own, they often end up liking these books—a good teacher, after all, expands his or her students' options by opening them up to new things. But it's a strong boy who picks the *Anastasia* series over the *Shiloh* series when other boys are watching! We're told that boys like action and information. But isn't it a stereotype that boys must have action, that they don't like romance, that they're not interested in relationships? Too many teachers, librarians, and children's book authors are making suggestions about how we all can convince boys to read more, based on these stereotypes. Give them action. Write about sports. Throw in some car chases and crash scenes, a battle or two, a wise but harsh mentor, a few farts or burps, and, of course, No-Girls-Allowed. It seems as if they are telling us to kowtow to stereotypes. If boys glom on to the worst of the comics that have women with huge breasts, or if they become engrossed in a series where the dad is a bumbling idiot and mom just cooks and sews, where the author makes fun of overweight people, and homophobia lurks between the pages, we say UGH, let them watch some good movies instead!

While the world of boys' school achievement may need bigger solutions than we can offer in this book, we offer twelve tips for parents beyond the no-brainer *read to your son early and often!*

1. Don't assume that your boy isn't interested in reading, just because he's a boy.

2. Don't buy into the view that any reading is good reading. When boys

do their social networking on the computer they're also reading, but you can ask your son to be selective, to read something that widens his imagination, takes him to new places, and introduces new ideas. The old adage garbage in, garbage out, applies: he learns more than just how to read when he picks up that *WWE Kids* magazine.

3. Limit your collection of fart, gross, and burp books, and feel no need to start your three-year-old in lessons on sarcasm when they could be still adoring *Tell Me That You Love Me*.

4. Point out dads and grown men whom you see reading something other than a newspaper. Dad, read something other than the newspaper when you're at home so that you set a positive example for your son.

5. Don't be too afraid of violence in what they read, but do be selective. Good literature deals with violence well and often shows the vulnerability, pain, and horror of violence, which can be good lessons for your son to learn. Sadly, there is violence in the lives of boys, and books showing characters coping with it in a variety of ways helps them to cope too.

6. Help your boy choose books that may not look like boy books, such as *Junie B. Jones*, which one boy told us he likes because Junie is funny. Remind him that just as you can't tell a book by its cover, you can't tell a book by the gender of its characters.

7. Avoid any book made from a movie. In these cases, it might be just fine to say, "You've seen the movie, why read the book?" Tom Newkirk, author of *Misreading Masculinity*, says that boys have a unique relationship to pop culture and that authors should use it to their advantage. Parents should use media too. Suggest he write some fan fiction or design his own comic book to show off his creativity and take his favorite characters in different directions.

8. Ask questions like: Why do you think they show boys and dads fighting so much in these stories? Why are so many dads absent or killed off? To be able to have a decent discussion about this, you'll need to read what your son is reading.

9. As your son gets older, encourage him to imagine solutions other than fighting as ways to solve problems. If you can't find literature

where bullies are also human, keep up a conversation about stereotypes in literature so that you can ask your son, "How was the bully represented? What do we know about his life? Do you think that's fair or just a way writers like to depict good vs. evil in books?"

10. Talk with his teachers and encourage them to give students ample opportunity to choose books they really enjoy. Request that they invite both male and female authors to speak to the class about their work and the challenges they've faced. Prepare male authors beforehand and ask them to speak directly to the issue of male stereotypes.

11. Don't push him to read books that are too difficult for him because you think he *should* be able to read them. Start with something you think he'll like.

12. When your son spouts some stereotype such as "boys like action books," remind him of the less-action-packed books he's loved and try to help him keep an open mind about what boys can read—and enjoy.

Amid all the concerns about boys and reading, we've seen some hopeful signs. In our survey, we found real differences in the reasons why boys like their favorite TV shows and why they like their favorite books. They told us that they watch TV shows because they are funny or because they have lots of action. But their favorite books inspire something more. In their own words, the fiction they love "jogs [their] memory," and nonfiction captivates because "some of the things really happened." They choose fantasy books because they "have the most magical things." Books they love "give a good message," they're "incredible," "exciting," "awesome," "cool," "creative," "entertaining," and "unique." Take that, *WWE Kids* magazine!

BOOKS THAT HAVE COMPLEX CHARACTERS AND FEW STEREOTYPES
(Thanks to librarians and friends)

LITTLE BOYS

The Snowy Day by Ezra Jack Keats

Where the Wild Things Are by Maurice Sendak

The Story of Ferdinand by Munro Leaf

Owen and Owen's Marshmallow Chick by Kevin Henkes

The Reluctant Dragon by Kenneth Grahame

19 Girls and Me by Darcy Pattison

Wilfrid Gordon McDonald Partridge by Mem Fox

*The Stinky Cheese Man and Other Fairly Stupid Tales by Jon Scieszka

Where the Sidewalk Ends by Shel Silverstein

What Shall We Play? by Sue Heap

The Polar Express by Chris Van Allsburg

What Do People Do All Day and *Busy, Busy Town* by Richard Scarry

How to Heal a Broken Wing by Bob Graham

Kenny & the Dragon by Tony DiTerlizzi

Clancy the Courageous Cow by Lachie Hume

Bee-Wigged by Cece Bell

Pete & Pickles by Berkeley Breathed

Turtle's Penguin Day by Valeri Gorbachev

NOT SO LITTLE BOYS

Henry and Mudge by Cynthia Rylant

The Misfits by James Howe

Understanding Buddy by Marc Kornblatt

A Series of Unfortunate Events by Lemony Snicket

*Diary of a Wimpy Kid by Jeff Kinney

Hoot by Carl Hiaasen

Holes by Louis Sachar

The Spiderwick Chronicles by Holly Black

Chasing Vermeer by Blue Balliett

The Lion, the Witch and the Wardrobe by C. S. Lewis

Charlie Bone by Jenny Nimmo

Super Fudge by Judy Blume

* Even though they do play up the slacker boy and boys-love-everything-gross-and-stinky stereotypes. Hey, we have a sense of humor too!

Bridge to Terabithia by Katherine Paterson

Love That Dog by Sharon Creech

Elijah of Buxton by Christopher Paul Curtis

The Watsons Go to Birmingham: 1963
by Christopher Paul Curtis

The Invention of Hugo Cabret by Brian Selznick

Hatchet by Gary Paulsen

Shield of Stars by Hilari Bell

Masterpiece by Elise Broach

Fablehaven by Brandon Mull

Nobody's Family Is Going to Change by Louise Fitzhugh

Island of the Aunts by Eva Ibbotson

BIGGER BOYS

Tangerine by Edward Bloor

The Graveyard Book by Neil Gaiman

Harry Potter by J. K. Rowling

Inkheart by Cornelia Funke

Lion Boy by Zizou Corder

Artemis Fowl by Eoin Colfer

City of Ember by Jeanne DuPrau

The Hobbit and *The Lord of the Rings*
by J. R. R. Tolkien

Catcher in the Rye by J. D. Salinger

The Giver by Lois Lowry

Feed by M. T. Anderson

The House of the Scorpion by Nancy Farmer

Monster by Walter Dean Myers

I Am the Cheese by Robert Cormier

The Outsiders by S. E. Hinton

Repossessed by A. M. Jenkins

Hero by Perry Moore

The Mysterious Benedict Society
by Trenton Lee Stewart

The Farsala Trilogy by Hilari Bell

Tunnels by Roderick Gordon and Brian Williams

Twisted by Laurie Halse Anderson

The Gospel According to Larry by Janet Tashijian

Pirates of the Retail Wasteland by Adam Selzer

The Bartimaeus Trilogy by Jonathan Stroud

His Dark Materials trilogy by Philip Pullman

The Unnameables by Ellen Booraem

To Kill a Mockingbird by Harper Lee

HIGH SCHOOL BOYS

Daniel Half Human by David Chotjewitz, translated by Doris Orgel

America and *Life Is Funny* by E. R. Frank

The Book Thief by Markus Zusak

The Astonishing Life of Octavian Nothing, Traitor to the Nation, Vol. 1 by M. T. Anderson

The Perks of Being a Wallflower by Stephen Chbosky

Someday This Pain Will Be Useful to You by Peter Cameron

Spanking Shakespeare by Jake Wizner

The Curious Incident of the Dog in the Night-Time by Mark Haddon

CHAPTER 4

Do You Hear What I Hear?
What Boys Listen To

They may be in constant movement, fully plugged in, or appear sullen and silent, but boys' ears are wide open, and from young to old, they are listening to everything—words, music, and so much more. In school hallways, they're likely to hear: "That's so gay" or "what a fag." From their coach? "Man up" or "What are you, a bunch of girls?" On radio and TV? An explosion of jokes and gags about what a real man is, like those on the TV show *Two and a Half Men*:

> UNCLE CHARLIE: Do you think I've been a good role model?
> TEENAGER, JAKE: You drink, you gamble, you have different women here practically every night—you're the best role model a guy could want. They should put your face on money!

Or they hear in some of the most degrading rap songs, "God damn lil' buddy take off your clothes and let me see that apple bottom and that brown booty." And "Imma Buy You a Drank; Then Imma Take You Home with Me; I Got Money in the Bank." Now that's a pickup line any girl could refuse.

You need to watch out for what your son might be hearing, not only in the music he listens to, but also what his peers and adults outside the home tell him about what it means to be a boy. When experts on boys talk about the "boy code" or "Guyland" or the "tough guise" boys are expected to put on, they know the expectations and pressures are not just "out there" but are right inside their homes, their families, and their relationships. Even parents and teachers with the best intentions inadvertently support stereotypes that they want to defy.

We've all grown up in this culture and we know what gives a boy social power. It's a rare parent who doesn't feel anxious when his son shows little interest in sports or isn't into the over-the-top action and adventure marketed to him. And it's a rare boy who can be at peace with feelings and choices that are contrary to what's expected of him as a boy. That's in part because we're all exposed to a frightening number of messages in the media that assume all boys are into the same things and which, as a general rule, connect real boyness to a version of masculinity that invokes sexism and homophobia. In such a climate, no boy wants to risk being called a girl or a fag.

So when boys hear their parents talk to other parents about how much energy their young boys have, how fearless and agile they are, how much they love to be all rough and tumble, boys get the message that they are connected to other boys primarily in these ways—and that can feel safe to them. They also feel connected to other boys when they hear from adults that boys need a "tribe," a place to hang, more recess, and time to blow off steam together. In school boys may hear teachers talk about these same qualities as negatives— how impulsive boys are, how undisciplined, how boys are underachieving, or are "bullies," "tough," "bad." But in the antiintellectual climate of boys' media right now, boys can interpret those concerns as concerns about all boys and feel "normal" and even cool when teachers get mad. What they don't hear nearly enough, from parents and teachers and especially in the media—and believe us, they notice—is how smart they are, what curious students, what good readers, what rational, philosophical, peace-loving, complex people they're on the road to becoming.

What success stories do they hear? Usually not ones involving school unless it's a story of an exception, someone who failed at school going on to win the Nobel Prize or a C student who became president. Consider the narratives of athletic feats and accomplishments boys hear, read, and watch regarding their favorite sports stars. They hear stories about heroes, champions, the guy who kicks, hits, throws the winning goal or makes the game-winning run. They hear about rising and falling stars, winning, money, winning, rivalries, winning, injuries, winning.

What do boys who actually *play* sports hear? According to researchers Omli and LaVoie, they hear lots of yelling. And they don't like it. When these researchers asked kids what they disliked most about playing sports they said hearing people yelling from the sidelines. But not just any yelling. Parents yelling. Parents coaching. And parents arguing with the refs. Parents may do this kind of yelling for a good reason—to help, encourage, and fight against unfairness on behalf of their kids. But what do their boys hear? Anger. Judgment. Impulsiveness. The same thing boys hear in their media at a constant rate— that when there's an injustice, they have a right to bring out the big guns without forethought. They have a right to yell. They have a right to make a scene.

What else don't kids like? This may be surprising, but they dislike it when they hear their parents say mean things about other kids. That sense of fairness can work for them and against them, and it's our responsibility to be fair to our child's peers.

Boys also hear a lot from other boys and girls. Peers tell boys what it means to be a boy through their put-downs, punking, and name-calling. The popularity of the word *gay* to mean anything stupid or weak is only accentuated by the myriad names boys call one another to indicate that they're not man enough: fag, for example, and Gaylord. In our survey boys told us that boys are likely to call other boys names that indicate they're like girls—but instead of the "old-fashioned" term "sissy," boys now call one another Bitch, Ho, Whore, Skank, Pussy, Hissie-fit man, Douche bag, and Verbal. Verbal? Sadly, as one boy wrote, girls are associated with being more verbal than boys, and so it becomes a put-down if boys come across as articulate.

In large part because of a media culture that has made "mean girls" the latest social crisis, we seem to have forgotten that boys experience a lot of and suffer too from what psychologists have termed "relational aggression." In fact, while boys are more likely to be physically aggressive than girls, when it comes to social aggression, they can dish it out just as well and just as often. When researchers examined nearly 150 studies on social aggression, their findings challenged the popular assumption that when boys get angry, they duke it out and it's over. When it comes to relational aggression, boys give and get as good as girls. They too struggle with the psychological effects of name-calling, verbal attacks on their reputation, and manipulation of their relationships, although being a guy might mean they're more likely to hide the scars—until, of course, the pain is unbearable. One study found that adolescent boys exposed to relational forms of aggression are more likely to carry a weapon to school. Alas, we've seen how that can end up.

So when boys hear "Hey, faggot," it matters, regardless of how much he protests that it's just a euphemism for stupid. "To call someone gay or a fag is like the lowest thing you can call someone. Because that's like saying you're nothing," says a Latino high schooler in C. J. Pascoe's book, *Dude You're a Fag*. But it's also a term that's a big part of the pranking and joking relationships that bond boys, a way for boys to announce their masculinity and heterosexuality. Boys in Pascoe's study said they wouldn't use the insult against someone they actually knew was gay, but the joking and playful insults do underscore the anxiety boys are made to feel about masculinity. It's a "hot potato" term, Pascoe says, and that's what makes it such a powerful way for boys to contain and control one another. It can be tossed around as a joke, but its meaning is both clear enough and fluid enough "that boys police their behaviors out of fear of having the fag identity permanently adhere." That policing means no obvious displays of closeness or affection toward other boys, no emotional language, and no crying or caretaking.

This explains, in part, the steady stream of messages boys hear about going it alone, bucking up, being the strongest and the very best all by themselves, with no help from others. It's this conventional wisdom we live by, a wisdom deeply embedded in our views of masculinity, that Malcolm Gladwell takes on in his 2008 book, *Outliers*. In spite of what boys hear about what it means to be a self-made man, a hero, a maverick, "no one—not rock stars, not professional athletes, not software billionaires, and not even geniuses—ever makes it alone." Just listen to the postelection attempts to recast President Obama as one man alone, after the many stories he told about his mother waking him up to do his homework and the discussions about politics she initiated, the support of mentors and collaborators, including his grandmother, wife Michelle, and his mother-in-law, who watched the two girls during the campaign. As Gladwell's message underscores, success is always the result of relationships and social context. We should always remember that even Thoreau had his meals brought to him at Walden Pond.

Creating Identities through Music

What boys hear impacts who they are, and music is a big part of what they hear. As with toys and picture books, the music children hear at home starts out pretty gender neutral. In the car, little boys and girls alike beg to hear child-centered CDs like The Wiggles' "Wiggly, Wiggly World," Jack Johnson's "Curious George," or Bare Naked Ladies' "Snacktime," and laugh together at goofy tunes like Raffi's "Down by the Bay" or the silly "I'm My Own Grandpa." Sure, some of the songs have gendered themes, especially when it comes to jump rope rhymes and Mother Goose poems, but it's only when those big moneymaking companies like Disney and Kidz Bop L.L.C. enter the scene that the gender divide breaks wide open.

In *Packaging Girlhood* we wrote about music for four- to seven-year-olds that hijacks childhood; the way "I'm a Little Teapot" and the "John Jacob Jingelheimer Schmidt" type of songs are overtaken by Disney remakes of the latest big pop hit or "sing-along" video collections of songs from their popular movies. This means little kids can both hear and sing along with a 1950s version of gender, including lots of Prince Charmings on white horses rescuing lots of princesses who clean houses and pal around with animals. They can listen to and watch big-breasted Disney girls swoon over Hercules, who transforms from a puny "zero" into a WWE-like muscled "hero" in the movie: "Folks lined up/Just to watch him flex/And this perfect package packed a pair of pretty pecs."

Thanks for the image, Disney. Whether it's good guy Simba in *The Lion King* singing "I can't wait to be king" ("I'm gonna be the mane event/ Like no king was before") or bad boy Gaston in *Beauty and the Beast* ("For there's no man in town half as manly/Perfect, a pure paragon/You can ask any Tom, Dick or Stanley/And they'll tell you whose team they prefer to be on"), Disney has a way of letting boys know what it means to be a real man—powerful, brave, and built—even when they poke fun at him simultaneously.

Kidz Bop is another series of CDs that hijacks childhood—there are fifteen now, all big sellers—advertised online, between cartoons on Saturday morning, and tucked in McDonald's Happy Meals. Tweens sing "Kid-Friendly Versions of Today's Hits." This means a collection of wannabe pop stars singing tuneless sanitized versions of songs like the Shop Boyz hit "Party Like a Rock Star":

i try ta run and hold my pants
but these hoes won't let my thang go

Does it matter that Kidz Bop writers change up the lyrics before giving them to the kidz to sing? Of course you won't hear words like hoes or thang—at least that kind of thang. But it's a little late, don't you think? They've already introduced eight-year-olds to a song by a band that's singing some of the most sexually degrading lyrics out there. In a few short years they'll be singing along and learning how to put in the real lyrics, if their older siblings don't teach them first! They can also then go to YouTube.com and watch the original video of this and other Kidz Bop songs, like the ones with drug metaphors (Britney Spears, "Toxic"), political assassinations (Franz Ferdinand, "Take Me Out"), or sex on the side with an ex (Hinder, "Lips of an Angel").

But like lots of lucrative "tween" products, the point of Kidz Bop is to bridge childhood and teendom in ways that make kids feel older and more mature, and to want the things teens want. "It's time to party like a rock star," Wal-Mart gushes on its Web site under the category "children's music":

Coming off the heels of a 12-week concert tour and a national television appearance on *Good Morning America*, this best-selling, gold-certified kid audio series continues to grow with every CD release. And the KIDZ BOP brand just keeps getting bigger, with new toys, electronics, personal care goods and greeting cards all in the works for this year.

"Go on," the advertising copy reads on the Wal-Mart Web site, "give in to the demand . . . give them what they want!" But of course what *they* want is what Kidz Bop and their Wal-Mart pushers want them to want. Such desire has been manufactured and relentlessly marketed.

Though music can be soothing, educational, a way to learn about history, and a way into a world that's sweeter than the boy world they live in at school, it can also overexcite and incite and provide the background beat to an identity modeled after a troublesome gangsta, pimp, or player. But listening to music is also a private thing, and this is where boys show diversity in their interests. While mainstream advertising through magazines and pop-up screens invites them to listen to the newest, most commercial, overwrought mixes, degrading lyrics, and pumped-up raps, the boys in our survey, in the privacy of their rooms and earbuds, listen to *High School Musical*, Nirvana, Radiohead, Lil Wayne, the Beatles, the soundtrack to *Wicked*, old school rap, Red Hot Chili Peppers, and Queen. And many boys who love music cross genres all the time.

While we as parents might worry about certain lyrics or the lifestyle of particular artists as poor role models, it's not always the case that these lyrics and artists are actually that important to boys. In fact, many of the boys we surveyed didn't know or care about the lifestyles of the rappers and other artists they listen to. They had a vague idea that most are superdevoted to their music but also party, do drugs, and, if they're rappers, may have been in prison or taken a bullet or two. These are stereotypes, of course, but they do get the "hard work" part right. Some told us that Lil Wayne has gone back to college (he has), one even mistakenly telling us he's getting a Ph.D. They know that he worked in a recording studio before making it big. Most know that rappers like 50 Cent, LL Cool J, and P. Diddy didn't get to their positions at the head of their own companies by riding around in the hood pointing guns and singing "ain't no such thing as halfway crooks."

Where we should direct our attention is not toward the "music young people listen to today" (can't you just hear granny's voice?) but to lyrics and videos that degrade women and glamorize violence. Remembering that some of the most wonderful music was once banned (Cole Porter's "Love for Sale," the Beatles' "A Day in the Life," and Kurt Weill and Bertolt Brecht's "Mack the Knife" from *The Threepenny Opera*), we can't just say no without listening to it ourselves. We need to listen along with our kids and talk about the character-narrators of songs and the attitudes they portray, and distinguish between irony and full-fledged support of bad behavior.

We've negotiated our way around the shocking, the degrading, the political, and the fun sides of the music boys listen to. Along the way we've uncovered how their desire to be part of the music world, whether it's through their choice of musical instruments or their desire to pick up a guitar and rock out, is influenced by marketing stereotypes.

Playing Like a Boy

Plenty of boys we surveyed play instruments and make a big sound in their bands. Indeed, boys dominate the brass sections of school bands and orchestras, and they tend to monopolize the percussion section. For a boy who is active and has a lot of energy, parents are frequently given the advice to buy him a set of drums—presumably to help him to expend some of that energy. The message is that hearing oneself make a big sound makes a boy feel more powerful and in control.

Boys understand the power of the drum and the way playing the drums can confirm masculinity. In one study about musical instrument choices, every single boy under the age of fifteen said they either played the drums or would like to. Would a boy who loves the airy sounds of the flute dare to admit it? "Very carefully," says researcher Katherine Sinsabaugh, who studied boys and girl's instrument choice. After choosing a viola, a boy came to a lesson with a black eye—he'd been harassed for playing a "sissy" instrument. Boys who like "girl" instruments or even slow music risk being seen as not boy enough. Sadly, not just the flute and the violin but also classical music, orchestral instruments, and choirs are all associated with girls. Though the tone from a violin can be so moving that it can have the power to make someone cry, it doesn't announce masculinity. While Beethoven's symphonies can evoke splendor, transcendence, and majesty, it's now considered elitist to like Beethoven, and elitist is not male, or at least not "that" kind of male. When boys choose instruments (if they're allowed to choose them themselves) they are drawn to the symbolic power of certain instruments.

In fourth or fifth grade, children across the country are often given the opportunity to start learning an instrument, so the brass section usually ends up filled with guys who will blow big noises from tubas, trombones, euphoniums, and trumpets. The flute section is almost always all girls. The oboe, because of its reputation for being a difficult instrument to learn, attracts more girls who know they will work hard on their instruments; research also shows that the clarinet is considered to be a "girl" instrument. The percussion section of every school band has far too many boys standing around in the back, waiting for their special moment to hit their timpani or crash their cymbals, safely hidden from the music until they get the chance to let loose and bang. In the meantime, the kids in the rest of the orchestra are multitasking by reading scores, playing solos, playing in harmony, and keeping time.

We aren't the only ones who have observed this. Music teachers have bemoaned this fact for years, and research shows that such instrument choices are not the result of biased appointments to certain instruments. It's the kids and parents following their kids' impulses. In this case, while girls may lose out on the chance to make a big noise, boys lose out by having far fewer instrument choices and much more peer disapproval. Though a girl might be discouraged from playing the trombone by her peers, a boy who loves the viola may end up with a black eye.

As with so many other choices we give our kids, we think that their desires are pure and uninformed by the rest of society. But think about the movies they've seen, the TV they've watched, the commercials they've viewed, and who plays what instruments. There are some anomalies, like Lisa Simpson on sax, or since we're hard-pressed to find a media example of a boy with a violin, we'll mention that in Lyn and Mark's daughter's school, and Sharon's son's orchestra, boys play string instruments in equal numbers to girls. But these experiences occur because of enormous effort on the part of parents and teachers to make it acceptable for boys to play certain instruments. This shows that we can combat kids' early gender biases in instrument choices by presenting them with role models that defy gender stereotypes. That's just what researchers did with boys and girls selecting instruments. They showed them videos as well as live performances of gender-inconsistent playing—for example, a man on a flute, a woman on a trombone—and it did have an influence. It permitted kids to choose instruments they actually had a feel for, not as gender accessories. Moreover, when researcher Sinsabaugh interviewed students who had already chosen gender inconsistent instruments, she discovered that these were students who had been encouraged to research that instrument first.

But parents shouldn't be above negotiation and certainly shouldn't dismiss the reality that boys live with day to day. Another suggestion by music teachers is to make sure each child has a primary and a secondary instrument. For boys, this can be a way to "save face." Lug the tuba back and forth to school while playing the piccolo in the privacy of your bedroom? Well, maybe. We parents can open the world to our kids, allow them the world, while we're cognizant of the peer pressure in it. If we can rely on their own good sense that any kid can try any instrument, we can help them defy stereotypes and make big noises or little peeps, as well as beautiful music.

Band of Brothers

Why are rock-and-roll bands featured in the media as a quintessential boy activity, second only to playing a sport? Well, most bands are all-boy. But why? Some say this stems from rock and roll's history of bad boys and sexist lyrics, performances that have excluded girls. But let's look at it the other way around. What is peculiar to rock and roll that attracts boys? How has it been packaged for them through history as something essentially masculine or as a different way to be masculine than, say, through sports participation. There's something about rock and roll, maybe like drinking beer and playing sports, that tells them they're all-boy and they have power. This may be true in spite of the gender benders, the indie rock figures who have been gay and the heavy metal guys who glammed it up.

Until fairly recently the band has been *the* unit in rock and roll. Many preteen and teen boys still dream of being in a band, even before they pick up an instrument. Mary Ann Clawson, writing for *Popular Music* about a decade ago, researched adolescent rock bands and spoke of the ease with which boys entered into bands. One of the boys she talked with remembers someone saying to him, "Why don't you buy a used bass and we can start a band?" He actually hadn't played an instrument before then but bought one, and *voilà*, he was in a band.

This is the first little miracle of rock-and-roll bands for boys—you don't really have to be good at it when you begin. And miracle it is, providing an open and accessible invitation to music making amid all those messages about being the best, the champ, the hero. Sure boys admire those kids who have amazing skills. But much more than with sports, it's assumed that any kid can pick up an instrument, learn it, and be a part of the band. Clausen's research showed that almost all of the boys who started rock bands in their teens were self-taught. What confidence. As fun and cool as it is, it's great to see that it's such a self-motivated effort.

The second little miracle is that playing a rock band instrument is an activity that's typically taken up outside the realm of parental pressure to take lessons or practice. It represents change—where he is in his life, what his room represents to him now, what it means to look the part, and what he values. But there's no back alley sneakiness—hard to hide the sound of an amp or drum set. More often than not this is a kind of conversation about identity, maybe without lots of words, happening right at home. What a healthy and constructive way to be independent from one's parents.

These two miraculous qualities of starting a rock band feed into themes we've run into over and over again in boys' world—the theme that boys shouldn't have to work hard at something, that excellence and fame just happen, and the theme that they don't need parents or adults to initiate the activity for them, to tell them how it's done, to get them to practice, or to remind them of the foundational principles of music. But played out in this way, we see that these themes can offer him something healthy—providing both confidence to try something new and the faith that he can do it, as well as a form of independence through learning from peers.

These bands are typically formed through friendships and not by finding who's necessarily the best at what. No adult stands watch to make sure everything is equitable; no coach schedules tryouts and picks teams and demands discipline. There are heroes, but they tend to be historical figures like Jimi Hendrix, Stevie Ray Vaughan, or Kurt Cobain. They're not the guys who everyone listened to, but the guys who redefined an era, who played in a unique style, who most people, certainly most adults, didn't get at the time. In this way, playing in a band becomes something alternative and holds the promise of originality.

But what about the hero or antihero aspect of rock and roll? These figures, historical and present day, can be known for their drug use, partying, and bad behavior. Playing guitar can be wrapped up in that image. When a boy picks up an "air guitar" and plays it, he most likely imagines himself a hero, worshipped by fans, misunderstood by adults, maybe even a "bad boy." While he's practicing feeling skilled and in charge, he's also practicing something with his body akin to taking up space and creating a powerful physical presence. Political scientist David Whitson wrote that "body sense is crucial to the development of male identity" and learning to use one's body in "forceful and space-occupying ways" is crucial. The boy imitating the rocker is thrusting, smashing, jumping, screaming, and thrashing. He dominates the stage (or the basement).

Remember too that rock is amplified. Set up in traditionally male places of the house like basements and garages, novice rockers play loud. It's a form of domination; while they don't take up that much space, they take up all the air space in a room or house. They even invade outside space with speaker-to-window "sharing."

Journalist and BBC broadcaster Kevin le Gendre writes about the guitar as a substitute for a gun: "The hallowed Fender Stratocaster is as loud as a juggernaut, as sexy as a stripper and as dangerous as a Colt 45." Symbolically, a guitar is a weapon. This may be more true in the United States, where the angry, militaristic, heroic aspects of guitar playing are manifest among white boys, while black boys have been rappers—using language—or jazz horn players—guys with a horn.

This kind of domineering white male power can also be expressed in band titles. Clawson writes that newly formed boy bands tend to choose names that evoke power, such as Arson, Sniper, or Shark. They suggest armies or physical force or criminality and other forms of power. Names can announce something adolescent boys, in the throes of personal angst or change, feel or want to say but can't yet quite express with those first few chords and melodies. It's who they want to be, who they imagine becoming.

Practice Makes Perfect

Sure rock and roll provides mixed opportunities for boys—like anything that popular, it serves the needs of boys who want to be masculine as well as those who aim to reject the status quo. Even so, at least boys are playing around with these images in an area that's big enough for exploration and that can accommodate a variety of tastes and interests.

Then along came the computer games *Guitar Hero* and *Rock Band*. *Guitar Hero* takes all the wonderful miracles of rock and roll and converts them into a reduced, mainstream version of success. The idea that anyone can play guitar has been useful to boys for a long time, but Harmonix took advantage of it. It takes a little more effort to get up off of one's behind in front of a screen to start a "real" band. But why do so when guitar playing can be incorporated into a slacker lifestyle that requires a lot less? When a boy can turn on the TV, pick up his plastic instrument, and press colored buttons to produce a sound that's fairly close to the music his own guitar heroes have made?

With *Guitar Hero*, there's also the one man alone element rather than the group effort—every boy can become a hero, a champion, the best, the winner. It can be about speed, who can play the licks the fastest, and, lest we forget, it produces a single line, reduced homogenized guitar sound not from an instrument per se, but from a plastic toy (a very expensive plastic toy that costs as much as a used guitar). *Guitar Hero* tells boys what to listen to, what the important songs in rock are. The discovery of old and new rock and the sharing of it has long been a part of a love of rock and roll and continues over the Internet, but sadly, *Guitar Hero* most certainly minimizes this element of discovery and provides less of a place for community and history in a broader sense.

Tinkering with electronics has also long been a part of guitar playing; using the foot pedals that create different sounds from the same instrument, for example, is part electronics tinkering/part music making. Author and music professor Steve Waksman writes that this has been a way that guitar playing fortifies masculinity. The first *Guitar Hero* was set up to get any boy playing, so a novice could get basic technique. The second version mimicked more closely how real bands get started, so that different boys could play at different levels together on different instruments simultaneously. It also has a feature where an individual can slow down the music in order to practice a particular technique or lick.

As one reviewer wrote, "No other game can touch that giddy sense of euphoria as you rip up the frets and rock out to music you're near-as-dammit making yourself." But isn't this the point, that you're not making it yourself? That you're damn near doing it, like playing baseball or tennis on a Wii? Oasis guitarist Noel Gallagher says it trivializes music. As he told *Total Guitar* magazine: "I always tell kids playing a guitar is not a video game, there is no level to get to. You'll never master it and you'll never complete the game." It remains to be seen if playing *Guitar Hero* provides a kid with enough skill to join a live interactive rock band. In fact, a brief perusal of blogging on this topic led us to this entry: "Most of us who can play that well are shockingly bad at *Guitar Hero*, because of the disconnect between what the visual prompts demand and how our hands react to what we're hearing. I can't even make it through 'Iron Man' because I can't make myself resist *playing it*." If this is an indication of what's required of a kid with real musical ability, the robotizing of his hands and mind to match a prearranged solo with a track that doesn't change, suppressing his or her own instincts to the model, then the real miracle of rock and roll becomes banal everyday computer game repetition. Practice makes perfect, but for what? *Guitar Hero* offers all the social fun of being in a rock band, minus the talent.

Rock and Roll, Anger and Angst

Rock and roll, still the quintessential *teen* music genre, has the potential to provide boys a way to express all kinds of feelings and to choose among several competing identities. Rock-and-roll's history of rebellion is deep and impressive. Grounded in the blues, it has offered generations of teenagers a way to express their views about race, politics, war, and sex. It has been at the heart of social movements—Motown and the civil rights movement; counterculture rock and Vietnam War protests; punk rock and anticonsumerism. Today's rock and roll is less cohesive than it once was, less tied to history in this postmodern moment, but it provides no less an opportunity for rebellion and self-expression in a variety of forms.

Variety combats stereotypes, but in a sense, when it comes to rock, there isn't a choice not to rebel. Take a look at a recent collection of rock-and-roll portraits in the book *Fück Yöu*. It's a selection of rock stars giving the finger. That pretty much sums up one of the predominant emotions that rock serves to express. They're saying F-off to the world, but also, more importantly, to the camera, to indicate that it's about the music and not the fame.

Rock has always expressed heartfelt rebellion over values. Consider the protest songs of Bob Dylan and Crosby, Stills, and Nash, Bob Geldoff's Live Aid concert for Africa, or more recently when the bands U2 and Green Day joined to cover The Skids' song "The Saints Are Coming" to raise money for Hurricane Katrina victims.

> *A drowning sorrow floods the deepest grief*
> *How long now*
> *Until a weather change condemns belief*

This history of expressing pain and Rage Against the Machine, the name of one late 1990s rock group, isn't lost on the boys in our survey. One boy told us he loves the remake of Nena's protest song "Ninety-nine Red Balloons" by Goldfinger (perhaps because this is one of the *Guitar Hero* selections). For boys alienated in this world of superplayers and macho men, the punk band Green Day's rock opera *American Idiot* offers up rage that satisfies.

> *Well maybe I'm the faggot America*
> *I'm not a part of a redneck agenda*

Another boy wrote of the song by Mika, called "Billy Brown," in which a married man falls in love with another man: "Oh Billy Brown you are a victim of the times."

A lot of the media about "young people today," and "their music" focuses on hip-hop and sexually degrading rap lyrics, something we will address more carefully later. Post-Columbine, it was angst over the potential influence of "shock rocker" Marilyn Manson. But we mustn't forget that there have been worries about teen music in every generation, leading to arrests over obscenity as well as trials regarding the potential of music to incite suicide and other violent acts. When we research music, it's so difficult to tease apart what is exactly affecting kids. Is it the music? Is it the lyrics? Do kids who feel a certain way choose music to reflect and develop those feelings, or are kids so emotionally transformed by popular music that they do and feel things they wouldn't normally do and feel?

And what feelings are we worrying about? Anger, predominantly—anger directed outward; anger directed inward; angst that might lead to self-destructive acts. Yet the ability to direct and reflect anger and angst is core to so many genres of music that one can hardly fault rock for this. Anger is also an emotion that has enormous political potential when channeled into music that connects to a generation, as we've seen over and over. But many boys in our survey weren't referring to that kind of anger when they pointed us to songs and bands that smash guitars, fling their heads back and forth like head-banging monkeys, jump and snarl with ferocity, and scream lyrics with their mouths wide open. These boys watch videos on YouTube and listen to angry music from all eras—like Slayer's "Raining Blood." Heavy metal, of course, is known for its angry lyrics, performances, and sound, as well as the sexualized images and lyrics.

What's interesting, though, about performances that look so anguished and angry (watch YouTube videos of faces contorted in full expression, guitarists jumping up and down and twirling around like whirling dervishes) is that the rage and over-the-top emotion that they seem to express is in sharp contrast to lyrics that state how dead they feel. One boy in our survey wrote about "Descending" by Lamb of God, who sing

This God that I worship, a faded reflection
This demon I blame, a flickering flame

Another wrote of the group The Killers, who in their video sing "Smile Like You Mean It" in an empty house with ghost versions of family memories around. Alienation is also reflected in one boy's choice of the classic Rolling Stones song "It's Only Rock 'N Roll (But I Like It)," in which the singer asks whether the listener would be satisfied if he stuck a pen in his heart and spilled blood on the stage.

If I could stick my pen in my heart
And spill it all over the stage
Would it satisfy ya, would it slide on by ya
Would you think the boy is strange? Ain't he strange?

It's in some ways a good thing that boys can hear reflected in their music some of the angst and alienation that they must certainly feel in a world that does box them in. On the other hand this kind of music can perpetuate a male stereotype of angry or deadend young men who turn to violence for expression.

Anger and angst are real in the lives of boys. But so are a host of other emotions. Nevertheless, anger and angst are held up as signs of authenticity. Anything that's bubblegum or sweet feels "girly" and "inauthentic." Indeed, critic Freya Jarman-Ivens points out that the more music is "male," the more it is seen as authentic and meaningful; the more "female," the more inauthentic, like "teen-pop." When Johnny Rotten said "We mean it, man" or a rapper claims to be "keepin' it real," they are both speaking about male authenticity. Old school rap is often held up to be "authentic" as opposed to the newer, commercialized music that has come along. Comments at the bottom of YouTube videos constantly argue that the "old stuff" is better than the new stuff. And if the turn to classic rock gives boys some options, because they can search in decades past for something uniquely expressive, that's good. But there's still the problem that "authentic" is often used to mean painful.

Authors Hugh Barker and Yuval Taylor write in *Faking It: The Quest for Authenticity in Popular Music* that this quest for authenticity "has inspired countless musicians to make heartfelt, and often groundbreaking music . . . punk, house, grunge, garage, and hip-hop." They also argue that when you're performing rebellion, angst, and anger, there's often no room for change, and those musicians who begin "authentically" trying to express their alienation can't help but find the draw of commercializing it. For example, they argue that the antihero Kurt Cobain needed to self-destruct, so bound was he by the identity that served an entire generation. They ask whether after years of authentic nihilistic anguish, did he have to "fake" to live up (or down) to this image? How do you stay true to your alienated self and anticapitalist message when you've become a central figure and a commercial success?

So what else does rock and roll do besides give kids an opportunity to say "Fück Yöu" in music? In his 2003 book *My Son Is an Alien*, communications professor and cultural theorist Marcel Danesi reports that when asked "What do you read, watch, or listen to in order to make meaning in your life," teen boys between the ages of twelve to eighteen chose music much more often (70 percent) than reading novels or watching TV or movies. Music is how they make meaning. And since they spend so much time listening to music, it's important that they be able to identify a variety of sources, visions, and philosophies about life in and through what they listen to.

Rebels with a Cause: Alternative Music

Although we hear a lot about hip-hop, rap, and hard rock because of parental concerns about what kids are learning from this music, music for teens today is actually quite diverse, and as Danesi argues, reflects the fragmentation of the culture. Punk and Emo serve to "celebrate misfits and losers." Indie rock serves to glorify independence from mainstream. Androgynous lead singers show boys they don't have to be steroidal. Jam bands provide an alternative to speed and power; they take boys on a laid-back ride through chord changes, silly lyrics, and intellectually stimulating musical turns. A host of other forms help musical kids feel as if there is someone out there who is expressing how they feel. Clearly their music gives boys alternatives to macho images when they move out of the popular mainstream.

"Boy bands" and "boy" singers, indeed, make the most of the transition from boyhood to manhood, emphasizing a vulnerability that can't be seen in those forms of music that teach boys what it means to be a real man. And while jam bands (Phish, Disco Biscuits) are known for their weed smoking and other drug-using audiences, and in some ways reflect the slacker alternative to commercialized hard rock, a boy into these bands isn't necessarily a "stoner" but may be attracted to a kind of intellectual listening that awakens rather than deadens his senses.

Consider the boys who took our survey. They wrote that they loved rap, hip-hop, and rock from the last thirty years—the more hypermasculine forms of music. But they also prided themselves on their broad interests in music. Along with mainstream rappers and bands, our boys, ages fourteen to seventeen listened to:

"King of the Road"

Radiohead

"Saeglópur" by Sigur Ros

"Tarzan Boy" by Baltimora

"Sweet Home Alabama"

A few listened to the CD from *High School Musical.* Another boy found the music to a popular video game and compared it to Rachmaninoff. Still others are discovering Bach for the first time.

These alternatives do give boys a chance to explore emotions other than anger. We had never heard of Sigur Ros, a band mentioned by one of our survey boys, and so we looked it up on YouTube. Listening to this "postrock" band, one YouTube writer asks, "Step back and think about this for a second . . . is your soul easily interpreted?"

We asked in our survey: What song keeps going through your head? One boy wrote, "What a beautiful face/I have found in this place/That is circling all around the sun . . . when we meet on a cloud/I'll be laughing out loud . . . with everyone I see." These interesting lyrics come from an indie folk band of ten years ago, Neutral Milk Hotel.

Some of this other-than-rock-or-rap music spoke to what would traditionally be called a feminine side of boys. Of course, anything emotional that isn't raw or angry tends to be called "feminine." Any male singer using his voice in a way that's expressive and has range is also often called feminine. But in spite of this connection to the feminine in music, boys did not tell us that they listened with any regularity to any female vocalist. Actually, only one boy referred to a female vocalist or band—Avril Lavigne, initially in her career known to have been "one of the boys." We know boys who listen to Regina Spektor and Beyoncé, old Janis Joplin and Aretha Franklin, but for our survey on boys, these women didn't come to mind.

In the 1970s and 1980s "cock rock" bands like Foreigner and Van Halen, sporting big hair, tight pants, and that macho swagger, sang cheesy sexist lyrics. Music videos help keep this image fresh for new generations, so that when Puddle of Mud does a video of their poignant song "Psycho," it's filled with hot girls, oversexed references to the shower scene in *Psycho* the movie, and a crazy-acting Pamela Anderson.

Lets not forget about the music boys listen to in the video games they play, often the first place a boy will hear a Gregorian chant (*Halo*) or a string quartet (*Bad Company*). *New York Times* writer Vivien Schweitzer writes that in the game *Bioshock*, Rachmaninoff-like music plays while an evil composer, Cohen, shouts "Presto Presto" and incinerates "a hapless pianist and his instrument." Schweitzer points out that some rendition of classical music appears in plenty of video games. Music for the game *Battlefield* is played by a seventy-piece ensemble, and composers of music for video games aim to create music that reinforces the emotion of the action at that moment. Kids are beginning to download these tunes without knowing that they're inspired by Mahler, Schoenberg, Bartók, contemporary composers, and even an avant-garde string quartet.

What happens when the hypermasculine is paired with the stuff of nerdy intellectuals, John Williams's *Star Trek Wars* scores notwithstanding? We either get a way to bring boys into new media and music or one more way to hype up something beautiful to make it more masculine. Sadly, it doesn't seem to be a little of both.

There will always be angst, anger, and sex in music. That's all the more reason to stay current with your son's musical interests. Listen to his music, have discussions about the lyrics that point boys toward self-destructive acts when they are angry, ask him what it does for him to see and hear such incredible intensity in some of the harsher music he loves. Listen to these emotions, but most important, also point out his love of music that's joyful, silly, and romantic as he takes risks with music that expresses these other parts of who he is. Talk to him about what gets promoted by marketers and in what ways. Tell him music is far too important to him and his soul to be run by big label producers, and let him know that there's a strong history of rebellion in the field of music. Tell him to look for sounds, lyrics, and meaning outside of the mainstream. Of course, you won't just "tell him, tell him, tell him, tell him right now," as The Exciters once sang. But there are inroads to talking about music with your teenage son and topics to bring up when listening to music you love, and, more important, to music he loves.

Some of the greatest composers of all times rebelled, took chances, and produced wonderful music that the mainstream did not like. Of Beethoven's Ninth Symphony, one critic wrote, "But is not worship paid this Symphony mere fetishism? Is not the famous Scherzo insufferably long-winded? The

Finale . . . is to me for the most part dull and ugly . . . The unspeakable cheapness of the chief tune." Another critic found Wagner horrendous: "The overture . . . is a musical horror, a mixture concocted of bad taste and brutality in equal doses" and "Wagner is a man devoid of all talent. . . . The violins squeal throughout on the highest notes and throw the listener into a state of extreme nervousness."

See, these guys were rebels of sorts—your son can rebel too!

Mixing It Up: Hip-Hop and Rap

It's an enduring image from the summer of 2008: Michael Phelps, the Olympic swimming superstar, entering the pool deck with his fellow competitors, approaching the starting block, shedding his sweats and sneakers, removing his iPod earbuds, and mounting the block, preparing to win another gold medal.

What was he listening to on his iPod, just before the race? This was the burning question asked after his successful quest for a record eighth gold medal. Phelps told the *Today Show* on August 12, 2008: "I think I had Lil Wayne, 'I'm Me' . . . I think I had that on there.'" His answer surprised everyone, especially those in the hip-hop world, forever linking Michael Phelps and Lil Wayne, preparing their way for a joint appearance on the 2008 premiere of *Saturday Night Live* and prompting Lil Wayne to write a song in honor of Phelps.

What exactly did "I'm Me" have to say to Michael Phelps? Here's a representative verse:

Baby I'm me, so who you? fuck U, u not me
And I know that ain't fair, but I don't care
I'ma mutha fuckin Cash Money Millionaire

It had to be the beat, right? After all, Phelps is a nice, hardworking guy who is close to his mother and sisters. He couldn't have found inspiration to be the best swimmer in the world in these lyrics about making millions, insulting women, and saying fuck you to everybody else, could he? Maybe it was the in-your-face attitude, aside from the actual lyrics, that offered up the confidence and arrogance to stare down the competition and face history. Whatever it was, this is where we find ourselves when it comes to hip-hop and rap. It's an enormously popular, predominantly African American music genre that has become firmly planted in mainstream popular culture—approximately 70 percent of the audience for hip-hop music consists of white boys and young men—in large part because that popular culture has responded to hypersexualized and hypertough stereotypes about black men. Even boys of privilege, for example, white suburban boys, feel the need to pump themselves up with power before they metaphorically jump in the pool.

One has to wonder how hip-hop moved so far from revolutionary Grandmaster Flash & The Furious Five or the political resistance of Public Enemy, whose song "Fight the Power" provided the backdrop to Spike Lee's movie *Do the Right Thing*:

> *Our freedom of speech is freedom or death*
> *We got to fight the powers that be*

This genre now appears to be mainly composed of commercial sell-outs—and it has a lot of folks shaking their heads, including a lot of great hip-hop–inspired artists and rappers. How could Flavor Flav of Public Enemy, no matter how clownish he was when they made "Fight the Power," be the same guy sexing up a bevy of hot girls on one of the raunchiest reality shows on TV, *Flavor of Love*, a show that was the most popular nonsports show on cable TV in 2006?

Rap music has surely taken a beating in the past few years because of the sheer number of sexually degrading lyrics, like Nelly's crass rap: "I said it must be ya ass cause it ain't yo face, I need a tip drill" . . . "toot that ass up mama put that dip in ya back and let me tip drill." In 2007 the African American women students at Spelman College canceled a bone marrow drive sponsored by Nelly's foundation because he would not appear on campus to answer questions about the "Tip Drill" video, where he swipes a credit card through a woman's buttocks. African American record producers, media moguls, rappers, and the Spelman students all converged on *Oprah* to talk about a hip-hop reality in which, as Denean Sharpley-Whiting says in her book *Pimps Up, Ho's Down*, is "as much about images as it is skills and beats." And those images are primarily "the very public celebration and commercial trafficking" of sexualized black women.

"Tip Drill" may have summed up what many would say is the problem with contemporary hip-hop music, but as we've seen with rock and roll, or for that matter with R-rated movies and TV shows targeting young men, neither rap nor black rappers have the corner on the objectification and degradation of women—even though the hypersexualized stuff is popular in large part because it conforms to stereotypes of black men. Let's not forget Eminem and his songs, like "Superman": "Put Anthrax on a Tampax and slap you till you can't stand"—and that's one of the milder ones. Still, through verse and music videos, rappers send images of manhood and coolness too often tied to the objectification of women, to violence, and to materialism.

What's a parent of a boy to do? First, it's important to appreciate the complexity of hip-hop and rap. Some say that hip-hop is a lifestyle and rap is the music of that lifestyle; some associate hip-hop music with MCs and DJs, grafitti, and beat-boxing, all with more positive rhymes, as opposed to rap, which is more gangsta or commercialized. No matter. Either way, if your son is into hip-hop what you need to know is: (1) he's engaging with a wide range of messages, images, and products, and the music is central to all of it; (2) many of the artists your son may be a huge fan of like Nelly, 50 Cent, and Lil Wayne, offer some of the most sexually degrading and violent verse and videos in the music scene today; (3) your son is participating in a public conversation about who's most authentic, which means he is helping to define the culture of masculinity through his choice of music; and (4) hip-hop and rap are in constant motion; it's all about changing things up. The songs and artists we write about today will be different by the time you read this—but we suspect the general themes won't be.

If you hope to have any reasonable conversation with your son, and any influence when it comes to his love of hip-hop and rap, you have to appreciate that the artists he's listening to are not *only* involved in the music business; they are also entrepreneurs, parents, philanthropists, activists, actors, and even students making it big in a world that used to chew them up and spit them out. It's a world where "authenticity" and image are truly as important as talent.

WAYNE'S WORLD

Take Lil Wayne for example. He was far and away the most popular rapper on our survey. If you follow hip-hop, you might have seen Lil Wayne on the cover of XXL's tenth-anniversary issue, "a decade of dominance." (XXL is the most popular music magazine on U.S. newstands.) In this issue, he's pictured hanging with Bryan "Baby" Williams (stage name: Birdman) because, as the copy reads, theirs is "a bond that no man can tear asunder." Posing without a shirt, buff and covered in tattoos that say THUGGED, GANG BANG, ROLLS ROYCE, BLESSED, and MISUNDERSTOOD, among many others (and with tattoo tears rolling down his cheeks and the words FEAR GOD on his eyelids), heavily laden with platinum necklaces, earrings, and rings, Lil Wayne seems to be in control of the many messages he sends to your son. Looking into the camera, head cocked under his sideways Cincinnati Reds baseball cap (so we can see the authenticity sticker of course), he's holding a red bandana, typically a gang signal that the wearer is a member of the New Orleans Bloods.

In the *XXL* article, "Nobody Do It Better," we read about the photos and the interview that he and Baby say exposed "our pain, our gain, our losses, our loyalty." The photos were taken in the neighborhood Baby grew up in and evoke an earlier *XXL* cover, to symbolize all the changes the two have gone through since. This is a big part of hip-hop—the family tree, the arguments, the challenges, the betrayals, and a boy invested in these personal stories will find as much drama here as on any daytime soap opera.

As with most rappers, attitude is a big part of who Lil Wayne is; he calls himself "the best rapper alive," and much of the *XXL* interview is a chance for him to talk about his high profile and how others see and admire him. Self-aggrandizement is essential to the success of rap artists. At the same time, he comes across as thoughtful, honest, in touch with his emotions, and even humble. He deflects a question about being the best: "We're not on top of *the* game—we're on top of *our* game . . . It ain't even about being on top of *the* game." He also talks about the way he loves Baby as a son loves his father (Baby calls Lil Wayne Junior) and a much publicized kiss they shared. He talks about his reaction when other disgruntled rappers left his label: "I felt responsible. I lost my father when I was fourteen, and he left me with the house mortgage, and I had to step up, and I was my mama's husband at fourteen." He talks about a former love interest—"that's a very, very beautiful woman"—and another woman rapper he's been linked to—"I respect her. I respect a woman who know how to make her money," not by getting caught up in poverty and drugs but by "being able to rap about it and make people understand you and feel you."

This honest and respectful approach stands in stark contrast to the guy who raps about women and pens songs like "Pussy, Money, Weed."

Likewise, Lil Wayne raps *a lot* about drugs and says in the article, "I smoke weed and drink syrup all day." But he also admits that he records music every day, works harder than any other rapper, and couldn't do what he does if he were high all the time. The drug raps, he says, are because his audience, many of them in recovery, want to feel what it's like again vicariously, and his music can offer that. Whether you buy this argument or not, it's a pretty interesting point of view: sing it, don't snort it. It's also irresponsible and a terrible example for the boys who look up to him and buy his music. In a February 8, 2009, pre-Grammy interview with Katie Couric, Lil Wayne said, "I'm a rapper and that's who I am, Miss Katie. And I'm a gangsta, and I do what I want. And I love to smoke." He also insists he's not a role model for anyone but his own two children: "You worry about yours, let them worry about theirs, and I got mine." But of course we are worried about ours, and we worry more when ours idolize a rapper who has been busted for drugs repeatedly. We worry more, knowing that the most successful marketers sell to everyone, find angles that will reach the recovering addicts, the youngbloods wanting to try new stuff, girls who think pumped-up guys are hot, boys who want to empower themselves through image and violence, guys who hang on to the street narrative—just about everyone but parents.

Lil Wayne might rightly argue that the story boys *want* is the drug, gangsta, street story or the poor-boy-made-it-rich story. Producer Russell Simmons used the word *niggerize* to refer to the way artists imbue their work with a sense of urban grit and authenticity . . . for white consumers. Hood narratives rarely show hope or defiance to whites and often mix up poverty, crime, and misogyny with blackness.

If you're intrigued by the drama, the contradictions, the relationships, the complexity, you can see why your son would be also. Lil Wayne was popular not only with the high school boys in our survey, but he was also the favorite of preteens and middle schoolers. This is what those who market hip-hop and rap do so well—they sell the same artist in different ways to different audiences. The November 2008 issue of *Word Up!*, an entertainment magazine for younger teens who love hip-hop, devotes almost the entire issue to Lil Wayne. Not only are references to drugs long gone here, so is the hip-hop vernacular that gave the *XXL* interview a certain "street cred"— no clipped words, no "fuckin'" this and "I'm in this bitch" that, not even an "ain't." This issue asks if Lil Wayne is "changing his tough-guy image," invokes "clean-cut all-American boy" Michael Phelps to show that everyone loves Weezy, and assures the reader that "he's a genuinely nice and very real guy," "tough but tender!" We hear about his film, *Hurricane Season* ("Wayne has been thrilled to make friends in all aspects of show business"), his donations to Katrina relief and his dedication to his hometown of New Orleans, his new champagne and clothing lines, his Fashion Rocks performance at Radio City, his large entourage of stylists and the assistants he needs, even though he's an "every day guy," and how he's "the perfect mix of good humor, talent, and honest lyrics!" (They must think parents will read the magazine and not listen to the music.)

You have to do your homework if you want to talk with your son about hip-hop and rap. This means you have to listen to what he listens to. Go online and download the music and the lyrics, but remember, the story is not always or only in the lyrics, and a rapper's life is rarely transparent. You'll need to dig a little deeper, read a few articles about his favorite artist, check out the artist's personal and musical story on Wikipedia, go on the artist's MySpace page (Lil Wayne's is YoungMoneyEnt). Once you've done your homework, there are plenty of things to talk about with your son.

MONEY AIN'T A THANG, IT'S EVERYTHANG

Materialism garners a certain level of coolness and respect in hip-hop culture. In music and music videos rappers flaunt their money, cars, and jewelry. The more merchandise a rapper has, the cooler he is, the more respect he gains, and the more power he has. In their song "Money Ain't a Thang," Jay-Z and Jermaine Dupri rap: "In the Ferrari or Jaguar switchin' four lanes, with the top down screamin' out money aint a thang." In "Whatever You Like," T.I. showers his girl with cars, diamonds, and money:

> *Want it you could get it my dear*
> *Five million dollar home, drop Bentley's I swear*

If the lyrics aren't clear enough, in the videos the rappers are throwing their money around, driving expensive cars, and flashing jewelry. And always, always there are lots of hot girls sipping champagne, lounging by the pool, or just hanging around.

These images would all be absurd if they didn't come with pretty important backstories about rising out of poverty and racism to claim the American dream. Rap, especially the gangsta version, is about living a history of violence, experiencing the murder of friends, surviving drive-bys, starting with nothing, successfully playing the system—and of course rapping about it well. The story about any given rapper—whether true or embellished, and, again, it's usually a lot of both—not only gives him credibility, but also allows for transformation and redemption that feels like a superhero story for boys. A player (in the nonsexual sense) is someone who utilizes a game to his advantage, and fashion icons like P. Diddy have played fashion fully, as we talked about in chapter 1, What Boys Wear, bringing gangsta styles and images into fashion, transforming the marginality of ethnic into mainstream American. There's something truly ingenious here. At the same time there's something not right about "playing," especially when it suggests a lack of responsibility for past violence or when it involves the commercialization of something painfully difficult for so many, as when rappers show off their wealth in the midst of abject poverty, or sexualize women when they owe their success to dedicated mothers, sisters, and girl friends. These contradictions are ripe for discussion.

YOU'RE NOBODY UNTIL SOMEBODY KILLS YOU

Another topic for discussion should be the tough in-your-face, don't-mess-with-me attitude associated with gangsta rap, which offers language about manhood that, as Marlene Kim Connor says in her book *What Is Cool? Understanding Black Manhood in America,* can lead to violence. When Eminem rapped in his first single, "Just Don't Give a Fuck!," the rage beneath it came through: "So when you see me on your block with two Glocks/Screamin' Fuck the world like Tupac/I just don't give a fuck!"

Rap can also offer a story about revenge and survival, as with 50 Cent's song "Many Men," about his experience of surviving attempted murder: "better watch how you talk, when you talk about me/'cause, I'll come and take your life away." In their videos and on their CD covers, it's common for rappers to carry knives and guns as a form of protection and warning. In his documentary, *Hip Hop: Beyond Beats and Rhymes,* Byron Hurt underscores how rappers Tupac and 50 Cent are idolized because they both survived attempted murders and multiple gunshot wounds. The Notorious B.I.G., arguably the most respected and lyrical rapper, was murdered in a drive-by shooting. It seems to be true, as Biggie himself rapped, that "You're Nobody Till Somebody Kills You." And in these videos, there's certainly a choice of gangstas to identify with—the street gangster (with a 40 of malt liquor) or a champagne-drinking, sophisticated gangster, but never a schoolteacher or scientist.

It's important not to dismiss the desire boys have for power and respect and the attraction they feel to these images. In boy culture, as in hip-hop culture, reputation and image are seriously important, and boys who identify with these gangsta rappers find a way to talk back to the system, to vent anger and frustration, and also to connect with other guys in a "bros before hoes" bonding. The posturing and violence need to be addressed directly and talked about in very plain terms. It's also important for teen boys to appreciate how these images are constructed and how much that "authenticity" connected to violence is fabricated to keep rappers fresh and in the headlines. It doesn't mean his favorite rapper isn't talented, but he's part of a commercial world that ties popularity to authenticity and authenticity to street violence and sexualized women. The things 50 Cent raps about and the choices he makes are heavily influenced by what sells. That means "keepin' it real" isn't always based on reality and, ironically, doesn't always reflect what's real.

SUPERMAN DAT HO: SEXUAL DEGRADATION IN THE HOOD

Many younger boys will rap away, missing the meanings of lyrics. How many preteen boys (and girls) sang "Lollipop" by Lil Wyane with no idea that he's rapping about oral sex? How many middle school boys sing along with Soulja Boy's "Crank Dat" and never know what it really meant to "superman dat ho?" (You can check *Urban Dictionary* if you're not sure either.) Well, they no doubt understand the ho part; some hear that word pretty much every day in school.

But lots of teenage boys hear all the words pretty clearly and understand their meaning, and there's evidence to suggest that the sexualized lyrics and images in rap music have a lasting effect. Research shows that exposure to sexualized rap videos fosters negative perceptions of African American women in particular, and exposure to rap videos that contain images of women in degrading and subordinate roles leads to a greater acceptance of teen dating violence. Moreover, frequent television viewing and exposure to pop music leads to a greater acceptance of sexual harassment. One study, published in *Archives of Pediatric and Adolescent Medicine*, found that teens exposed to sexually degrading lyrics (not simply lyrics about sex—an important distinction) were almost twice as likely to start engaging in intercourse or other sexual activities within the following two years as were teens who listened to little or no sexually degrading music. This is an important study, because the researchers were able to follow children over time to determine what they listened to and then to document what behaviors they engaged in.

We know that many other styles of music offer lyrics that are degrading to women. Boys who love rap point out to us that there are rock and country music songs that are just as bad, and to be fair, most of these studies do tend to focus only on rap. So a conversation to have with your son might entail talking about why sexually degrading rap lyrics are so much more offensive to parents than similar lyrics in other genres.

RACISM AND THE BIGGEST COLORED SHOW ON EARTH

Parents from the generation that understood the music of the Black Power movement can see clearly that hip-hop has, as cultural theorist Jeffrey O. G. Ogbar, author of *Hip Hop Revolution: The Culture and Politics of Rap*, writes, "devolved into a mockery of itself . . . the Biggest Colored Show on Earth." Remind kids of the minstrel shows that were a part of our country's horrible history, shows in which white people in blackface stereotyped and lampooned black people as ignorant, lazy, buffoonish, and superstitious, in addition to musical.

Your son, if he enjoys rap, may actually be able to teach you a thing or two about racism and how it's talked about in that world. For example, rapper KRS-One has argued, according to Ogbar, that it's not the minstrel that's enacted but "the teacher" teaching "real facts" about life and the record industry, working against a white recording monopoly that's demanding hostile stereotypes. By real, KRS-One is not talking about bling and gangstas. Look for those lyrics that suggest defiance against the recording industry itself. They're out there. Ask your son to take a look at www.stop coonin.com, an organization of educators, artists, professionals, and activists who are concerned about the impact of negative portrayals of blacks in the media and the tendency for all people to internalize these inaccurate images. Or ask him about those who critique rap, like NYOIL, as Ogbar writes, who raps: "I've seen people on this drug. I've seen murders, death, theft, robbery, communities ravaged, beautiful families turned inside out behind money and this drug." Listen up, Lil Wayne.

ANOTHER KIND OF HOMEWORK

We know hip-hop has gone mainstream when Russell Simmons, P. Diddy, and Usher decorate a Martha Stewart Christmas tree in a 2006 TV ad for Macy's. P. Diddy has roots in gangsta rap (his possible connections with Tupac Shakur's murder have never been fully resolved), and Simmons, of course, was brokering deals and nurturing rappers from the beginning. They are survivors who've worked the system and played the game, remaking themselves into highly commercial fashion and music icons.

Hip-hop, however, has also spawned quite a few grassroots political movements your son should know about—the No More Prisons movement, voting campaigns, anti–police brutality. Rappers *can* be shrewd negotiators who work hard for their fame and for good causes. Look for those examples of rap artists, like Jay-Z, who give money to community projects.

There's plenty more to celebrate about hip-hop, and you can talk with your son about the influence of hip-hop on the wider culture, as well as on the culture of his school, where white kids and kids of color bond over music and fashion. You can also investigate and turn him on to a genre of artists known as MCs, who rhyme about love, hope, building better communities, and spirituality, issues that have long been at the center of African American culture. You might want to introduce your son to Common, a Chicago-based rapper who's worked with Kanye West and who's taken some heat for criticizing the direction commercialized rap has taken.

There's also hip-hop artist Nas, who takes on war, AIDS, and black-on-black violence in his verse. In "I Know I Can," the chorus sung by children, he raps, "I know I can/Be what I wanna be/If I work hard at it/ . . . I'll be where I wanna be." In his song "Get By," Talib Kweli, who was featured in Byron Hurt's film *Beyond Beats and Rhymes*, sings, "This morning, I woke up/Feeling brand new and I jumped up/Feeling my highs, and my lows/In my soul, and my goals." Joining Kanye West in his song "Classic," KRS-One raps, "This is the difference between MCing and rap/Rappers spit rhymes that are mostly illegal, MC's spit rhymes that uplift they people/Peace, love, unity, and havin' fun, these are the lyrics of KRS-One!"

The rapper Common predicts that hip-hop will change for the better as a result of the 2008 election. The former Black Eyed Peas front man, will.i.am agrees. In a January 19, 2009, *Time* magazine interview, he says, "Now that Obama's president it changes inner-city youths. They can now not just dream to be Lil Waynes or 50 Cents, but they can now dream to be Obamas."

Hip-hop is one of the most important media of this generation. Enjoy the beats and the brilliance of some of these guys, while wondering aloud about the spin and marketing machine that simultaneously creates the Lil Wayne in *XXL* and the Lil Wayne in *Word Up!* Our role as parents of teenagers is to broaden their perspectives, raise questions, and press for some integrity in this fragmented world. By its very nature adolescence is about a search for identity, so use your son's love of hip-hop and rap to help him think about what it means to bring together his outer image with his inner experiences and to think about how rap lyrics can raise us up or bring us and the communities we live in down.

I'm Still a Guy: Country Music

Country music appealed to some of the boys in our survey: Brad Paisley, Toby Keith, Rascal Flatts, the mix of bluegrass instruments with electric guitars and crossover artists like Kid Rock with a reckless urban edge, the longing for the old days of fishing, partying, and finding the right girl. As Kelefa Sanneh writes in the *New York Times*, "Country remains one of America's most vital commercial radio formats, driven by a singularly weird mix of teenagers and parents of teenagers, pop melodrama and old-school stoicism." Much like hip-hop in this way, country is a mix of loyalty to the past and a "need for glamour and novelty."

Country music is unabashedly pro-American and pro-guy and offers up to boys an image of a grown man (not a teenager, like so many other genres) they may like to become. This role model is often a gun-toting guy who wears Stetsons, cowboy boots, flannel shirts, or long black leather coats, who drives a pickup truck, calls the shots and also drinks them. He has a "save a horse, ride a cowboy" view of women, at least until he finds that beautiful girl next door and, if he doesn't drink too much and lose her, he'll work hard to be the kind of dad who remembers the kind of guy he was, has a daughter he adores, and warns the next country boy who comes along not to try the things he tried. The kind of man country music tells a boy he should look up to is one who'll set him straight but who's been there and done all that, kind of like the coaches we saw in sports movies.

For a while, country music's version of men and women seemed to be changing, maybe because of the likes of Faith Hill, Shania Twain, and the Dixie Chicks, among others, who softened or talked back to their men by singing the other side of the story: about cheating or abusive boyfriends getting their due, and about leaving rather than standing by your man if he's doing you wrong. Garth Brooks showed up as the emotional, wild, fun kind of family man who also had "friends in low places," and country singers started to cross-pollinate with pop music.

But then came 9/11 and the Iraq war. The Dixie Chicks spoke out against President Bush's decision to invade Iraq, and Toby Keith retaliated, separating the girls from the boys. Keith followed up with his unapologetically prowar anthem, "Courtesy of the Red, White and Blue (The Angry

American)": "You'll be sorry that you messed with the US of A/'Cuz we'll put a boot in your ass/It's the American way." The song hit number one on the country charts over the weekend of July 4, 2002. The lead singer of the Dixie Chicks, Natalie Maines, said the song was "ignorant, and it makes country music sound ignorant." Keith responded by displaying a doctored photo of Maines with Iraqi dictator Saddam Hussein as a backdrop at his concerts.

Since then, country music has become a lot more patriotic, and masculine, with Toby Keith leading the way. While the "she thinks my tractor's sexy" cowboy persona of the likes of Kenny Chesney and Brad Paisley remains a steady role model for boys, the military man has now become the subject of a number of ballads. The message of these songs, plain and simple: don't attack our troops; don't attack manhood.

The attraction of country is the simplicity—not just the hooks and melodies, but also the simple clarity of what it means to be a boy and a girl. Of the twenty-five number one country hits in 2008, only five were performed by women artists—specifically two young blondes: Carrie Underwood of *American Idol* fame, and nineteen-year-old Taylor Swift, both singing songs that make guys feel like guys, such as Underwood's "All-American Girl" and Swift's "Love Story." The other twenty number one hits are boys and men singing about being country boys and family men. Like professional sports or NASCAR, country music is primarily a male space. Sociologist Angela Stroud reported that 81 percent of the 175 top Hot Country Singles for *Billboard* from 2002 to 2004 were performed by male solo artists and described two familiar themes—men and women "are distinct and nearly opposite," and there are rules for what real boys and men *should* be and do.

Brad Paisley's "I'm Still a Guy," one of the most popular country songs as we write this book, has spent weeks atop the charts and gives life to the "men are men and women are women" message. Paisley sings songs that appeal to the old-style honky-tonk roots of country. His string of sweet and simple guy vs. girl hits have lyrics like this: "Well, love makes a man do some things he ain't proud of/And in a weak moment I might walk your sissy dog, hold your purse at the mall/But remember, I'm still a guy."

It's a message that embraces a "'boys will be boys' youthful masculinity," Stroud says. A guy may put up with a girl for the sake of love, but he's so out of there if given half a chance to go fishing, four wheeling, or drinking with his buddies. In country music boys get a big dose of the "I've got a pair" message. They also hear lyrics about behaving recklessly with the hopes of winning over girls and women, like in Dierks Bentley's "What Was I Thinking?"

about a guy who escapes from the police by driving through a cornfield; punches a much bigger guy in the face; and risks getting shot by a protective father. His music makes it seem like being a boy is all about screwing off, taking risks, and having impulsive, reckless fun.

But these messages are also mixed with a love and longing for a simple country life. Against a backdrop of riders flying through the air doing tricks on their dirt bikes, former *American Idol* finalist Bucky Covington sings, "When I lay down at night girl, give me your hand/I can take any hurt this world has to give/As long as I got you." When Kid Rock sings in "All Summer Long," "Splashing through the sand bar/Talking by the campfire/It's the simple things in life, like when and where" there's a wish to be carefree and in love. A pretty picture, unless you listen to some of the women of country singing about the men who beat them, who became drunkards, or who left them and their kids.

Country music tells boys what it means to be all-American—prom kings and queens, American flags and supporting the troops, Friday night football, driving your first car too fast, and kissing a girl under the stars. It's about having the time of your life. But country music also puts out videos of those like "Rough & Ready" by Trace Adkins, who in his sleeveless plaid shirt and beat-up ball cap drives his pickup, makes fun of the "pretty boys" in fancy cars, picks up his hot country girl in tight jeans and sings, "White T-shirt, Ain't afraid to work/Got a 'what-are-you-looking-at-asshole' smirk."

Country music combines a "badass" attitude with a hardworking stiff who's ready for a beer and a party because, as Alan Jackson sings, "It's four o'clock somewhere." But country music also tells stories about how life is and should be. There's responsibility a man needs to live up to, told through tear-jerking songs with tear-jerking images of true loves lost to disease and war. It tugs at something very real or at least real in a "this is what a family, a man, a woman, a good American life should be" kind of way. A real man does the right thing when it comes to work and family. He's a good father, husband, hard worker, and soldier. He's also romantic and vulnerable and afraid sometimes, although he shouldn't show it, especially to her. Country music gives these messages about how a man expresses longing, heartache, loss, and fear arguably better than any other music genre. In its plainspoken, simple truth-telling way, country can be more emo than emo.

Finally, there are some changes afoot—even country music has been influenced by this hype-beast media culture. A boy into country these days will find a version of pop music in groups like Rascal Flatts, a little R&B in the likes of Hootie & The Blowfish's Darius Rucker, and some rock and roll in Bon Jovi's crossover hits. But one of the most interesting developments in country music in recent years has been the emergence of the MuzikMafia, an eclectic group of musicians that founder (or "godfather" as the Muzic-Mafia calls him) John Rich of the duo Big & Rich describes on country radio station K-98.5 as "a bunch of oddballs, a circus of talent." The friends, who struggled in Nashville for years without much success, bonded together with the agreement that "if one made it, we'd shine a light on the others." It's a wildly loyal bunch that includes: Gretchen Wilson, of "Redneck Woman" fame; self-described "hick-hop" singer Cowboy Troy, who raps in three languages; R&B-influenced Damien Horne; entertainer Two Foot Fred; SWJ (Spoken Word Jen); visual artist Rachel Kice; and others. They call it "muzik without prejudice." It's what country music is all about, Rich explains: "always be open to the next idea."

The MuzicMafia Web site promotes the friends' videos, performances, and tours amid ads for Berkeley School of Music and causes like Nashville for Africa and Save Darfur: Stop the Genocide. Sure, some of the music is raunchy and falls into the same old stereotypes, but it's refreshing to see a collective within country music that crosses genres and boundaries to enact "the powerful idea of bringing a group of artists together, regardless of race, religion, background or muzikal genre."

As the working-man's music, country is also bound to be influenced by the economic crisis. As we send this book off to editing, John Rich's ballad "Shutting Down Detroit" is picking up steam. It's what country does best, tugging at heartstrings and tapping into a justified rage on behalf of working-men and workingwomen, in this case over losing their jobs and their homes in the wake of bank scandals and greedy CEOs. What better conversation—about manhood, vulnerability, and solidarity—could you initiate with your son than this?

From Raffi to Rap: Listen and Sing

What boys listen to and what they hear is every bit as important to them as the TV shows and movies they watch, and more important to most of them than the books they may (or may not) read. Be aware that even when a particular rapper or band puts out incredibly degrading lyrics or a hypermasculine approach in one song, they often turn around and put out something incredibly sweet in the next. Our theme of "the same old same old" with regard to boys' media holds less true in music, a genre that prizes experimentation. Music and lyrics are sometimes contradictory, and their messages can't always be pinned down. Although marketers promote a version of black masculinity to white boys that is stereotyped and offensive, many boys do adventure beyond the mainstream into alternative genres and artists, and into the history, politics, and discussions of what it means to be a man in this culture via "old school" music.

While Scholastic Book Club tells boys what to read, TV shouts at them nonstop, and action movies tell them who they can be and how fast and furious to act while becoming a hero, music seems to be an area where their choice is enhanced. Producers and marketers can't seem to keep up with the sharing and experimentation that new technology allows boys. Radio stations used to tell kids what to listen to (and even took money to do so, as in the payola scandal of 1959). Today boys can try something new in an instant by going online. This is the way to join with your son when you talk about music. Try to listen to what he's listening to and acknowledge the complexity of his choices. Download a song that he loves on your own iPod. If you don't like some of Phish's silly lyrics, think back to all the Raffi songs about beans trying on jeans and whatnot that you used to enjoy together. Then try to listen along to a fifteen-minute Phish jam and ask your son to talk about the musical changes (chords, tempi, mood) he's responding to. If you don't like a rap song your son is listening to, ask him if this rapper is connected in any way to the "old school" rap that was born of oppression. Talk about "real" vs. mass produced. If you hate the angst and volume, try to listen to the emotional message that underlies it. And, we're sorry to say— don't fight over what to listen to in the car! What better time do you have to hear his favorite music and have a real discussion about it?

As will.i.am said in that *Time* magazine interview, "Every piece of entertainment sends out messages to young people. . . . what's important is that parents educate their children to know the difference between entertainment and reality." Bottom line? Hang in there.

CHAPTER 5

Wanna Play? What Boys Do

If visitors from another planet landed in the boys' section of Toys "R" Us, they would assume the inhabitants of our world are obsessed with action, speed, risk taking, winning, and violence. They'd look at the rows of WWE action figures and guess that we run on some energy called "adrenaline" and are disciplined to obey via something called a good "smackdown." They'd see how much cars and trucks mean to us and how fast we must drive them. They might appreciate our love of science but also wonder why we're obsessed with stinky, gooey things. They might conclude that we are skilled at building complex structures from small parts, but where, they might wonder, do we live? Ours would seem to be a planet of superheroes and soldiers, but if we are so good at rescuing, protecting, and defending, where's the rest of the world worth fighting for? Where are the families? How do children grow? What do people eat? Who feeds them? How do families work? Who cares for us when we're sick and injured? Why is the world so dark and gloomy? Why is everyone so angry? They might think, quite mistakenly, that the world they've landed on is inhospitable and uninhabitable.

In this chapter, we explore how media and marketers package and sell toys, games, and activities to boys and how they so successfully present "choices" that reassert old stereotypes of masculinity. While the Toys "R" Us girl aisles are equally stereotypical, at least there are competing messages in the real world that encourage girls to question, to venture forth, to dare to explore the other side of the store. Not so for boys. Fear and anxiety keep them firmly in the boys' aisle, and marketers take full advantage of this, selling boys (and their parents) anxiety about not being the right kind of boy—not powerful, strong, athletic, or aggressive enough.

The differences in the ways marketers and media package girl and boy activities are telling. Girls are packaged in ways that accentuate caretaking or, more likely these days, their appearance and, increasingly, their sexuality. For boys it's different. They are packaged as powerful people—with power to build, fight, save, and protect. They're told repeatedly that the world is theirs to control, to take charge of. *You* have the power, slogans exclaim. It's a message designed to exhilarate, make a boy feel on top of the world, remind him repeatedly that he's the best, that dominating and winning are what boys can and should expect to do. This is the privilege offered boys.

There's no doubt that images of boys and men monopolize media; for example, they're the focus of 95 percent of sports programming. Also, the majority of characters in films, TV shows, comic books, books, and video games are boys or men. It's called a Game *Boy* for a reason. However, as we've said before, quantity doesn't equal quality, and there's more often than not a downside to all this presumed male power and control. Participation in sports is associated with more violent and delinquent activities in boys. Video games like *World of Warcraft* and *Grand Theft Auto* offer boys messages about violence and control that parents are justifiably worried about. From day one boys are taught the importance of cars and learning to drive, but no parent wants their son to mimic the speed and wild stunts shown in the media. As they get older, the stereotypical "hot babes" are not the kinds of girls we want them to date, nor does flaunting these trophies represent the kind of relationships we want them to have, and the love we want them to find.

We consider the impact media and marketers have on a boy's-eye view of playing, gaming, driving, sex, and other extracurriculars. We stroll through big box department stores and look at what boys are encouraged to play with. We look for the characteristics and qualities that are associated with boys in the toys, games, and activities they (and marketers) choose, and we consider how the available choices constrain your son and limit his options.

Put the Pedal to the Metal: Greeting Cards for Little Boys

You've survived another year.
Some skids, some scrapes, some near escapes
But still you made it through.
Some hope the coming year will be
A winning one for you!

—NASCAR birthday card

What better way to explore what's all-boy than to look at the cards he might get on his fifth birthday telling him how to celebrate. While girl cards are covered with mermaids, fairies, princesses, Barbies wishin', hopin', and dreamin', pop stars shakin,' and everyone "sparkled in magic," boys cards are all about action, whether it's NASCAR- and Hot Wheels–inspired ("run it, rev it, floor it . . . peel out, drive fast, awesome birthday blast!") or about NFL football ("time to tackle some cake!") and Major League Baseball ("hope your birthday is a grand slam good time"), or they're superhero-motivated ("action-packed wishes for you!"). In every way, shape, and form—through images, words, even activities and music—boys are told they are the "best"— the fastest, coolest, bravest, strongest, sometimes the smartest, but always the "winners."

Cards tell both boys and girls they should have fun, fun, fun on their birthdays; boys are given "boy ways" and girls "girl ways" to do so. In the musical variety of cards, boys hear the Darth Vadar theme song, NASCAR engines, and those four organ notes that play faster and faster at MLB games and are designed to rev up the crowd. While girls on cards look pretty, on one boy's card there's a cartoon character that burps in your face. Boys are invited to act *on* the cards—fold out a superhero into a fierce pose, spin a Shrek joke wheel ("What do you smell if Shrek hasn't bathed in a while? A foul ogre."). There's dynamite, and monkeys "gone bananas," a twenty-six-legged creature with furry eyeballs, a racing car that takes off with a "thunderous roar." There's sports, sports, and more sports. Boys' cards abound with words and images about the fun, competitive, winning side of soccer, baseball, football, basketball, skateboarding, and car racing. Getting down and dirty is part of the game and especially fun, as muddy handprints on the front of one card remind us. Cards tell boys they're expected to compete and become "super-boy," "champ," "winner," and "all-star." They are supposed to "dominate" in all areas, including "cyber domination." They should "push [their] limits" and be the "best" and make others "envy" them.

This pressure extends to valentines, which are virile beyond belief. Whether he picks up some Transformer, Superhero, Chub City, or Spider-Man cards, he'll be told that Valentine's Day is a day to rock!!! Boys are presumed to go "Ewwwww" at anything romantic, which is fine; pushing romance onto first graders is inappropriate. So when the Transformer card producers are looking through the possible messages to print, there will be a couple of reasons why "Your love has transformed me" won't cut it.

But we're struck at just how action-packed valentines cards are. *Pirates of the Caribbean* cards say "Have an adventurous Valentine's Day," but the cards also could have said "Shiver me timbers, you're a great Valentine" or "Ahoy, mate. Let's be Valentines." Instead it's all about adventure. The only low-key wish we found was on a Chub City card where one of the kids expresses "Have a chillin' Valentine's Day, friend!" and the picture shows him and his multiethnic buddies hanging out on a couch. Sweet, but as the only set of valentines featuring kids of color, perhaps a tad too close to hangin' out on the street corner.

Of course there are many of the typical over-the-top messages that scream boyhood. Valentine's Day can't just be sweet and fun. How boring! It's always "out of this world," "spectacular," or "smashing" (says a villain on a Spider-Man card who looks ready to smash his valentine). Valentine's Day has to be "legendary" as one *Pirates* card expresses. Another card says the boy who receives it is "going to the extreme" and "[his] awesomeness is out of control." Yet another card with an alien theme tells the boy to sample "megatons of sweets." Some of the valentines we looked over were downright scary. "I've been looking for you" one police car Transformer card says, dark and shiny, with nary a heart or flower. "Happy Valentine's Day, Bud" one Chub City card expresses, and while the message is just fine with us, the cool dude on it is showing his fists to the reader, lest the reader think he actually likes him. And since when did Valentine's Day become a competitive sport? "I am the greatest Valentine in the universe!" says one Transformer on his card. Another, "I will prove that I am the best Valentine!" Do they have WWE cards with wrestlers promising to crush and maim each other too?

Both birthday cards and Valentine's Day cards send messages about what boys are supposed to do. They're conversation starters and as such can help you talk to him about his own interests and uniqueness as well as his feelings of warmth, kindness, and sweetness, all of which may rarely be shown to him in cards, even when someone has shelled out $3.50.

Planes, Trains, Automobiles . . . and Guns: Boys' Toys

Knowing that we teach about gender and the media, at least once a year colleagues—very well-educated, informed, and intelligent people—will tell us that they are surprised to see their little girl run straight to the baby dolls or their little boy scream with delight at the sight of dump trucks. Really? Why wouldn't children react this way? In spite of our best efforts to offer children choices, they see how the world is gender coded. We've seen it in the cards they receive. We've seen it on their little T-shirts and Onesies. In the movies they watch. It's a message they get almost everywhere, and it's consistent. But it's also good to be reminded that there are exceptions. Sharon remembers fondly how her son used to love to push trucks around in a doll carriage in day care, and the kitchen was his favorite nursery school play station. Lyn and Mark's daughter loved dolls well enough, but she also had a fascination with marble runs and building sets. Children are complex little creatures.

Marketers know this about children, and so they don't start enforcing strict gender codes until after about age three. Toys sold to children under three are educational and, other than the incessant need to pinkify anything female, often gender neutral. Boys are offered up cuddly puppies, toys that play songs, farm animals, Play and Spins, and colorful rings to stack. We know that it's okay for boys to play with these toys because boys are pictured on the packaging. Predictably, they're featured on the packaging for trucks, tools, and "easy dunk" basketball hoops too, but you can also clearly see them on toys like the PlaySkool Dance Cam and the Amazing Color Copier, as well as in commercials on TV for these products. There they are— pushing musical shopping carts, seated in their Song and Story Learning Chairs, and coloring earnestly at PlaySkool desks. They are even pictured playing with girls!

Sure, some gender stereotyping still exists in the early years. There are lots of guy figures that come as part of the toys they're encouraged to play with; lots of little plastic men to identify with. These are often the usual suspects—men driving wacky cars, piloting planes, and rescuing whales (well, maybe rescuing whales is not so common, but the act of rescuing is). For parents who may be inadvertently pushing boys to be "real men" early, Fisher-Price offers them traditional fare like Roberto and His Loader, Michael and his Rescue Rig, and Eddie and his Boulder Worksite. For those parents anxious to have their sons model themselves after WWE wrestlers at the tender age of two, Fisher-Price brings them Tuff Rumblin' Guys, who work front loaders and dump trucks and have frighteningly steroidal physiques. That may be yucky, but our point is, it's hard to care or worry too much about the few steroidal Tuff Rumblers when boys from birth to three years old have a whole world of choices, from Roberto to a Fur Real Friend!

After age three, however, their world sadly narrows to exclude songs, dolls, kitchens, and shopping. Even art seems forbidden to boys, as Roberto, Michael, and Eddie lead the way into Boyworld. In a recent trip down the Toys "R" Us gender-coded aisles, we didn't see a single package for a doll, a cooking set, a kitchen, or a shopping cart that featured a boy in addition to a girl. It's clear that routine family activities are for girls, when even the "pizza party" and "cupcake party" kits don't show little boys. Don't boys like pizza and cupcakes? We guess not, if they have to make them themselves.

Boys' toy world narrows to planes, trains (but just a few), and automobiles. Nothing's wrong with planes, trains, and automobiles. As kids play with vehicles their vision expands beyond their homes and they imagine themselves in cities, countries, and even galaxies. As they work out traffic congestion and plan trips around the house and yard they learn visual spatial relationships and develop creativity. But we have two questions: (1) Why are these the ONLY toys for boys? and (2) Why do so many of these simple toys transform into fighting, blasting, and exploding toys? Why do they have to *be* guns?

Let's not forget building kits, which are great toys for kids, but they are marketed specifically to boys. LEGOs, Lincoln Logs, Erector sets, and blocks—all kids should have these. Building sets of late, however, are, in essence, either gun or transportation sets. After the LEGO sets for ages two to five years, which include fire trucks, gas trucks, Thomas the Tank Engine, and police cars, LEGO sets for older boys ask them to help create Fierce Creatures, Troll Battle Wheels, and a Tower Raid. Mars Mission sets don't feature explorers or science equipment but fighting vehicles like the MT-61 Crystal Reaper. Aqua RAIDERS! Star WARS! Bionicles ready for a "TOA undersea ATTACK!" When did LEGOs get so aggressive? And there are spies, racers, and city scenes. Cities? For LEGO, *city* means boats, trains, and helicopters—not pet stores, bakeries, houses, skyscrapers, and parks.

It's sad that boys who love to build are encouraged to use all the raw LEGO material to build the same old stuff—planes, trucks, automobiles, and buildings. It's unfortunate too that many of the vehicles are just weapons on wheels. There are plenty of boys who will play Parcheesi rather than Rhino Rampage and beg parents for an Easy-Bake Oven, but they simply aren't represented. This lack of representation impacts boys in one of two ways: (1) when they make those choices for themselves they are embarrassed or don't think of themselves as "real" boys, or (2) over time they are encouraged to transform themselves into mutant-Transformer-Bionicle boys who love all weapons, all massive machines, and all explosions, and nothing else.

We're not against guns, per se. Gerard Jones writes, in *Killing Monsters*, that gun play in childhood is universal in cultures where firearms exist. Children develop fantasies of their destructive power, he argues, and guns symbolize this wish. He also makes the argument that the guns kids play with today are more fantasy-based and not as real-looking as say the pistols boys played with in the 1960s. But take a look at the guns these days and imagine the fantasy that goes with them!

We agree that children need toys to help them express and work out all their feelings, rage included! Some kids will be drawn to act out violent fantasies with action figures or guns or other kinds of play, which does not imply that they will become adult killers. It very well could be a way to express imagination and creativity, to become a person more at peace with his own fantasies or fears of destruction and anger.

What happens, though, when a whole generation of boys have fantasies of violence imposed on them? When they're told that this is what boys love to do, what boys need to work on? When they're given detailed story lines based on PG-13 movies? Guns per se aren't the problem. The problem is when other kinds of toys are excluded, or when guns become a part of so many toys for boys.

For example, what the heck happened to Nerf? Wasn't Nerf supposed to be the soft alternative to toy guns? Last we checked, you could pop orange foam balls in the air and catch them in rugbylike rackets. Nope. Not anymore. Couldn't find those. Nerf is, however, ominously still present in toy stores throughout the United States. There is the Nerf N-Strike Tech Target, the N-Strike Rapid Fire AS-20 (machine gun–type blaster), a gun called the Buzzsaw, another called the Hornet AS-6. There is the Attack Unit, the Recon CS-6, Firefly REV-8, and 2008 election favorite, we guess, the Maverick. These were gunlike contraptions with soft orange bulletlike projectiles that emerge in groups, somewhat akin, we conjecture, to semiautomatics. Not "dangerous," per se . . . but "lethal."

With Nerf gone violent, what could we expect from toy vehicles? What do the following Hot Wheels sets suggest?

T-Rex Rampage "Destroy an entire city" Ages 4+

Shark Park "It's crunch time." Ages 4+

Volcano Shoot-Out "Defeat the evil volcano." Ages 5+

It suggests to us that Hot Wheels thinks boys not only like cars, but that they like cars that can be used as weapons.

Killing isn't everything. Those that don't shoot and destroy can always race. The Fireball Raceway with nine (two or three aren't enough, you loser!) high-speed crash zones has an "exploding" meteor core. We thought the object of the raceway was to make it through to the end of the loop de loop! Matchbox fares better with a shuttle mission, haunted house, and garage adventure. But as the cars get larger, so does the aggression. Remote-control cars have Morphing Missile Launchers and are called things like

Mutator. Car sets often feature police chase scenes. Big trucks like Tonka and Cat still look solid and inviting, but their packagers can't resist calling them "massive machines," all sixteen inches of them. And just in case there's any doubt about who should be playing with these toys, Hasbro has their Tonka trucks clearly labeled: "Built for Boyhood."

Trains are a parent's best bet. Somehow, thankfully, they haven't been transformed to evoke much violence. No exploding locomotive or ten-car super smashup (not yet at least). Starting from Thomas the Tank Engine and moving on to larger Lincoln Logs "Ready to Run" train sets, these seem tame by comparison. There's the cobranding we see all over toy products, as in the Hogwarts Express and the Polar Express sets. But both of these represent great books that boys might have read or will read. And the Polar Express sweetly boasts that it comes "with Santa's bell." Trains are still about transportation . . . and imagination.

Planes? Not so much. One stands out from the rest. The Air Hogs Blue Sky, which is "Enviro Friendly" and shouts "Just pump it up!" on the package. But it's unlikely to last long in a sky filled with Havoc Heli, Havoc Cyclone, Hyper, Viper, Sky Hornet, Air Raptor, Twin Thunder, and a squadron of other fighter planes. The pump up is going down!

Toys are not only for fantasy life. They prepare kids for adulthood by introducing a fantasy version of the grown-up toys and gadgets they'll covet later. The gadgets with tech-sounding names that encourage boys to believe that some toys are super awesome prepare them to purchase big boy and grown men toys that are packaged the same way. Little about this play prepares them for the houses they'll live in, the suppers they'll cook, and the children they'll take care of—unless these tasks all involve explosions, attacks, and battles. Of course, we hope for their sake and for their future families' that they don't.

Super Strong, Super Cool: Action Figures

"Action figures" are synonymous with "boys' toys"—at least for boys between the ages of three and eight. After age eight, says *Toy Directory*, a toy industry Web site, marketers commonly assume that boys begin to lose interest in toys like action figures and turn instead to electronics, like computers and video games. So we visited our local Wal-Mart to look at the new toy offerings for boys. The first thing we noticed was that "action figures" have their own dedicated aisle in the toy section, filled with black, blue, red, and green packages of plastic figurines in the form of popular characters from movies, television shows, and video games.

Remember G.I. Joe? The first action figure, introduced by Hasbro in 1964, G.I. Joe was an eleven-and-a-half-inch-tall plastic solider, sailor, or marine targeted at boys. He had moveable body parts and changeable uniforms and weapons. When his clothes were off one could see that his physique, while muscular and toned, was relatively average.

Today, however, G.I. Joe's presence in the action figures aisle is almost nonexistent, even though he's now a muscled-up guy with huge weaponry. His only hope is to star in his own TV show, video game, and movie because contemporary action figures are now marketing tie-ins to shows and films rather than stand-alone toys that encourage boys to develop their own story lines for playtime. He's done the TV show and the video games, and as we write, *G.I. Joe: The Rise of Cobra* is on the horizon. But a look at the trailer tells us that, like the Transformer movies, it isn't something five- and six-year-old boys should go to. You can bet, however, that the movie will be advertised incessantly between their favorite Saturday morning cartoons.

So it's no wonder, after comic books, cartoons, and three blockbuster films with high-profile young actors, Spider-Man is the most ubiquitous action figure of all as we write. Almost half an aisle top to bottom displayed blue, red, and black packages of Spider-Man and his friends and enemies from the *Spider-Man 3* PG-13 film (all marked ages 4+). Most are only about six inches tall or so. The various Spider-Men (all in their red and blue spandex costumes) have different powers or characteristics—ranging from Super Punch Action! to Super Stretch Web! to Multiple Spinning Webs! to Four Web Projectiles! There's also a Peter Parker Quick Change Spider-Man. Spider-Man's enemies include the Sandman, the Goblin (with Disk Attack!), and Dr. Octopus (with Grabbing Tentacle Attack!). For the slightly younger set, there's a Superhero Spider-Man and Friends collection (designed after the cartoon show rather than the most recent movie)—Hang Glider Spider-Man, Firefighter Spider-Man, and Deep Sea Spider-Man. He can do anything! If a little boy wants to be part of the action, in the same aisle as the action figures there's a two-piece Spider-Man Costume, Spider-Man mask, and other assorted Spider-Man accessories (including actual web-spinning contraptions that kids can strap on to their wrists).

Finally, as if all this Spider-Mania isn't enough, across the aisle from the Spider-Man action figures we found a singing Spider-Man plush toy, a soft caricature of Spider-Man with a big head and little arms and legs. Squeeze one hand and he sings "Itsy Bitsy Spider." Squeeze the other hand and he sings the Spider-Man theme song. It's enough to make our spider senses tingle. Some clever marketer has found a way to forever connect a beloved nursery rhyme and game to the lucrative Spider-Man franchise. They call it "cradle to grave brand loyalty." Critics call it highjacking childhood.

But perhaps the appeal of Spider-Man goes deeper for boys, the messages resonating with something closer to home. There's the heroic dimension, yes—it's cool to be a hero, to do what's right, to defeat the bad guys, to save the day. There's the obvious appeal of the radioactive spider bite and its effects—the thrill of climbing walls and spinning webs and swinging through the streets of the city. But as a little boy gets older, the real appeal will have more to do with the Peter Parker-to-Spider-Man transformation. It's the kind of guy Peter is—an average, even nerdy, teenage boy who cares for an elderly aunt and loves a girl out of his league, a boy whose power and motivation catches him by surprise. Peter, who sews his own costume and designs his own web shooters, is the unlikely everyday hero, the underdog given his chance to show the world what he can do. Of course, little boys who play with action heroes may not know all this about Peter Parker, but they do know that it's not just the "superhuman" physical power they like; it's also the power and potential for a real boy to "save the day."

The other action figures that are impossible to miss in the toy aisles of Wal-Mart, Kmart, Target, and Toys "R" Us these days originate from WWE. These are figures (slightly larger than Spider-Man) that represent real-life stars from those various WWE shows and events we wrote about in chapter 2. Boys don't have to have seen WWE to get the basic premise, and parents can't miss the blatant marketing of uncontrollable violence. Packaged in black, silver, and gold, they are categorized by labels like "Ruthless Aggression," "Adrenaline," "Impact!," and "Classic WWE Stars." All of the figures appear shirtless, most with tiny wrestling briefs. Their bodies (dwarfing Spider-Man's relatively normal frame) are grossly out of proportion—chests, arms, necks, thighs are abnormally pumped and cartoonishly exaggerated. While the real WWE wrestlers certainly don't look like normal men, but have bulked themselves with weight training and possibly steroids, these figures wildly exaggerate those exaggerated physiques even more.

But what really strikes us about these action figures is the appeal to emotional hardness and invulnerability. The expressions on their plastic faces are so angry, aggressive, and threatening—particularly so for the few figures that represent men of color. The message for boys who are watching and buying is that the only stance is an offensive one—the only emotion is rage, the only response is aggression. The image these fighters project to little ones is "don't mess with me or you'll be sorry!"

If WWE is all about competition, winning, and taunting the weak, boys need the full setup to practice their bullying. To oblige, there's a replica of the golden championship belt that wrestlers vie for on various shows and a model of a wrestling ring in which action figures can perform. Adults know it's a pumped-up orchestrated farce. Boys who are too young to distinguish fantasy from reality, don't. They believe in the power and pain, the competition with one's rivals, the humiliation of one's victims. Playing John Cena or Battista doesn't invite talking to each other or sharing stories, taking care of or protecting other adults or children, journeys of discovery or heroic deeds—just adrenaline rushes that catapult the biggest and most aggressive into the winner's circle.

Like Spider-Man, these action figures are primarily marketing tools. Although we know some little boys who watch WWE with fathers or older brothers, most boys younger than age ten aren't watching Friday night *SmackDown*. So for them, WWE action figures serve as one big commercial, developing their awareness and piquing their interest in the real thing. And that's enough—whether it's the show or just the action figures, related toys, and games, boys get the message that aggression and violence are the avenues to power they will have as they get older.

What about those boys who aren't particularly engaged by superhero narratives or ultimate combat games? What about those with parents who outright reject the militarism of G.I. Joes? For those boys, and there are millions of them, contemporary action figures don't have much to offer. Are marketers and manufacturers too busy hawking and hyping the latest films to develop action toys for boys that appeal to a wider range of interests and emotions?

Fisher-Price introduced their Rescue Heroes action figure line in 1998, and the popularity of these heroes soared to new heights after 9/11. At least Rescue Heroes represent real-life men (and women)—they are paramedics, firefighters, construction crew members, police officers, even wildlife workers. No super strength, no over-the-top aggression, these toys represent all the hard, good work of so many unsung heroes.

Unfortunately, the same old stereotypes of what a hero is apply to these action figures too. Of the sixty-two Rescue Heroes listed on the Fisher-Price Web site, only three are women. The men have active, heroic, clever names like Rip Rockefeller, Matt Medic, Captain Cuffs, Billy Blazes, Perry Chute, Cliff Hanger, and Gil Gripper. The women have mundane, descriptive names like Wendy Waves and Maureen Biologist (hardly a celebration of the real women heroes who rescued others on 9/11). The men's boxes have pop-up advertisements with exclamations such as, "With real digging action," "Now with Rescue Pliers!," "With Ejectable Handcuffs!" and "Extendable Fire Hose!" The men are heavily muscled ("ripped") and broad-shouldered with strong square jaws and oversize hands and feet. Some wear dark sunglasses that obscure their eyes. None are smiling. The women have hourglass figures with small waists and large breasts; they all have abnormally small heads, pretty faces, and smiling lipsticked mouths. How do they rescue anything with those rail-thin arms and belly-button-revealing clothes? Affirmative action for women may have kicked in at the rescue hero fire station and construction site, but the real work of rescuing, little boys are reminded, is for men.

A DIFFERENT KIND OF HERO

Parents sick and tired of the rough-and-tough fantasy world of most action figures can go for the ultimate superhero: Jesus! In the summer of 2007, Wal-Mart announced that it would test sales of biblical action figures whose makers, one2believe, say are aimed at Christian parents who want an alternative to all those toys and action figures that "glorify evil, destruction, and promiscuity." The toys, based on biblical stories, include a three-inch figure of Daniel in the lion's den, a twelve-inch talking Jesus doll, and a thirteen-inch Samson action figure. Six months later, the Minneapolis *StarTribune* tells us that "Jesus is selling out."

You bet he is. Are proceeds for Jesus dolls going to Christian charities or just lining one2believe's corporate pockets? Are the Chinese workers who make the dolls making a living wage? What part of the story isn't being told? You can buy Mary, the mother of God, but of course there's no adoring Mary Magdalene. You can buy Samson, but no Delilah and her sharp accessory. How can we believe for a minute that this is about offering up peace and love in an overly aggressive and violent toy sales climate when the Spirit Warrior action figures are built like WWE action figures and sold to boys in the most graphically violent ways. Take the Web site description of Spirit Warrior Samson, for example, with huge muscles bulging and fists held high in fighter pose:

> Samson was one of the strongest men who ever lived. . . . he killed 30 men in one night without any weapons; and he even used the jawbone of a donkey to single-handedly defeat one thousand men!

Then there's Spirit Warrior Goliath, huge and menacing, teeth and fists clenched. Boys learn he "was a giant Philistine warrior. Standing over 9 feet tall, he towered over all of his enemies! Because of his great size and strength, he became one of the most important soldiers in the Philistine army." What spirit exactly is Goliath a warrior for? Where's David? What's really being sold here? (We're surprised they didn't go so far as to create a sexy Jezebel to give the Bratz girls a run for their money.) Pandering to the same aggressive pumped-up stereotypes they say they're marketing against makes this marketing campaign onenot2believe.

Extreme Performance! Even on Training Wheels

Teaching your son to ride a bike for the first time is one of those unforgettable parenting moments. Running alongside his wobbly handlebars, holding on to the seat, experiencing that split second when you feel him catch his balance and pick up speed, and you know it's time to let go; you slow to a jog, and watch him fly down the sidewalk. It's symbolic of all those letting gos ahead—practice for the first day of school, the first bus ride, the first school dance, college!

But long before he can master a bike or even a big wheels, he can drive a car. Yes, a car; and not just any car, a motorized boys' car. In the face of a wide-open world of possibilities, it's ironic that manufacturers and marketers would limit his options so early. There are the pink Barbie-esque vehicles and there are the Urban X Street Monsters—nary a wheel in between. It would be an unusual parent of a son who would encourage him to choose the shocking pink Dazzler over the black and blue Fast Lane or the "Green Machine with 180° spin technology." At least if he chooses the fire truck with siren sounds and emergency lights he can imagine that his speed is in the service of a good deed, or if he loves the John Deere tractors with carts, he can take farm animal toys on a hayride! The rest are full of action-packed BMX-style something or other with pneumatic wheels and purportedly high-tech accessories.

Funny, if we're led to believe that all this action, speed, and technology are what it takes to make a three-year-old boy go "Yippeee," why is the little boy on the box of the Happy Songs Coupe the one who looks the happiest? The faces of the little boys riding many of the other "machines" are aggressive, as if they're saying "grrrrrrrrr," with teeth showing. Some boys are just serious. Driving, even at age three, we're led to believe, is serious business.

It ought to be, given the selection of motorized vehicles little boys can choose from. They tell a story of boyhood that rolls over and demolishes the Happy Songs Coupes of the world. Many of these motorized vehicles mimic grown-up wheels, for example the Arctic Cat and the Harley-Davidson, as well as sports cars and Hummers. There isn't a minivan or station wagon in the bunch. Nor is there a little VW Beetle or, heaven forbid, a hybrid! (We know, we know, none of them actually run on gas. But why couldn't their overhyped boasts of technology put in a plug for "clean" running?)

The colors tell us boys are bold—The Arctic Cat is fluorescent green, the Harley red, the race cars red or black, and the Vtwin 750 Kawasaki comes in fluorescent green or army camouflage. There's some kind of KFX "ninja" power wheels (like the ubiquitous princess in girls' toys, ninjas pop up in the strangest places), and a T. Rex version. The KFX features "aggressive, oversized tires, color-detailed shock covers and an updated 'real' handlebar configuration (including a battery charge indicator), as well as updated colors and graphics." Color? Graphics? Sounds like they're selling a computer game.

On this day at Toys "R" Us, the Barbie cars were parked in between the T. Rexs and the KFXs, as if to stop a fight, or at least to slow down the one-sided adrenaline rush. Toy motorized Cadillacs also come in Barbie or black. The black version looked like a pimpmobile, and it's not just any ol' Cadillac but the gas-guzzling Escalade 2008, BPRO version, EXT Cadillac. We're sure none of those letters make a difference to him, but they're included to indicate that it's a high-tech version.

As we walked by the even higher-priced models, like the Jeep Hurricane, we noticed that the boy pictured in the front seat on this package looks happy-ish in a serious kind of way. Maybe he's concentrating on the "monster traction" of those wheels. The most expensive vehicle, $599, was the Polaris Ranger RZR for "your little outdoor enthusiast." When did being a three-year-old outdoor enthusiast become the equivalent of tearing up terrain? Why would an outdoor "enthusiast" need an electronic radio with MP3 input and an electronic LED speedometer? On the packaging a green lightning bolt with a personified snarl holds his fist up aggressively, promising "24 volt superpower extreme performance" all at $3^1/2$ to 7 mph. We have to ask, Wouldn't a plain old bike go faster?

In a nostalgic mood, we took a look at those plain ol' bikes, starting with twelve-inch wheels on up to the eighteen-inch wheels. Until then we hadn't realized that "hyper" was a positive term. Of course it's not positive when bandied about in schools—it's usually followed by a parent-teacher conference and a conversation about ADD—but in bike packaging, yes. There were bikes called "Hyper" in all sizes. In the youngest styles there was still some sweetness (joyous colors and cheerful accessories), even if each one reflected some cobranding and marketing partnerships, from Diego, to Speed Racer, to Tony Hawk, to Spider-Man and Tonka. Where did all the Schwinns go? The plain old bike brands? Tonka looked promising, but the marketers had to hype it up with "dual shocks," call it a "MIGHTY bike," and include a little sports bottle that says "Thirst Extinguished." Extinguished. Not quenched. Why? Because a kid who rides a fourteen-inch bike wants to feel mighty and demolish things like . . . thirst? There were no My Little Pony bikes in "boy colors" (probably because, like so many products, these Ponies have been sexed up "girly" style), no backseats for stuffed animals or dolls on their bikes, no baskets, no streamers. What do boys get instead? All those techlike numbers and letters, lots of horns and gadgets to make noise, and promises that they will go like a "Flash" and be "Hyper," even on training wheels.

As they get older, the girls will ride on bikes called Divine and Paradise Cove or choose ones that reference *High School Musical* or *Hannah Montana.* Woe to the elementary school boy who races by on one of those babies when he could be on a bike called Ignition, Action Zone, Release, Vault, Engage, or Fallout. Sadly, when he gets bigger he will only be asked to be more aggressive and violent on his Nuke or Spitfire.

It's interesting to us that so many of these bikes do not seem to advocate competition and challenge, except if cobranding with Speed Racer. Nor did many allude to going fast, although there was a bike called Rushmore. Instead, the imagery was all about technology, out-of-control risk taking, and aggression. Today, perhaps it's more important to have the best and coolest ride, rather than to *be* the best.

We left the store thinking about our own kids, wondering what they were feeling and thinking the moment they realized no one was there to hold them up as they rode their wobbly bikes down the street, one of their first real tastes of DIY (Do It Yourself) freedom. Were they in the Action Zone, were they Hyper? Did they feel like a Thruster or a Competitor or some other prepackaged version of bike riding, or did they just feel like anything in life was possible?

"Gro to Pro": Sports Stuff

Learning to ride a bike and learning to really love and play sports happens around the same time, and when parents think of their sons and sports they think of them participating in something big, something American, something almost patriotic. They see the empowerment sports affords a boy, the personal power when he runs his hardest and plays his best, or when he understands and perfectly executes a new play. They see that power reflected in the eyes of others as his teammates and parents in the stands cheer him on. Parents believe that their sons will feel a connection to and support from his teammates, as well as admiration for his coach. In sports there's the promise of a perfect recipe for growing up strong and healthy, with friends and a mentor. Of course we want our sons to have these experiences and to feel this kind of power. But what do sports media tell boys about the power and entitlements they "deserve" when they play?

Children Now, a children's advocacy and research group, reported in 1999 that "98 percent of U.S. boys ages eight to seventeen consume some form of sports-related media, 82 percent do so at least a couple of times a week, and 90 percent watch televised sports. Although the study is ten years old now, it's hard to imagine things have changed very much. If anything, the growth of cable, satellite, and pay-per-view TV, the proliferation of sports video games, and the ability to watch and look up favorite players and teams on the Internet give boys more access and invite their interests more than ever before.

Not only does playing and watching sports cross all socioeconomic classes, races, and ethnicities in the United States, but sports are also among the most heavily marketed and packaged domains in our culture. Major professional sports leagues and the networks that televise their games spend countless millions to advertise and promote their respective leagues, teams, and stars. "Sports talk radio" is popular in every major media market. There are two major cable channels devoted to all sports all the time— ESPN and ESPN2, and the daily SportsCenter wrap-up show on ESPN is among the most popular cable television shows in the United States. A thirty-second commercial spot during Super Bowl XLII carried a $2.7-million price tag.

We'd like to think that experiencing sports and marketing sports are separate, but when little boys are introduced to sports at the age of two or three, it's in the context of a culture saturated with images and messages about professional athletes. Even as those first balls are tossed, caught, and kicked, boys are getting messages about what it means to be an athlete and the kind of person—the kind of male athlete—who plays these games. As balls meet Wiffle bats, mini–soccer goals, or four-foot-tall plastic basketball hoops, those "Little Champs" are invited not just to practice shooting because they love to, but also to "Dunk'n Cheer," "Adjust and Jam," and "Gro-to-Pro."

It's unavoidable, really. Unless your son is raised without any media whatsoever, has no social life outside your home, and wears a blindfold and earplugs to school, he's going to hear a media story about sports and athletes. As we've seen, sports stars are everywhere and endorse everything, from toys to cars to energy drinks, clothing lines, and alcohol, to cologne and watches, and of course, athletic wear and equipment. Sports marketing infiltrates pretty much every aspect of boys' lives these days. It's offered up as the answer to a boy's reluctance to read (give him sports magazines and biographies of famous players) or his dislike for math (turn it into sports stats or game plays), the answer to his insecurities about fitting in (buy the right jersey or the sneakers endorsed by a favorite player and be instantly recognized as part of a tribe) or his desire to seem cool, strong, and brave (watch the best and learn to walk the walk, talk the talk). In show after magazine after movie after book after commercial, he's invited into this world. Hey, even if he's not on the football team, he can be in the know by watching SportsCenter, listening to sports radio, and playing fantasy football online.

When little boys play sports, their love of the game is mediated incessantly by messages from the wider culture. Local teams carry the names of professional teams—"Red Sox," "Yankees," and "Cubs." Baskets in school gyms may be lowered to eight feet (instead of the regulation ten), but little boys will have already been introduced to the stars of the NBA, like LeBron James and Kobe Bryant, sporting jerseys with their names and numbers and wearing sneakers they endorse. The NBA makes it very easy for even little boys to follow their favorite teams and their favorite stars. They simply go to NBA.com to find out every detail of every team's, coach's, and player's life. Click on a team's Web site to find player profiles, news, schedules, results, standings, and stats. For football, "Pop Warner" teams begin at an early age, where little boys are outfitted in oversize pads and helmets that make them look a lot like Rick Moranis's character "Dark Helmet" in *Spaceballs*. On teams named after prominent NFL teams, like the "Patriots," "Giants," and "Steelers," they learn the rudiments of blocking, tackling, throwing, and kicking.

So is a sport something a boy *plays*, something he belongs to, or is it an identity? For many boys it's all of the above, which means that all this packaging of sports should really matter to you as a parent. If playing sports is a form of power for boys, what does it teach them about the use of power and what entitlements go with talent and expertise? What does it mean for him to "Gro to Pro"?

Getting His Game On

IT'S JUST PART OF THE GAME

For a parent, the most troubling part of athletic participation is the violence associated with sports. Aggression is an essential part of competing, but violence seems to be an add-on. In a survey of 12,000 children ages ten to seventeen, Children Now reports that 57 percent of boys said they see violence in sports "often." In spite of that, sports news is generally positive in its representation of sports figures, or so the boys perceive. Children Now points out the networks' adulation of those figures who "kill," "destroy," or "take aim," who "play with pain," "take hits," "engage in reckless acts," and "show guts in the face of danger and disaster." Boys get a confusing packaging of hero worship and violence. Children Now documents a steady stream of "fights, near-fights, threats of fights or other violent actions . . . often verbally framed in sarcastic language that suggests that this kind of action is acceptable." In their sports programming, boys repeatedly hear a troubling narrative—that serious competition justifies violence.

So what do boys learn? According to a study of 4,200 high school athletes by the the Josephson Institute's Center for Sports Ethics:

- More than half (51 percent) of the boys (30 percent of the girls) thought it was okay for the coach to argue with an official to get the referee to change his calls later.

- Nearly half (47 percent) of the boys (19 percent of girls) thought that trash-talking was acceptable.

- Thirty percent of the boys (16 percent of girls) thought it was fair to throw at a batter who had hit a home run the last time up.

Are the gender differences explained by different public behaviors of their role models, male and female athletes? Hardly, since women receive just 6.3 percent of sports coverage on TV sports news and even less on ESPN and SportsCenter; there are really not enough women to impact girls either way.

It's more likely that we all just see a *lot* of violence and aggression coming from male athletes.

The Children Now report suggests it's the everyday trash-talking and aggressive acts, the idolatry of big egos, and the media-hyped rivalries that have the biggest impact on boys. During the 2008 Summer Olympic coverage, we were struck by the great effort host Bob Costas put into fanning the fire of any and all rivalries, such as his accusation that the French swimmers were "talking trash" about the Americans and the airtime he gave to a "gloating" U.S. relay team when they won the race in question.

Parents might be surprised to know that the TV parental guidelines ratings to gauge sex, violence, and profanity don't apply to sports programming. So boys have come to expect brawls like the one between the Indiana Pacers and the Detroit Pistons on November 19, 2004: "Officials stopped the game with 45.9 seconds remaining after pushing and shoving between the teams spilled into the stands and fans began throwing things at the players near the scorer's table." After all was said and done, Ron Artest was suspended for seventy-two games, Stephen Jackson was suspended for thirty games, and Jermaine O'Neal was suspended for twenty-five games. What's the lesson to boys? Crime doesn't pay? We think not, given that this fight was so exciting it was broadcast repeatedly for weeks afterward, and it still can be found easily on YouTube.

Why does this matter? Studies tell us that boys who play sports manifest elevated levels of aggression and violence. Those who play team sports with high levels of physical contact (e.g., ice hockey, football, basketball), and participate in high body contact individual sports (e.g., boxing, wrestling) are more likely to engage in violence outside the sports settings and are more likely to exhibit delinquent behavior. Is this a price we have to pay?

THE EASIEST WAY TO CHOOSE "GUY"

Sports is one of the last real female-free zones, "where guys can be guys," argues Michael Kimmel in *Guyland*. Or at least that's the way it's packaged and sold; in reality, girls and women make up 40 percent of all athletes in the United States. The all-guy nature of sports applies mostly to media coverage of sporting events, which of course is supported by school teams that segregate girls from boys, some at ridiculously early ages.

When a female reader asked *ESPN* magazine columnist Bill Simmons how she and other sports-savvy women might convince guys to let them watch the game with them, he was pretty frank:

> Guys like watching sports with other guys. It's nothing personal, we just do. We're not asking for that much—football on Sundays, a weekend in Vegas, the occasional male bonding night at the ball-park. Throw females into the mix, and we can't make the same in-appropriate jokes or emit the same noises. We never forget for a single second there's a girl in the room—so why bother?

Simmons then listed ten things the reader could do to be accepted, includ-ing wait on (as in bring beer and nachos to) the guys watching.

Even though sports is a female-free zone, when women do appear they are typically portrayed in stereotypical ways—as sex objects, often cheering the men on. In the NBA and NFL games, for example, cameras cut to close-up shots of the cheerleaders, often focusing on breasts and butts. In boys' lives, cheerleaders emerge in middle school, and with them boys' entitle-ment to being cheered for. While cheerleading has its own interscholastic competitions (and pressures), sports programming makes it next to impossi-ble to shake the sexualized version of the sport. School cheerleaders cheer not only for the boys' football, soccer, and basketball teams, but also for the girls' soccer, field hockey, and basketball teams; however, they know which teams are *really* valued. In one junior high we know of, the cheerleaders (who were cheerleaders for both the girls' and boys' teams) put up a collage in the hallway featuring only the boys' football team's names and numbers. The message? Cheerleaders are there to cheer on a certain kind of athlete—a male with dreams of being a superstar.

Playing sports is also, as boys learn at a young age, "the easiest way to choose 'guy' over 'gay'—and make sure everyone gets the right idea about them." As one young man told Kimmel, "[Playing sports] was the only way to be a guy in my school. I mean, you could be smart, but you better not show it. You could be, like, talented or artistic or whatever, but you better not show it. Everyone was always going around saying, 'that's so gay.' . . . And the one thing they never said that about was sports."

If this is true, then there's more than a little anxiety behind all that sports watching and playing, and that makes for a great marketing climate. One of the surest ways to sell a product is first to create anxiety. By using sports stars to sell products, humorously or seriously, marketers make boys anxious about not matching up to an ideal of masculinity—big, tough, cool, risk taking, aggressive—that will prevent others from thinking that he's a girl or he's gay. Then the boy is convinced that purchasing a particular product will help him overcome his fears, embarrassments, and shortcomings.

The good news for parents is that being successful at sports not only protects a boy from being called gay but also gives him permission to do well academically, show sensitivity, and stick up for kids who are bullied. So the superhero mantra holds here as well: with great power comes great responsibility. And even if their favorite player doesn't live up to this credo, boys certainly can.

BEING THE BEST, NOT DOING YOUR BEST

Superstars, superheroes, Super Bowls. Everything worth a boy's attention in sports is super. Take for example Fox Sports' supersize cgi robot football player mascot, "Cleatus"—a name awarded on the basis of a "name the robot" contest among fans. Cleatus is the epitome of hypermasculinity—from his extraordinarily broad shoulders (enhanced by supersize shoulder pads) to his muscular arms and legs to his high-energy warm-up antics. He doesn't speak and actually receives a good bit of hate mail from avid NFL watchers because he interrupts the game so frequently, but he sends a superhero, Transformer-like, larger-than-life message to younger boys who are watching. To drive home the point, boys can have their own ten-inch action figure Cleatus, available online and in stores like Toys "R" Us.

Like this "iron man," all sports superstars are represented as superheroes. This representation sends the message that the goal of playing sports is not the love of the game, not playing for the sake of playing, the satisfaction and success of teamwork, but to be the star, the hero, the best of the best. Sure, there's something important there about aspirations, but doing one's best, something any boy can do, is different from *being* the best, something available to the smallest percentage of boys, who must have a lot more than heart and hard work on their side.

Consider LeBron James, who, even before he was drafted into the NBA, signed a seven-year shoe contract with Nike worth more than $90 million. Since then LeBron has become a superstar in the NBA—one of the best players in the league, and not surprisingly, given the expensive Nike price tag, one of the most recognizable, marketed aggressively via print, television, and Internet advertising.

The way superstars like LeBron are marketed sends a set of complex messages to boys. LeBron's "Better Than Me" commercial for Nike offers something deeper and more emotional than simply idolization of a star athlete. The ad follows LeBron from being a little boy playing basketball with his friends, to becoming a teen star, to his present-day status as a pro, performing a slow-motion dunk in front of adoring fans. LeBron speaks to his young fans over these images in a sincere, man-to-man style about inspiration, overcoming challenges, and the quest to become great—something he invites all young boys to become. In the end, he says, "I am LeBron James./ You don't want to be me./You want to be better than me."

Sincere, even humble, yes. But what does it mean to be better than LeBron? His message is that a boy, if he never gives up, pushes himself to improve, and dedicates himself to the game, can be better than his hero. But can he also be better than him by reading? By doing his chores? By working well with others? The message is nonspecific—but we know why LeBron is great, and it's not for any of these mundane tasks. Instead, we are led to believe he's one man against the world, who's on a personal journey that takes great heart, humility, and belief in oneself. This may be an inspirational ad, but of course, in reality LeBron has things going for him most boys don't and never will. He's six foot eight, for one thing. His image is handled by sponsors, for another.

Perhaps the more packaged an athlete is, the more endorsements, the more people invested in his image, the more important it is for him to insist it's all from the heart. (That's why so many hearts are broken when a player switches teams for a few million more!)

As a brand, LeBron needs to appeal to everyone. Take the Nike commercials that feature him, Eddie Murphy style, playing four different characters or family members at the same time:

> *Wise LeBron*—The old sage who keeps LeBron grounded, who often makes references to his past basketball prowess, claiming, for example, to have attained a quadruple double in the state championship game. He also likes to keep Athlete LeBron in his place by talking about what "Michael" (that is, Michael Jordan) did.
>
> *Hip LeBron*—The hip/slick business/ladies man. Often too busy talking on his cell phone to participate in other activities.
>
> *The Real LeBron*—LeBron James, the NBA star, as the public knows him today.

Kid LeBron—A play on LeBron's youth compared to other NBA players; he is a youngster just looking to have fun. Short, almost dwarf-like.

Even though LeBron is, in a sense, making fun of himself, each commercial also includes some representation of superior athletic accomplishment. The Real LeBron makes an extraordinary dunk in a basketball game in which all four characters participate, the Hip LeBron executes an Olympic-quality high dive into a swimming pool in which the Real LeBron and the Kid LeBron are "training." In the end, however, they all say the same thing: LeBron is larger than life.

The Indianapolis Colts' Peyton Manning is also larger than life. The latest in a series of handsome, tall, talented, fearless, and almost always white NFL quarterbacks, he's the icon of masculinity. Peyton appears in print, television, and Internet advertisements for some of the NFL's biggest sponsors, including Sprint, Sony, MasterCard, Gatorade, DirecTV, Xbox, and the American Red Cross. He also appears in ads for NBC, ESPN, and the NFL network, which televises NFL games. On March 24, 2007, his thirty-first birthday, he hosted NBC's *Saturday Night Live* with musical guest Carrie Underwood. The episode earned the show's highest rating in more than ten months in the metered markets. During his opening monologue, Manning alluded to his most-marketable status by joking that he had accomplished two of his life goals: his team, the Colts, winning a Super Bowl and his appearance on over half of America's television commercials.

Look at these ads and ads featuring other superstars. Most are selling fast cars and fast-food, alcohol, and video games. Ads in magazines like *ESPN* are filled with athletes doing their best to associate products with their larger-than-life image, like superstar running back LaDainian Tomlinson of the San Diego Chargers for Campbell's soup ("Eat More Protein, Eat Less Turf") and Tiger Woods for TAG Heuer watches, ("What are you made of?"). Other ads don't need the stars, as long as they reverberate the sports superstar qualities in the magazine, like the Geico cavemen ("You don't win games by catching a ball. You win by having the will of the warrior"), Levi's 501 jeans (Live Life Unbuttoned), Gillette shampoo (Take Charge of Your Hair), an online giveaway contest (The only way to make this prize better would be to wrap it in bacon), and of course lots of alcohol ads, like Jim Beam ("The men rode into the saloon" is never followed by "and ordered Merlot").

In spite of their inspirational stories as well as stories that show humble beginnings, sports superstars model themselves after superheroes. They date or marry famous women like Victoria Beckham, Halle Berry, Eva Longoria, Jessica Simpson, and Madonna. They join the world of rap stars and "players," drive cool cars, have *lots* of money. They are invincible.

SPORTS AND DANGER

This invincibility is admired. Violence, risk taking, and danger are especially prevalent in "extreme" or adventure sports, like skateboarding, snowboarding, BMX racing, and surfing. The Children Now study found that 27 percent of the *commercials* during such televised sporting events placed actors in dangerous situations. We found some of the most extreme shows and ads on specialized commercial Web sites. Here boys can find portraits of their favorite athletes creating that adrenaline rush by testing the outer limits, doing spectacular stunts, wiping out, and playing hurt, all in the service of selling amped-up energy drinks, cool equipment, or X Game athletes themselves.

Of course playing sports is good for boys. But we need to ask, can we separate the way we want our sons to play sports from what they're taught about sports in the media? Our colleague Bill Pollack, author of *Real Boys*, says that playing sports has the potential to enrich boys' lives by encouraging healthy emotional expression, by helping boys experience the power of friendship, connection, and affection among teammates, by boosting self-esteem as boys experience a sense of mastery, and by teaching lessons of resilience and the ability to face loss. We add, imbibing a media-laced version of sports 24/7 has the potential to turn your son's dreams of sports stardom into dreams of being a hypermasculinized, self-mutilating, sexist, superhero superstar—he may not be able to buy just one part of the whole package.

We spoke with the people who began the program "Play Like a Champion Today—Sports as Ministry" at Notre Dame. They attempt to undercut the idea of superheroes in sports and sports-as-violence by training coaches to work differently with boys. To them teamwork means something different from how it's usually played out. They have the brilliant idea that players should have as much ownership over the game as the coaches do. They teach coaches how to lead team discussions about moral issues that come up when kids play games. They ask that, in K-6 grades, coaches commit to giving each child equal playing time. If it's not okay for a kid to tell another kid "you can't play," they ask "why should an adult have the right to say you can't play"?

There are other great coaches out there trying to undo stereotypical ways of playing sports. Jeffrey Marx wrote *Season of Life: A Football Star, a Boy, a Journey to Manhood*, about Joe Ehrmann, a former NFL star who now coaches at a private high school. Ehrmann begins his practices by gathering his boys together and directing a team chant: "What is our job as coaches?" he asks the boys, and they answer "To love us." "What's your job boys?" he asks: "To love each other." Some may ask, what does this have to do with sports? Well, if sports is about winning, not much. But if it's about playing with and learning from other people, it means everything. "Masculinity ought to be defined in terms of relationships," says Ehrmann, "and taught in terms of the capacity to love and be loved." Now that's a message about sports we don't expect to hear on ESPN or *Monday Night Football* anytime soon—wouldn't it be super if we did?

The Fastest Man Wins: NASCAR

Speaking of super, no discussion of boys and sports would be complete without NASCAR. The hottest cars and the most famous drivers speed around an oval track at velocities of almost two hundred miles per hour; the roar of the cars and of the crowd is deafening; the competition is fierce, and when cars jockey for position, bumper to bumper and side to side, the potential for a fiery crash lurks around every corner. This is the reality of "big-time" NASCAR auto racing—powerful stories, compelling images, and plenty of messages about masculine daring and skill. It's one of the oldest "extreme sports" around. No wonder so many boys tune in or head to the track.

NASCAR (the National Association for Stock Car Auto Racing) is the largest sanctioning body for stock car racing in the United States. Stock cars are supposedly "regular" cars that can be purchased by regular consumers and are driven on highways and byways all over the country (in contrast to race cars—like those raced in the Indianapolis 500—that are specially designed and constructed only for racing). In reality, however, modern stock cars resemble production models (like the Chevrolet Monte Carlo, Ford Taurus, or Toyota Camry) only in name and look. Underneath they're as specially designed and constructed as any race car.

NASCAR is the second-most-popular professional sport in terms of television ratings in the United States, ranking behind only the National Football League. Seventeen of the top twenty attended sporting events in the United States have been NASCAR races, and there are an estimated seventy-five million NASCAR fans who purchase over $3 billion in annual licensed product sales. According to NASCAR, these fans are extremely brand loyal; consequently, more *Fortune* 500 companies participate in NASCAR than any other sport.

NASCAR sponsors several racing series each year—the most popular and prestigious is the Sprint Cup series, in which about fifty drivers compete in thirty-six races held in nineteen different states from February through November. Typically more than 100,000 fans attend each race, and even though there are plenty of women and girls in the stands as well, make no mistake about it—NASCAR is about masculinity. Best-selling mystery writer Janet Evanovich, a fan herself, said it well, "The noise and the testosterone rolled off the track, rushed up the stands, and almost knocked me over."

More specifically, NASCAR is about white southern masculinity, but even so, it's a kind of masculinity any boy can love. For one, stock car racing reflects a romanticized version of the working-class hero. Boys can identify with the "good old boy," whether or not they're good, or old, or from the South. Drivers "are folk heroes" according to the *Encyclopedia of Southern Culture.* The good old boy is linked to a sense of nostalgia that's considered conservative and even backward outside the South, but within southern culture he's been immortalized in popular literature and country music songs as "blue collar, an outdoorsman, a patriot, something of a populist, basically conservative—a man's man." And, "like the cowboy and his horse, the good old boy needs his car."

NASCAR drivers are also superheroes of a kind and thus imbued with some religious mythology. As former *New York Times* writer, Robert Lipsyte wrote, "The beatification of Dale Earnhardt Sr. as a man's man who sacrificed himself to shepherd his flock to the finish line, a hero who in death evoked both John Wayne and Jesus, presented America with its biggest joint jolt of sports and evangelical Christianity." Could he be simply just a guy whose luck ran out? Or is he instead a superhero, once a little guy who achieved great things, and then died for racing's sins?

Then there's the aggression. Why else was Dale Earnhardt called "the intimidator"? Why else did Jeff Gordon, after he shoved racer Matt Kenseth (after the race), say proudly that now fans can see what kind of man he really is? (He explained, he's no longer afraid of what the public may think!) David Caraviello, writing for Nascar.com, says, "that's all part of the sport. It's not the speed, but the 'leaning' on other cars. It's that physical nature—the rubbing part of the racing—that sets NASCAR apart from more delicate forms of auto racing." Like the bullies that walk down the halls and push their shoulders against the smaller guys who didn't move away fast enough, part of the sport is pushing other cars to the side. In defense of this aggression, Caraviello says it's natural: "the prospect of forty-three drivers denying their nature for three solid hours each Sunday becomes about as likely as Kevin Harvick and Juan Montoya opening a bed and breakfast." No, they don't use the word *sissy*, but "opening a bed-and-breakfast"? Not for real men, and NASCAR is for real men.

Just as country music has changed over the years, so has NASCAR. It has become mainstream America as the rough-and-ready stock car heroes have been replaced by corporate-sponsored, polished, and heavily marketed drivers of the new century. Marketable and good-looking Jeff Gordon, for example, sells Pepsi, Fritos Corn Chips, Quaker State Motor Oil, OnStar, and, like Tiger Woods, TAG Heuer watches. These are manly products no doubt. The movie *Talladega Nights* makes this point by having Perrier sponsor Will Ferrell's archrival, Jean Girard!

This shift hasn't been easy. Just ask Jeff Gordon and Jimmie Johnson. Both have been enormously successful and both have been booed on a regular basis, Gordon because his record and slick image created a comparison to good old boy Dale Earnhardt Sr. that fueled a media frenzy and fan-based rivalry with Dale Earnhardt Jr., and Johnson because he's, well, a clean-cut nice guy from California. "When Johnson's name is announced to the crowd during prerace introductions," Jeff Gluck of SceneDaily.com, an online publication covering NASCAR says, "boos rain down on the California native like a thunderstorm of hate. You'd think he just walked onstage and burned an American flag."

Jeff Gordon says it's because, like himself in his earlier days, Johnson hasn't offered anything yet for the crowd to identify with, no "personal issues." "People want to find a way to connect to you. Until they see you going through some of the same things that they're going through, sometimes they don't have that connection." Just like WWE, NASCAR fans like the stories, no matter how dramatic, the loves and losses, the rivalries and competitions. These kinds of stories always require a little trash-talk, don't they? What do you do with a guy like Jimmie Johnson who doesn't play the game, who instead says things like, "What's wrong with good competition and people that respect each other and teams that respect each other?" and "I think we get warped into reality television shows and perspectives that you need to be in fistfights and all these different types of things"?

For boys NASCAR is a world of power and danger and speed—dominated by great machines and skillful, daring, courageous—dare we say it?—superhuman drivers. As such, this provides another way in which boys, in an attempt to emulate their favorite NASCAR heroes, may be encouraged to go too fast and too furious. Men overwhelmingly dominate, and even a female race car driver like Danica Patrick kowtows to the good ol' boys by posing in her bikini. It's a man's world.

But it's also a world for little boys. Sanjay Gupta, reporting for CNN, says that NASCAR is almost like Little League, "with boys and girls starting at six or seven and moving up through the ranks as they get older, all the while dreaming of becoming the next Rusty Wallace, Carl Edwards or Dale Earnhardt Jr." Immediately out of Pull-ups, little boys can wear NASCAR underwear and sleep in their big boy beds on NASCAR pillowcases (cobranded with M&M's). And then there's the Pinewood Derby, which just about every Cub Scout participates in, a Scout-sponsored beginning to lifelong racing interest. It's hard to knock and hard to bear this charming activity for dads and sons that takes weeks of planning and work, only to have little hearts dashed in thirty minutes at the "races."

If your son loves racing, you can talk to him about the "bad boys" of NASCAR who bump other cars, recklessly causing huge pileups and endangering lives. Tony Stewart, according to racer Rusty Wallace, in 2004 was "driving like an idiot and taking a bunch of cars out." Wallace said at the time, "He needs to get his emotions in check. He's a good kid, but I'm not respecting him at all right now, and half of the garage is not respecting him. He's going to have to get out there and start earning the respect of his peers again. He's screwed up a lot of good cars here because he's pouting." So there's immaturity and there's maturity.

You can also use the "nice guys" of NASCAR to start a conversation about the different ways to be a guy, and the cost of staying true to yourself. But don't forget to help him think about the corporate side of this and other sports, and about how when an outsider (from the big city?) achieves success, it can make a little guy feel littler, a poor guy feel poorer, in ways that make him want to boo a Jeff Gordon or a Jimmie Johnson. Finally, as Sanjay Gupta noted, successful drivers "need to combine hours of focus and split-second timing, hours of patience and moments of aggression." Catch that? No violence. Moments of aggression. Just enough to pull ahead.

Full Throttle Drinking

You can't watch a sports event on TV these days without seeing commercials for beverages—that is, energy drinks and beer. Just like sports, these drinks are all about action and competition, getting the go to go faster or the go to get that girl. Then again, with all the gorgeous women surrounding guys drinking beer, they don't actually need to work hard and get up off their couches or barstools and go get anyone. Work is not really the point anyway, unless you're a young Budweiser Clydesdale who wants to make the A-team. Beer ads are selling leisure time, slacking, hanging with the guys, and hitting on the girls. And the next day, when you're all leisured out, energy drinks bring you back to form.

ENERGY DRINKS

Full Throttle, No Fear, Adrenaline Rush, Assault, Monster Energy, Gatorade Tiger, Red Bull, Rockstar, Amp, and Pimp Juice. It's tiring just reading the names of the most popular energy drinks on the market today. Whether these drinks are promoted by extreme and elite athletes or tough, womanizing hip-hop stars, boys are getting the message loud and clear that being a man is a draining task. With the help of these cans of masculine raw energy they too can be amped up, or energized to the max, ready to live life just this side of coked out.

In recent years there's been an influx of energy drinks into sports competitions, bars, music videos, and grocery store aisles. Each drink targets a different demographic, but other than the pink energy drinks hawked during Fashion Week in New York, they are all aimed at boys and men. There are two broad categories through which energy drinks are promoted: music and sports. These categories are not mutually exclusive, but there's a distinct divide between the drinks made by hip-hop stars for the club scene, like Nelly's "Pimp Juice," and the ones made for elite athletes or those who want to be like them.

It's likely that coffee chains reached down to hook younger customers with those special Frappucinos and supersweet coffee drinks. But when a kid can get up to three times the caffeine (in some cases, fourteen times more caffeine than a can of cola) in an energy drink that comes with an inviting warning that tells them NOT FOR KIDS, now that's a product! All the better when those kids see their sports stars and favorite artists guzzling the stuff. Little boys have grown up on scenes of very big boys dumping tubs of iced Gatorade over their coach's head in the spirit of playful celebration. Even though Gatorade has no caffeine, it's designed to give energy to hardworking athletes. Of course, all that sugar and sodium isn't good for kids, but little boys are still encouraged, as they were in the 1990s, to "be like Mike" and drink tons of the stuff.

Energy drinks like Red Bull, Monster Energy, and Gatorade Tiger are marketed to literally "amp up" boys' and men's intensity. Whether it's Gatorade's depiction of Tiger Woods as "an athlete who embodies mental strength, physical power, and technical perfection," or Monster Energy's cry to consumers to "declare war on the ordinary," the message of these drinks is that they will help you measure up (or "Man Up," as the slogan for No Fear says), for without them, you just aren't worthy of playing the game at all. A man's man, as Rockstar, suggests, deserves a man's drink:

> Bigger. Better. Faster. Stronger. ROCKSTAR is the world's most powerful energy drink. . . . ROCKSTAR is scientifically formulated to provide an incredible energy boost for those who lead active and exhausting lifestyles—from athletes to rock stars.

Monster Energy takes it one step further:

> The MONSTER packs a vicious punch but has a smooth kick ass flavor you can really pound down. So when it's time to unleash the beast within, grab a MONSTER and GO BIG!

Vicious punch? Kick ass? Pound down? Over-the-top isn't just about buzz and energy, it's also about an attraction to violence and risk taking.

Red Bull sponsors dozens of extreme athletes and features their tricks, stories, and interviews on their Web site. Boys are told that Red Bull athletes are experimental, unique, and always pushing the limits. One "Red Bull Experiment" featured Robbie Maddison, Australian motocross star, as he shattered the world record and cleared an entire football field on his motorcycle. Prove your masculinity, this "experiment" says, by risking it all to be the best. Red Bull's challenge, "Flugtag," is a flying competition that encourages the ordinary guy to prove himself extraordinary by building the "most outrageous machine." The slogan? "Designed by amateurs, built by volunteers, and piloted by the incredibly brave." Maybe anyone can help build such a machine, but only the few with "extreme daring" can fly one. You can be *that* guy, they suggest.

Monster Energy takes its notion of bravery from the military and defends the honor of its "troops." In a press release from the company about Ryan Villopoto's crash in a supercross competition, Monster Energy tells its consumers that they're willing to stand behind their extreme athletes no matter what, "Monster Energy will continue to stand up for and defend its athletes . . . the M-Claw logo represents a lot more than sponsorship money. It represents family."

Monster Energy uses that "band of brothers" inclusion and loyalty so important to military and fraternity recruitment to appeal to boys. Veterans will tell you that it's true of military service—extreme risk taking earns extreme loyalty, and both the risk taking as well as the loyalty can be dangerous. However, it's not enough simply to belong. Anyone can join the online "Monster Army" as a private, but to move through the ranks to general, to transform from "regular athletes to Monster Army Soldiers," a boy has to prove himself worthy—improve his skill, rid himself of fear, and prove his bravery in extreme sports. To rise in the ranks of Monster Energy, a boy has to "declare war on the ordinary" and become the biggest and baddest. Skater Jason "Wee Man" Acuna, known for doing risky tricks on reality shows like *Jackass*, works for Monster. On the Monster Web site, Wee Man says in a video that he begins his day with a Monster Energy drink called Heavy Metal, does tricks in the skate park, and then ends with shooting a few practice rounds with his gun. As he tells the camera aferward, "Now you know what it takes to be Wee Man all day long" (which apparently includes also referring to yourself in the third person).

Another recent addition to the energy drink market is Pimp Juice. Inspired by the song of the same name by rap star Nelly (who co-owns and endorses the drink), Pimp Juice is marketed as the "#1 Hip Hop Energy Drink." As one of the first celebrity-driven energy drinks on the market, it's an example of hip-hop and pop stars using their appeal to younger audiences to market and sell non-music-related products (rapper 50 Cent made $400 million when the Coca-Cola Company bought the firm behind his energy drink, Formula 50). Pimp Juice was also greeted with some controversy when it was first introduced. A number of groups and organizations called for a national boycott, because it glorifies a negative stereotype of African American culture. (Nelly, as we discussed in chapter 4, What Boys Listen To, has also been roundly criticized for his portrayal of African American women as sex objects in his raps and videos.)

One might think that a military troop and a pimp have little in common, but the same language used for Monster Energy drinks about energy and honor is used for Nelly's drink, implying that a Pimp is someone to respect. Check out this online ad for the "Extra Strength Formula":

> Nelly's Pimp Juice drink is truly a high energy caffeinated beverage worthy of gracing the inside of your pimp cup. Buy Pimp Juice now

and be the first to walk your street with a glorious pimped out aura that will attract the opposite sex like something out of a rap music video.

Red Bull and Monster Energy show boys, even the young ones—as one eleven-year-old told us, "I used to be addicted to Monster. I'd have three or four a day"—what it means to be daring, violent, and over-the-top. Nelly's Pimp Juice shows boys how to earn street cred and get hot babes. But Gatorade uses Tiger Woods to suggest a different way to earn respect: focus, confidence, and control in competition—a good idea, since the caffeine-free content calls for a "Quiet Storm" approach.

No ordinary men (pimps, monsters, heroes, and Tiger), these are no ordinary drinks. There's little camaraderie or group wackiness as in some of those earlier Mountain Dew commercials. Energy drinks are about building yourself up, energizing yourself, so that you alone can make it to the top. "You can get it if you really want . . . if you try, try, try," says the soundtrack to Red Bull's "Flugtag" competition. But of course trying isn't enough, and what we never hear about are the millions of privates in the army who are never promoted, the millions of boys consuming these drinks who aren't close to being the best at anything, but who keep pushing through the pain convinced that this is the only way to be the best that they can be. It doesn't matter really; these drinks are about constructing desire, and perhaps it's enough just to identify with Tiger Woods, who says, "The greatest thing about tomorrow is I will be better than I am today." Better, though, in what way? At your sport? Kind of a narrow outlook, we say. The truth is, of course, that Tiger can never rest or stop running the race, and that someone younger, better, and cooler will come along in due time.

Energy drink consumption was up 20 percent in 2008 among eighteen- to twenty-four-year-olds, with sales expected to top $9 billion in three years, according to Beverage Marketing Corp. The number of male drinkers has risen by 64 percent in the past five years. And marketers are finding newer ways to sell to kids.

Marketed to boys and boy athletes in particular, there's no evidence that any kid athlete needs the extra carbs from these, nor that they will improve his game and make a man of him. While nobody dies from drinking too many energy drinks, or perhaps it's very rare for someone to die and their deaths have not been conclusively attributed to drinking energy drinks, research shows a range of associated medical problems; some kids are already addicts, and a few have been hospitalized with racing heart rates and the sweats.

Of course marketers will claim that energy drinks, as opposed to sports drinks, are only marketed to adults. But they're not. "The fact that they are not using more traditional advertising venues begs the question: If adults are their primary market, how come they are only using the tactics that are popular with teens?" says James Mosher, an attorney with the Pacific Institute for Research and Evaluation who researches the effects of alcohol marketing campaigns on young audiences.

Mosher was talking about an energy drink with 12 percent alcohol content, sold in small colorful bottles, easily slipped into a teen's pocket as he's leaving the store or house: Spykes. When they came out, they were available in flavors like mango, chocolate, and lime and infused with caffeine as well; MSNBC wondered if this was "a booze buzz for teenyboppers." They are now off the market. Critics claimed that Spykes were of course being marketed to kids: "I think it's one more outrageous example of the predatory marketing practices of the alcohol industry," said Susan Foster, vice president and director of policy research at Columbia University's National Center of Addiction and Substance Abuse. Anheuser-Busch, who made the drink, was more interested in the cross between energy drinks and alcohol. As Mosher explained, "A big part of the market is using energy drinks as a mixer with booze with the idea that the caffeine will keep you partying all night."

The drinks themselves may be bad enough, but what do boys learn from the messages that support drinking these drinks, advertised as they are as a way to be an amped man, or, to the younger set, to become one someday. Red Bull gives you "wings" and Monster Energy gives you that "big bad Monster buzz," but neither gives boys and young men the tools to deal with the withdrawal from the thrill. Who needs the tools anyway, if you can come down by chugging a few beers?

BEER AND BABES: THE MAN LAW

Drinking beer, as any boy who watches TV can see, is a distinctly masculine experience. Not wanting to binge, we limited ourselves to watching just twenty-five beer commercials on TV and online (featuring five different types of beer). In these, only one featured women drinking beer. That should tell any boy: beer is for men. But more than that, beer drinking brings men together either to be men, or to poke fun at what it means to be a man, together.

While energy drinks market a certain kind of hyped-up competitor, beer markets an image of a loveable loser. Loser or not, he's still a guy's guy, and that's what's important.

Plenty of beer commercials not only humorously show men telling sexist jokes, behaving childishly, bonding through sports, and making rules concerning manhood, but they're also meant to poke fun at the guys doing it. What kind of humor is it? It's a strange sort, where guys tell guys that guys are supposed to be a certain way and agree together that it's kind of stupid but that they're going to pursue this guyness anyway. Male solidarity and the sexualization of women portray a particular brand of masculinity but also serve to make fun of the kind of guy who drinks beer with the guys and hopes to get hot women.

In his book *Uneasy Pleasures: The Male as Erotic Object*, Kenneth MacKinnon points to the "contemptuous irony" of men in advertising. The "deflation of the male ego" in such advertising often provides the humor, as men are routinely presented as onlookers in beer commercials to laugh at what their buddy has just done to make himself look stupid. Is this a form of male humiliation of other males? Not really, because the onlookers are not superior to the clumsy idiots; they're buddies. Keystone Light commercials claim their beer "is smooth, even when you're not." In the process of buying beer, each guy ends up making some sort of foolish mistake in front of a sexy woman and experiences some degree of humiliation, more humiliating indeed because another guy is watching and laughing in "the joke's on you" or a "you've been punked" kind of way. The ads are funny, not because the guys in the commercials are losers, but because they're regular guys trying to live up to an ideal that even guys know is unrealistic and phoney, and they've been caught in the act. There's something really funny about having your worst fear acknowledged and realized. We don't think these ads are so contemptuous, because once that fear is acknowledged and realized, guys together can thumb their noses at the snooty rest of us (women especially) who expect anything more of them.

Media ecologist Lance Strate describes beer commercials as typically located in "self-contained environments" (often outdoors or at a bar) that "[free] men from the constraints of civilization, allowing them to behave irresponsibly." Sociologists have long pointed out that in the United States at the turn of the twentieth century, as men no longer were primarily laborers and were forced to take on less strenuous office work, a variety of all-male places where men could preserve their threatened manhood were established— pool halls, bars, and men's clubs. Many of the commercials we watched reflect this idea that men need a place of their own, a place in which they are free from criticism, and most importantly, a place where they can act like men, even if it's in the kitchen while their wives are having a wine party in the next room.

This sense of threatened territory is featured in a series of Miller Lite ads. The ads show a group of men sitting around a table in some sort of glass house in what appears to be a large, dark building. In their supersecret hideaway they discuss what it means to be a man, eventually forming a "Man Law." In one of the commercials a man poses the question, "Are women allowed to keep things in the garage fridge other than Miller Lite?" One of the men replies, ". . . the garage is the only sovereign territory we got left." The joke, of course, is that women have taken over every other male space and the men, like women of another era perhaps, are relegated to secret meetings and meager attempts to hang on to what little they have.

Like most humor, these jokes are funny because there's a bit of truth to them—both a social truth that men are told they should be in control of their worlds and a social reality in which women have encroached on traditional male space. These ads suggest that beer is the last bastion of true masculinity, as well as the only thing guys have left in a world of successful women.

We think this message is not lost on boys who watch these ads, and who have seen this concept before in cartoons about "no girls allowed" clubs or tree houses. Even the littlest of boys are sure to understand that big boys, men, and dads need their own territories away from women and girls, but they probably are confused about why. In fact, the commercials aren't really clear about why this is a problem anyway, except that women and girls, for some reason, want to make men less manly. That is, except when they're there in skimpy clothing for the purpose of making men feel more so. Explain that to your eight-year-old.

Women make men feel more manly by desiring them. Like a competition, seduction is "the highest form of challenge" for these guys, argues Strate. Men in beer commercials pick specific types of women to seduce. Consider again the Man Law commercial, in which a cowboy character's girlfriend shows up unannounced at the hideaway. Burt Reynolds is ready to lecture the cowboy about the Man Law that he broke—never ditch your friends for a girl ("remember, it's bros before hoes")—when he sees her and drops the lecture. The implication here is that for some girls—really hot girls—there are exceptions. But only because their presence makes the men feel all the more manly.

The seduction of these kinds of babes is repeated over and over again. Coors Light ads show off the "Coors Light Twins"—busty blondes who dress in skimpy clothing and act as cheerleaders in a series of ads entitled "Here's to Football!" There are plenty of pool parties with women in bikinis, but there are also ads that poke fun at girls who look hot but who, upon closer inspection, have crooked teeth or manly voices.

Does it really matter that beer ads, like MTV videos, portray women as sex objects? Boys are watching for sure, but are these ads harmful? Maybe not on their own, but the whole point is that they resonate with other messages and media boys are consuming—films like *College* and *American Pie* that advocate a kind of attitude toward sex and women that has a little (maybe even a lot) to do with coercive and nonconsensual sex after drunken partying. Believe us, working on real college campuses, we know the problem with this. Boys watching these ads get the message that when guys get together to drink, either they're going to be laughingly humiliated in some outrageously fun way, or they're going to get some!

We wish these ads didn't fill living rooms on family weekends. We wish beer wasn't so heavily associated with the fun and competition of sports. But mostly we wish that boys got the messages that there are a number of ways to get together for fun and pleasure without drinking, and we're not talking about smoking weed. It's not that it's wrong for little boys to see grown men having fun together. But with deaths related to alcohol, addiction, and accidents so prevalent, why must every get-together for guys be accompanied by beer?

Big Guys, Big Guns

In these times of war and images of military personnel returning home with post-traumatic stress disorder (PTSD) and missing limbs, it's really difficult to talk to our sons about the disconnect between war media and real war heroes, between war heroes and the realities of war. But if we don't, we allow media to define war for our kids. What they'll get are images of explosions and men always escaping those explosions in the nick of time. They'll get adrenaline rushes from shooting a gun that's taller than they are if stood on end. They'll get the sense that all military men are brave and loyal and will never accept defeat. Indeed they'll get a message that only men are in the military. They'll also get the impression that rather than accidentally harming children and families living in war zones, troops are primarily involved in saving them, carrying them to safety, and showing them what life in America can promise. Sure these images come from a recruitment video for the National Guard, but they're also a part of the stories boys get in video games, movies, and comic books about what it means to be in the military.

The National Guard recruitment videos have been shown in over 24,000 movie theatres (65 percent) across the United States since the first one was made in September 2007. Parents taking their kids to movies like PG-rated *Marley and Me*, must sit through a three-and-a-half-minute film featuring the alternative-rock group 3 Doors Down singing "Citizen Soldier." The lyrics to this moving song are impressive. Calling out to people in war-torn areas the lead singer croons, "On that day when you need your brothers and sisters to care, I'll be right here . . . holding the light for the ones that we guide from the dark of despair." These are lyrics of caretaking, and they acknowledge that the National Guard are brothers and sisters of those in need.

But take a look at the video that accompanies these moving lyrics, a video produced by LM&O Advertising Inc., who had a $450 million contract with the National Guard. The video uses "complex pyrotechnics and the computer generated imagery" familiar to the video's director Antoine Fuqua, who directed the crime thriller *Training Day*. It takes viewers through the explosions of at least three wars—the Revolutionary War, World War II, and the Iraq war. The overtitles counter the lyrics' message of unity with statements like "I fired the shot that started a nation," "I am expert," "I am professional," and "I will never accept defeat." I, I, I—the same macho I'm the best, I'm the only one, I'm in control, I will win, messages we hear constantly in boy-targeted media. Sure, there's a moment of caretaking but it's so ridiculously stereotyped that one wonders how some bloggers could call the video inspirational. A blue-eyed blond boy in the rubble of war is lifted by a soldier and returned to his very pretty mom, the only woman in the film. In addition to that scene and those titles, there are the requisite big guns, men rappelling down from helicopters to rooftops, and men throwing grenades. Shockingly, there is also the statement "I stepped forward when the towers fell." Of course this was the National Guard in its finest hour, but we all know now that the Bush administration was wrong to connect the Iraq war to the bombing of the World Trade Center. There was no connection— except in recruiting films, we gather, where any ploy to pull the heartstrings of patriotism is used.

This video was followed in November of 2008 by a tougher message. Kid Rock screamed his lyrics: "They call me WARRIOR. They call me LOY-ALTY!" and "If you ain't gonna fight, get out of my way." Another blonde child kisses her daddy good-bye. But in this video, a Middle-Eastern-looking little boy also appears. He is frightened when his ball rolls in front of a jeep but reassured when the U.S. soldier throws it back to him. Message: they've come to help, not hurt. But wait a minute? Who's that? Interspersed with scenes of a family man going to war are scenes of NASCAR driver Dale Earnhardt Jr. suiting up and racing. Turns out he's driving a National Guard–sponsored car, and as Lieutenant General Clyde Vaughn points out, males eighteen to twenty-four are the prime audience for NASCAR, the same group from which the National Guard recruits. The general puts it in simple terms: "People will look at the partnership this way: 'The Guard is a great way to serve. It's a first-class organization. And I like Dale Earnhardt Jr. So does the guard. I'm going to have to think about that.'" In other words, an insulting "Me like cars. Dale like cars. Dale like Guard. Me join Guard." Any kid exposed to the thinking of ad men generals like this one will surely be insulted, whether or not they're inclined to like cars and the Guard!

Then there's the "U.S. Army Experience Center," which opened in August 2008 at the Franklin Mills shopping mall in northeast Philadelphia. "Departing from the recruiting environment of metal tables and uniformed soldiers in a drab military building, the Army has invested $12 million in a facility that looks like a cross between a hotel lobby and a video arcade." This twenty-first-century recruiting center has dozens of personal computers loaded with military video games, Xbox 360 video game controllers, and a series of interactive screens describing military bases and career options in great detail, as well as a lounge where potential recruits can hang out and listen to rock music. But the real fun comes from the "opportunity" that prospective soldiers are given to "fire" from a real Humvee on enemy encampments in battleground scenes projected on a fifteen-foot-high screen that has "deafening sound effects," or to join helicopter raids in which "enemy soldiers emerge from hideouts to be felled by automatic gunfire rattling from a simulator modeled on an Apache or Blackhawk helicopter." While recruiters say that the intent of the center is to "dispel misperceptions about Army life," critics, like Jesse Hamilton, a former army staff sergeant who served two tours of duty in Iraq and is now a member of Iraq Veterans Against the War, argue that the use of video games glamorizes war and misleads potential recruits. It's "very deceiving and very far from realistic," says Hamilton. "You can't simulate the loss when you see people getting killed."

Your son doesn't have to go to the movies or the mall to become a virtual soldier and experience what it's like to be part of "today's premier land force." In the privacy of your own home, he can download (for free) and play

America's Army, the "official" video game of the U.S. Army, rated T for Teen. A recruiting tool since 2002, America's Army combines promotional material with cool visual effects that create a "fast-paced, action-packed, information-rich experience that immerses visitors in the world of Soldiering in the U.S. Army." The imagery in the video game is all the same—machine guns fire, helicopters, soldiers scaling walls, but if we had any doubt that the goal was recruitment, rather than entertainment, Lawrence Kutner and Cheryl Olson report in their book *Grand Theft Childhood* that "the Web site refers to real-world army recruiting fairs across the country as 'upcoming missions.'"

The Peace Coalition, a grassroots citizen organization that began as an interfaith service in New Jersey, writes about children playing war games. They say that when children play war games they learn to:

- Create two sides, "ours" and "theirs"

- Solve arguments by fighting

- Use guns and other war equipment as toys

- Praise and reward the use of violence and physical strength

- Start fights and make enemies

- Pretend people don't suffer and die in a war

- Make war seem like an okay thing to do

- Make boys seem more important than girls.

One could argue (and our colleagues at the Campaign for a Commercial Free Childhood do) that war is sold to boys through toys. But even if you don't want to go that far, the Guard recruitment rock songs and the army video games are admittedly, up front, in your face, selling war to boys. How?—the fun of blowing things up, the ready-made peer group that has a fratlike feel, gadgets and technology, heroism. But what's missing? The boredom? The fear? The harm? The environmental destruction? Leaving the ones you love? Coming home injured physically or psychologically? The guilt and regret? Death? Certainly what's missing are some of the same aspects of war that went missing from the news when former president Bush put a ban on certain kinds of reporting. As CNN correspondent Jessica Yellin reports, "The press corps was under enormous pressure from corporate executives, frankly, to make sure that this was a war that was presented in a way that was consistent with the patriotic fever in the nation and the president's high approval ratings." A record number of troops are committing suicide: army suicides are at a twenty-year high and have been rising during the first five years in Iraq and seven years in Afghanistan. A record number of troops are returning with PTSD. The Guard and the army have major recruiting problems. But war is fun?

So what's a parent to do? Show your young sons the documentary made by Sheila Devins with James Gandolfini, *Alive Day Memories: Home from Iraq*? In this documentary, men and women who have returned from war show a mixture of pride, fear, symptoms, missing limbs, regrets, shame, and patriotism. Do we want to counteract our sons' fantasies of glory with this kind of reality? Maybe not with the kind of graphic and frightening detail that's in this particular documentary, but maybe yes. We need to do this not only because war is glorified in an unrealistic way, but also because the idea of being a man through violence is glorified. Indeed, this must play a part in the enormous problem of female military personnel being raped and sexually harrassed by other military personnel.

War is violent and takes an enormous toll on those involved, and parents will want to point out the problem with packaging it up as manhood personified and romanticizing it by using familiar messages about bands of brothers, loyalty, and protection of the weak. Since there's nothing we as parents can do about the National Guard recruitment video on the screen, short of walking out of the theater, why not use it to start a conversation about the images you've both just seen—what's there and what's not there? If he's a teen, broaden the conversation to the realities of war we don't see, and talk about the appeal to emotion these media techniques allow. The media that sells a sanitized, emotional, or pumped-up version of war is predominantly targeting boys. Since war can require the ultimate sacrifice, the least we can do is offer the truth and help him fully understand the options in front of him.

The Need for Speed

In 2008 Bravo Sports released the Pulse Kick 'N Go scooter, a reengineered version of the original Kick 'N Go from the 1970s. Guess why it has a pulse? It's a "classic racing machine" with "high performance Chromoly steel frame, band braking system and state of the art high speed polyurethane wheels."

In a press release, the CEO boasts that when he first tried it out he "ripped" around the warehouse for a "thrill" and had a "blast right from the very first kick." But CARU, the children's advertising industry's self-regulatory forum, which examines advertising directed to children under twelve, was not so thrilled. They didn't like the commercial on the Web site where a boy, around eight or nine, is riding the scooter down a residential street with several kids cheering him on. The announcer says, "Part rocket . . . part science . . . part kid. Introducing the Pulse Kick 'N Go, loaded with turbo fastronomic kick 'n go technology, which means . . . the more you kick it, the more it screams." Putting aside the reference to kicking something until it screams, CARU was interested in the way the video approvingly created an illusion of speed through high-speed photography (which blurred the background) as well as with racing sound effects. They didn't like that Bravo Sports showed a kid riding in the street without elbow and knee pads, and they didn't like that Bravo Sports created an illusion that the scooter raced faster than it actually did. We don't either. If boys are encouraged to get on their first scooter and do everything James Bond did in his last flick, what's a parent to do when he starts driving?

FAST AND FURIOUS: TEEN BOYS AND DRIVING

A few years back we remember coming across a greeting card that was gender specific and meant to be sent to parents of a newborn. Congratulations on your baby boy! Soon he will be saying two letter words: MAMA, DADA, and [turn the page] HONDA. (The baby girl version said VISA, not HONDA.) You might say that boys are born to drive, like girls are born to shop. In greeting cards, cartoons, advertisements, movies, song lyrics, video games, and other media in boys' worlds, they learn that boys love cars, boys love to drive. This makes getting your license a huge deal, getting a car even huger. (Buying insurance, paying for gas, having the car inspected—not so much.) A rite of passage of sorts, like first sex and first beer, getting a driving license is big in the lives of teen boys.

What they learn from their parents is that cars are a big responsibility. What they learn from their media is that cars:

1. represent freedom;

2. get you hot babes;

3. announce who you are;

4. prove masculinity; and

5. that the only way to really confirm the above four points is to drive your car fast and furiously.

Why else are insurance rates for teen boys so high? If in every other aspect of their media they are encouraged to be reckless, to prove their masculinity, to get ahead or be left behind, why should we expect anything different when they get behind the wheel?

As parents, we want our sons to be able to drive, to get themselves where they need to be in places where there are no public transportation, to experience freedom, and to get a lot of practice before they're truly out on their own. The laws support this. Many states have a junior operator's license that sometimes has curfews for driving and often says the teen is not permitted to drive other people for a period of time. Some states have higher driving ages, giving teens a chance for further brain development—that part of the brain that accounts for planning ahead and self-restraint. And many states have very watchful police departments, ready to give a ticket for—driving a friend on a junior operator's license; speeding; doing a rolling stop at a stop sign; not fixing that loud muffler; and making illegal U-turns. In fact, in some states, they are so vigilant that a high percentage of teens have their licenses revoked for a lengthy period of time. Would a boy rather this than be called a wuss for safe driving or refusing a friend in need who wanted a ride? Probably.

For boys, peer pressure and a need to impress their friends while driving is a real problem. One National Institutes of Health study showed that boys and girls drive faster and more recklessly when they have a male passenger. Is the stereotype that boys love speed influencing their driving? Do they have to prove they're not afraid? (Even girls know from action movies that guys love a hot babe who loves a car chase and then can jump out and repair an engine!) Or are kids afraid to look cautious in front of someone who might see that cautiousness as wussy?

Afraid to look cautious? You betcha. The Pluggedin Online Web site, affiliated with Focus on the Family, a Christian nonprofit group that reviews media aimed at kids, makes the point that in *2 Fast 2 Furious* the film's racing moves "beg to be copied . . . Trying to impress Monica, Brian accelerates to 120 mph while staring intently at her sitting beside him in the passenger seat. Then he brakes to a stop at a red light before redirecting his gaze to the road. Pulling up beside them, Roman smirks, "Did he do the stare-and-drive thing? I taught him that!"

This review also points out that *2 Fast 2 Furious* costar Eva Mendes told Jay Leno that to do that scene they slowed the car down to about 15 mph. We're not sure how many teen boys were watching Leno that night and how many think that stunt was done in real time as opposed to those who imagine toy cars in a production studio digitally reproduced for action! Of course, most boys won't try this specific stunt, but it would seem that there's a mound of approval waiting for those willing to try any stunt.

Then there's the *Need for Speed* series of racing games that say a lot to boys about what the need for speed now means, which is no longer just racing and winning. Perhaps the makers of these games learned a thing or two from Vin Diesel in *Fast and Furious* and his replacement, rapper-actor Tyrese, in *2 Fast 2 Furious*, which celebrate the bad guy origins of the hero: he's a criminal racing for respect. *Need for Speed* becomes *Need for Speed: Most Wanted* and then *Need for Speed: Carbon*, all of which use the bad guys getting the badder guys' device. In this series of racing games a kid plays a lone racer (yes, one man alone in these cars!) returning to his home city only to find it dominated by rival racing groups who disrespect him, one of which includes the guy who stole his girlfriend. As in *2 Fast 2 Furious*, for speed racing to be cool, police also have to be the bad guys. In *Need for Speed: Carbon*, for example, the driver must avoid capture and gets points for the money he costs the state in the damage done to public property.

With *Grand Theft Auto* and *Need for Speed*, with a wild car chase and a cool car in nearly every "guy" movie, with all those messages that boys must be over-the-top in image and ready to take dangerous risks, what else can we expect when boys start driving? Blame lack of parental discipline. Blame testosterone. Blame peers. Why not also blame the media?

FAST AND NOT SO FURIOUS: SNOWBOARDING

Snowboarding, a sport that has gained momentum in the past two decades, has a special place in the lives of boys who live up North. Snowboarders have long been known to be one part jock, one part slacker, and one part risk taker. A store in Maine even calls itself Slackers. Another company is called Smokin' Snowboards, obviously a play on speed and on the impression that snowboarders like to smoke weed.

Even so, snowboarding can be an extreme sport where the laid-back stoner culture exists hand in hand with a devil-may-care stunt-driven approach to the slopes. While many snowboarders are mellow, they practice a lot and do amazing things on their boards, take risks, and are over-the-top in the things they will try.

Marketers take advantage of inside jokes among users of their products and in so doing tell newly interested kids what kind of identity goes hand in hand with being a snowboarder. Take the boards that are sold to them from the Vermont Company, Burton Snowboards, that have graphics of cartoon characters self-mutilating. First, these kitschy graphics have a kind of stoner quality to them, as in a stoned boy staring at his hand. In fact, the name of the line is Primo, and whether or not the manufacturers knew this or not, *Urban Dictionary* tells us that's the name of a hollowed-out cigar filled with a mixture of marijuana and cocaine. The Primo line shows a set of cartoons with blood dripping down hands that are being mutilated. We see someone cutting off his or her fingers, driving nails into them, slicing them off with razor blades. One shows a dog biting one of these fingers. In one called "Number One" someone is snipping off his fingers or having his fingers cut off in order to sew on a foam rubber finger of sport team support. On another board, called Peace, fingers are bloodily cut off to leave the two fingers that form a peace sign. On yet another, Metal Horns, horns are created on a hand by a vicious dog biting off the middle two fingers. The message is clear. Snowboarders are extreme. They can take that self-mutilation as they "tear" down a mountain and do crazy stunts. It's even considered a badge of honor.

In the wake of a rise in self-mutilation (cutting) among high school girls and boys, parents and antiviolence advocates protested these snowboards. These horror cartoons, done tongue in cheek (or so say the owners of Burton), disturbed parents. One nonprofit group that provides classes to boys who have been physically and sexually aggressive in schools made the brave decision to turn down the charitable snowboarding program that Burton has for years provided them. In a culture where inflicting self-pain, through dangerous stunts and throwing oneself at the slopes, is sometimes encouraged, why do boys also need the suggestion of self-mutilation?

Think about the boards named Primo and Fix with "kits" like the one called "420," which suggest illegal drug activity (4/20 is considered by many to be "national weed smoking day," originally referring to police lingo). Kaboodle.com says, "Although Burton claims to have no idea what it's used for, we think you can figure it out. This handy satchel is crush-resistant and watertight for raucous riding, and has a sleeve for an extra lighter, since you always forget where you put that other one. The wallet-size 420 Kit has a removable baggie to keep your stash fresh and elastic loops to secure a couple prerolled delights." There's something especially sleazy about the way manufacturers and marketers collude with kids to pull one over on parents. Most parents most likely don't know the connotations of 420 and will be likely to see this kit as a little box for whatever. They might, however, get some other references. The "Fix" snowboard, for example, is purportedly in the shape of a 55 mg pill, and the caption says: "Getting This High in the Park Should be Illegal." It's as if they're saying to boys, "Your parents are so lame and so out of touch; but we get you, we know what's cool and what you're into."

When marketers say "we know who you are" they also mean we *create* who you are. Burton is no exception, expanding their brand by introducing new identities. Stoner? Slacker? How about player? Alex Kuczynski wrote in the *New York Times* about Burton's "template for life" and how Burton sells a "Liquid Lounger, a knapsack with speakers, which also folds out into a chair. Inside are a knife, dice and a miniature martini shaker." The Burton Hook-Up Kit, although supposedly for the ladies, is stocked with items they might need after a hookup—a toothbrush and thong underwear—and sounds to us as if this is exactly the present a stupid guy will give a gal! Sure it may be for girls, but they're marketing an image to boys with this item. And images imply behaviors. Take the board shaped like a condom called, of course, Condom—"So Raw the Park Needs Protection." Ouch.

Recently, Burton introduced the Love boards, which we mentioned earlier. Picturing naked women, here's the Web description:

> Hi. My name is "Love" and I'm on the market for someone looking for some serious action, no matter where they like to stick it. I enjoy laps through the park, long hard grinds on my meaty park edges.

While the company has a record of supporting women's and antiviolence organizations, as well as giving free snowboarding trips to at-risk youth in Vermont and elsewhere, these ideals are pushed aside if a new demographic can be served. "Fast" takes on new meaning, and just as action movies get ridiculous with their sexual innuendoes by using car themes, snowboarding marketing hype has its edgy innuendoes with "laps around the park" and "long hard grinds." While these jokes may be as old as B porn movies from the 1960s, they're brand-new and edgy messages to each generation of boys.

FAST, FAST, FAST

Fast invades all aspects of boys' lives, especially through the media. The joke is that "real" boys are speedy—that this is just a part of who they are. They're shown whizzing through the kitchen and picking up some "fast-food," whizzing down a hill, whizzing down a street. Boy media revs them up further with fast edits from one scene to the next rather than long cuts or growing narratives. Everything's quicker, impulsive, speedy. Their favorite books are graphic novels and manga. The music that accompanies their media pumps them up. It's exhausting. No wonder so many want to opt out, slack, and get stoned.

Parents can help boys slow down, not by "grounding" them or clipping their wings, but by talking to them about how there are urges everywhere in media to do things quickly and to enjoy that sense of speed. As our good friend Rich DeGrandpre writes in his book, *Ritalin Nation*, the antidote to all this speed is deliberateness. We can break sensory addictions by asking our sons to accompany us on walks in the woods. We can challenge our own paradigm of work, work, work by inviting them away from their homework not into a world of slackerdom but out for some relaxing time, letting them know that even hard workers do take breaks. We can talk about consciousness with them and the difference between simulated and hands-on reality. This doesn't mean saying no to everything fast and hyped. It just means helping them to find places and activities beyond the world of slacking that are not.

Boys Will Be Players: Sex Acts and Media

In fifth grade, in schools across the nation, when the boys are separated from the girls to receive their sex education about puberty, reproduction, and wet dreams, they're often given a takeaway, sort of a party favor, in the form of a related product. No, not a condom, but a stick of deodorant. Besides branding them for life as an Old Spice user (now renamed Red Zone because, we guess, sailors are no longer considered as cool or rugged as football players), it gives them a message about sex and boyhood. Girls also get deodorant, but peach-scented Secret doesn't come with a slew of ads connecting her body smells to whether or not she'll get lucky. For boys, what begins as a message akin to what "rude bunny," the cartoon character found at stores like Hot Topic, says on girls' "revenge" T-shirts—BOYS ARE

SMELLY—winds up as a message to boys that they need cleaning up before girls will like them. It is, after all, a deodorant "that appeals to your Friday night date, and your Saturday night date, and your Thursday night date." You know, because all those fifth-grade players have dates lined up. The gift of a deodorant to boys is a special boy message that *boy* means dirty, smelly, gross stuff, so clean up if you want to get some lovin'.

Along with the message that boys are smelly and gross, there will also be plenty more messages about boys as unstoppable sex machines. Boys' sexuality is depicted in films and on TV as uncomplicated. They are just ready to go, driven, always heterosexual, thinking with and controlled by their penis, sometimes to their embarrassment, and eager to dive into a new sexual life as an adult unambivalently and with total enthusiasm whenever, wherever, and with whomever. If they are ever depicted as insecure, this insecurity seems to be about being chosen by girls, being cool enough to be of interest to girls, but never about the wanting. That's a given. No longer are they ever pictured as Allan Felix (Woody Allen) in *Play It Again, Sam* saying with excitement before a date, "I really have mixed feelings about this!"

Rarely are they depicted as not wanting to have sex. Do they ask, "Am I really attracted to this girl?" Not unless she's played up as someone any viewer would consider gross and unappealing. Occasionally boys, or the men in movies that boys watch, are shown as torn between a night out with the boys or a beautiful girl offering herself up to him in exchange for letting down his buds. We know that in real life boys do refuse sex, and research shows that when they don't want to have sex but go ahead and do it anyway, they regret it. Interestingly enough, among college-aged boys, over half report having sex they regretted the morning after for the following reasons: alcohol, not wanting the same things their partner wanted, lack of condom use, and that it was inconsistent with their morals.

It's not only in the movies where teen boys' real sexuality remains unexplored. Whereas scholarly writing about teen girls and their sexuality (often treated as what makes them vulnerable and precious) abounds, researchers have, by and large, stayed away from teen boys and their sexuality. We wonder why. It may be difficult for a father or a grown man to imagine anything beyond the standardized view of teen boys' sexuality—which includes unfettered (except by their own awkwardness or zits) access to all those supposedly hot and ready teen girls we see so much of in the media. Is it just a stereotype that fathers of teen boys take an "atta boy" stance as their sons go out into the world of dating? When the media report shocking examples of sexual misconduct on the part of boys (the incidents most likely to make headlines in the current media circus), we seem to hear only from those fathers willing to defend their sons with a public "boys will be boys message" and very little from the fathers who struggle with what to say to their sons at these moments. As men age, perhaps they fall prey to an idealization of teen male sexuality, picturing boys "at the ready" in a way the older male sometimes no longer is? Is the more complex conversation, the one that includes feelings of ambivalence, conformity, and fear of being called gay, too difficult to take on? Is it more important for the media to publicly present those dads who prop up their sons, representing a culture where boys are supposed to be hypersexual to prove their manhood? Teens have long been a screen for our projections, with parents wanting to redo their own adolescence through their children. But this version of adolescence they picture and want their sons to have is an illusion best laid to rest.

The work of sociologist Peggy Giordano and her colleagues is a noteable exception to the lack of research on boys' sexuality. They argue that boys, regardless of race and social class, are more emotionally engaged in their romantic relationships and also feel more awkward and less confident than all those stereotypes and media depictions suggest. In a study of 1,300 teenagers, boys described how it felt to be on the other end of those long awkward silences on the phone, to feel nervous and uncertain about a new romance. They described the pressure they felt to initiate sex and their anxiety about performance. They talked about the intensity of their feelings for girls who "were there for them," how much it meant to be able to disclose their real selves to someone, and how difficult it was to hurt someone they no longer loved or how much they hurt when a relationship "crashed and burned." They also talked about the social experience and power girls had in their relationships, especially in the beginning stages. Now and again, the researchers discovered a "player," but their study suggests that the "big man" stereotype that sociologist Barrie Thorne described just doesn't exist—in fact, most boys distance themselves from this image. Still, it's a highly valued social role and the belief in it, propped up by all those movie and TV studs and players, keeps boys believing and prevents them from talking to other boys about what they really feel and think. The same boys who expressed their love for their girlfriends expressed concern that other boys would tease them for being controlled by a girl and thus not matching up to the big man ideal.

But it's not only that we're missing another side of (or the real story behind) boys' sexuality, it's also that the media bombardment of these messages about the only way to be sexual makes it difficult for boys to recognize their own ambivalences, hesitancies, and insecurities with regard to sex. Boys in college who've had "regrettable sex" may do so because at the time they didn't even know they didn't want to have sex! Listening to boys talk about their relationships, psychologist Deborah Tolman was struck by how much peer pressure there is for boys to show that they can do sexual things with girls, even when they aren't feeling it. The more they engage in these activities, the more masculine and popular they are in the eyes of other boys. Being a player and having several girlfriends, said one boy to her, shows your friends "that you are macho or more of a man." The expectation that they should want sex all the time with whomever they can "get it from" reduced the time to pause and consider whether they were actually ready or wanted to do so. When Tolman says that girls need to know they can say yes before they can convincingly say no, we think for boys it's just the opposite— if they understand why and when they can say no, they're more likely to say yes at a time and place and with a person who feels right to them.

How are boys expected to deal with all the messages about being out of control, having body parts that seem disconnected or out of their control, having desire that they are told is boundless, and having smells that offend? They are told that they should take control, and when it comes to sex, the control message is the player message. This message starts early with bibs that say CHICK MAGNET and Onesies that say LOCK UP YOUR DAUGHTERS. As we've noted earlier, the player is invulnerable, always cool, but suavely not invested in the game, even as he plays it.

We parents should ask ourselves, How are our sons coping with the un-relenting messaging of boys as players? Is it just a buddy thing, something they play at when they're with their pals as they share in the objectification of girls? Or is it something that makes them feel totally inadequate, like porn pictures of men with extraordinarily large penises or booty-shaking music videos with guys surrounded by hot babes? Are our own efforts to prop boys up—telling them that they're cool and in control, with the intent of helping them avoid feeling out of control or protecting them from the worst kinds of insults—contributing to a culture that can only make him feel inadequate by comparison?

What about love? What about passion? Don't teen boys long for passion while they play it cool as the player? Giordano's study about boys' romantic feelings suggest they do. Is passion always presented as uncontrollable lust? No, not always. In many of the movies we watched of men standing alone against the odds, of fantasy figures fighting the good fight, of boys searching for long-lost fathers, there was the girl next door. She props him up when he's at his lowest point. It's with her that a hero can be vulnerable and show a passion that looks to any viewer like the intermingling of love and sex. She's not the girl he thought he wanted, the one with the fake boobs and flashy clothes. She's the one who's been there all along when he was a jerk and/or failed at something. She's the sweet Renee Zellweger character, Dorothy, in *Jerry Maguire*. Alas, in this story of love boys are essentially being offered an age-old madonna/whore dichotomy refigured as the sexpot vs. the chaste girlfriend.

Passion and a longing for death are entwined, as the famed scholar de Rougemont wrote in *Love in the Western World*. This is especially true in boys' media: where there is love there is often a concomitant message about bravery, risk, and death. Whether it's Hans Solo staring passionately into Princess Leia's eyes as he's frozen in carbonite, the loss of love that compels Spider-Man to fight evil, or the varied cinematic versions of passion that drive a Bruce Willis character in *Die Hard* movies to risk his life to save the world, love and death are almost always part of the same story.

What does this suggest to a boy harboring feelings of awkwardness and uncertainty? Like so many of the over-the-top emotions that boys are presented with, passion is depicted as so violent and disruptive an emotion that it can make a man do anything and put himself in all sorts of danger, enduring all sorts of pain for the woman he loves. And thus for boys, when they want someone and actually feel something for them, they are in danger of humiliation and rejection, so this mixture of lust and longing needs to be transformed into acts where invulnerability is glorified. In a story we see over and over, from *Shrek* to *A Knight's Tale* to nearly every superhero movie, the hero is set up to be strong, to put himself in danger and prove his love, not by his tenderness in the love scenes, but in his willingness to fight for her and prove his worth.

The danger-driven performance of love and passion in boys' media make it especially difficult for boys who are gay or questioning their sexuality. All that pressure on boys to be a player and demonstrate to other boys that they can get girls, whether as dates or as sexual partners, Tolman says, is designed to establish themselves publicly as heterosexual and to avoid being the target of homophobic harassment and (humiliating/shaming) labeling behaviors. TV and movies, especially the funny movies like *Blades of Glory*, *Borat*, and *Step Brothers*, are filled with not-so-subtle warnings to boys who dare to express anything other than strict codes of male heterosexuality.

Of course true love doesn't exist in media and marketing for boys who are gay or questioning their sexuality. If they're lucky enough to live in a more liberal city they may see coupled gay men, even with adopted kids, living what seem to be boring, middle-class lives. If they rely on TV, they'll get abundant messages that gay men long for love too but have as much difficulty finding Mr. Right as the women of *Sex and the City*. They might hear stereotypes about the sleazy underbelly of gay city life that has more to do with homophobic fears than reality. Or they might be able to peek into a gay bar where there are gay partners and singles having a good time. What they won't see very often, as with heterosexual media fare, is an intermingling of lust and love.

Psychiatrist Harry Stack Sullivan wrote in the 1950s that integrating lust with love is a lifelong task for boys. He described the need to replace the sense of loneliness that can emerge in early adolescence with real intimacy, and the importance of connecting those intimate feelings with sexual desire. Today's media, with its stark, over-the-top macho messages makes this process so much more difficult for boys, and they are at their most vulnerable when feeling both.

We would like to see more movies and TV shows that put boys in complex situations, that don't send them off to fight a dragon or save the world the minute they get into a situation where they begin to love someone. We would like to see movies and TV shows that reveal more than that one side of his sexuality, the side that shows him wanting to screw anyone in sight. Sure that's a part of adolescence too, but it's the only part of adolescent sexuality he'll see reflected unless his family owns some chick flicks. And funnily enough, even though he sees it reflected everywhere, he'll still worry that he's strange and perverse for feeling that way. No amount of *American Pie* can comfort him on that score. He can't be all about getting some without feeling disgusting, and can't fall in love without feeling like a sissy. And that's sad.

The Pornification of Boyhood

None of the boys who filled out our survey admitted to looking at pornography, although when asked about things they want to watch but their parents say no to, boys as young as eleven answered "nasty videos," "any too adult stuff," and "sex channels." Clearly boys are interested, parents know boys are interested, and experts who study youth and pornography tell us that most teens and many preteens, particularly boys, have viewed porn.

One study from Canada is telling, and we would be naïve to think that the boys in our survey are all that different from Canadian boys. Sonya

Thompson at the University of Alberta anonymously surveyed more than four hundred thirteen- and fourteen-year-olds from both urban and rural schools across the province of Alberta. She asked them about how and how often they accessed sexually explicit media content on digital or satellite television, video, or DVD, and the Internet. Ninety percent of males and 70 percent of females reported watching at least once. More than one-third of the boys reported viewing pornographic DVDs or videos "too many times to count," compared to 8 percent of the girls surveyed.

A majority of the students (74 percent) reported viewing pornography on the Internet, 41 percent saw it on video or DVD, and 57 percent reported seeing it on a specialty TV channel. Nine percent of the teens reported they accessed pornography because someone over eighteen (typically a friend or older sibling) had rented it; 6 percent had rented it themselves; and 20 percent viewed it at a friend's house. The study also revealed different patterns of use between males and females, with boys doing the majority of deliberate viewing, some even planning social time around viewing porn with male friends. Girls reported more accidental or unwanted exposure online and tended to view porn in same-gender pairs or with mixed groups.

More evidence about young people's exposure to pornography comes from Janis Wolak and her colleagues at the University of New Hampshire's Crimes against Children Research Center. Wolak's team asked a national sample of parents for permission to interview their ten- to seventeen-year-old children about exposure to Internet pornography. Just under half of the parents agreed to allow the children to speak privately with the researchers by telephone. Between March and June 2005, the researchers interviewed 1,422 children and found that:

- Forty-two percent of youths age ten to seventeen had seen Internet porn in the past year.

- Two-thirds of youth exposures to Internet porn were unwanted. Unwanted porn found its way to 17 percent of ten- to eleven-year-old boys and 16 percent of ten- to eleven-years-old girls. (However, not all unwanted exposure to porn was unintentional; 21 percent of the time, kids knew they were entering X-rated Web sites but weren't quite sure what they were in for.)

- Boys were exposed to Internet porn far more often than girls, and boys were nine times more likely than girls to actively seek out Internet porn.

- Teens, especially those age sixteen to seventeen, were far more likely than younger kids to view online porn, either accidentally or on purpose. For example, more than two-thirds of boys sixteen to seventeen had been exposed to online porn.

- Most youth said they were not upset by the images they saw.

What should we make of the findings from these studies? It should come as no surprise that kids are curious about sex. With the majority of porn being made for boys and men, it's also no surprise that boys are seeking out the stuff that's explicitly for them. But there are consequences. For example, watching porn could undermine attitudes about sexual behavior, values like respect and a commitment to procuring verbal consent. Exposure to deviant or offensive sexual behavior could introduce ideas to young minds that will color their sexual expectations, especially if there's no one they can turn to for a reality check.

Those who seek out our friend and colleague Gale Golden, associate professor of Psychiatry at Fletcher Allen Hospital in Vermont, for help with porn addictions (typically adult men whose addiction has cost them their relationships and sometimes their jobs), often talk about early compulsive use of pornography. These men may have been particularly vulnerable, just as boys already angry and impulsive are more likely to lash out after watching too many violent films or engaging in hours of violent video games.

We have other concerns about boys' exposure to pornography, concerns that are shared by Jackson Katz, author of *The Macho Paradox*, and Robert Jensen, author of *Getting Off: Pornography and the End of Masculinity*. We worry about the messages that pornography sends to boys about the sexual objectification and exploitation of girls and women. We worry about the effects of seeing degrading acts "performed" by women, and sometimes teen girls, in pornographic videos and on pornographic Web sites and the ways these acts are increasingly alluded to, and thus normalized, in PG-13 films and ad campaigns targeting teen boys. If boys and young men are conditioned to relate sexually to girls and women only as objects or body parts, interchangeable and anonymous, rather than as unique, complex human beings, then boys and young men's sexual and relational lives run the risk of becoming severely impoverished. If it doesn't affect their relationships, couldn't porn affect their real sex life after building fantasies about perfect women with perfect bodies? Naomi Wolf writes that for avid porn users, "real naked women are just bad porn."

What about the racism in porn? *The Porning of America* authors Carmine Saracchino and Kevin Scott write that interracial scenes are considered at the bottom of the list of undesirable porn acts for performers but that they are also "immensely popular with consumers, [suggesting] an implicit desire in the viewers to see porn stars lower themselves—regarding sex with a black man as a degradation, and thereby combining racism with misogyny."

Speaking of the "over-the-top" action marketers love to give boys—in commercials, in movies, in video games, on TV—sex in porn is always over-the-top. The women are delirious with pleasure or are being demeaned in more violent porn. This, of course, creates unrealistic expectations in heterosexual boys with regard to what real sex is like—it's not being sweet, funny, attentive, sensitive, interested, and knowledgeable that makes a man good in bed these images tell him; it's size and authority.

The boy who watches WWE, MTV, or simply connects to friends' MySpace pages are also likely to see images that come from the world of porn. Many of these can be every bit as demeaning and objectifying as triple-X Internet porn. Take the porn-inspired advertisements a boy might see, as we wrote about earlier, on the Axe deodorant site, or in an Old Spice ad of a blonde twenty-something woman licking a very phallic ice-cream cone with her eyes closed in sexual ecstasy. As Saracchino and Scott pointed out when they write about this ad in their book, the words *eat* and *eating* are paired with *it* four times in a single ad, and the headline says: "This is simply a picture of a woman eating a vanilla ice-cream cone" (nudge nudge wink wink). The byline on the bottom, which says "keep it clean," plays on boys' anxiety and shame about dirtiness, reminding them to use the deodorant and stay clean if they want girls to give them blow jobs.

Debbie Nathan, in her book *Pornography*, writes that kids cannot be shielded. They are exposed to pornographic images everywhere. America has truly been porned—and so censorship for a variety of reasons is not the answer. Her alternative is media literacy. She writes that media literacy advocates are now asking for curriculum units on pornography. Teens could then start asking, "Why are these pictures being shown to me? Is what I am seeing a true and realistic image of what sex is like? Why are other people drawn to these images? What important things are not shown? What are the circumstances that led these individuals to be filmed or photographed? Could an adult help me better understand what I'm seeing?"

Parents can and should do their own media literacy talking at home. It is important to acknowledge the difficulty of having the kind of conversations with boys and young men that all these authors and researchers, including coauthor Sharon Lamb, in an earlier book, write about. For many boys, pornography may already be inextricably linked to their sexual pleasure, given that heterosexual boys and young men tend to masturbate to images and videos of nude women. Because sexuality is an intensely private experience for most boys, and its link to pornography is also intensely private and even taboo, it's very difficult to get boys to talk about their use of pornography and its relationship to his developing sexuality. But we can only try.

SEX ED CAN INCLUDE PORN ED

We strongly recommend that you do not allow pornography to become your son's primary sex educator. Don't blame, shame, or condemn your son for being curious about and titillated by porn. Share your opinions, beliefs, and values about the harmful lessons that porn teaches him. Fathers, in particular, need to tell their sons how most porn degrades women, as well as the boys and men who view it. Tell your son that sex can and should be an outgrowth of a loving, committed, respectful relationship, not a forum for male self-gratification and the exploitation of women. Discussions about sex and sexuality are among the most difficult discussions you will have with your children. But isn't it better to have these discussions, even admitting to your son that you are somewhat uncomfortable talking about these topics, than to surrender his heart and mind to pornographers?

Boys also need to see how their media presents women as sexual gatekeepers, while boys are presented as always wanting it. They are going to be faced with some Mars/Venus problems, given that women are fed nonstop romance, while men are fed nonstop porn. We need to address with them how pornography teaches and invades a fantasy life that could be richer. Have a sense of humor and laugh when you discuss how porn creates a version of sexuality that's far from reality—even play your teen son the scene from *When Harry Met Sally* when Meg Ryan imitates an orgasm while eating a salad in a restaurant. If you're a parent who feels strongly that media censorship is wrong, tell your son that you're not against pornography per se but against narrow versions of pornography that are degrading to women and make guys feel as if they have to be superstuds.

Finally, why can't schools discuss porn in health classes? Or in media literacy classes? Once your son understands the drugs, corruption, and exploitation behind the porn industry he may feel very differently about it. Discussions about airbrushing and digitizing women's bodies, and the harm that derives from sexualizing all sorts of images and experiences that aren't necessarily or don't need to be sexual, should be part of boys' education as well as girls'. Sex ed needs to move forward fearlessly to include discussion about what "healthy sexuality" is. Adults don't have all the answers, but it's at least worth opening up a dialogue. Some religious groups, parents, and kids will take offense, but they need to know that sex education now involves more than just how and when to do it; it involves learning how to be in and cope with a flashy world of marketing and media that sexualizes everything in our culture 24/7. There are ways to think about this that pull for kids' ethical responses, questions about gender equality, autonomy, and caring that ask them to consider what kind of world they'd like to live in—and we should invite them into these kinds of ethical discussions. In this way, we make them sexual citizens in a 24/7 XXX world.

Blood, Guts, and Glory: Just Another Day at the Screen

Boys and video games—the quintessential toy, technology, extracurricular activity, love that defines modern boyhood play. Boys told us they love games where they can perform like rock stars, jump or kick like sports stars, fight like warriors, or kill enemies with some of the most impressive weapons of modern combat. By playing video games, a boy can *become* a hero; he can turn the tide of battle or make the right decision to change the world. Gone are the ghost-eating Pac-Men and mushroom-jumping Marios. In fact, America Ferrera and Carrie Underwood are selling Mario to girls in a recent ad, and as we know all too well, that's the kiss of death in terms of boy interest! Modern video games convey excitement and fear in ways barely imagined when Atari's video Pong first displaced foosball in bars across the United States. Like "embeds" in the Iraq war, boys can now easily imagine what it might be like to be in the trenches. Let's look at a few of the most popular games and explore the worlds they invite boys to enter.

SHOOT 'EM UP

Halo, Half-Life, and *Bioshock* are examples of first-person shooter (FPS) games. Boys who play these games rarely see the main character's face because they assume his persona. They *become* him, shooting his gun, keeping track of his ammo, monitoring his health. If he sees a group of enemies, the player as the hero can run at them, firing as he goes. Then, if an enemy tank shows up, the player can jump on top of it, stick a grenade in, and jump off the tank as it is exploding, just like any movie action hero.

Avatars—players' representations of themselves or alter egos in computer games—are often unstoppable, with bodies like WWE wrestlers and unfailing strength. For example, *Halo's* Master Chief is a seven-foot, thousand-pound soldier who fights off an alien foe known in the game as the Covenant. Like other avatars, which are cartoon characters of sorts, he can be designed to meet any boy's (or general's) fantasy, more robot, or 'bot, than man. When other marines fail in one-on-one combat against Covenant soldiers, the Master Chief can destroy legions of the invading army.

Playing on a boy's desire not only to be recognized as powerful, but also to be deserving of that power—a desire, as we've seen, that's been honed through years of media messages—value or worth in such games is measured not only by successful battles but also by admiration from others around one. Often nonplayer characters (NPC) celebrate the arrival of the lead character. As a superior officer screams to a scared marine in *Halo*: "The Chief is gonna jump in this tank, roll across the bridge, and blow up any inhuman son-of-a-bitch dumb enough to get between him and the Prophet of Regret!"

Admiration quickly becomes worship, and it, like the fear evoked in enemies, rises exponentially. For example, when the Master Chief is celebrated for killing an alien, a boy playing *Halo 3* feels his status rise through the NPCs cheering him on as well as the enemies running in terror. A boy can experience the strength of the Master Chief as his own, and as Lawrence Kutner and Cheryl Olson say in *Grand Theft Childhood*, these experiences can boost confidence.

But do we want our boys gaining confidence through creating fear in others or even through the cold and distant admiration of followers? What other possibilities are there? In these games, not many. In these games, you are the celebrated hero or the lowly follower. In *Gears of War*, another popular FPS game, the player again wages war against an alien force, except it's from the vantage point of a person looking over the main character's shoulder, seeing his snarl as he turns back and faces the player, and watching him shrug at the gore he leaves behind. But even behind the leader, the player is not a follower. He feels as if he *is* Marcus Fenix, an unflinching, fearless ex-convict: mankind's only hope. And as a hero for boys, Fenix is very cold. He cusses apathetically, behaves too cool to care whether he lives or dies, and acknowledges atrocities as a part of life. In this way, Fenix and other video game heroes like him show boys how to cope with fear, which is to be too cool to feel it, too hard to cry, and too above it all to care. When an NPC, a junior soldier, shows admiration, "Are you THE Marcus Fenix?" he answers simply, "Yep." The admiring soldier says, "Cool!" to which Fenix responds, in that understated action figure style, "Not really . . ." Even after a close-quarters brawl and a graphic kill using a chain saw Fenix only says, "Ahh . . . blood, guts, just another day on the job."

But fear is not altogether lost. It's preserved by the NPCs. When in *Halo* the Master Chief dies, the soldiers around him begin to panic, saying things like, "We're done for!" and "Who's gonna save the Earth?" One soldier in *Gears of War* says to Fenix, "I used to have nightmares about those things when I was a kid." These expressions of NPCs' fears remind the player that what's going on in the game is indeed something to be feared. But these fears are not included in order to teach boys, hey, it's okay to be afraid. They exist to reassert the value of the invulnerable hypermasculine lead avatar, the only character with whom boys are really asked to identify.

The *Grand Theft Auto* series is an example of a third-person shooter game (TPS), where you're not a character in the game, but you see the character you're controlling. In *Grand Theft Auto IV* it's Niko Bellic, a Balkan immigrant navigating the gangster underworld. *Grand Theft Auto* is also an example of an M-rated game that is enormously popular with teen and college-aged boys, in large part because it's a clever and funny satiric take on the games' various locales, such as Miami, Las Vegas, and Los Angeles. In *Grand Theft Auto IV*, the creators spoof New York. In an April 30, 2008, review for *The Pace Press*, Carlos Cabrera gushes:

> Every single corner contains incredible detail, right down to the blackened gum stuck to our sidewalks. City landmarks look as if they were pulled right off our streets, and their new names reflect some sort of a subtle joke on the actual structure; the isle of Manhattan now takes its original, Native American name. The Lincoln Tunnel is now the Booth Tunnel and the dilapidated Domino Sugar Factory makes a cameo as the Twitchins Sugar Factory. So much of the charm of this game is not just in the gunfire or the detail, but the execution.

Of course middle school boys playing won't get the charm, a concern because *Grand Theft Auto IV*, like its predecessors, is enormously violent. This is the game that has received all the sensationalized media coverage because players can have sex with prostitutes and then kill them. Yes it's true that

Niko can maintain his health by using the services of a prostitute, which would work against killing them for the pure fun of it, but this hardly registers as positive. That particular sex education, combined with a new battery of lethal weapons and the ability to drive drunk and partner with other online players to cheat, stab, shoot, and beat, make it all the more important for parents to take note of the M (not meant for anyone under seventeen) rating. As Common Sense Media reports in an April 23, 2008, article, "Grand Theft Auto IV—Parents: M means M!," "eighty-seven percent of boys under 17 have played an M-rated video game, and only one percent say their parents have ever stopped them from playing one." We're not exactly saying that parents should make sure that wherever their son goes, this video game will not be in the house, but parents ought to know what is in these games and at the very least talk to their sons about the content and their objections.

As boys live out their video game fantasies, they're invited into a world where serious violence and harm are entertainment. And so what? Aren't the majority of movies your teen son will see this summer full of the same excessive force, lurid blood splattering, strong language, and a smattering of ironic jokes to show we all know this isn't real? Well, actually no—not to this extent. In these games, avatars do M-rated violence with M-rated animated effects, whereas even the most action-packed PG-13 movie stops short of these kinds of graphics. For example, in *Gears of War*, players can curb-stomp a fallen enemy (stomping on someone's head on the edge of a curb) in a gruesome display of power. In *Bioshock* the player can set enemies on fire and watch them run around, pleading to be put out while flailing their arms. In *God of War*, a game set in ancient Greece, the player can rip out a Cyclops's one eye in a gory attempt at humor. This level of violence connected with humor and callousness invites something a little deeper, a little closer to the bone.

It's this kind of realistic and soulless violence that researchers tell us is the most damaging to children. Boys who are victims in other areas of their lives can feel not only heroic admiration in these video games, but also the power of revenge that they can't exact in real life. And as every parent knows, even for boys who aren't victimized on a daily basis or who generally feel pretty good about themselves, there's the worry about the ways these increasingly realistic-looking games can desensitize them to violence.

One may ask, But isn't this fantasy violence? My son won't be running into a Cyclops, nor will he probably ever see someone's eye gouged out? For sure—but he will learn and practice over and over again a certain attitude toward violence that minimizes the harm and horror, and maximizes emotions such as pride, callousness, too-cool-to-care-ness, and the guilty pleasure of rubbing it in when you emerge a victor. And like the difference in the level of graphic violence, the attitudes that appear in shooter games won't appear in PG-13 movies boys watch, except in the bad guys. In the movies that a parent might be tempted to compare these games to, it's always the bad guy who rubs it in. The good guy, although violent, shows remorse and respect. So what does that M really mean? That a boy needs to be Mature enough not to identify with a hero whom he will follow day in and day out, through adventure after crime scene after conflict after battle after war? Whose son is *that* Mature?

PARENTAL GUIDANCE REQUIRED

There's such a broad range of video games available to boys of every age that it's impossible to review them all. Online gaming sites and video game magazines promote games designated E for Everyone alongside T for Teen and M for Mature, and boys know they can go online and watch trailers for most any game or try out the newest games. Boys watching the reality show *From G's to Gents* online will see a short ad for 50 Cent's violent video game *Blood on the Sand* at virtually every commercial break. His interest piqued, he can check out the trailer on YouTube and see something much more graphically violent—a video game, crime adventure, and more Middle East war. He can see 50 Cent's Humvee's driver shot, blood spurting from his chest; his car careening over the men shooting at him; a camo-clad 50 Cent gunning down enemies, beating attackers up, breaking their necks with a crack, standing in the open door of a rising helicopter as he lets out a barrage of machine-gun fire on the enemies below, jumping out of the helicopter just before it crashes, just in time for another mano a mano fight. Are the guys he's fighting terrorists? No, this is personal: someone has stolen his property, a diamond-encrusted skull, and 50 Cent and his G-Unit (also the name of his clothing line) is on a violent rampage to get it back.

Each new video game is more visually sophisticated and sensational; each hero more bulked up, more entitled. In the case of *Blood on the Sand*, game designer Tim Austin and crew "didn't really want a game where you're spending all your time hiding behind cover . . . so there's a lot of point rewards for getting out and getting in the faces of your enemy." That means more neck breaking and kicks to the back and groin, more beaten and bloodied faces. Nick Breckon, writing for the online computer game forum

Shacknews, says in response, "That's what I'm talking about. If I'm playing a 50 Cent game, I don't want to run around daintily dodging bullets and hiding behind potted plants. Cover is for punks."

Should parents be concerned about violent video games? Clearly, yes. There's no doubt that the barrage of realistically violent games can impact even the boys who aren't already prone to violence. But it's also important not to be alarmist. Lawrence Kutner and Cheryl Olson, cofounder and directors of the Harvard Medical Center for Mental Health and Media and authors of *Grand Theft Childhood: The Surprising Truth about Violent Video Games and What Parents Can Do*, offer parents some important suggestions:

1. Do your homework. Kutner and Olson report that the majority of the 42 percent of preteen and teen boys who routinely played violent video games "said their parents were ignorant about video games in general and about their own game playing in particular." They recommend understanding the terms gamers use and the distinctions between types of games, like FPS, TPS, and MMORPG (Massive Multiplayer Online Role-Playing Game, like *World of Warcraft* [WoW]). They suggest asking questions and inviting your child to tell you about the games he plays and using your own awkwardness and unfamiliarity to your advantage—let him teach you. Only then can you have a real conversation about the costs and benefits of playing, and the nature of the messages the game imparts.

2. Put video games in perspective. There's a lot of violence in the world, and some of it is much more real and scary than M-rated video games. While Kutner and Olson found a positive relationship between kids who play M-rated games and aggression, delinquent behavior, school problems, and even victimization, they warn that a relationship does not mean causality. It's not clear if attraction to violent games causes aggression, for example, or if kids who are already aggressive are attracted to these games. Moreover, the actual number of kids who engage in violent behavior compared to the percentage of kids who play video games is really very low. How to reframe your perspective? Bring him your world. Acknowledge that you don't think he's going to be gunning down the neighbors, but that he might love these games as much as he does because he

doesn't feel powerful in his own world. Appreciate that he may be more interested in and engaged by the story line of the video game he is playing than he is by the blood and guts. Bring him your perspective on the attitudes in the game. As with all other forms of media we address, it's important to initiate conversations about what makes these games so fun and attractive, and also to help him to think critically about the messages they impart to him about what it means to be a man.

3. Teach media literacy. Research and then let him in on how marketers and video game producers see him in such a limited way: Boy = lots of violence. Talk about product placement and the selling of certain political ideologies. Kutner and Olson also warn against the free online recruitment games or those with social and political agendas. Whether it's *America's Army*, designed to introduce your son to U.S. Army soldiering, or it's *Kaboom: The Suicide Bombing Game*, where players direct an Arab suicide bomber to explode in a city street, it's important to discuss the intent and different persuasive techniques of the game's creators.

4. Use the tools available. Kutner and Olsen also suggest using the parental controls, Internet filters, and software already available, but we sure know how hard it is to figure those out. We agree with them when they say that blocking sites is no match for a kid's desire to be part of what he sees as boy culture. The best approach is being involved and doing all you can to impart a healthy dose of media literacy with a side of parental values. As with all media, your opinion counts and will count more if you take his media seriously, perhaps even more seriously than he does.

Your Place or MySpace

If you have a computer and a teenager, you can assume that he's wired and he's online. Through technology like his iPod, his cell phone, and Web sites like YouTube, MySpace, Facebook, and more, your son is connected to a world of people you don't know, and he is able to gather and distribute all kinds of information. The Pew Internet & American Life Project claims that 87 percent of twelve- to seventeen-year-olds are online, and more than half of them have created a home page, a blog, a photo album, or a video clip. More than twice as many children ages ten to twelve report using social networking sites in 2007 as did in 2006.

There's no getting around the fact that he's going to be steps ahead of you in understanding and using this form of communication and information gathering. Some kids prefer communicating via text message, while others love spending time on Facebook or MySpace—and most use all of these forms of networking. By the time this book is published, teen and preteen boy preferences will have changed again, and they will be responding to and creating new social networking venues. As we write, however, boys tells us that MySpace tends to be best for sharing music, and Facebook can get really superficial, as it is often used as a forum to post photos of you and your friends. Many boys text and generally can't be bothered to e-mail. They also love YouTube, where they can send their friends to watch bands, hilarious sketches, pirated episodes from British TV, heartfelt rants, and so on. It's also a place where boys can gain an audience by making their own home movies.

You might wonder why so many adaptations, upgrades, and new technologies are necessary. Do people think teens need this to stay engaged? Is it capitalism gone mad? Is it marketers taking advantage of boys' love of new gadgets? Here may be where marketers and media moguls have more in common with parents than teens. They too are out of breath trying to catch up with kids and the "pirates" inventing new forms of communication and information gathering to fit their needs. Mark Zuckerberg, the Harvard student who started Facebook, invented *when he was in high school* a program that helped kids get access to music they liked based on other preferences, and just posted it on the Web. Plenty of other teens and preteens are working on their next new big thing. Who knows who or what is coming down the pike?

We can't tell you that, like "boy TV," these venues only offer a narrow range of stereotypes because YouTube, as well as Facebook and MySpace, are full of things created by boys for boys—all types of boys. Sure, marketers constantly invade and try to shape these things, and what boys invent and share has been influenced by media, but this is different. It shifts and morphs, and a boy can make or choose something absolutely amazing in one moment (take a look at the clever movies two boys—"Yabo Productions"—post spoofing different types of kids liking different kinds of music) or something totally disgusting and horrifying in the next (like "Two Girls, One Cup"— we'll let you discover that one on your own). Each of these gets shared in an instant with a number of other friends, and then your son moves on to something new and different.

While the media is constantly renewing parental panic that kids will expose too much about their lives on social networking sites, engage in sexting, or come into contact with online predators, they rarely talk about the loneliness that having TMI (Too Much Information) about other people's social lives can bring. Imagine if you sat down at your computer right now and looked at a list of three hundred friends. Imagine if each one sent back a slew of photos of the parties they went to last weekend (sort of like getting those Christmas letters where other people's families seem to be having so much fun and other people's kids are achieving so much). You might feel a tad out of it, lonely, inferior, and, in spite of the line that says "You have 300 friends" on your page, even friendless. John Cassidy writes in *The New Yorker* that "clearly one of the reasons that [Facebook] is so popular is that it enables users to forgo the exertion that real relationships entail." He cites a recent Harvard grad who says, "It's a way of maintaining a friendship without having to make any effort whatsoever."

Facebook is a great tool for keeping tabs on friends who live far away, and it can be nice to check in with local friends to see what they are up to that night. Plus, having hundreds of friends on Facebook means that you will probably be introduced to new people, which is where the networking part comes in. It might even mean that your son has thought considerably about who he is and how he wants to represent himself to others. Besides sending and receiving messages instantly on Facebook, kids can create their own social groups and invite people to join. People organize themselves into subnetworks as they find people with similar interests. And some of these interests are noteworthy. Take for example the two high school students Nick Anderson and Ana Slavin who created Dollars for Darfur, wherein they were able to recruit thousands of peers through Facebook and MySpace.

Of course there are marketers ready to dissect and grab onto your son on Facebook. They use the information your kid puts up there to target him specifically. Sharon created a Facebook page to do a little research, and *voilà*, a wrinkle cream ad a day appeared! Facebook also allows your son to spread ads virally, declare himself a fan of a brand, and offer up "social demographics and pyschographics" to advertisers. Some companies even sponsor groups he can join to discuss products. Corporate-sponsored friends!

But while marketers target kids and encourage them to give up personal information to advertisers, this doesn't seem to worry parents as much as privacy issues of another kind. First, and especially for younger boys, parents don't want unseemly people getting info about their kids. (Facebook brags that it protects kids from this and that only kids thirteen and up can join, but how they verify this, we don't know.) Parents are also worried about the "tomorrow factor." What happens the next day, they might ask their son, when someone shows some authority figure in your school a photo of you drinking what looks like a beer at the football game? You're not only busted; you might also be expelled. And what about tomorrow's tomorrow? When someone interviewing your son for a job sees him doing something obscene or even just shows him slacking off in two hundred pictures on Facebook?

Somehow, we think, some smart kid will figure out how to solve this problem. Matt Mason writes in *The Pirate's Dilemma: How Youth Culture Is Reinventing Capitalism,* that teen rebels have been working for years on new ways of sharing information. It's inspiring to see that over the years, huge corporations haven't been able to keep up with them. As Dart Adams, self-proclaimed "information junkie" and blogger of "Poisonous Paragraphs" writes, hearing the same forty songs played over and over again on the radio sends teens to new and interesting technologies and places where they can't be had. He says, "This in turn pisses off these big businesses and corporations. They are usually slow to adapt to change and they want to stay in power. . . . The way they see it, these pirates are causing them to lose money. The way the consumer sees it, we weren't going to spend the money because the product doesn't fit our needs anymore." Isn't this what happened with record albums to CDs to iPods and the craziness over Napster, and the new decisions from groups like Radiohead to give their music away for free but ask for donations? No longer tied to a recording company, they told their fans to pay whatever they wanted for the CD.

There's so much more to talk about regarding new technology than just a boy's "let me" and a parent's "show me how it works" of social networking sites. Issues regarding ingenuity and youth outsmarting marketers abound; issues regarding social class, race, gender, and sexuality are ever present when someone talks about three hundred friends (what does "friend" mean, what does his list reflect about him?); and perhaps most important, issues that have to do with his own identity, beliefs, and creativity.

Try to be on your toes with this medium. Not because it's better or worse than other places he can go or things he can do, but because it's so much a part of his life, and so important to being a preteen and teenager today, and because there are all sorts of social and ethical dilemmas that arise for conversation. Doug Johnson in *Learning Right from Wrong in the Digital Age* writes about the kinds of moral dilemmas kids face. What if he's sent sexually explicit material he doesn't know quite what to make of? What about finding out accidentally about someone else's password? What if someone's posting offensive images or spreading some gossip you know isn't true?

You can ask your son to avoid harming others, to respect the privacy of others, and to try to be honest and trustworthy online.

That means that it's one of, if not the, primary venue for the important questions and issues that a teenager will deal with, like relationships, self-image, identity, privacy, and independence. Many of the parents we know have their own Facebook accounts now, but there will always be something new to catch up to. Check out Candice Kelsey's book *Generation MySpace*, as well as Y-Pulse blogger Anastasia Goodstein's *Totally Wired*. Since they cover an ever-changing media landscape, these books will obviously be out-of-date eventually. So, in addition, why not start a Facebook group called "ParentsCluelessAboutKidsTechnology" or "TechieParentsStaying1Step Ahead." You and your three hundred new friends can help one another figure out this brave new world!

To Do Is to Be

After reviewing all the things a boy can do, a parent might think it best to keep his or her son locked in his room with his homework, but we do recognize the good in all of these activities. Participation in sports can offer boys healthy competition, exercise, teamwork, strategy analysis, and fun. Bike and scooter riding are also great exercise if your son doesn't love sports. Video games teach strategy and spatial abilities, online gaming teaches social skills, and, of course, every kid needs to express some aggression once in a while through fantasy play and competition.

But overall, we're here to provide a thoughtful critique of our son's media world. Teens who read our books are dismayed by this and ask us, "Why didn't you describe what's good about these things?" Our goal is not to describe bikes, blocks, guns, and video gaming but rather to expose the media and marketing stories embedded in and surrounding your son's world that tell them how to be a boy. Any one of the things we've described in this book could impact boys positively, if only so many of them didn't conform to such strict gender stereotypes. Is a scooter really more fun if a kid believes it's going 60 mph when it's only going 5? Well maybe, but fantasies of power can only go so far. Your son's empowerment as a boy needs to come from positive experiences, not from stories about how powerful he is when he destroys, kills, and dominates—especially when these stories are created by people willing to say and do anything to sell him a product.

CHAPTER 6

Rebel, Resist, and Refuse: Conversations with Our Sons

Toward the end of our survey, we asked the boys to tell us how they think parents can talk to their sons about some of the issues we brought up. Nearly two hundred of them gave us their heartfelt answers, quite a few interpreting our question to mean how they can specifically talk with their fathers. They may have been picking up on a media-created desire that the most important talks are father-son talks. Or perhaps they were expressing an actual longing to include their fathers in conversations about what's important to them. Their answers were very important to us in our work, so we want to let these boys speak for themselves before we share with you our own ideas about the most important conversations to have with your son.

How should parents talk to their sons about issues in boys' media? Many answered: "Calmly," "just calmly," "just sit down and talk," "just sit down," "person to person," "man to man," "no yelling," "try to recommend the good stuff and guide [us] away from the bad stuff," "be nice, patient and don't get frustrated," "don't rush into it, take it easy, and let the kid do the talking," "always take it slow, don't scream. Just sit down and wait until the kid is calm. When a kid is calm, he will usually want to talk to parents." Sound advice, we think, and so telling that they have to warn parents not to yell. They want calm. They want reason. They want to listen and be heard.

They like openness too. One boy wrote, "Just keep things out in the open, and casual. Not everything has to be a lecture, because some kids just tune out when they hear that tone of voice. And now that I finished this survey, I have to go do my homework (I had no idea [the survey] would take this long)."

Another wrote passionately, "Leave us alone. It's my room. It's a free country. Say please, ask nicely. Just be honest, pleasant, helpful. No yelling. Don't mention chores or protected sex or drugs. Don't be demanding. Don't repeat what I already know." Another wrote, "They should try to remember what it felt like being a teenager. Teenagers naturally have a tendency to rebel against their parents, and if parents try to interfere in their teenagers' lives too much, it just makes it worse. Sometimes you need to let go of the small things in order to win the larger battles." Wise advice, indeed.

What suggestions do boys give when it comes to talking about their behavior? "Don't address it as a bad thing, or even as a question. Explain that they have done some questionable things and they only want to talk so they can regulate the good from the bad, but not to punish or scare." On the media, they told us they want parents to "be open and honest, be real and authentic. Give good reasons why you don't want them to listen to or watch something specific. Don't just say 'NO, because I said so.' Watch, listen, or do something together and then discuss it and teach them to make good choices about media and entertainment."

Following this excellent advice we recommend that parents do sit down with their sons and play the video games, watch the TV shows and movies, participate in the activities, and discuss with their sons what they see and hear. As our survey respondents say (echoing what we told parents of girls in *Packaging Girlhood*), don't just say "no." And why? Because "no" shuts down discussion, and how are kids to learn if they don't have an opportunity to discuss what they like? Also, consider this: how will they be able to share what they like about their world if there's an atmosphere of impatience or criticism; how will you as a parent be able to share and listen if you can't even for a moment honor their choices but instead treat them as "bad" or "questionable"?

Reality-Based Parenting

It's important to creatively initiate and maintain conversations with boys from a young age, and media and marketing strategies are great vehicles for those conversations. Let's be realistic. Boys are engaged with media. So why not use it for good? Why not turn the tables and, using the material meant to narrow his options, invite him to engage with it in order to develop a keen sense of observation, a vocabulary that will help him critique media messages, and an ability to see through the hype, which will, in the end, open up his world. It's satisfying to use the very images, messages, and strategies employed by media to undo the power of media messages, to help him identify and hold on to the complex person he is by teaching him to question and reject the narrow version of boyhood marketers package and sell. This is media literacy at its finest.

The media provide countless fodder for conversation. After listening to the boys in our survey and analyzing the media messages and products they say they love, we've focused on three topics for each of four age groups: little boys, preteens, middle school, and high school. The topics of our conversations reflect themes about boys but also topics that parents are hearing about in the media. These topics reflect the stereotypes used in countless ad campaigns, movies, TV shows, books, and magazines, all designed to create anxiety in boys about whether they're boy enough, to distance them from the influence of parents (yes, we believe this is purposeful), and to make boys feel more powerful and dominant, and yet not empowered. (If they were too empowered they just would say no to marketers.) Marketers use every marketing strategy possible to hook boys in: make them feel bad so they'll buy a product that promises something better; encourage them to react against their lame naysayer parents and buy that product that will make them feel cool and independent; ask them to buy into a version of manhood that promises success in the form of control over girls, other boys, and over pretty much everything else in their world.

Our point of view is guided by the reality-based model we first presented in *Packaging Girlhood*. The reality is that you can't turn off the world. These days, TV, movies, the Internet, music, clothing, toy manufacturers, fast-food restaurants, and even publishers are all part of one big media network. But we also don't have to accept it at face value. The important part is bringing him along. So when you're talking with your son, we suggest you start young and follow these general principles.

DO YOUR OWN WORK.

Become familiar with what's out there. Watch what he watches, listen to his music, read his books and magazines. Know what messages this world sends him. These messages change fast and so do the techniques for grabbing his attention. Marketers have to stay one step ahead of your son, and they pay people a lot of money to figure out just how to do that. You can't begin a conversation if you don't know what he's engaging with and if you haven't really considered why you find it problematic or offensive, or what's funny, exciting, or attractive about it. You may need to watch far more *Family Guy* than you ever would want to, leave the rap on the CD player in the car long after the phrase that made you want to scream, or quietly munch your popcorn through another multiexplosion car crash, but it will be worth it.

LISTEN TO WHAT YOUR SON LIKES AND WHY HE LIKES IT.

We know it's not easy, but suspend judgment. Get to know his world from his perspective. Don't assume you know what all that slackitude means to him or why he loves the rapper Lil Wayne. Ask him and then really hear what he has to say. You might be surprised. It's okay to see the fun and good in what he likes and also to remain concerned. It's okay to learn something you didn't know and even to change your mind. One mother of boys told us that her teenaged son loved shock jock radio, especially Howard Stern. Initially she railed against it and worried about what he was taking in. Finally she decided to listen. Yes, a lot of it was as bad as she imagined, but some of it wasn't, and there were so many topics to debate. She ended up listening more often and talking with her son about the bad and the good of the shows. He still listened to Howard Stern, but now he had the added advantage of another voice and viewpoint, this one from someone who knew him, loved him, and believed in him.

Another dad told us that watching TV with his preteen son helped him to see that a conversational "point of entry" for his son was the environment. (A number of parents we spoke with identified this as one positive media message.) Knowing this, the dad told us he and his son are "tracing the origins of consumer goods, where the plastic comes from, where the electronics are made, by whom, under what conditions, the global warming implications. Not to 'ruin' it, but to give his son a sense of the connectivity of it all." Sure he may still want to buy cool gadgets. But he'll do so with a little more connection to the world around him. If we don't investigate alongside our sons while still admiring cool technology and fun stuff to buy, we can't find those points of entry.

This leads us to the final step.

BRING YOUR SON THE WORLD ON YOUR TERMS, THROUGH YOUR BROADER VIEW.

After you've become familiar with his media and can talk about it with some knowledge and after you've asked genuine (not leading or loaded) questions, it's your turn. Share your point of view, as well as your discomfort and what worries you. Help him notice the bigger picture, like the environmental impact. Acknowledge that playing violent video games can be fun (after all, didn't you like zapping aliens in those early video games?) but that it also connects him with a lot of other stuff he might not have noticed or thought about.

It's important to parent from a place of maturity and thoughtfulness, not from a place of fear or anxiety. The way to reduce the fear and anxiety we have about the impact of media on our sons is to invite him in early to a way of watching, reading, and listening that develops and uses his emotional intelligence and his critical thinking skills, and then to really explore these issues together.

Whereas most people assume girls are willing, and even want to talk to parents about the issues in their lives, most also assume boys are either unwilling or unable to talk, and that the best way to reach boys is through action or doing things with them, hoping that an opportunity for conversation will arise. In fact, some of the most popular books about boys perpetuate this myth. Doing active things with boys is good, and lots of talk happens spontaneously when parents and their sons are doing yard work, playing catch, or making dinner, but recent studies indicate that boys are so much more emotionally available than we thought and they desire communication with parents and peers more than we have given them credit for. Sure it's fun to join in with the other parents bemoaning the silence of adolescent boys, but remember those conversations you have and have had where he needed you to just listen, or he was so angry about a teacher or he was so exuberant about a game or an activity he participated in that he couldn't wait to tell you about it. The boys in our survey support both this research and your own inkling that your son does want to talk to you.

So, with a chorus of boys' voices shoring us up, we offer a series of conversational topics by age. We help you zero in on what might be most helpful in raising your son's awareness of the way marketers and the media narrow the possibilities for him and sell him an identity story about power, domination, and ruling, or slacking as an inadequate alternative.

These topics are ones we think are essential, given what's out there, but your son may be pulled by different marketing strategies or drawn to different images and messages than the ones we have discussed. Even so, your strategies should stay the same: do your own work, listen, and bring him the world on your terms. If you are fully open to his world (and calm, remember, calm), you will have a way of talking about it and a way of teaching him how to challenge it too.

And remember the advice from one of the great kids who wrote to us: when you have these conversations, try not to mention chores!

Talking with Your Little Boy

INTRODUCING THE *S* WORD

As soon as he's old enough to be sorting out gender and asking what makes a boy a boy and a girl a girl—ages three, four, and five—you can introduce the *S* word: *Stereotype*. Maybe not even the word at this young age, but the idea. He'll be getting messages everywhere in the media that as a boy he should love all those other *S* words like *superheroes*, *speed*, and *sports*. He'll get the message that boys are hyper, tough, and over-the-top, that emotions (other than aggression and anger) are for girls, and that he should enjoy grossing people out with farts and burps. Because these expectations are so pervasive in media, you can begin this conversation pretty much anytime and anywhere. We recommend you start with the next trip to the toy store. Thanks to all those pesky marketers, all you'll need for a lively conversation has been carefully planned and laid out for you in the pink and blue/black aisles of Toys "R" Us or Wal-Mart.

A stereotype is an oversimplified message repeated so often about a group that we think it must apply to everyone in that group. The concept may be too big for him to grasp right now, but the important message to convey early on is that you want him to develop his own interests and you love what makes him uniquely his own little person. You also want to get him in the habit of questioning media images and what they tell him about being a boy, so that he notices when his world gets smaller and more limited. As you observe and question, so will he. Soon he'll be saying, "That's weird. Boys aren't really only like that. *I'm* not like that and I'm a boy."

You have one very big thing in your favor with little boys: they love you openly. They want you around. They think you know everything worth knowing. They're much more likely to believe you than a thirty-second commercial or even a row of action figures. So jump in. You might think that distracting him from media images is the best approach at this age, but trust us, it won't work for long. Stereotypes are so pervasive and marketers are so clever about grabbing his attention, that the best approach is a direct one. You are inoculating him, in a sense, by giving him what he needs to fight and resist the toxic messages that will, in time, discourage him from toys, activities, and people that nurture all sides of his personality and provide him with the social and emotional intelligence so important for a rich and full life.

There are countless images and messages to question. As you walk through the store, notice aloud who's on the cover of board games and the ways toys are packaged. Wonder aloud why there are only boys (or only girls) present on the boxes of fun toys or the advertisements and images plastered around the store. Observe colors and activities that either invite him in through extreme excitement or discourage his interest. At ages four or five, his natural tendency is to believe as fact whatever the media presents to him, so your job is to question and remind him always that you know his world is much richer and more complex than what he's being sold in stores and on TV. You might ask, "Why don't we see any boys playing with these cuddly stuffed animals or with these dolls? You love your teddy bear, and it's so important for little boys to know how to care for babies so when they grow up to be dads they'll know what to do." As a dad you might say, "I wish I had had more practice taking care of babies from an early age. I learned when you were born, but your mom had dolls to practice with." He may still choose the action figure over the doll, but at least you've made another option possible.

A number of parents we talked with raised concerns about how violent boys' media has become, and how much action-packed violence reaches them at such an early age. You might be surprised to know that we aren't against buying your son a toy gun, although we support day care centers and preschools that ban gunplay. In fact, if he gets into LEGOs or Playmobil, you won't be able to avoid them. Almost every parent of a grown boy, many of them pacifists, will tell you that his/her son went though a gun phase. If they forbade them, their little boys bit their toast into the shape of a gun. Guns are fantasy play, and yes, it's unfortunate that there are *so* many of them and they've become bigger and more powerful. But, like Barbie and Bratz dolls for girls, we encourage you not to overreact about this. While you fill his world with healthy and fun alternatives, don't forget to talk about the guns you see all around.

A conversation about wanting and even buying a toy gun is a great way to get at stereotypes because toy gun marketing is focused so exclusively on boys. After you listen to why he wants a toy gun ("Because they make noise" or "I want to kill bad guys") and let him know what makes you uncomfortable about buying him one ("In real life they can hurt and frighten people"), point out that not every boy or man even likes guns. If he's a little older, say, six or seven, tell him that stereotypes are things we're told are true about all boys, but which really aren't true for some boys, and that sometimes they make boys want to be "like everyone else" when really, every boy is unique. You might point out that because we see so many boys in media having such fun with guns or action figures or fast cars, it's hard to tell sometimes if you like something because it seems like "everybody does" or "all boys do" or because you do really like it. You can say also that you worry that there are *so* many guns, superhero action figures, and fast cars and not enough of the things you also know that he loves to do, like playing with his train set or drawing. Maybe, you can say, "We'll just be sure that we spend lots of time doing those other things too so we don't forget how important they are to you."

BUY ME THAT!

When your son enters any new social setting, whether a day care or elementary school, he's thrown into a whole new peer group of boys trying to be boys. We know from the psychological studies of the late Beverly Fagot that boys as young as two years old attempt to shape other boys' toy preferences by telling them not to play with certain toys and calling certain toys "girl" toys. When we show our students this research they are shocked. How can boys as young as two know what's a boy toy and what's a girl toy? They barely know the difference beween boys and girls! Marketing, my dear, marketing. Because of studies showing that two-year-olds can identify dozens of brand-name products, marketers scurry to find creative ways to reach the littlest ones. Sure, parents and siblings teach boys about what boys should play with and what boys should desire, but even by the age of two boys have been exposed to all kinds of marketing—even what might be called "viral" marketing—that is, boys telling other boys telling other boys. This kind of marketing occurs throughout their lives. It's built into ads where boys tell other boys what's cool and what's not. Thus parents are competing not only with marketers, but also with other kids acting as marketers. And it's pretty hard for parents to compete with peers who do the advertising *for* marketers once they've been sold a bill of goods.

It's also hard for parents to compete with the high-powered nature of these ads, which include ecstatic expressions of joy and powerful, determined, real-kid faces and bodies in action. Marketers overstimulate. They teach boys that the only kind of fun to have is fun that demands a high level of excitement. Like the scooter we described in the last chapter, which implied that riding on a scooter can only be fun if the child is doing it in a dangerous way, whizzing, with no protective gear, past houses in the middle of a street. What happens if a parent points out that that's a tad dangerous? The parent is set up to be the killjoy, the one who doesn't want Johnny to have any fun! The peers? They're the ones who get it; they're the ones to listen to.

To deal with this, parents need to appreciate how a child's motivation or desire for a product can be increased by a perceived threat to his freedom. Psychologists have shown this to be true when two-year-olds are denied access to a cookie. Given a choice of two cookies that they have an equal preference for, they will strongly desire the one behind the Plexiglas, the one they can't get to, rather than the one they can reach, simply because someone has said they can't have it (this is called reactance theory). Marketers play on this issue all the time. They set up parents as the bad guys who say no, and they enhance desire in kids by telling them that their parents won't want them to have something. More often than not it's the mom who's pictured as trying to ruin all the fun and the dad who secretly wants to join in.

Marketers also worry about psychological reactance in response to their own ads. How can they create brand loyalty if consumers feel that being loyal to one brand interferes with their freedom to choose a different brand? Why, they simply give a kid a choice within a brand! So if your son loves Nike, and has loyalty to that brand, the illusion that he has a number of choices in the Nike line and that the choices are always being updated gives him the feeling that he is still exercising his freedom. Marketers love boys with "relational proneness," which is a marketing term for taking advantage of a boy who wants to build loyalty or a relationship with the company he buys from. This is one you can take to the bank with him, though, and as he goes online, searching out information about the company and digging its cool graphics or style or market-right-to-you-because-we-know-you strategy, be right up over his shoulder, pointing out that this is strategy and not a real relationship.

So while you may not be able to argue with his peers, and may end up giving in to the latest trend toy, you can still try to beat marketers at their own game. You have three strategies: (1) make the things you love and want for your son extraexciting; (2) take back the language of choice and freedom the marketers use so effectively by connecting it to things you value or want for him; and (3) teach him about marketing, share with him your dilemmas, and help him to understand the persuasive intent of advertising.

Make the things you love and want for your son exciting.

It may feel a little phony to exaggerate and hype up the things that you love and want for him. But don't we do this all the time, with things like broccoli casserole for dinner? "You're going to loooooove it! Look how cheesy this is. This is the best ever!" You can compete with advertisers with your own emotional expression, repetition, and sharing of things that mean something to you. So ratchet up the excitement level and turn up your fun volume with little ones when it's time to sled outdoors, build a sand castle, or delve into your favorite book. With those a few years older, six and seven, sharing your excitement can be enough. They want to identify with you; they want to know why you love the things you love.

Take back the language of choice.

Marketers do a great job of using language that gives the illusion of endless options and freedom for your child to choose. Listen to the ads that target him and you'll hear not only a message of possibility—"Choose from ten different actions!" and "Make dozens of monsters!"—but the constant reminder that he's in the driver's seat, able to make things happen (with the products and story lines they provide, of course): "You have the power!" You're in control!" This sets parents up to be the ones reminding him that no, he isn't always in control, and no he can't have anything he wants. Alas, thanks to these marketing strategies, we, as parents, become the people he reacts against. The trick is to take back this false impression of complete power and control and channel his attention and energy toward things that can give him real power, a sense of control in those parts of his world you want him to master. So instead of "No, you can't have it," consider how to create an alternative choice or another option that's attractive and use the language of choice and power. How about the choice to build something original with you instead of buying a prefab building set; how about the power to organize a neighborhood ball game or to create a puppet show?

Teach him about marketing.

Teach your son to identify marketing strategies. Teach him how advertisers edit fast and short cuts from scene to scene to make a product seem more exciting. Complain when you hear popular songs used to market deodorant or cars, even suggesting to your child that some of their favorite musicians have sold out. Ask them for examples of how marketers could be digitally changing reality to fantasy in order to sell things. Do what our friend Heather, a Canadian filmmaker, does with her children—teach them the game "find the lie in the commercial." If you start when they're young, they'll naturally be able to pick out the more subtle lies as they get older.

Finally, share your dilemmas with him.

Explain that you too think toys or activities or CDs sound interesting and cool, but that you go through a process in your head so you don't jump to buy everything in sight. Invite him into that process. Consider aloud whether and how you've been affected by advertising, what appeals to you about a product, and also what makes you suspicious. Appraise the thing you or he wants to buy in terms of the actual enjoyment it might bring. Ask him to come up with shared rules about impulse vs. considered buying. As he gets older, review some of his and your own poor vs. successful purchases. "Was that DJ studio really worth spending all that Christmas money on?" "Let's look down the line and think about how you might actually use this new piece of technology and for how long?" "Remember when I bought myself that pasta maker I never use?"

Overall, remember that your relationship means a lot to him. In fact, speaking about relationship, that's one thing you have that marketers don't— a real relationship with your son. Use this advantage to talk about ideas and values, offer him genuine choices, and let him know you want the best for him. In the long run, genuine relationship trumps advertising every time.

BOYS VS. GIRLS

There are plenty of media messages in your little boy's world suggesting to him (1) that girls and boys live on entirely different planets, and so have nothing in common and (2) that girly things, and by extension girls, are yucky and no fun and real boys should stay away from them. As we've seen, the boys vs. girls message comes from their animated movies, TV shows, and commercials, but also from their books, toys, and even the cards they receive on their birthdays. They also get reinforced in schools, where teachers, with the best of intentions, can make assumptions about interests and personalities based solely on gender. Too often the message, when it comes to gender, is all or nothing. All-boy, or all-girl. Any sign of crossing over to girl territory for boys is an invitation to a world of pain.

It's easy to buy into this either-or world when rows of cotton candy pink and princess paraphernalia all but chase boys out of certain spaces and opportunities. Animated movies, whether classic Disney or new Pixar, introduce young children to traditional romance as pretty much the only option for male-female relationships, and before you know it those sweet rescue scenes are replaced with cool pickup lines. There's even a dating primer of sorts written by a nine-year-old boy, Alec Greven, entitled *How to Talk to Girls*, that's made him a media star. Alas, the focus is on romance and boys' desire to get girls' attention rather than on their desire to have a new friend in the fourth grade. It's truly a shame that Mars and Venus appear so early. Boys and girls have much in common, and when the lines are drawn so young they have virtually no opportunity to experience one another as just children, as friends defined only by their interests, inner qualities, and personalities.

We're not so much against what self-described social philosopher (and marketing consultant) Michael Gurian touts as "*viva la difference*" as we are against a media reality in which difference stands for limitations and boundaries around certain activities and interests. Most of the media and marketing translation of boy vs. girl comes down to boys who are angry and tough and into over-the-top action vs. girls who are caring, nice, and into relationships. Not a great deal for either gender, especially when tough means "show no vulnerability" and nice means "show no assertiveness." But in the wake of boy experts' concern that such gender boundaries do little to hone boys' sense of compassion or nurture a range of important human emotions, it seems obvious that the media's version of such difference is a really bad deal for boys.

Friendships with girls can offer opportunities for boys to talk about their feelings, to experience relationships, and let go of the pressure to always be the best, the coolest, the funniest, the toughest, the most disinterested. But let's be very clear. We're not saying boys should or could be girls; we're saying that, because boys and girls have different strengths, needs, and potentials, being in genuine friendships with one another is a very good thing. Without this opportunity boys and girls rely on media versions of gender rather than on real experiences, and in media "*viva la difference*" often means "*viva la stereotype*."

The good news is that parents of young boys are able to dictate who their kids play with and what kind of media they ingest. Encourage him to stay in relationships with girls by setting up playdates that include female friends or suggesting he invite them to his birthday party. (Too often parents support this gender-segregation in play, and their children follow along.) Reality checks can go a long way as well. One mother told us when her son was five she heard him chasing a female friend around the house shouting, "Boys are better than girls." She couldn't imagine where he got this message.

Most of his good friends were girls, and he wasn't watching much more than PBS shows on TV. She took the time to stop and ask him a series of direct questions: "Do you really think you're better than Molly?"; "Do you think Daddy is better than Mommy?"; "Do you think Molly's daddy is better than Molly's mommy?" The answer to each was a thoughtful, "No, no, and no." "Well, then", said this mom, "that just isn't true, is it?" "No, I guess not," he replied, and then he was off again, running and playing with Molly. Mom didn't hamper his fun and excitement or ask him to tone down his play— just to think about what he was saying. More often than not, young children just need us to check in and provide a reality that's a little more complex and closer to home.

Challenging the typical media stereotypes of boy-girl relationships early on is also important because so much of the media version of what it means to be a boy or man depends on put-downs of girls and girly stuff or comparisons to girls that make boys look tougher, braver, or smarter. Competition can be a very good thing, but not competition that has, built into it, a disparaging view of a category of people. Though some educational shows provide great lessons on diversity and the importance of knowing a person from the inside, this kind of everyday sexism often goes unaddressed. It's not only girls who are affected by these comparisons and messages, it's also those boys who don't match up to the media ideals of tough, cool boys. In a world where there are just two stereotypical choices—all-boy or all-girl—these boys are virtually in no-man's-land. The teasing, bullying, and name-calling they'll endure down the road is directly connected to a version of boyhood and manhood that puts down or labels weak those characteristics—like gentleness, compassion, and thoughtfulness—that are associated with femininity. These qualities define many little boys as well—and would define more of them if boys weren't warned so early not to be *that* kind of boy.

We encourage you to talk directly to your son about these narrow versions of what a boy can or should be. You can start a conversation whenever there's a girl vs. boy situation in a movie or TV show (think of the genius Dexter and his pinkified ditzy sister DeeDee in the cartoon *Dexter's Laboratory*) or when a gentle, sweet, or smart boy is labeled nerdy and uncool, like Carl in *Jimmy Neutron* or Cody in *The Suite Life on Deck*. The gender put-downs can be reversed as well, especially when it comes to all those cartoon boys, slackers, and geniuses alike, who are pushed around by mean, smart-alecky girls. There's always a chance for a reality check. Talk about his friends who are girls and how their relationships are so much more fun than the boy-girl fighting he watches on TV. You might ask, "Where are girls like your friends?" "Why are there so few girls and boys who are real friends or buddies on TV or in movies?" "Why do they make boys feel weird or wrong for liking to do what girls like to do?" "Why is it okay for a girl to hang with boys and not for boys to hang with girls?" Or remind him of the friends you've had or have that cross those gender lines, and recall the fun time he's had with friends who are girls or girl cousins or classmates. Try to think of activities that aren't gender-coded, like sports that both girls and boys like to play or listening to music or their mutual love of animals or the outdoors.

The more you break down this gender either-or, the more you prepare the way for healthy relationships not only with girls but also with other boys who have a wide range of interests and qualities. The wider his circle of friends the more options will become available to him and the more likely his choices will be based on what he really likes and not on what he's supposed to like because he's a boy. He won't be any less "all-boy," but what it means to be "all-boy" will grow and expand to include the things and the people he loves.

Talking with Your Preteen

FATHER KNOWS SQUAT: MEDIA DADS (AND MISSING MOMS)

The long list of TV shows with bumbling fathers includes some of his favorites: *The Simpsons, Drake & Josh, Malcolm in the Middle, The Fairly OddParents, Family Guy, The Proud Family, Danny Phantom*. We could go on. If you watch any amount of TV with your preteen son, you'll see the pattern: stupid, dorky, newspaper-reading dads, and moms who are nagging them. The commercials between the shows aren't much better, with dads living in a perpetual childhood, bothering their kids who want to do homework or competing with their kids for waffles—and losing! Those lucky moms, if they're there at all, get to roll their eyes and act all high and mighty.

Who likes these images in shows and ads? Not dads. In a 2008 Father's Day survey of 320 men aptly titled "Note to Marketers: Dad Is Disappointed in You," 75 percent of respondents "couldn't think of one commercial that spoke to them with any relevance" and "more than half said the way dads are portrayed in media and pop culture is out of touch with reality." John January, the vice president and executive creative director at Sullivan, Higdon & Sink, the ad agency who conducted the survey and the father of three young children, said of the results,

Marketers need to know they . . . are talking to a generation of dads who see themselves as more deeply involved with their children than their own fathers were with them. Humor still applies. But that humor should come from where dad is really at today. Much of the marketing to men we see is remarkably stereotypical. On one hand, you see oversexed Peter Pans with little motivation or common sense. On the other, you see the dumb dad who, if he isn't reviled by his family, is at least ignored by them.

So why are there so many of these dorky dads? What purpose do they serve? These are great conversations to have with your preteen son because, while stupid dads are not just a "tween" TV phenomenon, it's where your son gets his first big dose of this message. That's because it's more than just an easy, cheap laugh—you know, the guy who's supposed to be in charge and who thinks he's in charge, but who isn't really? It's also part of what makes TV for this age group work: make the dads god-awful dorks or get rid of moms altogether so the tween stars can shine in a smart, independent, weirdly overmature sort of way. It says to the seven- to twelve-year-olds watching, "You are no longer children, you're cool teenagers." It's a calculated move designed to hurry kids along the road to independent consumerism because, of course, the shows are there to sell commercial products. What better way to get a share of that multi-billion-dollar market than to teach kids to ditch parental concerns? This is why the tweens in these shows hang out in cool teenlike bedrooms and enjoy the pseudo-drinking party scenes with hot girls at dance clubs and on the beach. It's also why parents on TV are lamebrained. Attentive parents would just ask annoying questions, like, "Is there an adult home to supervise the party?"; "Is this gadget a good investment?"; or "What about saving for college?" Bumbling dads, however, can be fooled or played. And missing moms? Heck, yeah!

But we think there's something more going on here, especially given the strain on father-son relationships we saw over and over again in boys' media. It's frankly just weird to see all that father anger and disappointment in sports movies and then to notice that the bumbling dads in these TV shows have affectionate relationships with their sons—they're dumb but lovable characters who would do anything for their kids. They don't judge, they join in on the slacker lifestyle, they're one of the boys, just another kid for mom to parent. We wonder if these bumbling dads, like all those boy slackers we've seen, are there *because* of the macho ideal of the great coach, the superhero, the action-figure-babe-magnet guy in so many movies? Who can live up to that? Is a bumbling dad funny because that male ideal is so entrenched or because it's now open to question? Are boys laughing and also thinking how cool it would be if they had a dad who hung around and played video games a little more or said, "To heck with work, let's play a little ball?" Why do only the media "loser" dads make the choice to spend time with their sons? Well, in part because of reality. In that Father's Day survey, the number one obstacle to being a better father was work responsibilities. So maybe there's some truth to the stereotype, but why don't we see how dads do struggle and at times make good choices? Is this what it has come down to: bumbling dads with lots of time and energy for their kids, or super-successful guys with neither?

Well, as we've said before, listening is important, and parents might want to ask their sons what these bumbling-dad messages say to their sons. What makes a bumbling dad funny? Why does he think there are so many of them? And don't forget the moms. On the surface they look like they get a better deal than dads, and maybe in some ways they do. But when media dads are stupid and making messes, those pretty, high-strung moms are set up as goody-goodies who either suffer with their additional man-child, nag him to do better, or settle for clean-up duty.

The best thing parents can do is counter these media parents with reality, and lots of it. The reality, of course, is that real teenagers aren't partying all the time or making decisions without input from parents and real pre-teens need and want a lot of their parents' attention, advice, and affection. The reality is that lots of dads are parenting more than ever and better than ever, in spite of work pressures, family responsibilities, and financial strains. Here are a few suggestions, just to underscore that reality: save the newspaper reading until after he's in bed or in school unless you plan to read with him and discuss the contents; work out family disagreements democratically when possible; model an egalitarian relationship with your partner that involves negotiating responsibilities; and remind your son that this is the way good marriages or partnerships really are. Point out the patterns in his TV shows, especially the bumbling dads and nagging moms, but also the movies where dads who have been slackers lose their wives and their children and then will do anything, *anything*—become Santa Claus, dress in drag, hold up a bank, become a superhero or sports star or super coach—to prove their love and get them back. Let him know that being larger than life isn't what being a dad is all about; it's the small everyday things, like being there to help with homework, playing a board game, and taking turns making dinner. If you walk the walk, you can talk the talk and let him know how it feels to see all that you do summed up by Homer Simpson.

STINKY BOYS AND DISRESPECTFUL TEENS

It's tricky to talk with your son about stereotypes of boys as stinky, sarcastic, wild, and disrespectful. For parents, the problems are pretty clear. What used to be called "mischievous" is now downright horrific behavior. With one extreme prank after another, some defiant boy (and sometimes girl) character is always thumbing his nose or giving the finger to authority. For little ones exposed to commercial TV, however, engaging with stinky, smelly, gross things is so commonplace that being reined in is tantamount to taking away his freedom! For preteens, this stuff and the attitude that goes with it are associated with a teen slacker-dude image that can mean anything from not picking up your room and ignoring homework to partying, experimenting with drugs, and exhibiting general malaise.

A parent might ask, What's the harm? Why quibble over a few farts and burps, something we all love to giggle about, especially when they're unexpected and interrupt anything too proper and polite? But it's not just a few, and they're pretty much all targeted at boys—defining him as smelly and messy simply because he's a boy. It's an image that's insulting. Pardon the pun, but it smells a little like a setup. Why? Because soon enough this behavior will get connected to rudeness and disrespect, to bullying, teasing, and stupidity, and even to crazy antics that can get him or someone else hurt.

This behavior is present throughout boy-targeted literature, TV shows, and movies. It starts to seem like *every* comedic cartoon in a preteen boys' repertoire is filled with the stereotype of smelly, stinky boys, whether it's Patrick in *SpongeBob SquarePants*, Jimmy's friends in *Jimmy Neutron*, or the boys in *Ned's Declassified School Survival Guide*. In the movie *The Benchwarmers*, bullies hold a boy down and fart in his face; Adam Sandler does the same thing to his arrogant boss in the movie *Click* (after he's stopped time with his clicker of course). It's a scene that repeats over and over, a cliché move for all those movie stars who act like sophomoric boys (Adam Sandler and Will Ferrell, for example), and designed to ensure an appeal to their preteen audiences. It's the lowest common denominator, and, again with a pun, it's aimed straight at your son.

Maybe the sheer volume of this stuff makes the stereotype a little easier to address. Because it's omnipresent, you can ask little boys to help spot it with you. Naming it as a stereotype helps take away its power to define for boys what boys are made of. For the youngest boys, you can point out how frequently their favorite lead characters in books and on TV are gassy and messy. Praise them for what they do in a polite or an organized way and point out to them that you know plenty of grown-up men with wonderful manners. Let them know you think they smell delicious and lovely most of the time.

Parents can also explain to boys why they're seeing so much of this stereotype. Give him a bit of history about how in "the olden days" grown-ups liked to make kids sit stiffly in uniforms in rows of seats and made them color inside the lines, how creativity was stifled. Let him know how grown-ups today don't want to be those kinds of commandants who repress kids, but want them to try new things, find their passions. It's good that rules have been relaxed to encourage comfort, individuality, and creativity. But also tell him that sometimes even grown-ups go overboard. Remind him that it may be funny in a book or on a TV show when they make kids full of mischief and gas and uncontrollable antics, but in real life it would be inappropriate and rude to act like that at Aunt Robin's or Uncle Gary's house. Rail against the BOYS STINK buttons they sell at novelty stores targeting girl buyers, and give your son creative outlets for messiness and creativity. Play therapists used to let kids fingerpaint to help them get a little messy. Parents can help boys create a mess in the kitchen and clean up with them, or pile a bunch of pillows and toys and blankets in front of the TV for a movie night. Sure, boys can be messy. They poop and they fart, but so do girls, also a valid point to be made to your son! It's a parent's job to channel that love of goopy, gross, messy, and smelly fun into activities and not to define it as "quintessentially boy."

Disrespect is another matter. We can love satire and irony, and laugh at farts. We can cheer when "just a kid" shows up some authority figure with a pole up his behind, so to speak. But when it comes down to it, a parent has to draw the line at disrespect. If we are going to worry about the violence in their video games, we should also worry about the nonstop disrespect of adults we see in boys' media. Of course, TV and movies set up authority figures to deserve this kind of treatment. They're stodgy and wrong and sometimes evil. And we understand why parents want to celebrate some forms of resistance and rebellion. This isn't exactly new stuff—"Question Authority" was a motto of the 1960s too. In fact, we want to celebrate it. But carefully considered rebellion, resistance, and refusal are different from the kind of lack of restraint found in TV and film. There's a clear line between expressing oneself and reacting impulsively to what one doesn't like, between taking a stand and playing cruel practical jokes on a teacher. Talk to your son about how some of his impulses to talk back, to give a teacher the finger, or to play a prank are straight from a TV culture that says that this is what teen boys do, and if they don't they're wusses or dweebs.

While parents can certainly engage him around stupid or hypocritical authority and support his "you're not the boss of me" feelings, they can also bring their own world to their son, a world in which they too have to live with authority figures that may not be so smart, even though they have power. But in your world, it's important to learn how to exist in these situations and to be strategic, to learn from others who are not just authority figures but real people, and to learn to live with others who annoy him or make him feel small. It's your job as a parent to teach your son how to engage with these people and their issues rather than to seek revenge or rebel for the sake of a cheap laugh, impulsively assert his own power, or avoid the issue altogether in a slackerlike way that says "who cares?" Show him *you* care.

THE THRILL OF VICTORY AND THE AGONY OF DEFEAT

In *Guyland*, sociologist Michael Kimmel says we need to talk to guys about sports—about what it means to them and the place it occupies in their lives. We think we also need to talk to boys about the media's version of what sports is and should mean to them, the way it affects their experiences of watching, relating to, and playing the games they love. There's so much here to talk about, given what they hear from sports radio, sports TV announcers, sports commercials, and the characters in sports films. They learn a lot about strategy, draft picks, skills, rules, discipline, sure, but they're also learning about how to have relationships, and specifically, how to have relationships with other guys and with men.

Who's the most important man in the world for most boys? Dad. More often than not, media gives boys the impression that the only place boys and dads can bond is over sports, and that without this bonding, a boy will grow up angry and with one big excuse to misbehave. When a dad changes over the course of a film, suddenly he sees his son for the winner he is. Finally he becomes the kind of dad every boy ever wanted. Maybe it's the male film producer's deepest hope; maybe it makes for a powerful film; but it doesn't reflect reality. Real fathers and sons bond over lots of things, like building a tree house, doing cool science projects, hunting, or fixing the car.

Aside from these stereotypical activities, they also bond over cooking, taking care of younger siblings, playing music together, and helping neighbors. How often do we see fathers impressed with their sons in these arenas in the media? Barely ever. This means that dads and sons who aren't into sports rarely see themselves reflected in media. This is something dads can address directly with their sons.

While playing sports is wonderful in all that it promises—physical health, competition, friendship, a feeling of inclusion and camaraderie—the experience is only as good as the coach and the team. It's a medium for all kinds of experiences and relationships—good and bad—and if we want the good to prevail, we have to be in the game too. This means not only talking about what it means to be a part of a team and how to support one another, but also what it means to refuse to participate in experiences that hurt or debase others. Parents would do well to begin such conversations the first time their son joins a T-ball or soccer team, and offer him the opportunity to practice ways of handling the pressure to be part of a team that makes some feel superior and others inferior.

We don't hear enough about the qualities of athletes and coaches outside winning. Occasionally we'll hear about a superstar's favorite foundation or charity, and the best coaches talk about what players can give back to their schools and communities. But when it comes to media, nothing trumps the attention given to a winner. Take Michael Phelps, for example, AP's 2008 Male Athlete of the Year, awarded USA Swimming Foundation's Male Performance of the Year, United States Olympic Committee's SportsMan of the Year, and *Sports Illustrated*'s Sportsman of the Year because, well, he's a "superstar": "He turned a pool in Beijing into the center of the universe, captivating millions with his exhilarating achievement." Wow. The universe? Are we reading a superhero comic here? He swam eight amazing races, the result of years and years of hard work; he deserved the gold and the accolades for sure. But the expected $100 million over his lifetime? Not so much. When you're put on a pedestal so high, it's a long fall, as we saw when Phelps was photographed smoking marijuana.

The superstar narrative is one boys hear over and over, drowning out almost anything else. What it means, essentially, is that this is what being an athlete is or should be about. The guy Phelps beat by one-hundredth of a second? No one cares about him, even though (and we think this is important to remember) so many more boys will know the agony of defeat than the thrill of victory. Of course we want our sons to win, and sure, admiring a winner motivates boys to do their best, but it doesn't help boys to see those who don't win pummeled, put down, and dismissed as they are in image after image, story after story. As a parent you can bring other stories to the attention of your son and talk back to the sensationalized and often arrogant commentary of media sportscasters and writers. We need to let our sons know they can and should be treated like human beings whether they compete hard and win or compete hard and lose.

Parents can use sports media to raise questions about so many things—father-son relationships, how his life is reflected in sports, and how sports fits into his life. We can talk about who has advantages and about how to use those advantages for the good of the team; about what makes a good winner and a good loser; about what it means to be the kind of parent or coach we rarely see in media. We can also prepare ourselves for the moment when he may decide sports are not for him or when he chooses to give up a sport that's no longer fun, that asks things of him he's not willing or ready to give, or because teammates are disappointing, a coach unfair. All this encouragement to be himself means he'll know when too much is too much and he'll know he can stand up for himself or others. There's so much out there telling boys to be disrespectful and smart-alecky to authority and yes, sports can sometimes straighten this out, much the same way that parents think military school will make a kid less impulsive. We know also that there are times when we want him to question, to know his own limits, and to walk off the field if he or his teammates are in danger, or to stay and fight the good fight. If he can make these kinds of considered choices, he'll be a real superstar.

Talking with Your Middle Schooler

SCHOOL AND SMARTS

There's a weird contradiction in boys' media when it comes to intelligence and school success. If there's a scientist, brain surgeon, "genius," or a trouble-shooting, problem-solving techie, he's likely to be male. But there's a hitch—these guys are also likely to be social outcasts, dweeby scientists, and nerdy brainiacs, especially in recent years. It seems as though men have to choose brains or brawn—they can't have both. Reality shows that attempt to transform dweebs into players like *Beauty and the Geek*, *Made*, and *The Pickup Artist* and shows starring nerdy guys like *The Office*, *The Big Bang Theory*, and *Chuck* have given this stereotype new life.

This smart geek vs. dumb cool guy is all pretty silly stuff, unless you're in middle school. There media stereotypes impact reality in ways that can feel pretty harsh as boys and girls are seen as "types" and often cruelly judged. Boys can admire Bill Gates, glasses and all, because of the big bucks he brings in; they can even get it that, in the long run, the joke's on the cool popular guys who put more energy into looking good and checking out hot babes than doing their math homework. But when it comes to walking the halls of middle school, it's a lot harder to make the connection between studying and success. When language arts or math starts getting really hard, the media offers boys a way out that saves them face—they can be cool slackers, not failing students. They can choose not to care.

When we asked parents what bothers them most about the messages boys get in their media, one message we heard a lot was the concern that for boys liking school and being smart aren't cool. They've heard all the talk about boys struggling academically, and they know the media that boys consume doesn't help matters. The images and messages work both ways for boys. If a middle school boy is studious or plays in the band, if he wears glasses and is a late bloomer, he's likely to be seen as smart and cast with the brainiacs. If he developed early and he's athletic, if he's caught the eye of a popular girl, he's cast with the jocks, and it's assumed he's not into school. The stereotypes are so ingrained that they hold even as they're being spoofed. As professors, we're not immune to it either. We've all been pleasantly surprised when that amazing paper or intellectually sharp comment comes from the star hockey player in the back row or the slovenly guy with the baseball cap over his eyes, especially because he's hid his interest so well.

Middle school is a great time to challenge media stereotypes of all kinds because: (1) kids feel increased pressure to conform and fit in; (2) they're tuned in to media; and (3) they don't like to be played, even or maybe especially by their media. Explaining to a sixth or seventh grader how those reality shows work can really get their attention—the way they slice and splice to create a dramatic scene; the way they prevent contestants from sleeping to ensure lots of fighting and drama; the way they choose contestants who reflect a certain type of guy. It's a great way to get them to question the other messages and messengers in their media. Don't forget to put the emphasis on the *they*—the writers, producers, and directors, the marketing executives, the CEOs—who make the decisions. Why do *they* always pair the nerdy-looking smart guy with the popular hot dumb guy? Why do *they* make it seem like boys never like school? Why do *they* never show an intellectual guy who's cool or edgy, unless sarcastically so? He'll catch on, and soon he'll be wondering why, in a culture so obsessed with technology and so taken with the latest scientific discovery, it is considered weird and abnormal to be smart—and show it?

SHOOT 'EM UP

Like most parents, we think that there's too much violent media at the expense of a whole range of other options. We certainly have read and accept the research that overwhelmingly supports the negative effects of violent media on kids over time, but we also know that this research applies to kids in general and not necessarily to your son in particular. Kids are individuals, and how a boy responds to such media depends a great deal on other factors and, especially, his relationship with you! We know so many great boys who are drawn to the killing in video games, who love war movies and gangster rap. In this day and age it's silly for anyone to take a simplistic view that if a kid watches, a kid imitates. It would be akin to saying that one trip to McDonalds will give your son high cholesterol.

But the debate rages. On the one side, though the media is more violent than ever, there has been no comparable rise in violent behavior. On the other, excellent scientific studies show that increases in the frequency of viewing and playing violent media are related to increases in aggressive behaviors and thoughts and decreases in strong negative reactions against violence. This may be particularly true when the violence is justified, such as in the superhero and action hero movies we discussed in earlier chapters, or when the child identifies with the one doing the violence. In a psychological study of elementary schoolchildren, frequent violent video game play early in a school year almost doubled the risk of getting into physical fights later in the school year (increasing the risk from 26 to 46 percent). If kids had other risk factors for aggression, there was an 84 percent chance of a physical fight (compared to 16 percent for children with no risk factors). This research, though startling, suggests that media violence is really just one of many factors that shape behavior.

Our motto is that you can't turn off the world, so learn to read it well. We also take the view that the narrowness of what's offered to boys—what the steady stream of violent and sexually degrading media teaches them about what it means to be a boy—is even more problematic. Sure, he won't go out blasting people after watching American Gangster on video, but he might get aggressive with his little brother. If he views a gangster, superhero, or action hero movie several times a week, while playing violent video games and tuning into Law & Order–type TV, he very well may grow up with more propensity to bully others, show verbal aggression, and not respond with concern when real-life violence occurs. More importantly, when asked to come up with solutions to interpersonal problems, violence might come to mind, blocking out other options that would help him in difficult situations and give him opportunities to develop mature relationships. When he's asked what makes him and other guys male, he might say with pride his ability to "take it" or his ability to be roughed up, or even the need to seek revenge. That is, this might affect his identity, his very self, and his understanding of himself as male, whether or not it leads him to join a backyard extreme wrestling club.

It's hard to measure what life experiences and narratives are gained and how they exacerbate or mitigate a boy's response to media violence, and it's hard to control for all the other positive influences in a boy's life. Because there are these other positive influences we don't go overboard and advise parents to say no to all violent media. We ask you to have discussions about violence with your son and make sure that he has other kinds of nonviolent influences in his life. So, if your son is playing *Grand Theft Auto*, is he also reading novels? If he's into shooter games, is he also having individual, team, and group experiences where problem solving and interpersonal skills are enhanced? You can teach a boy who loves first-person shooter games to limit his play time and also to love animals and take care of things. They aren't mutually exclusive. The world really is a lot more interesting than the dark, digital, mazelike corridors, even if he can "get to level ten with just five minutes more, Mom. Pleeease?" So you can join in, shoot a few bad guys if he'll let you, even celebrate when he finally kills the villain. These games and media are a part of a boy's world, and it's your job as parents to make it just a part and not the whole; to fill up those other spaces with the things you value, the things he's interested in, and the people he has fun with and learns from, so that violence isn't everywhere he looks and the Master Chief doesn't define manhood.

THE *F* WORD

Ask your son to tell you the most popular and deeply cutting insult he hears in school today and he'll tell you it's any and all variations of the word *faggot*. Boys in our survey confirm this. So do studies that tell us that kids hear antigay slurs such as "homo," "faggot," and "sissy" as often as twenty-six times a day or once every fourteen minutes. There's a reason all those boys in our survey told us the only thing they wouldn't wear is something that looks "gay." There's a reason why nearly 70 percent of gay youth report they experience some form of harassment or violence in school, 40 percent say they don't feel safe there, and 30 percent of gay teens drop out of school annually, nearly three times the national average. When you ask kids why they use this word, they'll say it means "stupid" or "lame," but in actuality they'll take those classic insults any day over the *f* word. Why? Because it might stick, and in middle school, that's the worst possible outcome. As we complete this book, tragically, two eleven-year-old boys living in different parts of the country committed suicide after enduring relentless homophobic harassment at their schools.

Why is this word so big with kids? Because it's shocking to adults? It expresses the anxiety of anything too feminine crossing into boys' worlds? It sounds "cool"? Maybe. But it also has a lot to do with boys' media and the inevitable steady stream of *f* words coming out of actors' mouths in both PG-13 and R-rated movies. It's the catchall insult of the day—everybody who wants a laugh uses it. Debbie in *Knocked Up* uses it in a rant against a bouncer. Comedies like *Benchwarmers*, *The Comebacks*, and *Wedding Crashers* unleash a steady stream of gay jokes, mostly as insurance that the close male friends in the movies are straight. Even Will Smith, called "the most likable actor in the world" by the *Los Angeles Times*, uses it in *Hancock*.

Spencer Fennell, describing himself in an article for the online writers' cooperative, Helium, as "just a high school student who likes to write rather than do homework," says this about all the degrading language in media:

> If you want to stop the slang words that attack homosexuals and mentally retarded citizens, stop the obscene television programs that encourage profanity and rudeness (not to mention violence). Don't get me wrong, i like some of the television programs, but there are certain ones that take it a little too far and i know when to stop watching a show due to the shear rudeness and disrespect to society.

This is the starting point for conversations: the fact that your son does know there are limits, even if he laughs with his friends. He also knows that there are different ways the *f* word and gay jokes can be used in movies. In *Step Brothers*, for example, it's the evil younger brother of Will Ferrell's character who taunts him for his childlike nature and dreams of being a singer. We're clearly meant to see gay baiting as part of what makes the bad guy bad. The gay character in NASCAR racing spoof *Talladega Nights* represents all that is refined and cool when he beats Ricky Bobby, again played by Will Ferrell (do we detect a pattern?). Their end-of-the-race kiss is funny, yes, but not homophobic. These movies have their own issues, but they are qualitatively different from those movies and TV shows that throw out gay slurs to shore up an anxious man's manliness, and you can affirm these distinctions while watching with your son.

Working in schools, we know that lots of kids use variations of insulting words for gay without actually knowing what they mean. So be sure he understands what people are saying. Then let him imagine hearing them as a guy who's gay or questioning his sexuality: the shame and anxiety of being discovered, the fear of walking the halls hearing these comments as someone who's out of the closet. Ask him to imagine where he might go for support. Is there a Gay-Straight Alliance in his school? That's important, because 70 percent of schools have no training for educators or staff on how to stop GLBTQ bullying or harassment, and 95 percent of school counseling services have few or no resources for this group of students.

Finally don't miss an opportunity to mention when you hear about an artist, actor, or athlete who either comes out or refuses to join in on the homophobic jokes. In the meantime, you can mention rapper Kanye West's rant against homophobia at a Madison Square Garden concert:

> Open your fucking minds. Open your minds. Be accepting of different people and let people be who they are. You know how many people came to me calling me gay cause I wear my jeans the fresh way? Or because I said hey, dude? How you gonna say "fag" right in front of a gay dude's face and act like that's ok. That shit is disrespectful. . . . I've flown across the world y'all, and I've come back here to tell you—open your minds and live a happier life.

(Okay, so in this case we'll forgive that *f* word).

Talking with Your High Schooler

RISK TAKING AND SELF-HARM

One of the typical ways parents are taught to view adolescence and adolescent behavior is that it's a time of risk taking and that adolescent brains are not fully developed, and boys especially don't yet have the capability to self-regulate and fully restrain themselves. A boy's gotta do what a boy's gotta do? Laurence Steinberg, who has written about a new perspective on risk taking, affirms these views. He explains that logical reasoning abilities of fifteen-year-olds are similar to adults, but he asks why the millions of dollars spent on drug awareness, driver's ed, and abstinence education haven't worked to contain our teens? Neuroscience provides some answers in terms of puberty and brain development. But also, these programs fail to consider the intersection of brain development and psychosocial factors such as impulse control, emotional regulation, delay of gratification, and resistance to peer influence, all of which continue to mature over the next several years and onward.

Impulse control? How does a teen develop impulse control when marketers constantly urge him to buy now and "just do it"? Emotional regulation? There's no emotional regulation in the over-the-top, action-packed, full-speed-ahead, the-fun-never-stops world of boy media. Delay of gratification? What does that mean to a boy who loves the Cartoon Network? Waiting? Saving? We think marketers want boys to say "why?" or "no way" to those worthy efforts. And resistance to peer influence? Every part of their media tells them that parents are lame and peers are the true role models.

If you approach your teen son with concern over the influence of peers and risk taking, he's likely to dismiss you as a lame parent. That doesn't mean you shouldn't do it, but be prepared. You can also be direct and say in the former case, "It seems as if you're not totally yourself with your friends, that you may feel in some ways that you're freer and the world has no consequences when you're out in the world." Steinberg suggests an approach of putting up natural barriers, and argues that simply raising the price of cigarettes and being more vigilant about liquor sold to minors is likely to deter them. But that doesn't teach your son anything about his own desires and anxieties, and in truth, we don't think this approach really helps when it come to risk taking and media and peer influences; it merely puts obstacles in their way. We, as parents, can't be with our kids every minute, so it's important to talk about what he wants and why.

Make this a conversation about the media and not about his impulsivity. Point out in his media how there are few models for considered judgment, and be on the lookout for articles, books, or documentaries about well-respected guys who are reflective and thoughtful about their choices. We've listed movies we like, as well as books, and there are great documentaries like *Kids + Money* and *Merchants of Cool* about the pull of consumerism and media that you can watch together. Maybe even more importantly, tell him that you think teens are maligned in the media and that the majority don't engage in reckless behavior. It just makes good headlines when they do, especially if they do so after watching reruns of *Jackass*.

Watch your own risk taking too! Do consider that media role models offer risk taking to your son as a way of coping with pain. Painful emotion in adolescence feels so much more painful because of teens' inability to emotionally self-regulate. They're given very few models in their media of men coping with their strong emotions through reaching out to others, through conversation. The lucky boys will pick up a guitar or a pen and write poetry. The less fortunate will punch a wall, swear at their parents, or pick up a knife and cut. Karen Sternheimer in her book, *Kids These Days*, makes a good point that most of the behaviors that are problematic in adulthood start in adolescence, but we tend to think of them as adolescent problems and create hype about teens being crazy.

Take, for example, drinking. It's older adults, says Sternheimer, who are most likely to use and abuse alcohol and drugs with deadly consequences, but our concern about teens overshadows that fact. Perhaps rightly so. As a parent, you don't want your son drinking underage even if his drinking isn't as bad as some far-gone middle-aged man. But you also need to understand that drinking is a marker of adulthood in a society that has few formal rites of passage. Buying into the media's view of him as binge drinking every weekend, when he probably isn't, won't get you very far. Instead, acknowledge the media's moral panic, appreciate that he might have a different reality, and know that what's most important is that he doesn't use alcohol, drugs, or other self-harming behaviors as a way to cope with problems.

Cutting is on the rise in boyhood, so much so that it's no longer considered to be just a girl problem. But rather than joining in on the new panic about teens these days, consider that boys want to and do feel strongly, and so little in their media teaches them how to self-soothe without harming themselves (such as slamming a fist into a wall) when they're angry. Labeling this kind of behavior as just boy behavior, due to testosterone or innate aggression or even too much violent media, will lead parents to miss something really important in their son—that he's in pain and needs help coping with it. And so the next time you and he watch a Herculean man get so angry he throws a car, breaks a mirror, or pounds a wall, it's time to talk about what your son can do when he's that angry.

Engaging with a teen around his pain is tricky. Sometimes when you give a label to his negative emotion, like alienation, he may feel as if you're criticizing him. You could say, "You seem to be feeling awful. I wish I could help. Can I?" You want to hear his thoughts, but as some moms have told us, being there at the right moment is all you can hope for. That's why we advocate sharing media with your son. When you're up late at night watching that action movie or listening to the music he's listening to in the next room, you may have an easier time talking with him about how the men they see and listen to deal with strong emotion. Your son may say something like "that's how guys do things. They suck it up." And you can agree, pointing out that it's how boys have been taught to deal with strong emotion for a long time. Ultimately, you want to provide him with alternative ways of expressing pain other than just bottling it up and then hitting someone or hurting himself. The more a mom or dad can bring feelings into the conversation, the more the talk around them and about them can be helpful.

And drugs? So many of us want to tell kids how dangerous they are or how smoking weed will lead them to squander their lives or become addicted to harder drugs. But one of the most important conversations to have with your son is about how using drugs to enhance or tamp down feelings is a poor choice. Share your deep concern when you think he's making choices that numb him to pain and to the world around him. Let him know you want to help him to be strong and tolerate difficult feelings and hope that he'll turn to you to work through them. He may send you packing in the moment, but later he may be open to your help. Let him know that the world around him presents unhealthy solutions to problems and that marketers don't care about him. Media folk want him to get a big kick out of slacker potheads because they're funny, and beer companies don't really care if he drinks and drives.

A little gender education never hurts either. Agree with him that there are expectations for boys to be hard and unfeeling and few examples of productive solutions to pain and sadness. Explain that sometimes the best solutions might look "girly" because girls are the ones who are supposed to be good with feelings and relationships. But also let him know that you know who he is—a kid with lots of feeling inside—and that your job as a parent is to help him find productive and nondestructive ways to express it.

TALKING SEX: YOU VS. THE MEDIA

There may be no one your son wants to talk to less about sex than you, but you've got to do it. If you don't, you let the media educate him—the media, not books, not sex ed class; his peers, yes, but peers who've been saturated with the same media stereotypes. And what will the media teach him? That girls are sexual trophies, toys, performers for his delight. That if he has any sexual feelings toward other boys, he ought to feel ashamed or be prepared to be condemned. That boys want to have sex all the time in every way possible. That all the other boys are getting some, so he'd better get some too. That romance is a girl-thing.

Thankfully, if you're listening to his music, watching some TV with him, going to the movies, or looking over his shoulder at his Facebook page, you're bound to see a good conversation starter. You'd probably like to start a conversation about condom use or respecting women, but it's difficult. There's a disconnect between the TV show you just watched about a serial killer raping then murdering and his own sexual development—it would seem. But why not use this kind of show as a jumping-off point? Consent is consent, whether it's the rape of a prostitute or grabbing a girl's butt. You've got to have it.

One of the easier ways to start a conversation about sex is by discussing "over-the-top" sex. It's everywhere he looks. You'll see it in a movie or on TV as some woman screams with delight or moans with pleasure. Just call it "movie sex" or "TV sex." And tell him when he sees people slamming each other against a wall, ripping each other's clothes off, and sucking face that, well, "it just isn't like that," and most people would feel incredibly awkward acting that way with someone they had just met—unless they were drunk, and in that case they would certainly not look that sexy and they wouldn't have consent. Besides, you can add, "I really would like you to get to know/ like/love/marry (choose your value) someone before you pounce on them."

Help him see the gender disconnect too. Let him know that girls, from the age of three, have been sold their own set of narratives that have to do with romance. They want a Prince Charming, they want roses, they want Edward, the romantic vampire from *Twilight*, to adore them and only them, to be madly in love with them, so much that it sometimes turns him into a beast. A guy who hasn't grown up with sisters or who hasn't had many conversations with girls about romance will be baffled by girls' ideas and desires. One teen boy we know, who hadn't yet been in a relationship, asked of the movie *Annie Hall*, "Is that realistic? Do people talk that much and worry that much over relationships?" His older brother said, "Yup. Pretty realistic."

But boys hear enough about the "battle between the sexes." They don't need more on how to play a game, or play a girl, or play at all. Many of them want relationships, not just sex, and you probably want that for your son too. So tell him that.

When it comes to porn, it's best to acknowledge that 90 percent or more of guys use it occasionally. But let him know it should come with a warning: REAL GIRLS do not come airbrushed with digitalized perfect bodies and pumped-up boobs—but they're a lot more fun. Let him know that he might get a distorted view of real sex and real women if he views too much of this. The same goes for gay porn. Let him know if you disapprove of porn in general or if you merely disapprove of porn that's stereotyped, impersonal, and/or airbrushed.

There are conversations to have about birth control too, which is rarely, if ever, used in movie or TV sex. There are conversations to have about HIV and other STDs and the risks to your son and his potential partner(s). There are conversations to be had about pregnancy, abortion, adoption, and early fatherhood. We as parents can so often reduce talking about sex to talking about "doing it" and whether or not we approve. While we wait to broach the subject, they're living in a very real world out there and need a long-term view and as much information as you can give them.

Our advice is to take advantage of the sexualized world all around him and talk to him about it. He might not meet your eye, but he'll listen.

POWER AND PRIVILEGE

There's really no question that from all the media they consume boys get an eyeful, and an earful, about what it means to be a man. We may not like many of the messages or the images reflected back to them, but boys aren't exactly victims of media. The sheer volume of messages they get about power and control—whether it's the power over nature when they're shredding those mountaintops, the power to take the field, court, or diamond, the power to rescue or pick up hot girls, the power to fight evil, or to be evil itself—suggests something different from victimization. This is why we're not fond of the "boy box," an exercise widely used by boy advocates that shows up in media literacy and health curricula. It's an exercise aimed at showing boys the ways they are kept from expressing anything other than narrow gender roles. Boys are asked to call out all the rules regarding what it means to be a man, and the group leader, often a man who has some street cred (he's big and brawny, he once played pro football, he speaks their language), puts these themes into a box and asks boys what happens if they deviate, if they act "outside the box." We get it, and they get it too. Boys love to hear how they're "boxed" in, because it reflects back to them how much they feel they will be punished for not measuring up. Much of this book laments this pressure too. But this exercise can have the unintended effect of building up or reaffirming stereotypes we want boys to question. Without acknowledging how those who fit best into the box benefit the most and how what happens in that box impacts those outside the box—both boys and girls—we have only half the story.

One of the most important conversations that parents can have with their sons is about the privileged space media affords boys in the culture. Scholar and activist Peggy McIntosh was the first to use the term "privilege" to describe the advantages she enjoys as a white person in this society. Inspired by McIntosh's groundbreaking work, Barry Deutsch, a cartoonist from Portland, Oregon, developed a "Male Privilege Checklist," which he posted and continues to update on Alas!, his blog. Here are a few of the privileges he lists:

> I am far less likely to face sexual harassment at work than my female coworkers are; on average, I am taught to fear walking alone after dark in average public spaces much less than my female counterparts are; my elected representatives are mostly people of my own sex; I do not have to worry about the message my wardrobe sends about my sexual availability; I can be aggressive with no fear of being called a bitch; I will never be expected to change my name upon marriage or questioned if I don't change my name; if I buy a new car, chances are I'll be offered a better price than a woman buying the same car.

Pointing out that men are privileged, Deutsch says, in no way denies that bad things happen to men or that men do not work hard, do not suffer, or are not at times discriminated against too. "In many cases—from a boy being bullied in school, to a soldier dying in war—the sexist society that maintains male privilege also does great harm to boys and men." We just think you need to talk to your son about both sides—the costs and benefits of accepting this kind of privilege.

We've taken the liberty of adapting Deutsch's list to generate a few items of our own that define some aspects of "boy privilege" in media. We've added, along with the privileges, the cost to boys:

1. I can choose from an almost infinite variety of children's media featuring positive, active heroes of my own sex. I never have to look for them; male protagonists are the default. Cost: If I identify with them, however, I'll need to become a superhero; most of these "choices" represent stereotypes that leave little room for my unique qualities.

2. I can turn on the television or glance at the front page of the newspaper and see people of my own sex widely represented, every day, without exception. Cost: These people must always win, dominate, and control. Maybe I want to dominate and control—it's better than being a weakling. On the other hand, what will I be missing out on if I choose that path, and what if these are impossible ideals anyway?

3. The media shows me that hot girls will always be ready for me and that I just need to learn how to play the game. An advantage is I'll never be shamed if I play along. Costs: But I might not always want hot girls. I might want a girlfriend and eventually to get romantic with someone I actually like. Still, magazines, billboards, television, movies, pornography, and virtually all of media are filled with images of scantily clad women intended to appeal to me sexually and make me feel like a stud. Costs: I'm pretty unaware of my own sexual development and weirded out by some of my fantasies, and have no one to talk to about them.

4. I have the privilege of failing, slacking off, and bucking authority because it will be seen as part of my adolescence and because slackers are cool. Costs: I may not get into the college I would like to, and I might not be able to have my dream career.

5. I have the privilege of calling the shots, and when I'm insulted or hurt, seeking revenge will be seen as seeking justice. A man's got to do what a man's got to do. Cost: But if I do seek revenge, I'm usually not very happy, and aggression tends to beget more aggression. I might get hurt. I might get killed.

The messages your son gets to be big, strong, tough, a player, the best, a winner, and a superhero/superstar send clear signals about the value of power and dominance. It's human to want power. It's good for our kids to aspire to be independent, to feel that they can create and master new things; that they can control their own lives. But as we've pointed out many times, these same messages, seen too often and taken too far, also have costs. They promise power and yet are not empowering. They interfere with his emotional development, connection, and empathy, with the formation of authentic and meaningful relationships; they set him up to meet impossible ideals, to ignore pressure and pain, to disconnect from himself and the wonderfully complex and interesting person he is. And in spite of the messages that boys want justice, this kind of dominance and power is patently unfair.

Since one of the primary features of privilege is its invisibility—think of water to a fish—you'll be tempted to talk with your son about only the disadvantages that you see in the media stereotypes that reflect his power and privilege. But try not to take just one side. It's truly important to acknowledge how good all that privilege feels, the benefit of having someone trust your opinion or see your authority without you having to prove it, the benefit of someone thinking you'll make a good leader because of your gender, their hope that you'll be able to solve some tech problem just because you're a guy. It's nice to be stereotyped at times if the stereotype's a positive one, even if you can't quite live up to the image. So first of all, acknowledge what feels good about being or aspiring to all those "box" qualities. If it didn't feel good to be strong and brawny, a lot of gyms would close, *Monday Night Football* would falter, and action figure sales would suffer. So discuss with your son how being strong and brawny affords him some privileges. And then decide whether it's worth it and what elements of who he is he must give up to attain that. You can then review all those other stereotypical qualities.

Also, on occasion, discuss gender inequities with him. Talk with your son about why the sports stars are usually men, while the main role for women is to be cheerleaders dressed in sexy uniforms. If he says that women play basketball too, talk with him about why the NBA and the NCAA Men's Basketball Tournament are broadcast on the major TV networks, while the WNBA and the NCAA Women's Basketball Tournament are broadcast on hard-to-find cable channels. You and your son can also talk about why 75 percent of characters in the top-grossing G-rated films from 1990 through 2004 are male, or why male characters dominate Newbery Award–winning children's books, popular video games, and toys that have anything to do with action, competition, and power. There are so few men in boys' media and boys' world who are willing to talk with them about gender inequity, so here's one area where we ask dads to really step it up.

Boys have a strong sense of justice, and you can easily appeal to it. Like white parents teaching their children about racism, the goal is awareness and education. We don't want boys to feel ashamed of their human interest in having power, in exercising entitlement, and going for the gold. But you can teach him to feel empowered through his capacity for criticism, by understanding the messages that push him to be someone he is not, and the parts of him that aren't recognized and utilized by marketers and media. You can teach him to think of gender equity as an attainable goal for all in our society, not something that only girls have to pay attention to. In this way, his understanding of marketers and media becomes one thread in his growing understanding of social justice in our changing world—and that's something a boy born and bred on superheroes can grab hold of!

NOTE TO ROLE MODELS: LISTEN UP!

The good thing about a superhero is that he'll rarely let you down, that is, unless it's Christian Bale, the actor who played the Dark Knight, who went ballistic on the set of *Terminator: Salvation*. Teens following the Dark Knight actor have heard about his rant and subsequent apologies, and most probably caught the replay on the Internet. But it's not just Bale. There are a host of other "superheroes" who have been caught behaving badly—they've been caught lying, abusing others, and doing drugs; that is, leading lives of unexamined entitlement that affect our sons. As we write, it's been a bad year for superheroes.

> *Christian Bale:* His rant was captured on tape, and it's directed at someone repeatedly and humbly saying "sorry" and "we can talk about this later" after that person accidentally ruined the shooting of a scene by walking into it to check a light. F**king this and f**king that. Bale doesn't let up for over three minutes straight. His explanation? He was in the middle of some intense work for *Terminator: Salvation* and, as he put it "mixed up fact and fiction."

> *Major League Baseball's Alex Rodriguez:* "In 2003, when he won the American League home run title and the American League's Most Valuable Player award as a shortstop for the Texas Rangers, Alex Rodriguez tested positive for two anabolic steroids, four sources have independently told *Sports Illustrated.*"

> *Teen hip-hop star Chris Brown:* ". . . then came the ugly scene that left Rihanna bleeding and bruised, Brown in police custody and the picture of them as hip, uncomplicated lovers in tatters." R & B singer Chris Brown allegedly beat his girlfriend, pop singer Rihanna, to the extent that someone called 911 and she was taken to a hospital.

> *Swimming phenom Michael Phelps:* The Olympic swimming sensation Michael Phelps was photographed inhaling from a marijuana bong. As a result, he's lost a major sponsorship deal and has been suspended from competition for three months.

Platinum-selling rap artist Lil Wayne: The Grammy-winning gangsta rapper has had repeated drug arrests. "After a consensual search of the vehicle, trained dogs sniffed out a grip of illegal substances: all told, agents discovered 105 grams of marijuana, 29 grams of cocaine, and 41 grams of Ecstasy . . . arrested by the Drug Enforcement Agency, along with two other people also riding in the bus. The DEA also found approximately $25,000 in cash and three registered handguns—one of which was registered to Lil Wayne in Florida."

Excuses and explanations follow. For Bale, he has a "potty mouth" and he was playing his character, "a guy who would talk that way." For A-Rod, it was the pressure to live up to expectations to be the best, and an appeal to a different culture four years ago that found steroid use more acceptable. For Brown, well, we're still waiting for an explanation as we write this, but his father tells us this is a "stumble," he tripped, "he loves people." For Phelps, he's young. As for Lil Wayne? He's a gangsta and he uses weed medicinally, for his migraines.

Have we heard real apologies? Well, yes and no. Bale calls his behavior "unexcusable." A-Rod qualified his apology and said he's "sorry for [his] Texas years," reminding fans that all of his New York years have been clean. Brown says he's sorry for "events that transpired" but the "media is wrong." Phelps said, "I acted in a youthful and inappropriate way, not in a manner people have come to expect from me. For this, I am sorry. I promise my fans and the public it will not happen again." And Lil Wayne? We guess that being a gangster means never having to say you're sorry. What decent gangster would admit to being a role model for kids? He was adamant in his conversation with Couric: "Never in my life would I ever say, that I ever set out to be an example for people on how to live their lives. If you need an example for how to live then you just shouldn't have been born, straight up."

We guess they didn't get the memo: you *are* our kids' role models, whether we like it or not, so "man up" to it. Don't say you didn't ask for it. Of course you asked for it. You went out looking for fans. You honed an image that would procure more fans. You do "shout-outs" to your fans. And your fans are loyal to you. You can't be just part superstar or a superstar when you feel like it.

How about taking a lesson from rapper T.I., convicted for drug dealing and weapons possession? His apology took the form of heartfelt community service, the result of a plea deal that reduced his prison term to one year. Each episode of his subsequent reality show, *T.I.'s Road to Redemption*, focused

on saving a child from gangs and violence, giving that child a reason to believe, as T.I. said in one episode, "who you are now ain't who you have to
be." He crisscrossed the country speaking to churches, schools, and Boys
and Girls clubs, hosting anti-gun and anti-violence rallies, supporting "Give
Back Your Gun Day," and giving money to rebuild urban communities. His
op-ed, "Responsibility Is a Lifestyle: It's Time to Bury Da Beef," teaches you
and the rest of the fallen heroes what a good apology sounds like:

> I made some bad decisions. I broke the law and will accept my pun-
> ishment. With deep reflection about where my life was headed, I
> have begun the process of redemption, and decided that before I go
> to prison, I want to speak to young people about responsibility as a
> lifestyle. . . . Now is the time for me to lead by example.

T.I. knows that with great power comes great responsibility. We not
only want our sons to be able to muster a decent apology, one that comes
without making excuses, playing dumb, having "bad weeks," forgetting about
former lies, using "that was then but I'm different now," or shoddy medical
arguments and the all-purpose "I'm just a kid." We want our sons to make
better judgments than you in the first place. What if each one of you said
exactly what you should have done differently and showed a little empathy
for those you disrespected? How about making reparations? How about putting in a little service to clean up the mess you've made?

Our kids do need heroes of sorts, so why not try to live up to the gift
those fans are giving you. How about taking a stand? How about telling boys
they don't have to be the best, if the road there means they have to compromise who they are and what they believe in? How about modeling someone
who chooses to be good and honorable, the kind of hero who has compassion as well as the courage to choose integrity over the all-mighty dollar?

Sorry about this rant, Lil Wayne, but we're keeping it real. And if you
say to us, as you said to Katie Couric and parents everywhere, "Nobody is
going to tell me what to do"—and believe us, parents of teens are really familiar with that line—we will say back, "Oh, yes we will. You may not want
to listen, but yes, we will. Get big, step up to it, if you can."

ABOVE THE INFLUENCE?

We love the Above the Influence anti-pot smoking Public Service An-
nouncements created for the National Youth Anti-Drug Media Campaign.

In one TV spot, three boys duck under a fence as one says, "You gotta try this." He goes up to a pony, pulls its tail, and gets kicked in the knee. As he doubles over in pain, the next boy runs over and does the same thing, with the same result. The third boy just shakes his head and walks away as the narrator says, "You know a bad idea when you see one." In another ad, a boy gets out of bed looking like an overweight football player, but as he peels off one graphic T-shirt after another with slogans like "I love this joint" and "Where's the fun at," he gets down to ones that say things like "be yourself" and finally to his last tee, which says "free." Unencumbered, he pulls on an Above the Influence sweatshirt and heads out the door. But our hands-down favorite is the funny fake documentary about kids into S.L.O.M.ming, which stands for Sticking Leeches On Myself. It's "a social thing," the kids say, "you hear people talk about slomming over the weekend." "It's hard not to get into it." Then the narrator: "What could you be influenced to do?" These are funny, and you know they get kids' attention when spoofs of these ads start showing up on YouTube.

We know how hard it is to be above the influence of all the marketing of cool and edgy. The people behind the marketing campaigns are incredibly savvy. They have paid lots of money to the right people, some of whom are developmental psychologists and social anthropologists, to find out what boys want and how to make them want it more. It's that desire they cultivate, that sense of "gotta have it," the fear of missing something important and fun, the "can't wait to have the latest thing" addiction. Listen to the boys in the film *Kids + Money* talk about consumption. Seventeen-year-old Sean Michael explains his sneaker addiction and how much it costs him "just to keep up."

> I'm trying to buy a new car, so instead of saving up . . . I'll go to the mall and I'll see a pair of shoes and I'll want the shoes right then and there. And since I can go and get these shoes and take them home with me, it's more like realistic for me . . . than to save up for something I'm not getting right then and there.

Cameron, also seventeen, talks about his need for money to buy clothes. "Clothes be important," he explains. "You gotta keep your rep up, you know. People gettin' clowned on . . . it's not a good feeling, it's cold . . . in front of the girls and all that." Cameron wants to be a rapper because "rappers get everything. They be in the movies, they go on TV, they own shows and radio, all the media. They own everything, pretty much."

It sometimes seems that media is so a part of us, so a part of our identities, that there's no getting above the influence. So why resist? This stuff is everywhere. Free choice itself has been co-opted by marketers defining it as the choice between brands of clothing, between the athletes worth following, the video games worth playing, between a limited number of high-profile movies marketed through endless toys, magazines, and trailers, all with the same narrow themes and stereotypes.

While it's true that you can't keep your son away from all these marketers reaching out to shape him into a little consumer before he's even out of diapers, and you can't fully protect him from media influences that sell the newest, freshest version of the same old stereotypes, you can help him observe this world, identify the lies, and question and criticize it. Doing such is in the service of real identity formation, real independence and autonomy. We're asking you to celebrate this possibility in him and put his natural powers of observation, his desire for fairness, and his ear for hypocrisy to good use. Truth, especially when it comes to marketing and media, is not just one thing but a deeply complex web. Start early, and as he grows up, introduce this complexity to him and trust that he can appreciate it and learn from it.

In the process, you will help your son reduce the anxiety that goes hand in hand with being a boy these days—anxiety, we're convinced, that's related to all kinds of problems, including poor school performance, risk taking, and violence. If we've said it once, we've said it a dozen times—media and marketers deliberately make boys and men feel anxious about being a "real boy" or a "real man," and then they sell products that are designed to help them "prove" their masculinity. But if you teach your son to question and critique the images and messages being sent by the media, to understand that the desire he feels for the products he sees is manufactured and manipulated, you'll help him increase his distance from marketers' schemes and reduce their power. In the end, he'll feel less anxious and more empowered simply to be himself.

There can still be wonder, enjoyment, and fun in your son's media. He can still laugh at the fart jokes, enjoy action and adventure, imagine being a superhero or even a powerful gangster. The bottom line is that you can be there with him, reflecting on the world around him, listening and also offering a voice he can internalize when he's out there alone—a voice that reflects his positive inner qualities as he's bombarded with a message about outer image. Remember, turning off the world is not the answer. Being by his side helping him to reflect on it is.

Notes

PREFACE

page xi over five thousand media images and messages: Aufreiter, Elzinga, and Gordon, 2003.

INTRODUCTION

page 6 Media targeting boys: Connell, 2005.
page 8 Our friend and colleague Bill Pollack: Pollack, 1999.
page 9 Material abundance seems to come without consequences: Kimmel, 2008b.
page 10 most tweens spend time traveling to after-school activities: Mickiewicz, 2004.
page 11 how sex is a vulnerable issue for boys: Kindlon and Thompson, 2000.
page 12 real people with their own losses and vulnerabilities: Gilligan, 2002.
page 13 Mooks are: Merchants of Cool, 2001; see also www.urbandictionary.com/define.php?term= mook.
page 13 old stereotypical scripts: Moore, Stuart, McNulty, Addis, Cordova, and Temple, 2008.
page 14 documentary films by Byron Hurt, Jackson Katz, and Sut Jhally: These books and films can be found in the Bibliography and in our list of recommended Online Resources.

1: BIG, BOLD, AND BRANDED: WHAT BOYS WEAR

page 20 Developmental psychologist Erik Erikson wrote: Erikson, 1963.
page 20 Sigmund Freud wrote about it too: Freud, 1923/1960.
page 21 general "pornification" of the culture: Sarracino and Scott, 2008.
page 21 "Younger hipper parents are looking for something": Howze, 2008.
page 25 They've carefully waded into these waters: Edwards, 2003.
page 31 the age of male customers for cologne and eau de toilette is getting younger : Facenda, 2007.
page 31 A spokesperson for Disney's cologne distributor: Facenda, 2007.
page 33 BusinessWeek called it "edgy humor": Hamm, 2007.
page 36 Diddy's clothing line, Sean John: Fleetwood, 2005.
page 36 "In this hypebeast kind of world": Ross, 2007.
page 38 "authentic," edgy, tough urban guy: Charles, Hurst, and Roussanov, 2009. See also, Fisman, 2008.
page 39 These cool, tough images clearly attract young: Yousman, 2003.
page 39 Jeffry Ogbar argues in Hip-Hop Revolution: Ogbar, 2007.
page 41 Bobbito Garcia, editor of Bounce: www.bouncemag.com.
page 41 "brothers like to coordinate": Just for Kicks, 2005.
page 41 It fits into a capitalist belief that people can create who they are: Miner, 2009.
page 42 to be "larger than life.": Just for Kicks, 2005.
page 42 high on angel dust: Just for Kicks, 2005.
page 43 owned at least one pair of Air Jordans: Just for Kicks, 2005.
page 43 selling the "authenticity" stereotype of the violent black man: Just for Kicks, 2005.
page 44 the faces of the new masculinity: Dines, personal communication, Feb. 23, 2009.
page 45 more or less cushion: Swoosh! Inside Nike, 2008.
page 46 As Robert Thompson, founding director of the Center: Cave, 2002.

2: SUPER SIZE ME: WHAT BOYS WATCH

page 48 forty thousand commercials each year: Wilcox, et al., 2004.
page 48 more important to boys than the character's gender: Calvert, Kotler, Zehnder, and Shockey, 2003.
page 49 recall more masculine than feminine behaviors: Calvert, Kotler, Zehnder, and Shockey, 2003.
page 49 according to a Kaiser Family Foundation: Kaiser Family Foundation, 2006a.
page 49 Boys see boys twice as often: Smith and Kelly, 2007.
page 51 hide what are perceived to be "weak" human emotions: Ruble and Martin, 1998.
page 51 Boys are more likely than girls to watch cartoons: Children Now, 1999a, 1999b; Leaper, Breed, Hoffman, and Perlman, 2006.
page 52 preschoolers play more aggressively after watching violent TV: Josephson, 1995.
page 52 more likely to act aggressively: Josephson, 1995.
page 53 author Brad Meltzer explains in an article for USA Weekend: Meltzer, 2008, p. 10.
page 55 the young men who Michael Kimmel writes about: Kimmel, 2008a.
page 57 "Kids don't just watch TV anymore": Business Ethics, 2007.
page 62 In 2006, The Kaiser Family Foundation found: Kaiser Family Foundation, 2006b.
page 62 Nick reports 77 percent of tweens do: Dee, 2007, p. 8.
page 65 As novelist and New York Times contributor Jonathan Dee writes: Dee, 2007.
page 66 Manhood is equated explicitly with the ability to settle scores: Katz, 2007.
page 67 make up nearly 40 percent of all viewers: WWE.com, 2008.
page 67 "soap opera for guys": Wrestling with Manhood 2002.
page 67 In his article "Masculinity as Homophobia," Michael Kimmel: Kimmel, 2003, p. 55.
page 72 male viewership of over three million: Johnson, 2007; Kaplan, 2007.
page 72 how a working-class guy makes it rich: Kaplan, 2007.
page 79 "a producer's ally on almost ally show": Rose, 2008.
page 82 Men comprise 83 percent of all directors: Rickey, 2006.
page 82 75 percent of characters in G-rated animated movies are male: Kelly and Smith, 2006.
page 83 life is about the journey, not the finish line: Cars, 2006.
page 86 sociologist J. C. Pascoe listened to high school-aged boys: Pascoe, 2007, p.55.
page 98 the "final girl" phenomenon: Clover, 1992.
page 100 One survey of third through eighth graders found: Singer, Slovac, Frierson, and York, 1998.
page 100 In studies of college students looking back on their lives: Harrison and Cantor, 1999.
page 101 even though Scream is somewhat satirical: Cantor, 2003.
page 101 Those who study the brain now speak of emotional memory: LeDoux, 1996.
page 103 "sickening, almost degenerate in its savagery": Germain, 2008.
page 103 over 250 people are killed: filmfather.blogspot.com/2009/03rambo-2008.html.

3: IT'S A GUY THING: WHAT BOYS READ

page 121 the stigma of being a boy reader: Porche, Ross, and Snow, 2004, pp. 345, 350, 356.
page 123 half chose "feminine" toys: Orenstein, 2008; Cherney and London, 2006.
page 127 it's all they see around them: Cherney and London, 2006.
page 128 . . . as children's book scholar Ellen Handler Spitz asserts: Spitz, 2008.
page 130 this lack of lead characters is just wrong.: Corbett, Hill, and St. Rose, 2008.
page 136 with author and comic book writer Gerard Jones: Jones, 2002, p. 66.
page 137 so a New York Times article claims, it's mostly adults are reading them.: Rabb, 2008.
page 139 empowering a generation to demand stories that reflected their realities: Peck, 2007.
page 154 David Hajdu tells us in his recent best seller: Hajdu, 2008.
page 155 superheroes were created by Jewish men: Dotinga, 2007; Fingeroth, 2007.
page 155 You had a bunch of young men whose parents were immigrants: Dotinga, 2007.
page 155 essential to their attraction to comic books: Fingeroth, 2007.
page 155 But when I imagine how it must feel to him: Morrison, Daniel, and Florea, 2008.
page 156 "I expected more valor.": Brubaker and D'Armata, 2008.
page 156 Fingeroth says, in an interview with "Mr. Media": Mr. Media Interviews Danny Fingeroth, 2008.
page 157 Peter (Spider-Man) saves the boy as his molten uncle explodes: Slott, McKone, Lanning, and Cox, 2008.
page 157 Icelandic flight attendants: Fraction, Larroga, and D'Armata, 2008.

page 157 expose her thonged bottom to A-is-for-all readers: Robinson, Guedes, and Magahaes, 2008.
page 158 babies' poop is often green and yellow: Bendis, Tan, and Gaydos, 2008.
page 158 what if Babar suddenly kicked butt and took names?: Fingeroth, 2004.
page 159 it didn't matter, but they had to be a guy: Welldon, 2005.
page 159 "we still tend to be a little nose-in-the-air about them": Frean, 2008.
page 159 in the state of Denmark: selfmadehero.com/manga_shakespeare/titles/hamlet.html.
page 160 world of mutants: selfmadehero.com/manga_shakespeare/titles/macbeth.html.
page 160 more to do with race and poverty than gender: Corbett, Hill, and St. Rose, 2008; Mead, 2006.
page 161 founder of the Guys Read project: guysread.org.
page 162 Tom Newkirk, author of Misreading Masculinity, says: Newkirk, 2002.

4: DO YOU HEAR WHAT I HEAR? WHAT BOYS LISTEN TO

page 167 the TV show Two and a Half Men: Dahl, 2008.
page 168 masculinity that invokes sexism and homophobia: Pascoe, 2007, p. 156.
page 168 they hear lots of yelling: Omli and LaVoie, in press.
page 169 When it comes to relational aggression: Card, Stucky, Sawalani, and Little, 2008.
page 169 more likely to carry a weapon to school: Goldstein, Young, and Boyd, 2007.
page 169 Pascoe's book, Dude You're a Fag: Pascoe, 2007, p. 55.
page 170 fear of having the fag identity permanently adhere: Pascoe, 2007, p. 54.
page 170 and not even geniuses—ever makes it alone: Gladwell, 2008, p. 115.
page 170 Obama as one man alone: Remnick, 2008.
page 173 they either played the drums or would like to: Green, 2002.
page 173 a boy came to a lesson with a black eye: Sinsabaugh, 2005.
page 174 the clarinet is considered to be a "girl" instrument: Eros, 2008.
page 174 not as gender accessories: Eros, 2008.
page 175 Mary Ann Clawson, writing for Popular Music: Clawson, 1999.
page 176 Whitson wrote that "body sense is crucial": Whitson, 1990, pp. 21, 23.
page 177 Kevin le Gendre writes about the guitar as a substitute for a gun: le Gendre, 2007.
page 177 newly formed boy bands tend to choose names that evoke power: Clawson, 1999.
page 178 Steve Waksman writes that: Waksman, 1999.
page 178 the first Guitar Hero: Waksman, 1999.
page 178 you're near-as-dammit making yourself: Whales, 2009.
page 178 Oasis guitarist Noel Gallagher: www.thisishullandeastriding.co.uk/showbiz/Noel-Guitar-Hero
    -authentic/article-666168-detail/article.html.
page 178 "I can't make myself resist playing it": http://meganmcardle.theatlantic.com/archives/2008/
    08/my_guitar_hero.php.
page 181 Indeed, critic Freya Jarman-Ivens: Jarman-Ivens, 2007, p. 3.
page 181 Authors Hugh Barker and Yuval Taylor: Barker and Taylor, 2007, p. x.
page 182 communications professor and cultural theorist Marcel Danesi: Danesi, 2003.
page 182 it reflects the fragmentation of the culture: Danesi, 2003, p. 87.
page 182 serve to "celebrate misfits and losers": Barker and Taylor, 2007, p. 286.
page 184 New York Times writer Vivien Schweitzer: Schweitzer, 2008, p. 31.
page 184 Of Beethoven's Ninth Symphony, one critic wrote . . . : Slonimsky, 2000.
page 185 Phelps told the Today Show: rap-up.com/2008/08/18/quote-of-the-day-michael-phelps/.
page 186 most popular nonsports show on cable TV in 2006?: as noted in Ogbar, 2007.
page 186 in her book Pimps Up, Ho's Down . . . : Sharpley-Whiting, 2007, p. 27.
page 186 of sexualized black women. Sharpley-Whiting, 2007, p. 12.
page 189 Russell Simmons used the word niggerize: Fleetwood, 2005.
page 189 Hood narratives rarely show hope or defiance to whites: Ogbar, 2007.
page 191 as Marlene Kim Connor says: Connor, 1995, p. 127.
page 192 Research shows that exposure to sexualized rap videos: Johnson, Adams, Ashburn, and Reed,
    1995.
page 192 frequent television viewing and exposure to pop music: Strouse, Goodwin, and Roscoe, 1994.
page 192 Little or no sexually degrading music: Ashby, Arcari, and Edmonson, 2006.
page 193 "the Biggest Colored Show on Earth": Ogbar, 2007, p. X.
page 193 white recording monopoly that's demanding hostile stereotypes: Ogbar, 2007, p.X.
page 194 The rapper Common predicts . . . : McLaughlin, 2008.

page 194 "they can now dream to be Obamas": will.i.am, 2009.

page 195 a "need for glamour and novelty": Sanneh, 2008.

page 196 Sociologist Angela Stroud reported: Stroud, 2007, p. 10.

page 197 He's a good father, husband, hard worker, and soldier: Stroud, 2007, p. 13.

page 198 "a bunch of oddballs, a circus of talent": youtube.com/watch?v=GoIXxFSq7og.

page 198 "always be open to the next idea": muzikmafia.com.

5: WANNA PLAY? WHAT BOYS DO

page 205 Gerard Jones writes, in Killing Monsters: Jones, 2002.

page 207 toys like action figures: Mickiewicz, 2004.

page 209 They call it "cradle to grave brand loyalty.": Linn, 2004.

page 211 that "glorify evil, destruction, and promiscuity": National Public Radio, 2007.

page 211 "Jesus is selling out.": Ewoldt, 2007.

page 211 Samson was one of the strongest men: www.one2believe.com/.

page 212 Boys learn he "was a giant Philistine warrior": www.one2believe.com/.

page 215 Children Now, a children's advocacy and research group: Children Now, 1999c, p. 2.

page 215 A thirty-second spot during Super Bowl XLII: Kiley, 2008.

page 217 In a survey of 12,000 children ages ten to seventeen: Children Now, 1999c, pp. 4–5.

page 217 According to a study of 4,200 high school athletes: Josephson Institute, 2006.

page 217 Hardly, since women receive just 6.3 percent of sports coverage: Duncan and Messner, 2005.

page 218 don't apply to sports programming: Messner, Dunbar, and Hunt, 2000.

page 218 "Officials stopped the game": ESPN.com News, 2004.

page 218 Jermaine O'Neal was suspended for twenty-five games.: Robbins, 2004.

page 218 Studies tell us that boys who play sports: Messner, 1990; Miedzian, 1991; Rowe, 1998.

page 218 more likely to exhibit delinquent behavior: Bloom and Smith, 1996; Endresen & Olweus, 2005; Nixon, 1997; Rowe, 1998; Watkins, 2000.

page 218 Michael Kimmel in Guyland: Kimmel, 2008a, p. 126.

page 219 Guys like watching sports with other guys: Simmons, 2002.

page 219 "the one thing they never said that about was sports": Kimmel, 2008, pp. 127–28.

page 220 He doesn't speak: Bricken, 2008.

page 222 he's the icon of masculinity: Black quarterbacks have become increasingly common in the NFL in recent years. Only one black man, however, has been the quarterback of a winning team in the Super Bowl (Doug Williams, of the Washington Redskins, the MVP of Super Bowl XXII in 1988). The recent conviction and imprisonment of Michael Vick, an exceptionally talented black quarterback with the Atlanta Falcons on charges of animal cruelty related to his participation in a dog-fighting ring, has unfortunately raised old racist stereotypes and questions about whether black men are really "fit" to be NFL quarterbacks.

page 223 The Children Now study: Children Now, 1999c, p. 10.

page 223 Our colleague Bill Pollack: Pollack, 1999.

page 224 "and taught in terms of the capacity to love and be loved.": Marx, 2004.

page 225 Janet Evanovich, a fan herself, said it well: Evanovich, 2008, p. 4.

page 225 NASCAR is about white southern masculinity: Parmley, 1989.

page 225 Encyclopedia of Southern Culture: Parmley, 1989, p. 1133; see also, web.wm.edu/amst/370/2002/sp3/Homepage.html.

page 225 "a man's man": Parmley, 1989, p. 1133.

page 225 "the good old boy needs his car": Ibid.

page 225 Robert Lipsyte wrote: Lipsyte, 2006.

page 225 David Caraviello, writing for Nascar.com: Caraviello, 2007.

page 226 NASCAR is for real men: Ibid.

page 226 an online publication covering NASCAR: Gluck, 2008.

page 226 "People want to find a way to connect to you": Ibid.

page 226 "I think we get warped": Ibid.

page 227 Sanjay Gupta, reporting for CNN: Gupta, 2005.

page 227 according to racer Rusty Wallace, in 2004: Owens, 2004.

page 227 as Sanjay Gupta noted: Gupta, 2005.

page 228 fourteen times more caffeine than a can of cola: www.cbc.ca/consumer/story/2008/09/24/energydrinks.html.

page 229 from athletes to rock stars: www.rockstar69.com/products.php.

page 229 grab a MONSTER and go BIG!: www.monsterenergy.com/product/locarb.php

page 230 "It represents family": www.monsterenergy.com.

page 230 and prove his bravery in extreme sports: www.monsterarmy.loopd.com/Members/monster/
Default.aspx.

page 230 Check out this online ad: www.xoxide.com/pimp-juice-energy-drink.html.

page 231 "I will be better than I am today": www.gatorade.com.

page 231 The number of male drinkers has risen by 64 percent: Francella, 2009.

page 231 attributed to drinking energy drinks: www.recipes.howstuffworks.com/energy-drink.htm.

page 231 a range of associated medical problems: www.cbc.ca/consumer/story/2008/09/24/energydrinks
.html.

page 232 the effects of alcohol marketing campaigns on young audiences: Childs, 2007.

page 232 "a buzz booze for teeny boppers": Huus, 2007.

page 232 "the predatory marketing practices of the alcohol industry": Childs, 2007.

page 232 "the caffeine will keep you partying all night": Childs, 2007.

page 233 Kenneth MacKinnon points to: MacKinnon, 1998, p. 100.

page 233 Media ecologist Lance Strate describes: Strate, 2003, pp. 83–85.

page 233 a variety of all-male places: Kimmel, 1996.

page 234 "the highest form of challenge": Strate, 2003, pp. 88–89.

page 236 the first one was made in September 2007: www.allbusiness.com/marketing-advertising/
marketing-advertising/5319074-1.html.

page 236 a $450 million dollar contract with the National Guard: myprfeed.wordpress.com/2008/05/31/
american-national-guard-3-doors-down-team-up-in-advertising-blitz/

page 236 who directed the crime thriller Training Day: www.allbusiness.com/marketing-advertising/
marketing-advertising/5319074-1.html.

page 237 "'I'm going to have to think about that'": Haskell, 2007.

page 237 a cross between a hotel lobby and a video arcade: Hurdle, 2009.

page 237 an Apache or Blackhawk helicopter: Hurdle, 2009.

page 237 "You can't simulate the loss when you see people getting killed": Hurdle, 2009.

page 238 "the world of Soldiering in the U.S. Army": www.americasarmy.com/

page 238 "upcoming missions.": Kutner and Olson, 2008, p. 154.

page 238 Make boys seem more important than girls: www.peacecoalition.org/facts/toys_are_for_fun
.html.

page 238 war is sold to boys through toys: Carlsson-Paige and Levin, 1990; Linn, 2008.

page 239 president's high approval ratings: Greenwald, 2008.

page 239 A record number of troops are returning with PTSD: Tyson, 2007.

page 241 when they have a male passenger: National Institutes of Health News, 2005.

page 241 Focus on the Family: www.pluggedinonline.com/movies/movies/a0000067.cfm.

page 243 "Although Burton claims to have no idea": www.kaboodle.com/reviews/burton-420-kit.

page 244 Alex Kuczynski wrote in the New York Times: Kuczynski, 2005.

page 244 "long hard grinds on my meaty park edges": www.burton.com/Gear/Default.aspx#/gear/pro
ductdetail/mens/boards/10419/206851000155/.

page 245 As our good friend Rich DeGrandpre writes in his book, Ritalin Nation: DeGrandpre, 1999.

page 246 "your Thursday night date": www.oldspice.com/products.html .

page 246 Interestingly enough, among college-aged boys: Oswalt, Cameron, and Koob, 2005.

page 247 especially in the beginning stages: Giordano, Longmore, and Manning, 2006.

page 247 sociologist Barrie Thorne: Thorne,1993.

page 247 not matching up to the big man ideal: Giordano, Longmore, and Manning, 2006.

page 248 "or more of a man": Tolman, Spencer, Rosen-Reynoso, and Porche, 2003.

page 249 Passion and a longing for death are intertwined: de Rougemont, 1983.

page 249 All that pressure on boys to be a player: Ibid.

page 250 integrating lust with love is a lifelong task for boys: Sullivan, 1953.

page 251 Sonya Thompson at the University of Alberta: www.cbc.ca/canada/edmonton/story/2007/02/
23/porn-teens.html.

page 251 Janis Wolak and her colleagues: Wolak, Mitchell, and Finkelhor, 2007.

page 252 Jackson Katz . . . and Robert Jensen: See Katz, 2006; Jensen, 2007.

page 252 "naked women are just bad porn": Wolf, 2003.

page 253 authors Carmine Saracchino and Kevin Scott: Saracchino and Scott, 2008.

page 253 As Saracchino and Scott point out: Ibid.

page 253 "*Could an adult help me*": Nathan, 2007, pp. 112–113.

page 254 including coauthor, Sharon Lamb: Lamb, 2006.

page 254 its relationship to his developing sexuality: Kindlon and Thompson, 1999.

page 256 as Lawrence Kutner and Cheryl Olson say: Kutner and Olson, 2008.

page 257 the charm of this game is not just in the gunfire or the detail, but the execution: Cabrera, 2008.

page 258 their parents have ever stopped them from playing one: www.commonsensemedia.org/grand
   -theft-auto-iv-parents-m-means-m

page 260 Cover is for punks: Breckon, 2009.

page 260 their parents were ignorant about video games in general: Kutner and Olson, 2008, p. 220.

page 261 The Pew Internet & American Life Project: Cassidy, 2006.

page 262 More than twice as many children: Oppenheim, 2008.

page 262 Mark Zuckerberg, the Harvard student who started Facebook: Cassidy, 2006.

page 263 "It's a way of maintaining a friendship without having to make any effort whatsoever.": Ibid.

page 263 "social demographics and pyschographics": Pagel, 2007; see also Smith, 2008.

page 264 teen rebels have been working for years on new ways of sharing information: Mason, 2008.

page 264 blogger of "Poisonous Paragraphs": Adams, 2008.

page 264 the kinds of moral dilemmas kids face: Johnson, 2003.

page 265 Check out Candice Kelsey's book Generation MySpace, *as well as Y-Pulse blogger Anastasia
   Goodstein's Totally Wired*: Kelsey, 2007; Goodstein, 2007.

6: REBEL, RESIST, AND REFUSE: CONVERSATIONS WITH OUR SONS

page 270 they desire communication with parents and peers: Way and Chu, 2004.

page 273 boys as young as two years old attempt to shape other boys' toy preferences: Fagot, 1985.

page 274 by a perceived threat to his freedom: Brehm and Brehm, 1981, p. 37.

page 274 simply because someone has said they can't have it: Brehm and Brehm, 1981.

page 274 Marketers love boys with "relational proneness: Darpy and Prim-Allaz, 2008.

page 277 that's made him a media star: Greven, 2008.

page 277 "viva la difference": michaelgurian.com.

page 279 In a 2008 Father's Day survey: www.wehatesheep.com/whatwedo/media/shs_FathersDay
   Findings.pdf.

page 279 John January, the vice president and executive creative director: www.reuters.com/article/press
   Release/idUS178970+13-Jun-2008+PRN20080613.

page 284 In Guyland, sociologist Michael Kimmel: Kimmel, 2008a, p. 126.

page 285 captivating millions with his exhilarating achievement.: Shipnuck, December 8, 2008.

page 288 In a psychological study of elementary schoolchildren: Gentile, Saleem, and Anderson,
   2007.

page 289 as twenty-six times a day or once every fourteen minutes: PFLAG, 2004.

page 290 There's a reason why nearly 70 percent of gay youth: Sexual Information and Education
   Council of the United States; www. siecus.org.

page 290 Spencer Fennell, describing himself: www.helium.com/items/824174-is-the-slang-use-of-the
   -word-retard-or-retarded-discriminatory.

page 291 That's important, because 70 percent of schools: PFLAG, 2004.

page 291 Kanye West's rant against homophobia: www.towleroad.com/2008/08/kanye-west-to-f.html.

page 292 logical reasoning abilities of fifteen-year-olds are similar to adults: Steinberg, 2007.

page 292 being more vigilant about liquor sold to minors: Steinberg, 2007.

page 293 most of the behaviors that are problematic in adulthood start in adolescence: Sternheimer,
   2006.

page 297 a "Male Privilege Checklist": www.amptoons.com/blog/the-male-privilege-checklist/.

page 300 "mixed up fact and fiction": Abramowitz, 2009.

page 300 "four sources have independently told Sports Illustrated": Roberts and Epstein, 2009.

page 300 uncomplicated lovers in tatters.: www.thefrisky.com/post/246-chris-brown-is-remorsefulfor
   -what-exactly/.

page 301 was registered to Lil Wayne in Florida.: Shepherd, 2008.

page 301 "he loves people": www.thefrisky.com/post/246-chris-brown-is-remorsefulfor-what-exactly/.

page 301 "then you just shouldn't have been born, straight up": Mancini, 2009.

page 302 We love the Above the Influence anti-pot smoking: www.abovetheinfluence.com/the-ads/.

page 303 "What could you be influenced to do?": www.abovetheinfluence.com/fun/slom.aspx.

page 303 "They own everything, pretty much": Kids+Money, 2008.

Bibliography

Abramowitz, R. February 7, 2009. "Christian Bale: 'I took it way too far.'" *Los Angeles Times*. www. latimes.com/entertainment/la-et-brief7-2009feb07,0,3864340.story.

Adams, D. January 7, 2008. "Dart Adams Presents Read a Book: *The Pirate's Dilemma* by Matt Mason." poisonousparagraphs.blogspot.com/2008/01/dart-adams-presents-read-book-pirates.html.

Ashby, S., Arcari, C., and Edmonson, M. 2006. "Television Viewing and Risk of Sexual Initiation by Young Adolescents." *Archives of Pediatrics & Adolescent Medicine* 160 (4): 375–380.

Aufreiter, N., Elzinga, D., and Gordon, J. 2003. "Better Branding." *McKinsey Quarterly*, Issue 4.

Barker, H., and Taylor, Y. 2007. *Faking It: The Quest for Authenticity in Popular Music*. New York: W. W. Norton.

Bendis, B., Tan, B., and Gaydos, M. 2008. *The New Avengers: Secret Invasion*. No. 47. Marvel Comics.

Bloom, G., and Smith, M. 1996. "Hockey Violence: A Test of Cultural Spillover Theory." *Sociology of Sport Journal* 13 (1): 65–77.

Breckon, N., February 10, 2009. "50 Cent Developer Video: Cover Is for Punks." *Shacknews.com*. www.shacknews.com/onearticle.x/57183.

Brehm, S., and Brehm, J. 1981. *Psychological Reactance: A Theory of Freedom and Control*. New York: John Wiley.

Bricken, R. January 16, 2008. "Chronicle of Unnecessary Toys: Cleatus." *Topless Robot*. www.topless robot.com/2008/01/chronicle_of_unnecessary_toys_cleatus.php.

Brubaker, E., Ross, L., Epting, S., and Bucema, S. 2008. *Captain America*. No. 44. Marvel Comics.

Business Wire, September 7, 2007. "4Kids TV(TM) Celebrates Sixth Season on FOX with Action-Packed Fall Line-up." www.allbusiness.com/marketing-advertising/sales-promotions-sweepstakes/5272268-1.html.

Cabrera, C. April 30, 2008. "*Grand Theft Auto IV* Brings Violence, Satire to New York." *The Pace Press*.

Calvert, S., Kotler, J., Zehnder, S., and Shockey, E. 2003. "Gender Stereotyping in Children's Reports about Educational and Informational Television Programs." *Media Psychology* 5 (2): 139–162.

Cantor, J. May 2003. "I'll Never Have a Clown in My House: Frightening Movies and Enduring Emotional Memory." Paper presented at the annual meeting of the International Communication Association, San Diego, Cal.

Caraviello, D. August 18, 2007. "Being Aggressive Is Part of a NASCAR Driver's Job." *NACAR.com*. racecast.nascar.com/2007/news/opinion/08/18/dcaraviello.aggressive.drivers/index.html.

Card, N., Stucky, B., Sawalani, G., and Little, T. 2008. "Direct and Indirect Aggression During Childhood and Adolescence: A Meta-Analytic Review of Gender Differences, Intercorrelations, and Relations to Maladjustment." *Child Development* 79 (5): 1185–1229.

Carlsson-Paige, N., and Levin, D. 1990. *Who's Calling the Shots? How to Respond Effectively to Children's Fascination with War Play and War Toys*. Gabriola Island, British Columbia: New Society Publishers.

Cars. 2006. Codirectors, John Lasseter and Joe Ranft. DVD. Disney/Pixar.

Cassidy, J. May 15, 2006. "Me Media: How Hanging Out on the Internet Became Big Business." *The New Yorker*.

Cave, D. August 5, 2002. "Air Jordans: What Changed Leisure Footwear Forever and Created the Wonderful, Hideous Behemoth of Contemporary Consumer Culture? It's Gotta Be Da Shoes." *Salon*. dir.salon.com/story/ent/masterpiece/2002/08/05/air_jordan/index.html.

Charles, K. K., Hurst, E., and Roussanov, N. Quarterly Journal of Economics. 2009. Conspicuous Consumption and Race.

Cherney, I., and London, K. 2006. "Gender-Linked Differences in the Toys, Television Shows, Computer Games, and Outdoor Activities of 5- to 13-year-old Children." *Sex Roles* 54 (9–10): 717–726.

Children Now. 1999a. *Boys to Men: Conference Report on Media Messages about Masculinity.* Oakland, Cal.: Children Now.

Children Now. 1999b. *Boys to Men: Entertainment Media Messages about Masculinity.* Oakland, Cal.: Children Now.

Children Now. 1999c. *Boys to Men: Sports Media Messages about Masculinity.* Oakland, Cal.: Children Now.

Childs, D. April 1, 2007. "Alcoholic Energy Drinks—A Threat to Kids?" *ABCnews.go.com.* abcnews.go.com/Health/story?id=2996316&page=1.

Clawson, M. A. 1999. "Masculinity and Skill Acquisition in the Adolescent Rock Band." *Popular Music,* 18: 99–114.

Clover, C. 1992. *Men, Women, and Chain Saws: Gender in the Modern Horror Film.* Princeton, N.J.: Princeton University Press.

Connell, R. W. 2005. *Masculinities.* Berkeley: University of California Press.

Connor, M. 1995. *What Is Cool? Understanding Black Manhood in America.* New York: Crown.

Corbett, C., Hill, C., and St. Rose, A. 2008. *Where the Girls Are: The Facts about Gender Equity in Education.* Washington, D.C.: AAUW Educational Foundation.

Dahl, O. August 18, 2008. BuddyTV Fall 2008 Preview: *Two and a Half Men.* www.buddytv.com/articles/two-and-a-half-men/buddytv-fall-2008-preview-two-22064.aspx.

Danesi, M. 2003. *My Son Is an Alien.* New York: Rowman & Littlefield.

Darpy, D., and Prim-Allaz, I. 2008. "Potential Effects of Psychological Reactance and Relationship Proneness on Relationships Marketing Programmes." Unpublished manuscript, University of Paris-Dauphine.

Dee, J. April 8, 2007. "Tween on the Screen." *The New York Times Magazine.*

DeGrandpre, R. 1999. *Ritalin Nation: Rapid-Fire Culture and the Transformation of Human Consciousness.* New York: W. W. Norton.

De Rougemont, D. 1983. *Love in the Western World.* Princeton, N.J.: Princeton University Press.

Dotinga, R. July 27, 2007. "Bird, Plane or SuperMensch? Jews and Superheroes Share a Rich History." *Wired.com.* www.wired.com/culture/art/news/2007/07/jews_comics_qa.

Duncan, M., and Messner, M. 2005. *Gender in Televised Sports: News and Highlights Shows, 1989–2004.* Los Angeles: Amateur Athletic Foundation of Los Angeles.

Edwards, T. 2003. "Sex, Booze, and Fags: Masculinity, Style, and Men's Magazines." In B. Benwell, ed., *Masculinity and Men's Lifestyle Magazines.* Malden, Mass.: Blackwell.

Endresen, I., and Olweus, D. 2005. "Participation in Power Sports and Antisocial Involvement in Preadolescent and Adolescent Boys." *Journal of Child Psychology and Psychiatry* 46 (5): 468–478.

Erikson, E. 1963. *Childhood and Society.* New York: W. W. Norton.

Eros, J. 2008. "Instrument Selection and Gender Stereotypes: A Review of Recent Literature." *Update: Applications of Research in Music Education* 27 (1): 57–64.

ESPN.com News. November 21, 2004. "Artest, Jackson Charge Palace Stands." sports.espn.go.com/nba/news/story?id=1927380.

Evanovich, J. August 24, 2008. "A Day at the Races." *Parade.*

Ewoldt, J. December 15, 2007. "Talking Jesus Doll Sales Are on the Ascent." Minneapolis *Star Tribune.* www.startribune.com/12535966.html.

Facenda, V. July 23, 2007. "Smells Like Profit: Disney Eyes Pre-Teen Fragrance Market," *Brandweek.* www.brandweek.com/bw/news/recent_display.jsp?vnu_content_id=1003615156.

Fagot, B. 1985. "Beyond the Reinforcement Principle: Another Step Toward Understanding Sex Role Development." *Developmental Psychology* 21: 1097–1104.

Fingeroth, D. 2004. *Superman on the Couch: What Superheroes Really Tell Us about Ourselves and Our Society.* New York: Continuum.

———. 2007. *Disguised as Clark Kent: Jews, Comics, and the Creation of the Superhero.* New York: Continuum.

Fisman, R. January 11, 2008. "Cos and Effect." *Slate.* www.slate.com/id/2181822.

Fleetwood, N. 2005. "Hip-Hop Fashion, Masculine Anxiety, and the Discourse of Americana." In H. Elam and K. Jackson, eds., *Black Cultural Traffic: Crossroads in Global Performance and Popular Culture.* Ann Arbor, Mich.: University of Michigan Press.

Fraction, M., Larocca, S., and D'Armata, F. 2008. *World's Most Wanted: The Invincible Iron Man (Dark Reign).* No. 8 Marvel Comics.

Francella, B. May 4, 2009. "Energy Drinks Power Up Margins." *Convenience Store News.* www.csnews.com/csn/sso/trendline/article_display.jsp?vnu_content_id=1003959118.

Frean, A. June 14, 2008. "Comic Books 'Can Get Boys in the Habit of Reading.'" *TimesOnline.* http://entertainment.timesonline.co.uk/tol/arts_and_entertainment/books/article4134092.ece.

Freud, S. 1923/1960. *The Ego and the Id* (ed. James Strachey). New York: W. W. Norton.

Gentile, D., Saleem, M., and Anderson, C. 2007. "Public Policy and the Effects of Media Violence on Children." *Social Issues and Policy Review* 1 (1): 15–61.

Germain, D. January 24, 2008. "Rambo Reeks of Depraved Violence." *Starpulse.com.* http://www .starpulse.com/news/index.php/2008/01/24/film_review_rambo_reeks_of_depraved_viol.

Gilligan, C. 2002. *The Birth of Pleasure.* New York: Alfred A. Knopf.

Giordano, P., Longmore, M., and Manning, W. 2006. "Gender and the Meanings of Adolescent Romantic Relationships: A Focus on Boys." *American Sociological Review* 71 (2): 260–287.

Gladwell, M. 2008. *Outliers: The Story of Success.* New York: Little, Brown.

Gluck, J. December 10, 2008. "Jimmie Johnson Proves That Nice Guys Don't Always Finish Last." *SceneDailycom.* http://www.scenedaily.com/news/articles/sprintcupseries/35866829.html.

Goldstein, S. E., Young, A., and Boyd, C. 2007. "Relational Aggression at School: Associations with School Safety and Social Climate." *Journal of Youth and Adolescence* 37 (6): 641–654.

Goodstein, A. 2007. *Totally Wired: What Teens and Tweens Are Really Doing Online.* New York: St. Martin's Press.

Green, L. 2002. "Exposing the Gendered Discourse of Music Education." *Feminism & Psychology,* 12 137–144.

Greenwald, G. May 29, 2008. "CNN/MSNBC Reporter: Corporate Executives Forced Pro-Bush, Pro-War Narrative." *Salon.com.* http://www.salon.com/opinion/greenwald/2008/05/29/yellin/.

Greven, A. 2008. *How to Talk to Girls.* New York: HarperCollins.

Gupta, S. November 17, 2005. "NASCAR Ride 'More Than a Little Terrifying.'" *CNN.com.* http:// www.cnn.com/2005/HEALTH/09/30/gupta.nascar/.

Hajdu, D. 2008. *The Ten-Cent Plague: The Great Comic-Book Scare and How It Changed America.* New York: Farrar, Straus and Giroux, LLC.

Hamm, S. July 2, 2007. "Children of the Web: How the Second-Generation Internet Is Spawning a Global Youth Culture—And What Business Can Do to Cash In." *BusinessWeek.*

Harrison, K., and Cantor, J. 1999. "Tales from the Screen: Enduring Fright Reactions to Scary Media." *Media Psychology* 1 (2): 97–116.

Haskell, B. September 21, 2007. "NASCAR's Dale Earnhardt Jr. to Drive National Guard Car." Army.mil/news.com. www.army.mil/-news/2007/09/21/4993-nascars-dale-earnhardt-jr-to-drive-na tional-guard-car/.

Herrett-Skjellum, J., and Allen, M. 1996. "Television Programming and Sex Stereotyping: A Meta-Analysis." In B. R. Burleson, ed., *Communication Yearbook, 19.* Thousand Oaks, Cal.: Sage.

Hip Hop: Beyond Beats and Rhymes. 2007. Producer, director, writer, Byron Hurt. DVD. Media Education Foundation.

Howze, J. February 1, 2008. "Children's T-shirts Get Risqué." *Times OnLine.* women.timeson line.co.uk/tol/life_and_style/women/families/article3289287.ece.

Hurdle, J. January 9, 2009. "U.S. Army Recruiting at the Mall with Videogames." *Reuters.com.* www .reuters.com/article/technologyNews/idUSTRE50819H20090110.

Huss, K. April 3, 2007. "A Booze Buzz for Teenyboppers? Anheuser-Busch Product So Adorable It Draws Fire from Alcohol Abuse Camp." MSNBC.com. www.msnbc.msn.com/id/17862137/.

Jarman-Ivens, F. 2007. "Introduction: Oh Boy! Making Masculinity in Popular Music." In F. Jarman-Ivens, ed., *Oh Boy! Masculinities and Popular Music.* New York: Routledge.

Jensen, R. 2007. *Getting Off: Pornography and the End of Masculinity.* Cambridge, Mass.: South End Press.

Johnson, D. 2003. *Learning Right from Wrong in the Digital Age: An Ethics Guide for Parents, Teachers, Librarians, and Others Who Care about Computer-Using Young People.* Columbus, Ohio: Linworth Publishing.

Johnson, J., Adams, M., Ashburn, L., and Reed, W. 1995. "Differential Gender Effects of Exposure to Rap Music on African American Adolescents' Acceptance of Teen Dating Violence." *Sex Roles* 33 (7–8): 597–605.

Johnson, P. April 3, 2007. "'Deadliest Catch' Survives High Seas, Lands Big Numbers." *USA Today.*

Jones, G. 2002. *Killing Monsters: Why Children Need Fantasy, Super Heroes, and Make-Believe Violence.* New York: Basic Books.

Josephson Institute. 2006. *What Are Your Children Learning? The Impact of High School Sports on the Values and Ethics of High School Athletes.* josephsoninstitute.org/sports/programs/survey/index .html.

Josephson, W. 1995. *Television Violence: A Review of the Effects on Children of Different Ages.* Ottawa, Canada: National Clearinghouse on Family Violence.

Just for Kicks. 2005. Directors, Thibaut de Longeville and Lisa Leone. Writers, Come Chantrel and Thibaut de Longeville. DVD. Image Entertainment.

Kaiser Family Foundation. 2006a. *The Media Family: Electronic Media in the Lives of Infants, Toddlers, Preschoolers, and their Parents.* www.kff.org/entmedia/7500.cfm.

Kaiser Family Foundation. 2006b. *Media Multitasking among American Youth: Prevalence, Predictors and Pairings.* www.kff.org/entmedia/7592.cfm.

Kaplan, D. March 30, 2007. "Killer Crabs: Why Deadliest Catch Is TV's Most Dangerous Show." *New York Post.*

Katz, J. 2006. *The Macho Paradox: Why Some Men Hurt Women and How All Men Can Help.* Naperville, Ill.: Sourcebooks.

Katz, J. July 16, 2007. Sport in Society blog. sportinsociety.blogspot.com/2007/07/analysis-of-wwe-misogyny-absent-from.html.

Kelley, J., and Smith, S. 2006. *Where the Girls Aren't: Gender Disparity Saturates G-Rated Films.* Los Angeles, Cal.: See Jane Program and Dads and Daughters.

Kelsey, C. 2007. *Generation MySpace: Helping Your Teen Survive Online Adolescence.* New York: Avalon.

Kids + Money, 2008. Filmmaker, Lauren Greenfield. DVD. Bullfrog Films.

Kiley, D. February 4, 2008. "Super Bowl Commercials XLII." *BusinessWeek.com.* www.businessweek.com/innovate/content/feb2008/id2008023_353659.htm.

Kimmel, M. 1996. *Manhood in America.* New York: Basic Books.

———. "Masculinity as Homophobia." In M. Kimmel and A. Ferber, eds., *Privilege: A Reader.* Boulder, Colo.: Westview.

———. 2008a. *Guyland: The Perilous World Where Boys Become Men.* NY: HarperCollins.

———. August 11, 2008b. Personal Communication.

Kindlon, D., and Thompson, M. 1999. *Raising Cain: Protecting the Emotional Life of Boys.* New York: Ballantine.

Kuczynski, A. October 27, 2005. "Preparing for Snow in the Ski Free Zone." *New York Times.* www.nytimes.com/2005/10/27/fashion/thursdaystyles/27CRITIC.html?_r=1.

Kutner, L., and Olson, C. 2008. *Grand Theft Childhood: The Surprising Truth about Violent Video Games and What Parents Can Do.* New York: Simon & Schuster.

Lamb, S. 2006. *Sex, Therapy, and Kids: Addressing Their Concerns through Talk and Play.* New York: Norton Professional Books.

Lamb, S. and Brown, L. 2006. *Packaging Girlhood. Rescuing Our Daughters from Marketers' Schemes.* New York: St. Martin's Press.

Leaper, C., Breed, L., Hoffman, L., and Perlman, C. 2006. "Variations in the Gender-Stereotyped Content of Children's Television Cartoons Across Genres." *Journal of Applied Social Psychology* 32 (8): 1653–1662.

LeDoux, J. 1996. *The Emotional Brain.* New York: Simon & Schuster.

le Gendre, K. May 4, 2007. "The Colour of the Guitar." *Catalyst: Debating Race, Identity, Citizenship, and Culture.* 83.137.212.42/siteArchive/catalystmagazine/Default.aspx.LocID-0hgnew0ua.RefLocID-0hg01b00100600f00g.Lang-EN.htm.

Levin, D. and Kilbourne, J. 2008. *So Sexy So Soon.* New York: Random House.

Linn, S. 2004. *Consuming Kids.* New York: The New Press.

———. 2008. *The Case for Make Believe: Saving Play in a Commercialized World.* New York: The New Press.

Lipsyte, R. November 21, 2006. "Nascar Values." *The Nation.* www.thenation.com/doc/20061204/lipsyte.

MacKinnon, K. 1998. *Uneasy Pleasures: The Male as Erotic Object.* Madison, N.J.: Fairleigh Dickinson University Press.

Mancini, E. February 5, 2009. "Lil Wayne Opens Up to Katie Couric, Says He's No Longer Addicted to Syrup." *XXLMag.com.* http://www.xxlmag.com/online/?p=36608.

Marx, J. August 29, 2004. "Joe Ehrmann: He Turns Boys into Men." *Parade.* www.racematters.org/joeehrmann.htm.

Mason, M. 2008. *The Pirate's Dilemma: How Youth Culture Is Reinventing Capitalism.* New York: The Free Press.

McLaughlin, E. December 9, 2008. "Rapper Common: Obama Will Change Hip-Hop's Attitude. *CNN.com.* http://www.cnn.com/2008/SHOWBIZ/Music/12/09/common.universal.mind.control/#cnnSTCText.

Mead, S. 2006. *The Truth about Boys and Girls.* Washington, D.C.: Education Sector.

Meltzer, B. August 29–31, 2008. "Why I Love Superman." *USA Weekend*. www.usaweekend.com/08 _issues/080831/080831superman-brad-meltzer.html.

Merchants of Cool. 2001. Director, Barak Goodman. Writer, Douglas Rushkoff. DVD. PBS *Frontline*. http://www.pbs.org/wgbh/pages/frontline/shows/cool/.

Messner, M. 1990. "When Bodies Are Weapons." *International Review for the Sociology of Sport* 25: 203–221.

Messner, M., Dunbar, M., and Hunt, D. 2000. "The Televised Sports Manhood Formula." *Journal of Sport & Social Issues* 24(4): 380–394.

Mickiewicz, M. November 14, 2004. "Keen on Tweens: Boys' Purchasing Power." *TDmonthly* 3 (2).

Miedzian, M. 1991. *Boys Will Be Boys: Breaking the Link Between Masculinity and Violence*. New York: Lantern Books.

Miner, D. 2009. "'It's Gotta Be the Shoes, Money!': Sneakers, Identity, and Consumption in the Making of an Authentic (Black) Basketball Culture." Unpublished manuscript, Michigan State University. www.dylanminer.com/shoes.pdf.

Miner, H. 1956. "Body Ritual among the Nacirema." *American Anthropologist* 58: 503–507.

Moore, T., Stuart, G., McNulty, J., Addis, M., Cordova, J., and Temple, J. 2008. "Domains of Masculine Gender Role Stress and Intimate Partner Violence in a Clinical Sample of Violent Men." *Psychology of Men and Masculinity* 9: 82–89.

Morrison, G., Daniel, T., Florea, S., and Major, G. 2008. *R.I.P. Batman*. No. 678. DC Comics.

Mr. Media Interviews Danny Fingeroth. February 26, 2008. www.blogtalkradio.com/mrmedia/2008/ 02/26/Danny-Fingeroth-DISGUISED-AS-CLARK-KENT-author-and-past-Marvel-Comics-editor-Mr-Media-Interview.

MTVNews. 2006. "The Best of 2006." www.mtv.com/news/.

Nathan, D. 2007. *Pornography*. Toronto: Groundwood Books.

National Institutes of Health News, August 25, 2005. "Teens' Driving Riskier with Male Teen Passenger, Teen Boy's Driving Safer with Female Teen Passenger." www.nichd.nih.gov/news/releases/ teen_passengers.cfm.

National Public Radio, *Morning Edition*. August 7, 2007. "Biblical Action Figures Hit Wal-Mart Shelves."

Newkirk, T. 2002. *Misreading Masculinity: Boys, Literacy, and Popular Culture*. Portsmouth, N.H.: Heinemann.

Nixon, H. 1997. "Gender, Sport, and Aggressive Behavior Outside Sport." *Journal of Sport & Social Issues* 21 (4): 379–391.

Ogbar, J. 2007. *Hip Hop Revolution: The Culture and Politics of Rap*. Lawrence, Kans.: University Press of Kansas.

Omli, J. and LaVoi, N. (in press). "The Perfect Storm: Background Anger in Youth Sports." *Journal of Sport Behavior*.

Oppenheim, K. April 2008. "Social Networking Sites: Growing Use Among Tweens and Teens, But a Growing Threat as Well? *Harris Interactive: Trends & Tudes*, 7. www.harrisinteractive.com/ news/newsletters_k12.asp

Orenstein, P. February 10, 2008. "Girls Will Be Girls." *The New York Times Magazine*.

Oswalt, S., Cameron, K., and Koob, J. 2005. "Sexual Regret in College Students." *Archives of Sexual Behavior* 34 (6): 663–669.

Owens, J. May 6, 2004. "NASCAR Bad Boy Stewart Tough to Figure." CBSSports.com. www.sport sline.com/autoracing/story/7309804.

Pagel, K. November 6, 2007. "Facebook: A Marketing Network." friendsclass.blogspot.com/2007/11/ facebook-marketing-network.html.

Parmley, I. 1989. "Stock Car Racing." In C. Wilson and W. Ferris, eds., *Encyclopedia of Southern Culture*. Chapel Hill, N.C.: University of North Carolina Press.

Pascoe, C. J. 2007. *Dude, You're a Fag: Masculinity and Sexuality in High School*. Berkeley: University of California Press.

Peck, D. September 23, 2007. "'The Outsiders': 40 Years Later. *The New York Times Sunday Book Review*. www.nytimes.com/2007/09/23/books/review/Peck-t.html?ref=review.

PFLAG, 2004. *Safe Schools Initiative National Survey Report*. www.pflag.org/fileadmin/Assessment _Report_2004.pdf

Pollack, W. 1999. *Real Boys: Rescuing Our Sons from the Myths of Boyhood*. New York: Owl Books.

Porche, M., Ross, S., and Snow, C. 2004. "From Preschool to Middle School: The Role of Masculinity in Low-Income Urban Adolescent Boys' Literacy Skills and Academic Achievement." In N. Way and Chu, J. Y., eds. *Adolescent Boys*. New York: NYU Press.

Rabb, M. July 20, 2008. "I'm Y.A., and I'm O.K." *New York Times*. www.nytimes.com/2008/07/20/books/review/Rabb-t.html?scp=1&sq=I'm%20Y.A%20.and%20I'm%20O.K.%20&st=cse.

Remnick, D. November 17, 2008. "The Joshua Generation: Race and the Campaign of Barack Obama." *The New Yorker*. www.newyorker.com/reporting/2008/11/17/081117fa_fact_remnick.

Rickey, C. February 8, 2006. "Oscar Is Hardly a Ladies Man." *GuerillaGirls.com*. www.guerrillagirls.com/posters/unchainedpress.shtml.

Roberts, S., and Epstein, D. February 7, 2009. "Sources Tell SI Alex Rodriguez Tested Positive for Steroids in 2003." *Sports Illustrated*. sportsillustrated.cnn.com/2009/baseball/mlb/02/07/alex-rodriguez-steroids/index.html?eref=T1.

Robbins, L. November 22, 2004. "One Player Barred for Season as N.B.A. Responds to Brawl." *New York Times*. www.nytimes.com/2004/11/22/sports/basketball/22brawl.html?scp=2&sq=ron+artest+suspended+for+the+rest+of+the+season&st=nyt.

Robinson, J., Guedes, R., and Magahaes, J. W. 2008. *Superman: Atlas Triumphant*. No. 679. DC Comics.

Rose, J. May 14, 2008. "On Reality TV, Less Sleep Means More Drama." *Morning Edition*. www.npr.org/templates/story/story.php?storyId=90406338.

Ross, D. November 30, 2007. "Mighty Healthy!" *Mass Appeal*. massappealmag.com/the-vault/issue-48/mighty-healthy/.

Rowe, C. 1998. "Aggression and Violence in Sports." *Psychiatric Annals* 28 (5): 265–269.

Ruble, D., and Martin, C. 1998. "Gender Development." In W. Damon and N. Eisenberg, eds., *Handbook of Child Psychology: Vol. 3. Social, Emotional, and Personality Development* (5th ed.). New York: Wiley.

Sanneh, K. February 24, 2008. "A Country Music Veteran Proves He's No Mere Hat Act." *New York Times*. www.nytimes.com/2008/02/24/arts/music/24sann.html?_r=1.

Sarracino, C., and Scott, K. 2008. *The Porning of America: The Rise of Porn Culture, What It Means, and Where We Go from Here*. Boston: Beacon Press.

Schweitzer, V. December 28, 2008. "Aliens Are Attacking. Cue the Strings." *New York Times*. www.nytimes.com/2008/12/28/arts/music/28schw.html?pagewanted=1.

Sharpley-Whiting, T. D. 2007. *Pimps Up, Ho's Down: Hip Hop's Hold on Young Black Women*. New York: NYU Press.

Shepherd, J. January 23, 2008. "DEA Busts Lil Wayne for Drugs." *Vibe.com*. www.vibe.com/news/news_headlines/2008/01/lil_wayne_arrested_drugs/.

Shipnuck, A. December 8, 2008. "Sportsman of the Year: Michael Phelps." *Sports Illustrated*. sportsillustrated.cnn.com/2008/magazine/specials/sportsman/2008/12/01/sportsman.2008/index.html.

Simmons, B. Oct. 2, 2002. "It's a Sport's Guy Thing." *ESPN Magazine*. proxy.espn.go.com/espn/page2/story?page=simmons/021003.

Singer, M. I., Slovak, K., Frierson, T., and York, P. 1998. "Viewing Preferences, Symptoms of Psychological Trauma, and Violent Behaviors among Children Who Watch Television." *Journal of the American Academy of Child and Adolescent Psychiatry* 37: 1041–1048.

Sinsabaugh, K. 2005. "Understanding Students Who Cross Over Gender Stereotypes in Musical Instrument Selection." Unpublished Doctoral Dissertation, Teachers College, Columbia University.

Slonimsky, N. 2000. *Lexicon of Musical Invective: Critical Assaults on Composers Since Beethoven's Time*. New York: W. W. Norton.

Slott, D., McKone, M., Lanning, A., and Cox, J. 2008. *The Amazing Spider-Man*. No. 581. Marvel Comics.

Smith, J. September 18, 2008. "Latest Data on US Facebook Age and Gender Demographics." *InsideFacebook.com*. www.insidefacebook.com/2008/09/18/latest-data-on-us-facebook-age-and-gender-demographics/.

Smith, S., and Kelly, J. 2007. *Now You See 'Em, Now You Don't: Gender and Racial Disparity in TV for Children*. Los Angeles, Cal.: See Jane Program and Dads and Daughters.

Spitz, E. May 24, 2008. Personal Communication.

Steinberg, L. 2007. "Risk Taking in Adolescence: New Perspectives from Brain and Behavioral Science." *Current Directions in Psychological Science* 16 (2): 55–59.

Sternheimer, K. 2006. *Kids These Days: Facts and Fictions about Today's Youth*. New York: Rowan & Littlefield.

Strate, L. 2003. "Beer Commercial: A Manual on Masculinity." In S. Craig, ed., *Men, Masculinity, and the Media*. Thousand Oaks, Cal.: Sage.

Stroud, A. August 2007. "Commercial Cowboys: Mainstream Country Music and the Production of White Masculinity." Paper presented at the Annual Meeting of the American Sociological Association, New York, NY. http://www.allacademic.com/meta/p182487_index.html.

Strouse, J., Goodwin, M., and Roscoe, B. 1994. "Correlates of Attitudes toward Sexual Harassment among Early Adolescents." *Sex Roles*, 31(9–10): 559–577.

Sullivan, H. S. (1953). *The Interpersonal Theory of Psychiatry*. New York: Norton.

Swoosh! Inside Nike. 2008. *CNBC.com*. www.cnbc.com/id/22492149.

Thorne, B. 1993. *Gender Play: Girls and Boys in School*. New Brunswick, N.J.: Rutgers University Press.

Tolman, D., Spencer, R., Rosen-Reynoso, M., and Porche, M. 2003. "Sowing the Seeds of Violence in Heterosexual Relationships: Early Adolescents Narrate Compulsory Heterosexuality." *Journal of Social Issues* 59 (1):159–178.

Tough Guise: Violence, Media and the Crisis in Masculinity. Producer and director, Sut Jhally. Writer, Jackson Katz. DVD. Media Education Foundation.

Tyson, A. May 28, 2008. "Pentagon: More Troops Suffering from PTSD." *The Washington Post*.

Waksman, S. 1999. *Instruments of Desire: The Electric Guitar and the Shaping of Musical Experience*. Cambridge, Mass.: Harvard University Press.

Ward, J. 2000. *The Skin We're In: Teaching Our Teens to Be Emotionally Strong, Socially Smart, and Spiritually Connected*. New York: The Free Press.

Watkins, S. 2000. "Black Youth and Mass Media: Current Research and Emerging Questions." *African American Research Perspectives* 6 (1). Retrieved June 5, 2003, from http:// www.rcgd.isr.umich.edu/prba/perspectives/winter2000/cwatkins.pdf.

Way, N., and Chu, J. Y., eds., 2004. *Adolescent Boys: Exploring the Diverse Cultures of Boyhood*. New York: NYU Press.

Welldon, C. 2005. "Addressing the Gender Gap in Boys' Reading." *Teacher Librarian* 32(4): 44–45.

Whales, M. 2009. "Guitar Hero II UK Review." *Ign.com*. http://ps2.ign.com/articles/746/746423p2.html.

Whitson, D. 1990. "Sport in the Social Construction of Masculinity." In M. Messner and D. Sabo, eds., *Sport, Men, and the Gender Order: Critical Feminist Perspectives*. Champaign, Ill.: Human Kinetics Books.

wil.i.am, January 8, 2009. "10 Questions for Will.i.am." *Time*. www.time.com/time/magazine/article/0,9171,1870496,00.html.

Wilcox, B., Kunkel, D., Cantor. J., Dowrick, P., Linn, S., and Palmer, E. 2004. *Report of the APA Task Force on Advertising and Children*. Washington, D.C.: American Psychological Association.

Wolf, N. October 20, 2003. "The Porn Myth." *New York Magazine*.

Wolak, J., Mitchell, K., and Finkelhor, D. 2007. "Unwanted and Wanted Exposure to Online Pornography in a National Sample of Youth Internet Users." *Pediatrics* 119 (2): 247–257.

Wrestling With Manhood, 2002. Writer, director Sut Jhally. DVD. Media Education Foundation.

WWE.com. 2008. Ad Sales. http://adsales.wwe.com/research/.

Yousman, B. 2003. "Blackophilia and Blackophobia: White Youth, the Consumption of Rap Music, and White Supremacy." *Communication Theory* 13 (4): 366–391.

Online Resources

(Some are for boys, some for teens, some for parents—check them out first!)

MEDIA LITERACY

www.media-awareness.ca
www.commonsensemedia.org
www.mediawatch.org
www.mediachannel.org
www.allianceforchildren.com
www.acmecoalition.org
www.childrennow.org/issues/media/
www.911media.org/about/
www.medialit.org
www.kidsfirst.org
www.ftc.gov/bcp/conline/edcams/ratings/ratings.htm
www.parentalguide.org

ADVOCACY FOR BOYS AND PARENTS AROUND COMMERCIALISM

www.commercialexploitation.org
www.pbskids.org/dontbuyit/
www.adaware.org
www.stayfreemagazine.org
mediasnackers.com/

GENERAL ONLINE COMMUNITIES AND RESOURCES FOR BOYS AND THEIR PARENTS

www.boystomen.info/index.html
www.cyberparent.com/boys/
www.pbs.org/parents/raisingboys/
www.pbs.org/opb/raisingcain/
www.michaelthompson-phd.com
www.hcz.org
www.scouting.org/
www.ymca.net
www.bgca.org
www.stand.org
www.cafemom.com

INTERNET SAFETY

www.fbi.gov/contact/fo/fo.htm
safekids.com
netsmartz.org

isafe.org
www.safeteens.com/
www.netparents.org/
www.netsafe.org.nz/home/home_default.aspx
www.protectkids.com/
disney.go.com/surfswell/index.html
www.wiredwithwisdom.org/
www.wiredsafety.org/
www.ftc.gov/bcp/conline/edcams/kidzprivacy/
www.kids.getnetwise.org

SPECIFIC TO THE ARTS

www.teenink.com—online magazine, stories, art, poetry by teens can submit
www.teenlit.com—publishes teen writing

SPECIFIC TO GAMING

www.gamerdad.com
www.gamerankings.com
www.gamespot.com

SPECIFIC TO SEX, DRUGS, AND ALCOHOL

www.abovetheinfluence.com
www.positive.org
www.advocatesforyouth.org
www.goaskalice.columbia.edu/
www.youthembassy.com
www.teenwire.com

SPECIFIC TO READING

www.guysread.com/
www.kathleenodean.com/boys.htm
www.menshealthnetwork.org/boys/info.php
www.literacytrust.org.uk/familyreading/parents/books.html#BoysInMind

NEWS AND ACTIVISM

www.Upcmkids.org—eight- to eighteen-year-olds' news bureau
www.Culturalenergy.org—world news with youth reporters
www.Pbs.org/merrow/listenup—youth media network
www.teenworldnews.com
www.Pinchmefilms.org—ten- to nineteen-year-olds' and adults social action media
www.Scenariosusa.org—kids creating social change
www.Mirrorproject.org—social change and awareness
www.Eecom.net—environmental and youth
www.alternet.org/wiretapmag/

Acknowledgments

We owe so much to our family members, friends, colleagues, and students who supported us, shared stories, helped with research, and offered advice along the way. Lyn and Mark wish to thank their daughter, Maya, for her healthy sense of adolescent irony and for providing a steady supply of great books to read. Many thanks to Lyn's brothers: David for his knowledge of NASCAR; Bill for his ongoing supply of father-son stories and for sending media Web sites. Lyn also expresses her deep love and gratitude to her sister, Susan, and parents, Diane and Lindy, for cheerleading her through this crazy life. A special thanks to Lyn and Mark's nephews, Camden, Kit, and Alex, for the great movie suggestions—how could you all be so different? Lyn thanks her childhood friend Connie Coleman, whose amazing twin sons, Nicholas and Nathaniel, have taught her so much about the complexity and compassion of preteen boys, and also her adulthood friend Betty Sasaki, her partner Ludger Duplessis, and sons, Jean Mark and Samuel, for their living testament to boys' expansive emotional lives. Mark also thanks his parents, Margaret and Richard, and his sister, Nancy, for their unwavering love and support during this project and all the rest.

Sharon must first acknowledge her sons, Willy and Julian, great and wonderful beings with huge senses of humor. She thanks them for their tolerance, their invitations into their worlds, their sharing of friends and media, the good the bad and the—well, ugly is too nice a word for "cupchicks." Her husband has grown to be one of her best and most loving supporters. And her best friends sustain her through all stresses in, around, and having nothing to do with writing this book. They remain Diane from third grade (whose children, Eric, Michael, and Emily were a help for sure), Kate from seventh grade, and Sarah from college. There's also Janet, Lorrie, Connie, Cathy, and glorious Bev.

Many children, teens, and parents helped us to write this book. Sharon's acknowledgments include Emma Shreefter, Julian's friends Nate and Angus Barstow (and perhaps even Angus's brother Charles!), and niece Jennifer. Eric Chubinsky offered very important information, as did his savvy parents, Peter and Edie. The sons of Kimberly Quinn-Smith, along with their mother and our mutual friend Dave Landers, gave us quintessential info on boys and men! Doris Orgel, Sharon's mother-in-law, was a most important informant about the world of children's literature. She was also enormously generous with compliments and advice. Sharon is indebted to Ellen Handler Spitz for her take on smelly, stinky boy books and to her son Nat and his partner Jason for their gift of a godson, Max. Larry Blum and his family shared wonderful insights about movies. Speaking of movies, Sharon relied often on the reviews of Margot Harrison in *Seven Days*, an alternative weekly in Burlington, Vermont, and wishes to thank Margot for conversations about movies and for sitting with her through a couple of rainy afternoons of boy flicks. Reebee Garofalo and Jeff Melnick were very helpful through short e-mail exchanges about boys, teens, and music. Ari Kirshenbaum and Molly Millwood made Sharon happy many a day working at Saint Mike's while also sharing lovely stories of Noah and his escapades with Spider-Man action figures. Buff shared stories of grown sons and keeps an eye out for press opportunities. Kim Swartz always provides insightful comments about gender, and Marty Machia has been fun and informative. Andrew Garrod and Sharon have talked about boys for years. When he writes about boys—read it! Mark Redmond, Lezlee Springer, Deb Sherrer, and a host of other Burlington activists were very helpful in analyzing the Burton LOVE snowboards.

Lyn wishes to thank Kenny Brechner, owner of Devany, Doak, and Garrett Booksellers, for his book reviews and recommendations, and literacy professor Elizabeth Marshall for her wonderful book suggestions. A special thank-you to colleagues at her nonprofit Hardy Girls Healthy Women for their sense of fun and unflagging support, and for believing that a world that supports healthy boys is a better world for girls. A number of parents of sons offered thoughtful responses to Lyn's frequent questions about their sons' media; special thanks to Anne Beldon, Catherine Besteman, Meg Bernier, Molly Docherty, Rebecca Green, Jan Holly, Michael Kimmel, Tarja Raag, and Linda Riley.

Mark would like to thank his colleagues from the Maine Boys' Network—Stephan Desrochers, Layne Gregory, Bernie Hertzberger, Julie Johnson, Bob Katz, Mark Kostin, Georgia Nigro, and Lisa Plimpton—for their friendship, support, and commitment to the success of all boys, in Maine and beyond.

We're grateful to our students at Colby College and Saint Michael's College for challenging us to think about the impact of media and cultural products, and for reminding us that things are always more complex than they first seem. A very special thanks to Aman Dang (Colby '08), who spent almost two years helping with various aspects of this project, from data entry and survey analysis, to teaching us the finer points of video games, to providing thoughtful and insightful movie reviews, to just chatting about boys and media. Thanks also to Katie Harris for her insight about hip-hop and Karina Carley for her helpful summaries and analysis of movies; Mark also wishes to thank his students in "Boys to Men," especially Keegan Albaugh, Celia Boren, Adam Choice, Todd Dixon, Ben Hauptman, Colin Hutzler, Jay Mangold, and Katie McCabe for their insights and ideas about boy-targeted media.

Adam Howard, Lyn and Mark's colleague in the Education Program at Colby, generously shared his insights about how social class is represented in the media and brought us up to speed on the ins and outs of contemporary country music. We are also grateful for the financial support Colby provided for this project, including summer research assistant funds and a small grant from the Interdisciplinary Studies Council. Denise Brault, the administrative assistant for the psychology department at Saint Michael's, and Sharon's research assistant, Joy-Anne Headley, were also particularly helpful.

Special thanks goes to Jean Kilbourne, whose groundbreaking work on girls and the media inspired many feminists, including ourselves, to enter this field. Thank you also to Joseph Pleck, Bill Pollack, Michael Kimmel, Sut Jhally, Jackson Katz, Gail Dines, Vic Seidler, and R. W. Connell for their important work on masculinity and the media, and for the insights of comrades Diane Levin, Susan Linn, Juliet Schor, Alexa Quart, Tomi-Ann Roberts, Deb Tolman, Monique Ward, Rebecca Collins, Eileen Zurbriggen, Janet Hyde, Gwen Keita, Leslie Cameron, and Joe Kelly, who have all taken up the cause of marketing to kids. Special thanks to blogger Amy Jussell at *Shaping Youth* for her endless energy and sharp eye for media madness. We wish to thank those colleagues who frequent the APA Division 46 Media Psychology listserv as well as the Action Coalition for Media Education (ACME) listserv, who were more helpful than they probably realize. Rachel Hare-Mustin is such a clever woman and Sharon is proud to still consider her a mentor! Sharon also thanks Jeanne Maracek, whom she relies on to test out any new idea—thanks, Jeanne, for your generosity. Nicola Gavey also shared insights regarding masculinity across the globe. We are all indebted to Carol Gilligan for her encouragement and her psychological work on boys, which grounded us at times when we got lost in the morass of boy's media.

We are so grateful to our agent, Carol Mann, who has been an ongoing source of support, enthusiasm, and wisdom. St. Martins Press has been wonderful to us, and our editor, Alyse Diamond, is a godsend. Thank you, Alyse, for loving this project as much as we do, for the funny cover art, and for bringing a good bit of fun to the editorial process.

Sharon and Lyn would be remiss not to thank each other for this wonderful journey and for an extraordinary friendship and support through the writing of two books. Our e-mail friendship has grown and spilled over into our lives, and sometimes is the realist and funniest part of our day. We're so grateful Mark Tappan joined us in this project, with his intellect, good humor, and strong feminist critique of manhood. And Mark says to Lyn and Sharon, "right back at 'cha!"

Finally, we owe considerable thanks to the six hundred boys who completed our survey and introduced us to the media they love. They surprised us, made us laugh, and taught us volumes.

Index